EAST ANGLIAN ARCHAEOLOGY

Hinxton, Cambridgeshire: Part I Excavations at the Wellcome Genome Campus: Late Glacial Lithics to the Icknield Way

by Alice Lyons and Lawrence Billington

with contributions by
Sue Anderson, Mark D. Bateman, Andrew Bates, Barry J. Bishop, Paul Booth, Steve Boreham, Lisa Brown, Rachel Clarke, Phil Copleston, Brian Dean, Michael Donnelly, Tom Eley, Carole Fletcher, Rachel Fosberry, Val Fryer, Anthony Haskins, Christine Howard Davis, Stephen Kemp, Scott Kenney, Jonathan Last, Ted Levermore, Louise Loe, Sarah Percival, Ian Riddler, Nicola Trzaska-Nartowski, Zoë Uí Choileáin and Helen Webb

illustrations by
Séverine Bézie, Gillian Greer, Frances Challoner, Sue Holden and Charlotte Walton, with aerial photographs by Alexis Pantos

edited for OA East by
Rachel Clarke and Elizabeth Popescu

East Anglian Archaeology
Report No. 178, 2023

Oxford Archaeology East

EAST ANGLIAN ARCHAEOLOGY
REPORT NO. 178

Published by
Oxford Archaeology East
15 Trafalgar Way, Bar Hill
Cambridgeshire CB23 8SQ

in conjunction with ALGAO East
www.algao.org.uk/cttees/regions

Editor: Kasia Gdaniec
Managing Editors: Jenny Glazebrook & Sue Anderson

Set in Times New Roman by Sue Anderson using Adobe InDesign
Printed by Henry Ling Limited, The Dorset Press

© OXFORD ARCHAEOLOGY EAST
ISBN 978-1-907588-13-6

East Anglian Archaeology was established in 1975 by the Scole Committee for Archaeology in East Anglia. The scope of the series expanded in 2002 to include all six eastern counties. Responsibility for publication rests with the editorial board in partnership with the Association of Local Government Archaeological Officers, East of England (ALGAO East). For details of *East Anglian Archaeology*, see last page

Cover illustrations
Front cover
Excavation of Ponds P and Q in Area J (Pond Q is in the foreground) looking north, with the Wellcome Trust Genome Campus European Bioinformatics Technical Hub building in the background

Back cover (left to right, top to bottom)
Bifacially flaked flint cobble (Fig. 3.6, SF 142) from Early Bronze Age shaft/pit; Late Neolithic/Early Bronze Age Beaker with slashed rim and moulded cordons (Fig. 3.13, No. 1); Conquest period/Early Roman copy of imported terra nigra platter (Fig. 3.15, No. 26); ?2nd-century AD circular plate brooch (Fig. 3.8, SF 39); Conquest period/Early Roman possible puzzle pot (Fig. 3.15, No. 24)

Contents

List of Plates

List of Figures

List of Tables

Contributors

Sue Anderson
Freelance human skeletal remains specialist

Mark D. Bateman
Sheffield Luminescence Dating Laboratory

Andrew Bates
Faunal remains specialist, formerly Oxford
Archaeology North

Séverine Bézie
Illustrator, Oxford Archaeology East

Barry Bishop
Freelance lithics specialist

Lawrence Billington
Post-Excavation Project Officer, Oxford Archaeology
East

Paul Booth
Coin specialist, Oxford Archaeology South

Steve Boreham
Pollen specialist

Lisa Brown
Prehistoric pottery specialist, Oxford Archaeology
South

Frances Challoner
Illustrator, formerly Oxford Archaeology East (finds
illustration)

Rachel Clarke
Post-Excavation Editor, Oxford Archaeology East

Phil Copleston
Ceramic Building Material specialist, formerly
Oxford Archaeology East (CCC AFU)

Brian Dean
Human skeletal remains specialist, Oxford
Archaeology South Burials Department

Michael Donnelly
Lithics specialist, Oxford Archaeology South

Tom Eley
Metalworking debris specialist, formerly Oxford
Archaeology East (CCC AFU)

Carole Fletcher
Finds Project Officer/Specialist, Oxford Archaeology
East

Rachel Fosberry
Project Officer: Archaeobotanist, Oxford
Archaeology East

Val Fryer
Freelance environmental specialist

Gillian Greer
Illustrator, Oxford Archaeology East (finds
illustration)

Anthony Haskins
Project Officer, Oxford Archaeology East

Sue Holden
Freelance illustrator (pottery from Late Neolithic/
Early Bronze Age shaft)

Christine Howard-Davis
Small finds specialist, Oxford Archaeology North

Stephen Kemp
Project Manager and worked stone specialist,
formerly Oxford Archaeology East (CCC AFU)

Scott Kenney
Project Officer, formerly Oxford Archaeology East

Jonathan Last
Prehistoric period specialist, formerly Oxford
Archaeology East (CCC AFU)

Ted Levermore
Assistant finds supervisor, Oxford Archaeology East

Louise Loe
Head of Burials Department, Oxford Archaeology
South

Alice Lyons
Project Officer (Post-excavation) and Roman pottery
specialist, formerly Oxford Archaeology East

Alexis Pantos
Freelance photographer (kite photography)

Sarah Percival
Prehistoric pottery specialist, formerly Oxford
Archaeology East

Elizabeth Popescu
Head of Post-Excavation and Publications, Oxford
Archaeology East

Ian Riddler
Freelance worked antler and bone specialist

Nicola Trzaska-Nartowski
Freelance worked antler and bone specialist

Zoë Uí Choileáin
Assistant finds supervisor and human skeletal
remains specialist, Oxford Archaeology East

Charlotte Walton
Formerly Illustrator, Oxford Archaeology East

Helen Webb
Human skeletal remains specialist, Oxford
Archaeology South Burials Department

Acknowledgements

The work was undertaken by staff of Oxford Archaeology East, formerly Cambridgeshire County Council Field Archaeology Unit. The authors would like to extend particular thanks to The Wellcome Trust Sanger Institute who commissioned and funded all phases of the archaeological work, as well as Fuller Peiser and Turner Townsend (and in particular Mat Temple) who commissioned the project on their behalf. Anthony Haskins would like to thank Bob Phillips and James Buckley-Walker for their assistance on site and Tim Waters for his input. The project was monitored by Cambridgeshire County Council's Historic Environment Team, most recently by Kasia Gdaniec, whose interest and support for the project is much appreciated.

The project and OA East team members were managed by Dr Paul Spoerry and Stephen Kemp, latterly with the assistance of Rachel Clarke, while individual aspects were supervised by Stephanie Leith, Stephen Kemp, Scott Kenney, Taleyna Fletcher and Anthony Haskins. Particular thanks are extended to Scott Kenney, who undertook the early stages of post-excavation analysis. The analysis and publication draft were completed by Alice Lyons, with post-refereeing revisions and additions being undertaken by Lawrence Billington.

Thanks are also extended to the many OA East site staff who worked in the field often in challenging conditions. Over the various stages of investigation, the project team has included the following: Emily Abrehart, Mary Alexander, Abby Antrobus, Robert Atkins, Tony Baker, Glenn Bailey, Celine Beauchamp, Emily Betts, Pete Boardman, Dave Brown, Louise Bush, Zoe Clarke, Kate Clover, Spencer Cooper, Ben Croxford, Simon Damant, Tom Dawson, Toby Driver, Jack Easen, Nick Fitch, Carole Fletcher, Taleyna Fletcher, Mike Green, Adam Howard, Richard Heawood, Mark Hinman, Sarah Hinds, Jeni Keen, Scott Kenney, Malgorzata Kwiatkowska, Stuart Ladd, Adam Lodoen, Chris Montague, Alison Morgan, Steve Morgan, Kathryn Nicholls, Steve Odett, Melodie Paice, Tom Phillips, Simon Pickstone, Ashley Pooley, Gareth Rees, Judith Roberts, Vicki Roulinson, Diogo Silva, Chris Swain, Helen Stocks-Morgan, Daria Tysbaeva, Stephen Wadeson, Kimberley Watt, Twigs Way, Robin Webb, Tam Webster and Sam Whitehead.

A number of volunteers, including Dave Whiter, Sally Lloyd, Jo Jones, Keith Matthews, Jane Matthews, David Crawford-White and Charles Rowland-Jones Chris Beard, Rick Kelly, Ray McMurray, Josephine Fried and Paul Comer are also thanked for their involvement over the years, in addition to the finds volunteers for assisting with the processing and marking of the flints. Thanks are also extended to the various skilled machine drivers, particularly from LOC Plant Hire.

Carole Fletcher and Phil Copleston are thanked for managing the finds at various stages of the project, assisted by Stephen Wadeson and Chris Faine. The authors would also like to thank each of the contributing specialists and the illustrators, whose work greatly assisted with the interpretation of the site. Barry Bishop, Zoe Outram (English Heritage Regional Science Advisor) and Deborah Priddy (English Heritage Inspector of Monuments) are thanked for their interest and advice in relation to the investigation of the flint scatters. Dr Mark Batemen and Samantha Stein (Sheffield University) are thanked for undertaking the OSL dating on the Palaeolithic flint scatter. The contribution of Alexis Pantos who provided aerial kite photographs of the Palaeolithic and Neolithic flint scatters is also appreciated.

The post-excavation phase of the project was managed by Rachel Clarke who also edited the volume prior to refereeing. Elizabeth Popescu edited the post-refereeing text and prepared the report for publication.

The index to this volume was compiled by Sue Vaughan.

Abbreviations

BP	Before present
CAM ARC	Cambridgeshire County Council Archaeological Unit (now OA East)
CAU	Cambridge Archaeological Unit
CCC AFU	Cambridgeshire County Council Archaeological Field Unit (now OA East)
CHER	Cambridgeshire Historic Environment Record
HSR	Human skeletal remains
MNE	Minimum number of elements
MNI	Minimum number of individuals
NHLE	National Heritage List for England
NISP	Number of individual specimens present
OA	Oxford Archaeology
OSL	Optically-Stimulated Luminescence
RIC	Roman Imperial Coinage
SFB	Sunken-featured building

Summary

Extensive archaeological investigations were undertaken in Hinxton, south Cambridgeshire by OA East (formerly Cambridgeshire County Council's Archaeological Field Unit, CCC AFU) between 1993 and 2014 on behalf of the Wellcome Trust. Centred around Hinxton Hall and the Genome Campus, to the south of the village, the excavated areas lay on either side of the River Cam within a 'borderland zone' crossed by long-lived prehistoric and Roman routeways, close to the modern county boundary with Essex.

Hinxton's post-glacial valley landscape of indigenous woodland, streams and seasonally flooded pools attracted Palaeolithic and Mesolithic communities to the area, to work flint and to hunt. The fills of one such 'pond' yielded a Terminal Palaeolithic 'Long/Bruised Blade' assemblage of national significance.

Tree clearance to permit exploitation of the fertile valley sides began in the Early Neolithic, with many small tree throws and a large hollow being utilised for flint knapping and other activities. The increasingly 'ritual' or ceremonial significance of the landscape is indicated by the discovery of a Late Neolithic/Early Bronze Age shaft containing a substantial assemblage of worked flint and Beaker pottery. This theme persisted throughout the later prehistoric and Early Roman periods, which saw the construction of two later Iron Age square enclosures – the largest of which appears to have been related to mortuary practices – followed by a small timber shrine. Burial of selected individuals, both in graves and as disarticulated remains, began in the Early Neolithic and continued sporadically through the Bronze Age and later Iron Age to Early Roman periods. The careful burial of a small dog alongside eggs and other offerings appears imbued with significance.

Agricultural exploitation of the valley seems to have been almost continuous until the Middle Roman period, with brief interludes perhaps resulting from flooding. It is largely represented by ditches demarcating fields, enclosures, tracks and droveways, including a formalised braid of the Icknield Way. Specialising in animal husbandry with a focus on cattle and sheep, the presence of two large corrals linked to major trackways potentially demonstrates stock management on a scale commensurate with supplying the nearby fort and Roman town at Great Chesterford. During the later Roman period, this farmland lay largely fallow, with only sporadic quarrying along the gravel terraces flanking the river edge, perhaps to provide building materials for construction and repair of the Roman town and its developing road network.

The immediate landscape was not resettled until the Anglo-Saxon period, although one of the major Roman field boundaries was re-established in the Saxo-Norman period and continued to influence the alignment of boundaries and associated settlement here for several centuries. The post-Roman period of activity at Hinxton is the subject of a companion volume (Part II).

Résumé

Des fouilles archéologiques ont été entreprises à Hinxton, dans le sud du Cambridgeshire, par OA East (anciennement l'unité de terrain archéologique régionale du Cambridgeshire, CCC AFU), entre 1993 et 2014 pour le compte du Wellcome Trust. Centrées autour d'Hinxton Hall et du Genome campus, au sud du village, les zones fouillées se trouvaient de chaque côté de la rivière Cam dans une «zone frontalière» traversée par des voies préhistoriques et romaines toujours en usage, à proximité de la limite administrative de la région moderne avec l'Essex.

Le paysage post-glaciaire de la vallée d'Hinxton, composé de forêts indigènes, de ruisseaux et de bassins inondés de façon saisonnière, a attiré les communautés paléolithiques et mésolithiques dans la région, pour travailler le silex et chasser. Les remplissages d'un de ces "étangs" ont produit un assemblage de "grandes lames et lames mâchurées" du Paléolithique supérieur d'importance nationale.

Le déboisement, afin de permettre l'exploitation des flancs fertiles de la vallée a commencé au Néolithique ancien, avec de nombreux petits troncs d'arbres et un large creux utilisé pour la taille du silex et pour d'autres activités. La signification de plus en plus «rituelle» ou cérémonielle du paysage est indiquée grâce a la découverte d'un puits, datant de la fin du Néolithique récent et du début de l'âge du bronze ancien, contenant un assemblage substantiel de silex travaillé et de poterie de type "gobelet". Ce thème a persisté tout au long des dernières périodes préhistoriques et durant le début de la période romaine, qui ont vu la construction de deux enceintes carrées de l'âge du fer – dont la plus grande semble avoir été liée à des pratiques funéraires – suivies d'un petit sanctuaire en bois. L'inhumation d'individus sélectionnés, à la fois dans des tombes et sous forme de restes désarticulés, a commencé au début du Néolithique ancien et s'est poursuivie sporadiquement à l'âge du bronze et plus tard à l'âge du fer jusqu'au début de la période romaine. L'inhumation soignée d'un petit chien à côté d'œufs et d'autres offrandes, parait imprégnée de signification.

L'exploitation agricole de la vallée semble avoir été presque continue jusqu'au milieu de l'époque romaine, avec de brefs intermèdes résultant peut-être d'inondations. Elle est largement représentée par des fossés délimitant des champs, des enclos, des pistes et des chemins de traverse, dont une branche pavée de l'Icknield Way. L'activité agricole est spécialisée dans l'élevage avec un accent sur les bovins et les ovins. La présence de deux grands enclos, reliés à des pistes principals, démontre potentiellement une gestion des stocks à une echelle proportionnelle à l'approvisionnement du fort voisin et de la ville romaine de Great Chesterford. À la fin de la période romaine, ces terres agricoles étaient en grande partie en friche, avec seulement des carrières sporadiques le long des terrasses de gravier flanquant le bord de la rivière, peut-être pour fournir des matériaux de construction destinés à la construction et à l'entretien de la ville romaine et de son réseau routier en développement.

Le paysage immédiat n'a pas été modifié jusqu'à la période anglo-saxonne, bien que l'une des bordures de la principale parcelle d'époque romaine ait été rétablie à l'époque saxo-normande et ait continué à influencer l'alignement des delimitations parcellaires, ainsi que l'occupation humaine qui lui est associée ici pendant plusieurs siècles. La période d'activité post-romaine à Hinxton fait l'objet d'un volume complémentaire (Volume II).

(Traduction: Séverine Bézie)

Zusammenfassung

Umfangreiche archäologische Untersuchungen wurden zwischen 1993 und 2014 im Auftrag des Wellcome Trust von OA East (ehemals Cambridgeshire County Council's Archaeological Field Unit, CCC AFU) in Hinxton, South Cambridgeshire, durchgeführt. Die Ausgrabungsgebiete, die sich um Hinxton Hall und den Genome Campus im Süden des Dorfes befanden, lagen auf beiden Seiten des Flusses Cam nahe der modernen Grafschaftsgrenze mit Essex in einer von „langlebigen" prähistorischen und römischen Wegtrassen durchzogen „Grenzgebietszone". Hinxtons postglaziale Tallandschaft mit einheimischen Wäldern, Bächen und saisonal gefluteten natürlichen Teichen zog paläolithische und mesolithische Gruppen an, um in der Gegend Feuerstein zu bearbeiten und zu jagen. Die Sedimentablagerungen eines solchen „Teiches" erbrachten einen Fundkomplex von endpaläolithischen Klingen („long blades" und „lame mâchurée") von nationaler Bedeutung.

Die Rodung von Bäumen, um die Nutzung der fruchtbaren Talseiten zu ermöglichen, begann im frühen Neolithikum, wobei viele kleinere Baumwürfe und eine große Mulde zum Schlagen von Feuerstein und zu anderen Aktivitäten genutzt wurden. Die zunehmend „rituelle" oder zeremonielle Bedeutung der Landschaft wird durch die Entdeckung eines Schachtes aus der späten Jungsteinzeit/frühen Bronzezeit, der eine beträchtliche Ansammlung von bearbeitetem Feuerstein und Becherkeramik enthielt, verdeutlicht. Dieses Thema setzte sich in der späteren prähistorischen und frührömischen Periode fort, während der zuerst zwei spät-eisenzeitliche quadratische Umfriedungen errichtet wurden – die größere hing offenbar mit Bestattungspraktiken zusammen – gefolgt von einem kleinen Holzschrein. Die Bestattung ausgewählter Personen, sowohl in Gräbern als auch als einzelne Überreste, begann im frühen Neolithikum und setzte sich sporadisch durch die Bronzezeit und spätere Eisenzeit bis in die frühe Römerzeit fort. Einer sorgfältigen Bestattung eines kleinen Hundes zusammen mit Eiern und anderen Opfergaben kommt anscheinend eine besonderer Bedeutung zu.

Die landwirtschaftliche Nutzung des Tales scheint bis in die mittelrömische Zeit nahezu durchgehend erfolgt zu sein, mit kurzen, möglicherweise durch Überschwemmungen verursachten Unterbrechungen. Bezeugt wird dies überwiegend durch feldbegrenzende Gräben, Einhegungen, Wege und Viehtriebe, einschließlich eines formalisierten Wegfächers des Icknield Way. Vor dem Hintergrund einer Spezialisierung auf die Tierhaltung mit Schwerpunkten auf der Rinder- und Schafhaltung, legt das Vorhandensein zweier großer, mit den Hauptwegen verbundener Gehege eine Bestandsverwaltung nahe, deren Ausmaß der Versorgung des nahe gelegenen Forts und der römischen Stadt Great Chesterford entspräche. Während der späteren Römerzeit lag das Land größtenteils brach. Lediglich die Schotterrassen entlang des Flussufers sahen sporadischen Kiesabbau, vielleicht für die Bereitstellung von Materalen für Bauarbeiten und Reparaturen in der römischen Stadt und an ihrem sich entwickelnden Straßennetz.

Die unmittelbar umgebende Landschaft wurde erst in der angelsächsischen Zeit neu besiedelt, wobei dann jedoch in sächsisch-normannischer Zeit eine der wichtigsten römischen Feldgrenzen wiederhergestellt wurde, die die örtliche Ausrichtung der Grenzen und der damit verbundene Besiedlung mehrere Jahrhunderte lang beeinflusste. Die nachrömische Sieldungsperiode in Hinxton ist der Gegenstand eines Begleitbandes (Teil II).

(Übersetzung: Christof Heistermann)

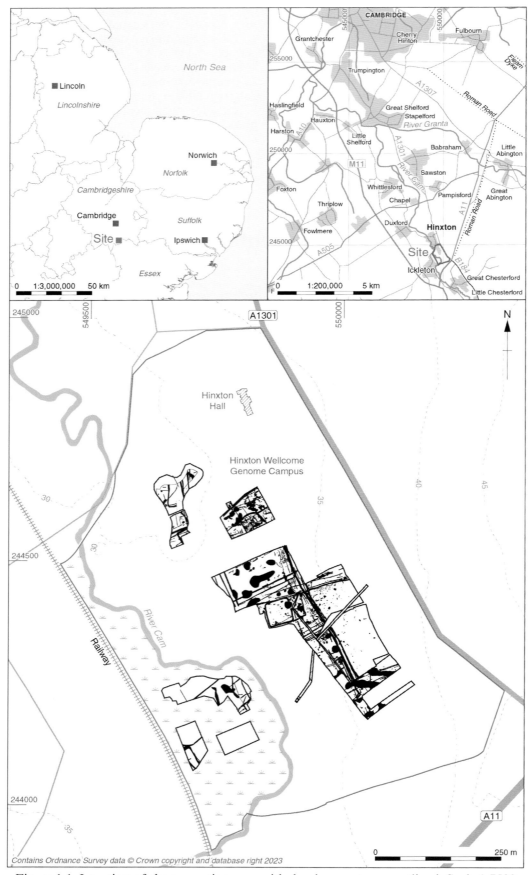

Figure 1.1 Location of the excavation area with development area outlined. Scale 1:7500

Chapter 1. Introduction
by Alice Lyons, Scott Kenney and Lawrence Billington

I. Project background
Fig. 1.1

Over a period of twenty-one years (between 1993 and 2014) an extended campaign of archaeological survey, evaluation, excavation and monitoring was carried out by Cambridgeshire County Council's Archaeological Field Unit, CAM ARC (now Oxford Archaeology East) on behalf of the Wellcome Trust Sanger Institute, in advance of the construction of the Wellcome Genome Campus (WGC). The survey area was centred to the south (and south-west) of Hinxton Hall (CHER 4272; centred at TL 498 446) in south Cambridgeshire and covered an area of approximately 30ha on both sides of the River Cam (Fig. 1.1). Within this area, c.16.5ha was examined by evaluation trenches and open area excavation. The work revealed a river valley landscape with a long history of activity and occupation from the early post-glacial period until the present day; this volume (Part I) presents and discusses the prehistoric and Roman remains revealed by this fieldwork, whilst the evidence for significant post-Roman re-colonisation and development of this landscape is discussed in a companion volume (Part II: Clarke *et al.* forthcoming).

The range and potential significance of the archaeological remains revealed during the trench-based evaluation of the site led to a requirement by Cambridgeshire County Council's Historic Environment Team that the area affected by development should be fully investigated and preserved both by record and *in situ* where possible. An archaeological management plan was subsequently agreed for the site (Thomas 2002), earmarking which areas would either be preserved under pasture or excavated in advance of development. As a result, an area of open grassland between the River Cam and the campus buildings has been set aside and managed, both to maintain species diversity and to preserve the below ground archaeological remains. Elsewhere, eight major phases of excavation have been completed.

II. Geology and topography
Figs 1.1 and 1.2

The excavations were located to the south of the medieval village of Hinxton on the southern edge of Cambridgeshire and on either side of the River Cam, close to the boundary with Essex. At this point, the Cam Valley has a wide, fairly flat base and is bounded by chalk ridges (up to 90m OD), which on the eastern side of the valley are topped by glacial till (Medlycott 2011a, 2, fig. 1.2). Within the valley bottom, sands and gravels (mapped as belonging to the first and second river terraces) flank alluvial deposits on the floodplain of the river (BGS Geology Map Sheet 205). Until the Wellcome Trust's development of the site, the survey

area was used for arable agriculture or lay fallow ('set aside'). The site is bounded to the east by the A1301 and to the west by a railway line.

On the eastern side of the Cam, the site lies largely on the gently sloping well drained river terraces which descend from c.40m OD (next to the A1301) to c.30–32m OD by the river. As described in more detail in Chapter 2.II, the main excavation areas here lay on sands and gravels (c.35m OD) at the foot of a chalky slope some 150m north-east of the River Cam (TL 499 422), whilst the Hinxton Riverside site to the west of the Cam, in the parish of Ickleton, was located on the floodplain itself (c.32m OD) (TL 497 441), within an area of peat and alluvial deposits.

III. Archaeological context
Fig. 1.2

Introduction
The immediate context for the site is provided by the rich archaeological record of Hinxton and its adjacent riverside parishes, including Duxford, Ickleton and Great Chesterford. More widely, the site is best understood in relation to the larger area of south Cambridgeshire and northernmost Essex, covering the upper and middle stretches of the Rivers Cam, Granta and Rhee — encompassing the ridges and escarpment edge of the south-west trending chalk outcrop to the south and east of the site and the topographically muted lowland river valleys to the north (Fig. 1.2). This landscape has a long and distinguished history of fieldwork, whilst over the lifetime of the Genome Campus project itself the area has benefitted from the major increase in developer-funded fieldwork over the last three decades. In the local area this includes the relatively large scale investigations undertaken at Hinxton Quarry in the 1990s (Fig. 1.2, No. 7; Mortimer and Evans 1996; Hill *et al.* 1999) and, much more recently, large scale evaluation (geophysical survey and trial trenching) of extensive areas to the east and north-east of the site associated with the proposed WGC Expansion Lands (Fig. 1.2, No. 21; Robinson-Zeki 2019) and the proposed development of land surrounding Hinxton Grange (Fig. 1.2, No. 20; Jones 2017). Further afield, recent work in the immediate hinterlands of Cambridge, in the Addenbrookes/Trumpington area, has revealed prehistoric and Roman remains on an enormous scale, providing a rich body of comparative evidence which also helps to contextualise the results of the Genome Campus fieldwork (Evans *et al.* 2008; Evans *et al.* 2018; Phillips and Mortimer forthcoming).

This rich regional record is drawn on extensively in later discussions (Chapter 5) while here, strictly for introductory purposes, a brief period-based summary is provided (Upper Palaeolithic to Roman), with selected sites and features recorded by aerial survey

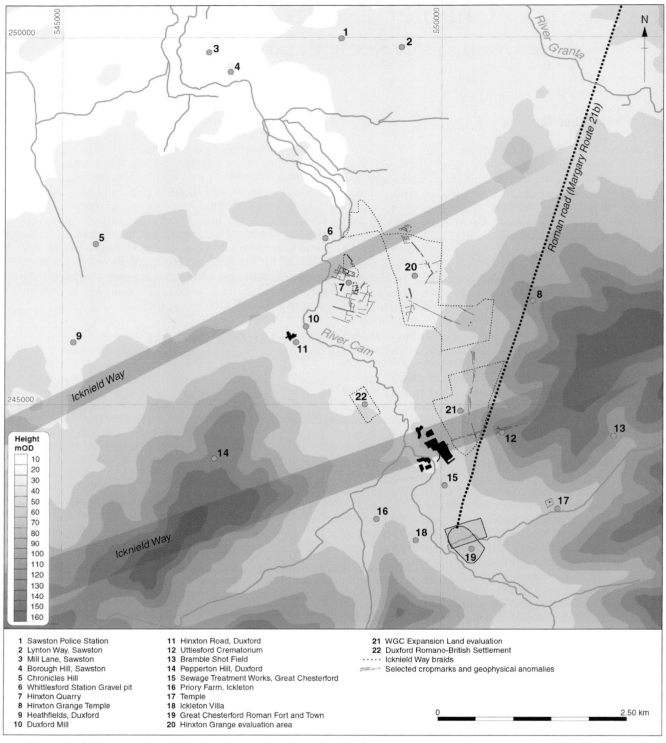

Figure 1.2 Topography of the local area showing selected sites, cropmarks and geophysical anomalies in the area. Scale 1:50,000

Height mOD
10
20
30
40
50
60
70
80
90
100
110
120
130
140
150
160

1 Sawston Police Station	11 Hinxton Road, Duxford	21 WGC Expansion Land evaluation
2 Lynton Way, Sawston	12 Uttlesford Crematorium	22 Duxford Romano-British Settlement
3 Mill Lane, Sawston	13 Bramble Shot Field	····· Icknield Way braids
4 Borough Hill, Sawston	14 Pepperton Hill, Duxford	Selected cropmarks and geophysical anomalies
5 Chronicles Hill	15 Sewage Treatment Works, Great Chesterford	
6 Whittlesford Station Gravel pit	16 Priory Farm, Ickleton	
7 Hinxton Quarry	17 Temple	
8 Hinxton Grange Temple	18 Ickleton Villa	0 2.50 km
9 Heathfields, Duxford	19 Great Chesterford Roman Fort and Town	
10 Duxford Mill	20 Hinxton Grange evaluation area	

and geophysics in the immediate hinterland of the site plotted on Figure 1.2. Prior to this, however, it is necessary to frame the site briefly in terms of its relationship to networks of routeways and communication, a theme that is of central importance to the interpretation of the prehistoric and Roman archaeology encountered at the Genome Campus.

Routeways, communications and connections

As will become clear, the prehistoric and Roman remains at the site are best understood in relation to their location within wider patterns and networks of settlement, communication and exchange. Whilst the character of such networks saw dramatic changes over the extended timescale considered here, this theme is no less relevant for the episodic earlier prehistoric (Upper Palaeolithic to Early Bronze Age) occupation and visitation of the site than for activity during the

Late Iron Age and Roman period, when major sets of trackways provide tangible evidence for its connection with the wider landscape.

Of importance here is the site's location at the nexus of two major, putative, corridors of movement and communication – 'the river and the ridgeway'. In terms of the former, the site lies just upstream of the position at which the Cam leaves its relatively constricted and heavily incised upper course through the chalk escarpment and the boulder clay plateau of north-east Essex, and enters the lowlands of south Cambridgeshire. Upstream of Hinxton, the river flows southwards to the watershed formed by the till-capped heights of the chalk escarpment, beyond which the south-flowing River Stort rises and runs to join the Lea, feeding into the Thames Basin beyond. Downstream, the Cam passes northwards through Cambridge and on into the south-east fenlands, ultimately meeting the canalised route of the Great Ouse south of the Isle of Ely and debouching into the Wash.

Meanwhile, perpendicular to the major north to south corridor formed by these rivers, along the exposed chalk downlands of the escarpment edge, runs the putative course of one of Southern Britain's famed prehistoric 'ridgeway routes', the Icknield Way. Celebrated and maligned in equal measure among archaeologists and historians (see Harrison 2003; Taylor and Arbon 2007, 39; Evans *et al.* 2018, 424–5; Bell 2020, 195–7), here it is sufficient to note the location of the site in relation to the traditionally understood routes of the Icknield Way – although it is clearly now best understood more as a corridor of movement occupying a broad belt along the escarpment as opposed to a set of individual well-defined route/trackways (*e.g.* Lyons 2011, figs 2 and 3; Ladd and Mortimer 2017, fig. 1.2), elements of which were later incorporated into and/or linked to the Roman road network. Largely following Fox (1923, ch. 4, map V), the main route of the Icknield Way through south-east Cambridgeshire has generally been understood to cross the Cam to the north of Hinxton, essentially underlying the modern A505, but most depictions of the route also show a secondary, southern route which Fox believed crossed the Cam at an 'ancient ford' at Ickleton (*ibid*; Malim 2000); it is this southern route that broadly corresponds with the evidence for trackways and river crossings revealed at the Genome Campus.

Notwithstanding the importance of the Icknield Way/chalk escarpment and the River Cam as natural corridors of movement and communication, it is equally important to emphasise their status as potential territorial/cultural boundaries – and thus as zones of interaction. As discussed in more detail below in connection with the Late Iron Age remains uncovered at the Genome Campus, this issue has loomed large in relation to the Late Iron Age of South-Eastern and Eastern England, with both the Cam–Stort–Lea valley and the chalk escarpment long seen as representing boundaries and zones of interactions between the various tribal groupings known from historical sources and numismatic evidence (see Medlycott 2011a, 9–10; Rippon 2018, ch. 2).

Upper Palaeolithic (*c.*12,700 to 9400 BC)

Evidence for Upper Palaeolithic activity has rarely been documented in the Cam Valley, although very small quantities of Upper Palaeolithic flintwork have come from excavations at Mill Lane, Sawston (Fig. 1.2, No. 3; Paul *et al.* 2016) and, further north, from Clay Farm, Trumpington (Phillips and Mortimer forthcoming). Prior to the excavations reported here, the only substantial assemblages known from the wider area were from south-east Cambridgeshire, at Rookery Farm, Great Wilbraham, where a small discrete Final Palaeolithic (*c.*1200–10,700 BC) lithic scatter appears to have related to a short episode of flint working and tool manufacture during the latter part of Late Glacial Interstadial (Conneller 2009), and at Whiteway Drove, Swaffham Prior, where large quantities of flintwork of Terminal Palaeolithic (*c.*9800–9400 cal BC), 'long blade' character have been collected from an extensive surface scatter on the fen edge (see Billington 2016, 322–9, fig. 7.12).

Mesolithic (*c.*9000 to 4000 BC)

As in many other parts of the region, Mesolithic activity appears to have been widespread along the Cam Valley, including in the immediate environs of the site although, with the evidence invariably consisting of small assemblages of flintwork from unstratified or disturbed contexts, the period remains poorly characterised. Thus, small assemblages of Mesolithic flints have been recovered from the gravel terraces of the Cam during programmes of excavation and surface collection at Hinxton Quarry (Fig. 1.2, No. 7; Pollard 1998; Mortimer and Evans 1996), Whittlesford (Hutton 2008; 2010) and Sawston (Fig. 1.2, No. 3; Paul *et al.* 2016), and during investigations of Great Chesterford Roman town (Fig. 1.2, No. 19; Medlycott 2011a, 9), whilst a very dense scatter of flintwork on the chalk ridge at Heathfields, Duxford appears to have included a major Mesolithic component (Fig. 1.2, No. 9; McFadyen 1999a and b; Last 2002; see Bishop 2012, 136–40). Perhaps more significantly, at least in terms of indicating the potential for well-preserved scatters of this date to survive *in situ* on the floodplain of the river, investigations at Duxford Mill recovered a small Mesolithic assemblage from beneath peat deposits adjacent to the river (Fig. 1.2, No. 10; Schlee and Robinson 1995). Further afield, small collections of Mesolithic flint from the upper Cam Valley, from Wicken Bonhunt and Newport (Jacobi 1980), demonstrate activity along the river valley, higher up on the chalk escarpment.

Neolithic (*c.*4000 to 2400 BC)

Neolithic activity is much better documented in the area – downstream of Hinxton, the Cam Valley and adjacent Gog Magog hills host an important complex of Early Neolithic monuments, including a pair of circular/oval funerary monuments at Trumpington Meadows, two causewayed enclosures (at Great Shelford and Little Trees Hill, Stapleford) and a long barrow at Copley Hill, Babraham (see Evans *et al.* 2018, 401–2, fig. 6.7). Upstream, records suggest the possibility that another causewayed enclosure once lay overlooking the river on the outskirts of modern Saffron Walden (Healy 2012a). Except for a few sites characterised by relatively large numbers of pits, such as Glebe Farm, Trumpington (Evans *et al.* 2018) and Dernford Farm, Sawston (Newton 2018), evidence for Neolithic settlement is more fugitive. In the immediate environs of the Genome Campus, the scale of Neolithic (and Early Bronze Age) activity on the gravel terraces of the Cam is best appreciated by the extensive and extremely dense ploughsoil lithic scatter sampled during fieldwalking at Hinxton Quarry (Pollard 1998; Evans *et al.* 2018, 408–10; Fig. 1.2, No. 7), with subsequent excavations revealing a small number of Early and Middle/Late Neolithic pits, and a single tree throw associated with a large assemblage of Early Neolithic pottery and flint (Mortimer and Evans 1996; Evans *et al.* 1999). Substantial assemblages of Neolithic pottery and flintwork were also recovered during the investigations on the river floodplain at Mill Lane, Sawston (Paul *et al.* 2016), while isolated Neolithic pits have been found at Priory Farm, Ickleton (Fig. 1.2, No. 16; Prosser and Murray 2001) and in the area immediately to the south of the Genome Campus, during monitoring at a sewage treatment works (Fig. 1.2, No. 15; Robertson *et al.* 2003).

Bronze Age (*c.*2400 to 800 BC)
Evidence for Chalcolithic/Early Bronze Age settlement in the area takes a similar, ephemeral, form to that of the Neolithic, with stray finds, lithic scatters and small numbers of pits testifying to activity during this period along the Cam Valley south of Cambridge – again, best represented locally by the multi-period lithic scatter and small number of cut features at Hinxton Quarry (Fig. 1.2, No. 7; Mortimer and Evans 1996). Ring ditches and round barrows, most of which can be assumed to belong to this broad period, form the most archaeologically visible traces of activity during this period and are well represented in the area. Published maps of such features show an extensive swathe of round barrows along the chalk escarpment in this area (Taylor 1981; Last 2000; Ingle and Saunders 2011). Most of these barrows were constructed in topographically commanding locations, on the chalk hills or on the upper sides of the river valleys: these include two ring ditches recently excavated at the site of Uttlesford Crematorium, located around 1km to the east of the Genome Campus and overlooking the site from the valley side (Fig. 1.2, No. 12; Network Archaeology 2017). Barrows do, however, occur on the lower lying terrace gravels, including one example at Hinxton Quarry (Fig. 1.2, No. 7; Pollard 1998). Elsewhere Beaker/Early Bronze Age funerary activity adjacent to the river is implied by finds in the northern part of Great Chesterford Roman town, including two Beaker vessels, a flint dagger, a probable Early Bronze Age urn and reports of an inhumation burial accompanied by a jet ornament (Fig. 1.2, No. 19; Medlycott 2011a, 9), whilst a complete beaker associated with the partial remains of an adult skeleton was recovered from a gravel pit next to Whittlesford Station in the late 1930s (Fig. 1.2, No. 6; Lethbridge and O'Reilly 1937, 74).

As in most parts of Southern Britain, the beginning of the Middle Bronze Age (*c.*1600–1200 BC) is traditionally seen as a major watershed in the region's prehistory, with the first evidence for large-scale land division accompanied by significant changes in material culture and funerary practices. One of the most outstanding discoveries of recent years has been the recognition and investigation of extensive field systems and settlement related enclosures of this date on the eastern side of the Cam Valley in the Trumpington/Addenbrookes environs (Evans *et al.* 2018, 418–27; Phillips and Mortimer forthcoming). The intensity of activity within this area compares favourably with the better known Middle Bronze Age landscapes of the Lower Ouse and western Fen edge (*e.g.* Pryor 1980; Evans and Knight 2001; Evans *et al.* 2009), but throws into sharper relief the relative lack of evidence for Middle Bronze Age activity in more upstream parts of the Cam Valley and across south Cambridgeshire more generally (Yates 2007, fig. 12.7; Evans *et al.* 2018, 426). Nevertheless, small-scale investigations in and around Sawston, at the police station (Fig. 1.2, No. 1; Cessford and Mortimer 2004; Mortimer 2006) and Lynton Way (Fig. 1.2, No. 2; Weston *et al.* 2007), have revealed elements of probable Middle Bronze Age enclosures, while ard marks cut by later Iron Age features at Hinxton Road, Duxford have been suggested to relate to Bronze Age cultivation (Fig. 1.2, No. 11; Lyons 2011). Most recently, possible Middle Bronze Age rectilinear enclosures/fields have been revealed by geophysical survey and trial trenching on the valley side to the west of Hinxton Grange (Fig. 1.2, No. 20; Jones 2017). Late Bronze Age (and earliest Iron Age) activity is similarly poorly represented in the immediate environs of the site – although this at least partly reflects the relatively low archaeological visibility of the unenclosed settlement remains that characterise these periods (Brudenell 2012, 74–98) and several of the excavations carried out in the environs of Cambridge in recent years have been of a scale sufficient to recover evidence of fairly widespread occupation (Phillips 2015; Phillips and Mortimer forthcoming; Evans *et al.* 2008, chap. 2).

Iron Age (*c.*800 BC to AD 50)
In contrast to the earlier centuries of the Iron Age, the latest part of the Early Iron Age and the beginning of the Middle Iron Age – between *c.*400 and 300 BC – has emerged as one of the most distinctive and significant periods of the later prehistory of south Cambridgeshire and the Cam Valley, although evidence in the immediate environs of the subject site is scarce. It is during this broad period that three of the hillforts/ring-works in the Cambridge environs appear to have their origins, at Wandlebury (Hartley 1957; French *et al.* 2004), the War Ditches (Pickstone and Mortimer 2012) and Arbury Camp (Evans and Knight 2002; 2008), whilst a series of major unenclosed settlements marked by mass agglomerations of grain storage pits has been uncovered at sites including Trumpington Meadows/Park and Ride (Evans *et al.* 2018), Harston (O'Brien 2016) and Edix Hill (Malim 1998). Recent work has also shown that at least some of a set of major linear earthworks laid out across the chalk escarpment may have had their origins in the period (Ladd and Mortimer 2017). The exact chronology and significance of these developments remains a matter of debate but in reviewing some of this evidence, Stephen Rippon has emphasised the importance of the area in terms of Iron Age political and cultural geography, representing part of a 'narrow communication route

from the lowlands of the South East Midlands up into East Anglia' (Rippon 2018, 99).

The Middle/later Iron Age was a period of major settlement expansion in the region – with hitherto little-occupied areas such as the boulder clays of west Cambridgeshire seeing large-scale 'colonisation' (*e.g.* Wright *et al.* 2009; Abrams and Ingham 2008), whilst the sheer density of settlement in many parts of the region seems likely to represent a real increase in the size of population – beyond simply reflecting on the increased archaeological visibility of the often ditch-enclosed settlements of the period. That said, Middle Iron Age settlement in the local area is relatively poorly documented. A settlement of this period was investigated on Pepperton Hill, some 2km to the west of the site (Fig. 1.2, No. 14; Price *et al.* 1997) and a series of Middle Iron Age storage pits at Hinxton Road, Duxford presumably relates to domestic-type activity, notwithstanding that associated finds assemblages appear to attest to large scale feasting and ritual activity (Fig. 1.2, No. 11; Lyons 2011). Within the extensive area subject to geophysical survey and trial trenching west of Hinxton Grange (Fig. 1.2, No. 20), at least two areas of Middle Iron Age settlement were identified, in the form of small groups of ring gullies, representing the remains of roundhouse structures, which in some cases may have been associated with wider systems of ditched boundaries and enclosures (Jones 2017).

The character of the Late Iron Age (*c.* 50 BC–AD 50) record in the wider landscape reflects its location on a major 'cultural' frontier, lying in the northernmost area of communities in South-East England which were strongly influenced by their connections with Romanised Gaul (see Hill 2007) – and the site's position in respect to Late Iron Age tribal polities has already been alluded to. More will be said concerning these issues below in discussion of the Late Iron Age remains revealed at the Genome Campus, but it is important to foreground some sites of this period known in the environs of the site. The area surrounding the pre-Flavian Roman fort and later town at Great Chesterford evidently saw Late Iron Age activity on some scale – the fragmentary evidence for which has recently been collated and reviewed by Maria Medlycott (2011a). In the area later occupied by the Roman town, a series of irregular enclosures detected by geophysical survey is suggested to be of Late Iron Age date, whilst early investigations of the town recovered Late Iron Age material including coins and pottery, although rarely from stratified or well-documented features/deposits. On the other side of the river to the town, rescue excavations in 1989 recorded several cremation burials belonging to an Aylesford–Swarling type cemetery, whilst overlooking the town to the north-east a masonry-built Roman temple appears to have been preceded by a rectangular timber-built shrine/temple of Late Iron Age/Conquest period date (Fig. 1.2, No. 17). Further Aylesford–Swarling type burials and cemeteries are known in the area; most relevant here is the group of cremation burials from Hinxton Quarry, found within a series of ring-ditches (Hill *et al.* 1999), but also includes an extremely richly furnished set of burials from Bramble Shot Field, to the east of Great Chesterford (Fig. 1.2, No. 13; see Medlycott 2011a, 217). Late Iron Age funerary and ceremonial activity of a rather different character was revealed at Hinxton Road, Duxford, where a mixed rite cemetery dominated by inhumation burials was found, associated with a small rectangular structure interpreted as a shrine (Lyons 2011). Funerary activity here was long-lived, probably from the early 1st century BC through to the 2nd century AD.

Roman

The Genome Campus site lies within a landscape that was extensively exploited during the Roman period. Key here is the Early Roman fort and subsequent large Roman town at Great Chesterford (Medlycott 2011a), which would have had a major impact on the development and economy of the surrounding area. It is not clear whether the fort was established in the immediate aftermath of the Roman invasion of AD 43 or was instead founded as a reaction to the Boudican revolts of AD 60–61, but it was evidently short-lived, with elements of its internal features being incorporated into the town established in its place. The occupation of the town and its extensive extra-mural settlement are suggested to have continued throughout the 4th century, with survival into the 5th century being postulated.

To the east of the Genome Campus site was a major Roman road. This followed the route of the modern A11 (Margary 1973, Route 21b) and ran north-eastwards from Great Chesterford, bridging the Granta at Pampisford and meeting Worsted Street (Route 24) at Worsted Lodge. This was one of a number of Roman roads that radiated out from the town of Great Chesterford, providing a network of routes linking the major contemporary settlements (Medlycott 2011a, 104–5, fig. 7.1). Adjacent to this road, to the north-east of the Genome Campus, excavations to the east of Hinxton Grange revealed a substantial building set within a wider complex of cropmarks which has been tentatively interpreted as a roadside temple or shrine (Fig. 1.2, No. 8; Heawood and Robinson 1998). Outside of the town, Romano-British settlement and land use on the terrace gravels flanking the river and on adjacent areas of the valley sides appears to have been intensive. To the south of the site, across the river in the parish of Ickleton, an elaborate winged corridor villa was partly excavated in the 19th century (Fig. 1.2, No. 18; Roach Smith 1849) and further north, in the southern part of Duxford parish, the cropmarks of a large complex of rectilinear enclosures associated with surface finds of Roman building material and pottery represent the site of a major rural settlement/farmstead lying immediately to the west of the River Cam (Fig. 1.2, No. 22; CHER 04210; NHLE 1004672). Further north still, on the eastern side of the river, to the north-east of the Genome Campus, the large-scale investigations at Hinxton Quarry revealed the remains of a Romano-British farmstead and associated field systems (Evans 1993; Gibson 2003; Mortimer and Evans 1996). Cropmarks of further probable Romano-British farmsteads/enclosures are known from further up the valley side in and adjacent to the northern part of the extensive area of evaluation fieldwork undertaken to the west of Hinxton Grange (Fig. 1.2, No. 20; Jones 2017).

Figure 1.3 Plan of all areas, trenches and features with prehistoric and Roman features highlighted. Scale 1:4000

Project name and grey literature report reference	Site code(s)	Date work undertaken
Hinxton Hall Park Evaluation (Leith 1993a; 1993a) and Excavation (Spoerry 1995)	HIN HH 93	1993–1994
New Lake Site Map and Record (Leith 1995a; Leith 1995b)	HIN HH 93	1994–1995
Earthwork Survey (Spoerry 1995)	HIN HH 95	1995
Observations along the route of the new water main between Hinxton and Great Chesterford (Roberts 1996)		October and November 1995
Genome Campus Extension Evaluation (Kemp and Spoerry 2002) and Excavation (Phase 1) (Kenney 2007)	HIN RIV 98, HIN RS 02, HIN GC 02	1998–2002
Ickleton evaluation (Kemp 2002) and excavation (Kenney 2007)	ICK GC 02/03	2002–2003
Genome Campus Extension Excavation (Phase 2) (Fletcher 2012)	HIN GEC 11	2011
Hinxton South Field (Haskins and Clarke 2015)	HIN GEL 14	2014

Table 1.1 Main evaluation and excavation components of the Hinxton Archaeological Project

IV. The investigation sequence
Fig. 1.3, Pls 1.1–1.2

This volume brings together the results of over two decades of fieldwork in what is now the Wellcome Genome Campus, with multiple phases of investigation having taken place since 1993 (Table 1.1). This has resulted in a large body of 'grey literature' reportage; the resulting reports form part of the site archive and are referenced below and listed in Appendix 1.

As noted in Section I above, the extent of evaluation and area excavation at the Wellcome Genome Campus has been dictated by the footprint of the development, itself informed by a management plan designed to mitigate, where practicable, against the disturbance and destruction of archaeological remains and resulting in several discrete areas of excavation, with widespread trenching having been carried out over other parts of the development area (Fig. 1.3). For the purposes of publication, the main excavation areas have been assigned a letter code (A–J), based on area designations originally used during the 1998–2003 fieldwork. These area codes are shown on Figure 1.3 and subsequent period-specific site plans. An aerial photograph of the core of the site before work commenced appears in Plate 1.1, with topsoil stripping in progress being illustrated in Plate 1.2.

Work began in 1993, with programmes of geophysical survey and trial trenching in the northern part of the site around Hinxton Hall (Trenches A–Q; Test Pit(TP); Shiel 1993a–b; Leith 1993 a–b). This was followed, in the winter of 1993/1994 by area excavation in Hinxton Hall Park (Area F; Spoerry 1995), alongside the excavation of a small trench targeting a geophysical anomaly some 100m east of the main excavation area (Trench U; Last 1997). Work continued in 1994 and 1995 with a programme of monitoring and excavation carried out in advance of the construction of a new lake to the west of the 1993/4 excavations (Area G; Leith 1995a–b). Survey of an area of upstanding earthworks was also undertaken at this time (Area L; Spoerry and Leith 1996), and the first programme of work was undertaken in the southern part of the Genome Campus, with the excavation of a series of trenches (Trenches AA–HH) and the monitoring of topsoil stripping along the proposed route of a new water main between Great Chesterford and Hinxton (Roberts 1996).

The next phases of work were carried out between 1998 and 2003 and were associated with a major southward expansion of the Genome Campus. Following programmes of geophysical survey and evaluation (Trenches 1–25 and 29–34; Kenney and Spoerry 2002; Kenney 2002), five areas were subject to excavation (Areas A–E; Kenney 2007). Simultaneously a programme of work was undertaken on the floodplain on the western side of the Cam, in the parish of Ickleton (Trenches 26–28; Kenney and Spoerry 2002; Kenney 2002), with a further phase of trenching (Trenches H1–H4; Kemp 2002), followed by area excavation (Area H; Kenney 2007). Most recently, two further phases of excavation were carried out in 2011 (Area E; Fletcher 2012) and 2013 (Area J; Haskins and Clarke 2015; Bishop et al. 2016), immediately to the east of Areas D and B.

V. Research objectives

Throughout the project's history, the various programmes of fieldwork and post-excavation analyses have been guided and informed by a series of national, regional and site-specific research aims, formulated and repeatedly updated with reference to relevant research frameworks and agendas (e.g. Brown and Glazebrook 2000; Medlycott 2011b; English Heritage 1997; Haselgrove et al. 2001). The final iteration of these Research Aims, which underpinned the last phases of fieldwork and the final stages and the preparation of this publication, were grouped under two overarching research themes: 'chronologies and processes of change' and 'landscape and environment', whilst – as intimated above (Section III) – a persistent and important theme running through the volume as a whole concerns the site's specific context in the regional landscape in terms of its relationship to routeways and boundaries. These general research themes, together with specific research questions and issues relevant to particular periods, are explored in detail in Chapter 5.

In addition to the project's research objectives noted above, the results of genome sequencing of human skeletal remains recovered from the excavations have been reported elsewhere as part of a wider study of Iron Age and Anglo-Saxon genomes from Eastern England (Schiffels et al. 2016). This included samples taken from two of the Late Iron Age/Early Roman burials reported in this volume (Skeleton

Plate 1.1 Aerial photograph, showing the two square mortuary/ceremonial enclosures (70H-Q60; reproduced with permission of the Cambridge University Collection of Aerial Photography © Copyright reserved)

Plate 1.2 Working shot, showing topsoil stripping in progress

(Sk) 1964; Burial Group 3B; Period 3.1 and Sk 1231; Burial group 4; Period 3.3), alongside samples from three of the Anglo-Saxon burials recovered from the site. Given that this study was designed to address genomic differences between Iron Age and Anglo-Saxon populations in the context of debates conceding the 'indigenous' or incoming status of Anglo-Saxon communities, its results are discussed more fully in the companion volume (Part II; Clarke *et al.* forthcoming).

VI. Phasing

The site phasing relates to the following chronological periods:

Period 1: Terminal Palaeolithic to Mesolithic (*c.*10,000 to 4000 BC)
1.1 Terminal Palaeolithic (*c.*10,000 to 9000 BC)
1.2 Mesolithic (*c.*9000 to 4000 BC)

Period 2: Neolithic to Bronze Age (*c.*4000 to 800 BC)
2.1 Neolithic (*c.*4000 to 2400 BC)
2.2 Bronze Age (*c.*2400 to 800 BC)

Period 3: Iron Age to Romano-British (*c.*800 BC to *c.*AD 410)
3.1 Middle to Late Iron Age (*c.*350 BC to AD 50)
3.2 Early Roman/Conquest Period, Phase I (*c.*AD 40 to 100 BC)
3.3 Early Roman/Conquest Period, Phase II (*c.*AD 40 to 150 BC)
3.4 Middle to Late Roman (*c.*AD 150 to 410)

Within the sub-phases of Period 2 (Neolithic and Bronze Age), further sub-divisions have been made based on radiocarbon dating and pottery types, as set out in Chapter 2. The overlapping date range between Periods 3.2 and 3.3 results from the fact that features attributed to Period 3.3 essentially relate to the same chronological period as those of Period 3.2, but are in most cases demonstrably stratigraphically later.

The post-Roman phases of the site's history (from the Anglo-Saxon to modern periods) are detailed in Part II (Clarke *et al.* forthcoming).

Chapter 2. The Archaeological Sequence
by Alice Lyons and Lawrence Billington
with Scott Kenney, Jonathan Last, Anthony Haskins and Rachel Clarke

I. Introduction and overview

This chapter sets out the sequence of prehistoric and Roman archaeology at the Genome Campus site, from the Late Upper Palaeolithic through to the 4th/5th century AD. The chapter is arranged chronologically according to the phasing scheme set out in Chapter 1.VI, and is prefixed by a brief description of the natural/geomorphological features/ deposits encountered during the investigations, which provides an important framework for understanding the archaeological remains belonging to the initial part of the sequence.

The earliest activity recorded at the site took the form of a very large Terminal Palaeolithic (Period 1.1) lithic assemblage derived from an *in situ* lithic scatter preserved within a natural hollow in the south-eastern part of the site (Area J). Probably dating to the very beginning of the Holocene (*c*.9500 cal BC), this represents a single, short-lived episode of activity by a group of highly mobile hunter-gatherers moving through what was then an area of relative upland on the margins of the great river valleys and plains now lost beneath the North Sea. From what is known of the history of Late Glacial and Holocene occupation in Southern Britain, it is likely that there was a significant hiatus between this activity and Mesolithic occupation of the area (Period 1.2). The evidence for Mesolithic activity was largely restricted to flintwork found within chronologically mixed assemblages collected from later features or from poorly stratified deposits, but includes some material from a series of possible pits or tree throws and from relatively undisturbed flint scatters preserved in some areas of the site.

Neolithic (Period 2.1) activity was better represented; a major assemblage of Early Neolithic pottery and flintwork recovered from buried soil deposits in Area J and a scatter of pits attests to episodes of settlement-type activity in the early 4th millennium BC, whilst a rare double inhumation burial of this date was also exposed in the same area. Middle and Late Neolithic activity was represented by small groups of pits and by residual/poorly stratified flintwork. Remains of Bronze Age (Period 2.2) activity included important evidence for Early Bronze Age (Beaker) settlement, including a possible structure and associated pits, together with a large pottery assemblage recovered from a midden-like deposit found filling the upper profile of a 'shaft' type feature investigated in the northern part of the development area (Trench U). Less prosaically, a small pit containing the remains of two near-complete Beaker vessels was found in the same general area (Area F): this feature may originally have been associated with funerary/ceremonial activity and the presence of a mound or marker of some kind is implied by the presence of a later inhumation burial interred immediately to the north-west, radiocarbon dated to the Early/Middle Bronze Age.

Evidence for activity from the Middle Bronze Age through to the Middle Iron Age was sparse; a number of stratigraphically early ditched boundaries may have represented the remains of a Middle Bronze Age field system, whilst residual flint-tempered post-Deverel Rimbury sherds hint at a Late Bronze Age/Early Iron Age presence. While there is some evidence for limited occupation of the site during the Middle Iron Age, the Late Iron Age saw the beginning of extensive and sustained activity that continued into Early Roman times, although current understanding of the layout and character of remains of this date across the development area as a whole is limited by the scale of area excavation. At least two major trackways running east to west were established on the eastern side of the river in this period, probably running from a ford or river crossing and following the putative 'southern route' of the Icknield Way. Adjacent to the one of the trackways, a regular rectangular enclosure was constructed. With its earliest phases appearing to date to *c*.15 BC to AD 30, it was associated with substantial assemblages of pottery and animal bone, together with a series of inhumation burials and disarticulated human remains, found both within the ditch of the enclosure and within its internal area.

The trackways and enclosure were superseded in the period immediately following the Roman Conquest by an agglomerated enclosure complex and field system laid out on a new alignment. This may have extended on both sides of the river and was linked by ditched trackways, presumably to aid the movement of animals and equipment. The presence of two possible post-built corrals indicates that animal husbandry was undertaken on a large-scale, possibly associated with supplying the nearby fort at Great Chesterford. This dramatic change in use of the landscape not only involved a physical realignment (from east–west to north–south) but, importantly, the ancient route of the Icknield Way was blocked. In general, this pattern of land use largely continued into the post-Conquest period, although a rectangular structure possibly representing a small shrine was present. Further land division, including the establishment of new trackways, continued into the Middle Roman period, although farming activity appears to have begun to decline. Some sporadic quarrying for the extraction of sands and gravels was undertaken along the valley terraces, after which the land lay largely fallow until it was re-settled by the Anglo-Saxons several hundred years later.

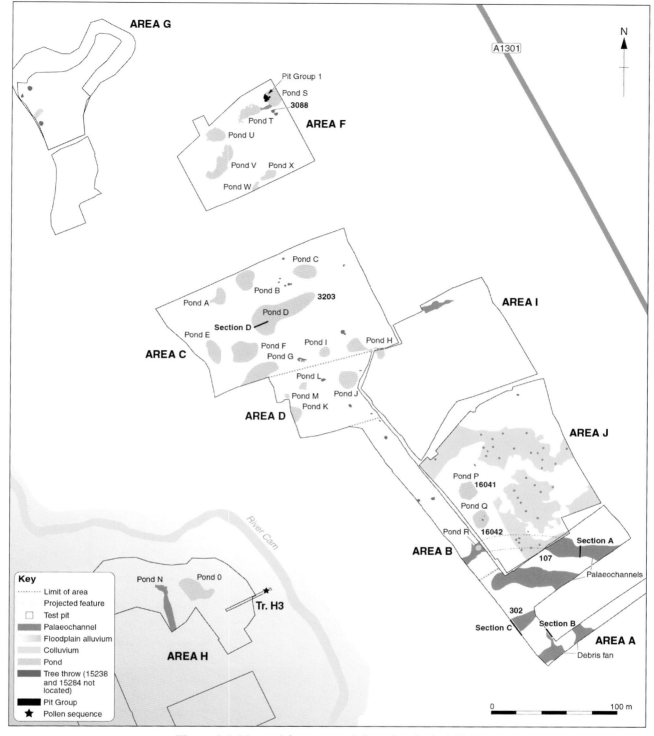

Figure 2.1 Natural features and deposits. Scale 1:3000

II. Natural features and deposits
Fig. 2.1

Investigation of the valley side and floodplain environments of the Genome Campus revealed numerous natural features and deposits, significant in archaeological terms principally because of their association with several large *in situ* prehistoric artefact scatters and with a more general 'background' scatter of flintwork. Most of these features and deposits originally formed as a result of geomorphological processes operating over the course of the Late Glacial and Early/Middle Holocene – the archaeological investigations at the Genome Campus facilitated a study of the geology and geomorphology of the site, co-ordinated by Steve Boreham of the University of Cambridge. The results of Boreham's analyses are set out in Chapter 4.IV and have been previously published elsewhere in support of a general model of the geological history of the Upper Cam Valley (Boreham and Rolfe 2009).

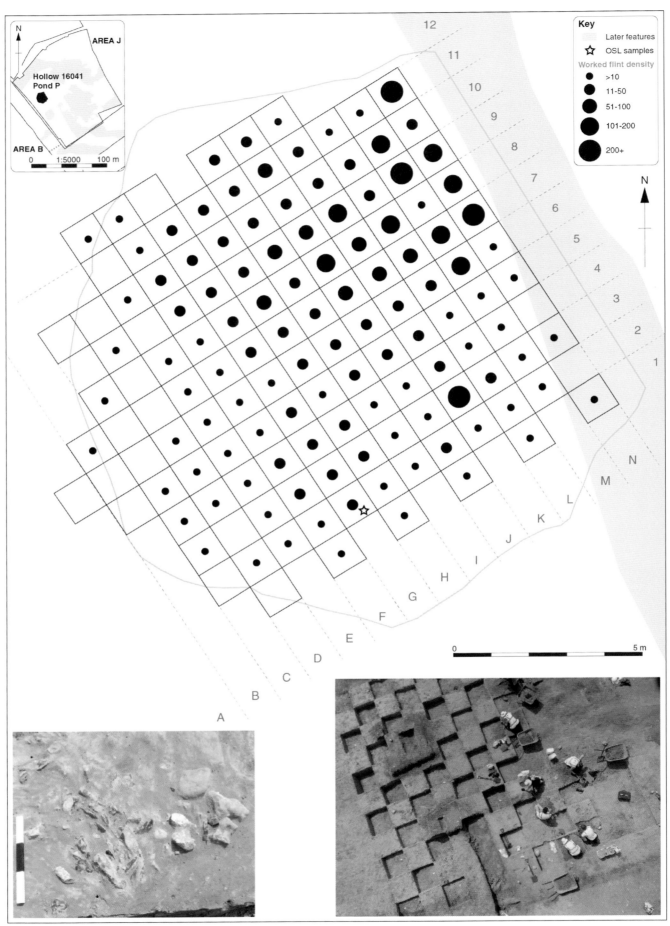

Figure 2.2 Period 1.1: Pond P, showing excavated grid squares and the overall density of worked flint.
Scale 1:100

As is detailed by Boreham and Rolfe (2009), the main areas of excavation on the eastern side of the Cam at the Genome Campus (Areas A–G) lay upon a thin but complex series of deposits of Pleistocene sands and gravels and solifluction deposits overlying the chalk bedrock. Exposure of these Pleistocene deposits during site stripping revealed a series of naturally formed features, with a number of linear channels/runnels, aligned perpendicular to the valley slope, alongside other irregular, oval/sub-circular hollows, some of which appear to have originally formed as a series of temporary pools, referred to here as *palaeochannels* and *ponds* respectively (Fig. 2.1). To the west, on the valley floodplain, trenches excavated on the eastern side of the river and area excavation on the western side (Area H) revealed sequences of Holocene peats and alluvium. These were recorded in detail during the initial trenching of Area H and yielded a pollen sequence which, whilst undated, appears to provide evidence for the local vegetation over the course of the Early and Middle Holocene (Chapter 4.IV).

Aside from sections mechanically excavated through the ponds and palaeochannels for the purposes of the geological recording described by Boreham (Sections A, B, C and D), most of these features were subject to investigation through surface collection and/or test excavation. The majority produced no finds, or relatively small quantities of flintwork (see below, Table 3.4), but in three cases (Ponds P, Q and R) they were associated with significant, *in situ* artefact scatters – described in detail in later sections.

On the lower slope of the valley side, particularly to the south-east (in Area J), more extensive areas of slope wash/colluvial deposits were also exposed, variably preserved within the undulating surface of the underlying sands and gravels. This material was examined in detail during the excavation of Area J, when systematic surface collection was carried out over the exposed colluvial deposits, alongside the excavation of thirty-nine 1 x 1m test pits (up to *c*.0.6m in depth) (Fig. 2.1), producing a substantial assemblage of over 500 worked flints. Alongside these colluvial deposits, numerous tree throws were recorded across the site. Although most of these features were simply recorded in plan, several were sample excavated and in some cases produced modest amounts of worked flint.

III. Period 1: Terminal Palaeolithic to Mesolithic (*c*.10,000 to 4000 BC)

Period 1.1. Terminal Palaeolithic (*c*.10,000–9000 BC)
by Lawrence Billington, with Barry J. Bishop and Anthony Haskins

Introduction
Aside from a few pieces of possible Late Glacial flintwork recovered as part of the larger multiperiod lithic assemblages from across the site, the evidence for this period at the Genome Campus consists of a single discrete flint scatter preserved within the fills of a hollow (Pond P) to the south-east (Area J, Fig. 2.2). The characteristics of the large lithic assemblage making up the scatter, and comparison

with contemporary sites known from Britain and adjacent parts of the continent, strongly suggests that it represents the remains of a single short-lived episode of activity belonging to a 'long-blade' industry of the Terminal Palaeolithic. In the insular context, such assemblages appear to date to the final years of the Younger Dryas (the climatic downturn at the end of the Late Glacial period) and the earliest Holocene: the results of OSL dating of the sediments associated with the scatter at the Genome Campus are consistent with this broad dating.

The discovery of this nationally important assemblage was made during the final phase of the project's fieldwork programme in 2014 and was entirely unanticipated. Whilst considerable resources were directed towards the excavation and analysis of the scatter, the potential for further analysis and research is very high. In particular, Bishop's analysis of the substantial assemblage of almost 4,000 worked flints, reported in Chapter 3.I, has been comprehensive in terms of cataloguing and classifying the assemblage, but only very limited refitting work has been undertaken and there also remains scope for more detailed technological/attribute analyses. Similarly, a 'pilot-study' of the potential of the assemblage for microscopic use-wear analysis, involving the inspection of a sample of 100 struck flints, has suggested that the material has considerable potential for future work of this kind (see Chapter 3.I). This analysis also resulted in the identification of possible black residues on two of the artefacts, one of which has subsequently been analysed and identified as pine tar (G. Langejans pers. comm.) – representing the first identification of a probable mastic/adhesive material on a Terminal Palaeolithic artefact from Britain.

Late Glacial pond/pool (Pond P)
Fig. 2.2, Pl. 2.1
This pool or hollow (16041), like the other examples exposed across the terrace, appeared in plan as a roughly subcircular area of reddish brown sandy silt, distinct from the surrounding coarser gravels and sands. Its north-eastern edge had been truncated by a substantial recut medieval ditch (see Fig. 2.2), but its surviving dimensions were approximately 18m by 13m.

Following the recovery of Upper Palaeolithic-type flintwork during initial investigation of the hollow, a strategy for related sampling was developed which aimed to maximise recovery whilst minimising disruption to the timetabling of the development. Following mechanical excavation of *c*.0.1m of the upper fill of the hollow (see below), a 1m grid was set out and work commenced with the excavation of alternate/chequerboard squares, followed by the almost total excavation of all the remaining grid squares. Individual context numbers were assigned to deposits encountered within each test pit and each deposit was excavated in 50mm thick spits, with individual artefacts being located to the level of the individual grid square, context and spit. The spoil generated during excavation was dry sieved on site where possible and a 20 litre bulk environmental sample was taken from a random context and spit within each square for the retrieval of smaller flints such as micro-debitage.

Plate 2.1 Overhead photograph of Late Upper Palaeolithic pond/hollow 16041 (Pond P) and Early Neolithic pond/hollow 16042 (Pond Q) in Area J during excavation, showing chequerboard sampling strategy

The hollow may have originated in the Late Glacial period as a pool/pond, as with other features of this kind described by Boreham in Chapter 4 (and see Boreham and Rolfe 2009). Excavation across the feature consistently revealed a sequence of three deposits. The lowest layer excavated within the hollow, which appeared to represent undisturbed deposits forming its base, was a compact layer of mid-brownish to yellowish red sand with frequent sub-rounded and rounded flints gravels and cobbles (15452). This was overlain by a light brownish grey silt, again up to 0.2m thick (15451). The uppermost deposit, exposed on the surface of the hollow, was a reddish brown silty sand up to 0.2m thick (15450), similar in composition and colour to colluvially derived deposits exposed elsewhere in Area J. Initial test pitting showed that the upper part of this uppermost deposit contained low densities of chronologically mixed flintwork, whilst the Terminal Palaeolithic flintwork was found in the lowest part of this deposit and throughout the underlying grey silt. Given constraints on time, the upper c.0.1m of context 15450 was therefore removed by a mechanical excavator. Additional spits were hand excavated into the underlying sands/gravels (15452), until such a point as no further finds were made (generally after the removal of one or two spits).

During the course of the excavations, OSL samples were taken from the sequence of deposits encountered in the hollow, as exposed in grid square G2 (see below, Fig. 3.1). The full results of this work are reported in Chapter 4.V. In summary, three samples were taken from each of the three deposits and the resulting date ranges suggest that the lowest 'natural' deposit (15452) was emplaced/last exposed before or during the early stages of the Last Glacial Maximum (c.29740–24130 cal BP). Dating of the overlying silt deposit produced somewhat ambiguous results, although the most archaeologically acceptable date range falls in the Late Glacial period, covering the final part of the Late Glacial Interstadial, the Younger Dryas and beginning of the Holocene (c.13340–10770 cal BP, 11390–8820 cal BC), whilst the uppermost, at least partly colluvial, infill appears to have accumulated in the later part of the Neolithic period (c.3370–2440 cal BC). With the flintwork appearing most likely to have originally been deposited on the surface of the silt deposits, this sequence is regarded as consistent with the Terminal Palaeolithic date indicated by the technology and typology of the assemblage.

The lithic scatter
Including a very small number of pieces derived from the fills of later features cut into the deposits infilling the hollow, a group of 3,817 worked flints was recovered. As detailed by Bishop (Chapter 3.I), the vast majority consist of flakes and blades and less than 4% has been retouched or shows convincing evidence for use, whilst cores provide only 0.6% of the total. Almost all of the flint derived from the upper two layers of the hollow, these providing 98% of the assemblage in roughly equal proportions. Overall, the assemblage shows a clear emphasis on the large-scale working of locally procured flint, with all stages of reduction represented from the initial stages of testing and preparing of nodules through to the discard of exhausted cores. The scarcity of retouched tools is typical of most assemblages of this date, although their presence, and that of pieces bearing clear macroscopically visible use-wear, does provide evidence that other activities aside from flintworking (*e.g.* butchery, wood/bone/hide working) were being undertaken at the site.

Our understanding of the distribution and taphonomy of the scatter should be regarded as provisional, given that a major programme of refitting would allow a much more detailed analysis of the scatter's formation, but it has been possible to gain some insights into the spatial organisation of flintworking at the site and the scatter's taphonomic history, as set out by Bishop in Chapter 3.I. Here, it is sufficient to note that the excellent condition of the flint assemblage and the very high potential for refitting clearly indicates that it represents an essentially *in situ*, minimally disturbed scatter, its distribution and composition suggesting that it probably derives from a single short-lived episode of activity. A basic distribution plot of the density of lithics is provided here (Fig. 2.2, and see Chapter 3.I, Fig. 3.1 and 5.II), showing very clearly that the greatest densities of material generally occurred in the north-eastern part of the hollow, with the number of pieces generally diminishing to the south and west and being largely absent from the hollow's western side. In the densest parts of the scatter values of above 100 pieces per metre square were common and dense clusters of flakes and blades were exposed. Burnt worked flint was very rare, but the presence of small quantities of unworked burnt flint – largely from the western side of the scatter – suggests that hearth settings could have been present in this area (see Discussion, Chapter 5.II).

Period 1.2: Mesolithic (*c.*9,000 to 4,000 BC)

Introduction
There was widespread evidence for Mesolithic activity across the site in the form of poorly stratified/ residual flintwork, albeit that there were no large coherent scatters comparable to that of the Terminal Palaeolithic and only one group of possible pits has been tentatively attributed to this period. With much of the Mesolithic flintwork occurring as a minority part of chronologically mixed flint assemblages – and with a relative dearth of chronologically sensitive, diagnostic, tool forms (just four microliths were recovered) – our understanding of the dating and tempo of activity in this period is poor. This said, it is very unlikely that Mesolithic activity at the Genome Campus predates *c.*8000 BC and much of the Mesolithic flint may reflect activity in the later part of the period (from *c.*7000 BC; see discussion in Chapter 5.III). The lower part of the pollen sequence obtained from organic floodplain deposits in Area H may reflect environmental conditions during this period (see Boreham, Chapter 4.IV), with woodland environments initially dominated by birch, pine and hazel giving way to oak, lime, elm and alder over the course of the Early and Middle Holocene.

A Mesolithic pit group
Fig. 2.3
In Area F, cutting the north-western quadrant of one of the ponds/pools (Pond S; 1529/1530), lay twelve features of varying form and size, some of which were confidently identified as deliberately cut features, but including others which may have been natural tree throw holes (Pit Group 1; Fig. 2.3). The most substantial and clearly defined pit (3114: 3.28m by 1.44m by 0.51m deep) was curvilinear – almost kidney-shaped – in plan, aligned roughly north-east to south-west, with concave sides and an irregular base.

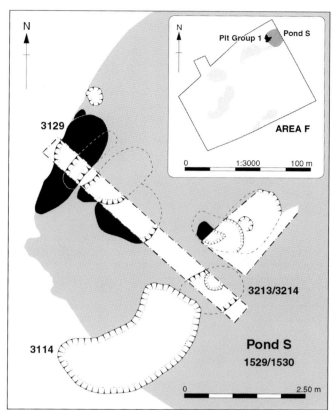

Figure 2.3 Period 1.2: Area F, Mesolithic Pit Group 1, cutting Pond S. Scale 1:80

Its primary fill was mixed yellow brown sandy clay silt, with areas of redeposited chalk, occasional flecks of charcoal and burnt clay. The overlying fill was a very dark grey sandy clay silt with a concentration of charcoal flecks in one area (3113), from which a substantial quantity of struck flint (133 pieces) was recovered, including a high proportion of core reduction knapping waste alongside fine blade-based removals and a serrated blade. The flint assemblage, in a good sharp condition, suggests a Mesolithic date for this feature (see Chapter 3.II). The similarities of the fills of this feature and those within the surrounding pits suggests that they may all have been broadly contemporary.

The Mesolithic flint assemblage
Pl. 2.2
The large, multi-period, assemblage of worked flint recovered from the fills of the natural ponds/ palaeochannels, colluvial deposits and fills of later features across the site evidently includes a substantial Mesolithic component (Bishop and Donnelley, Chapter 3.II), but given the difficulties in distinguishing between most of the products of Mesolithic and earlier Neolithic flintwork, it is very difficult to quantify the proportion of this material which dates to this period. In a number of cases, however, deposits infilling some of the ponds (Fig. 2.1) appear to have contained small but relatively coherent collections of Mesolithic flintwork. Notably, two of these assemblages (from Pond X (47 pieces) and Pond V (26 pieces)), were, like Pit Group 1, located in Area F – perhaps suggesting a focus of activity in this area. In the southern part of the

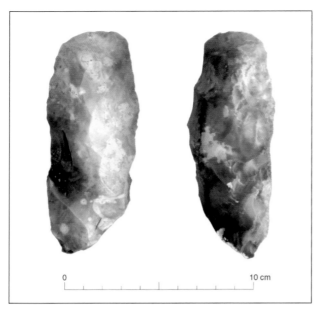

Plate 2.2 Mesolithic tranchet axe or adze (SF 529) from Early Neolithic deposit in Pond Q (16042, Area J). Scale 1:2

distinctive Mesolithic component including a very fine transversely sharpened axehead (Pl. 2.2) and a series of systematically produced prismatic blades.

IV. Period 2: Neolithic to Bronze Age (*c.*4000 to 800 BC)

Period 2.1: Neolithic (*c.*4000 to 2400 BC)
Fig. 2.4

Introduction
The availability of closely datable pottery, flint tools and a series of radiocarbon dates has made it possible to attribute the more significant of the Neolithic remains at the Genome Campus to three sub-periods: Early Neolithic (*c.*4000–3300 BC), Middle Neolithic (*c.*3300–2900 BC) and Late Neolithic (*c.*2900–2400 BC), with subsequent Beaker-associated activity attributed to the Bronze Age (Period 2.2; see below). The most significant remains date to the Early Neolithic, comprising a major midden-like accumulation of pottery and flint from a hollow/pond (Pond Q) and an important double burial, whilst Middle and Late Neolithic activity was largely represented by a few pit groups (Fig. 2.4).

Early Neolithic

Hollow/pond 16042 (Pond Q)
Fig. 2.5, Pls 2.3 and 2.4
This large hollow, which lay a few metres to the south of Pond P in the south-eastern part of the site (Area J), measured *c.*13m by 11m and was a maximum of

site (in Area B), test pitting of the upper fills of Pond R produced a moderately large assemblage of flint (243 pieces) which, although dominated by Neolithic material (see below), contained a small Mesolithic element including a microburin and a small number of fine blades and bladelets. Similarly, in Pond Q (Area J) – where a major assemblage of Early Neolithic pottery and flint was recovered – the lowest deposits infilling the pond produced flintwork with a small but

Plate 2.3 Early Neolithic pond/hollow 16042 (Pond Q, Area J), with Palaeolithic hollow 16041 (Pond P) to the north and the Genome Campus buildings in the background, looking north

16

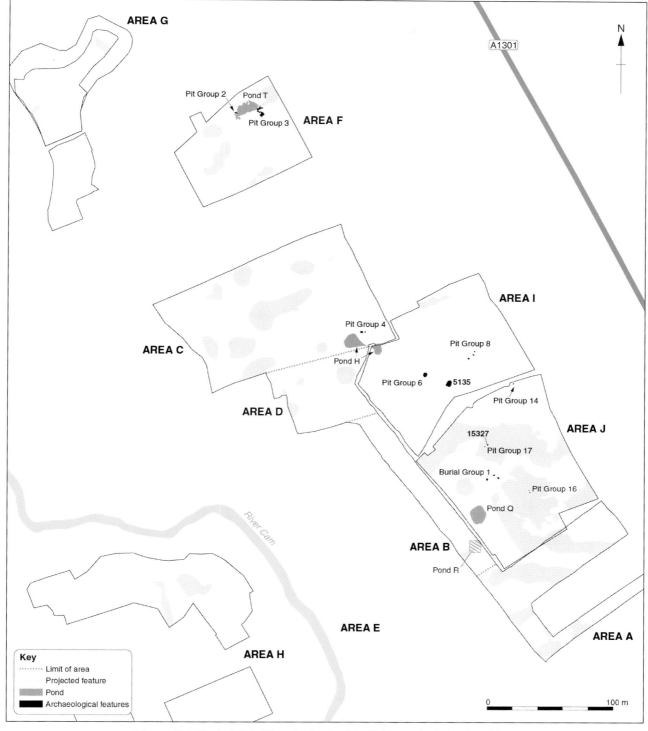

Figure 2.4 Period 2.1: The site in the Neolithic period. Scale 1:3000

0.3m deep with gently curving sides and a slightly undulating base (Pl. 2.3). The hollow was sampled through a grid of 1 x 1m squares, 74 of which were excavated – representing over 70% of the area of the hollow. A sequence of three main deposits was identified. The earliest deposit comprised a 'natural' gravel-rich greyish-brown silty sand (15697), which had an average thickness of 0.1m. Overlying this was a mixed layer of dark brown to red/black silty sand (15696) that measured a maximum of 0.2m thick and was interpreted as a probable buried soil horizon,

above which was a layer of mid greyish brown silty sand, which may have been partly colluvial in origin (15695). The hollow produced very substantial assemblages of pottery and flint, the vast majority of which derived from the upper two deposits. Bone was not, however, preserved and bulk sampling produced largely negative results, with sparse charcoal alongside a small number of poorly preserved (and potentially intrusive) cereal grains.

The pottery is made up exclusively of flint- and sand-tempered material of Early Neolithic date –

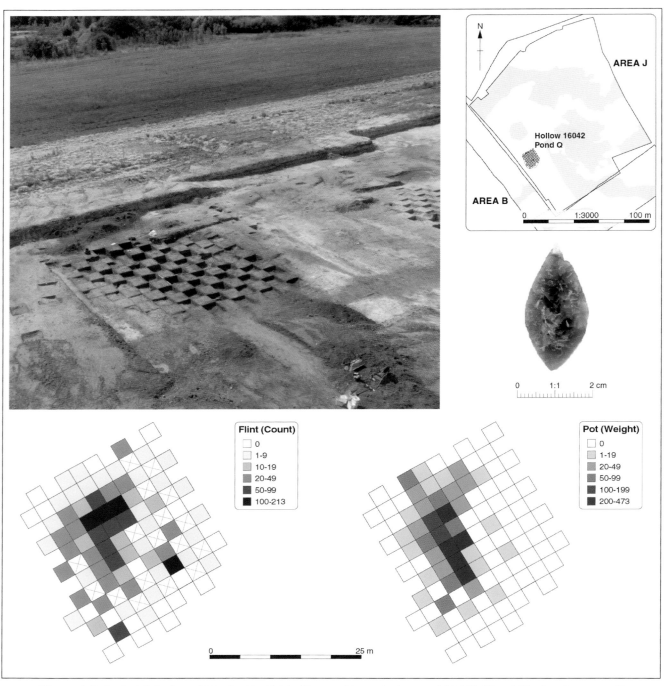

Figure 2.5 Period 2.1: Area J, Early Neolithic flintworking within pond 16042 (Pond Q) showing overall densities of pottery and worked flint, and a leaf-shaped arrowhead recovered during the excavation of the adjacent Pond P

with 643 sherds (2989g) including rims from twenty-one individual vessels (Chapter 3.VII). The flint assemblage is also dominated by Early Neolithic material (Pl. 2.4), although, as discussed above, it does include a small Mesolithic component, largely from the lowest ('natural') fill of the hollow, and a small quantity of potentially later flake-based material was recovered from the uppermost deposit. The flintwork from the 'buried soil' is in fresh condition and includes occasional refitting pieces, although the material from the upper, potentially partly colluvial deposit, appears to have experienced a somewhat greater level of disturbance. Plotting the horizontal distribution

of the pottery and flint shows that most of the finds were concentrated in an area close to the centre of the hollow, with a 'core' concentration covering some 5m by 3m, where densities of pottery and flint were up to 213g and 473 pieces respectively (Fig 2.5). As discussed in more detail in Chapter 5 – and in contrast to the Terminal Palaeolithic scatter in Pond P – the distribution, character and condition of the finds suggest that the scatter is probably best interpreted as representing a midden-like accumulation of material, as opposed to directly representing an occupation/activity area.

Plate 2.4 Selection of worked flints from Early Neolithic pond 16042 (Pond Q, Area J). 1) Fragment of polished axe (SF 533); 2) Laurel leaf (SF 534); 3) Bifacially worked implement -possible laurel leaf blank; 4) Bifacially worked implement; 5) Rod-like implement; 6) Rod-like implement. Scale 1:2

Double inhumation burial
Fig. 2.6
A rare example of a double inhumation burial of Early Neolithic date was located in the central part of Area J (Burial Group 1), lying within a shallow, poorly defined sub-rectangular cut (15188) aligned east to west. The latter measured 1.5m long and 0.9m wide and was 0.12m deep. It contained the remains of two poorly preserved adult skeletons: Sk 15189 and Sk 15190. Despite poor preservation, it was possible to establish that Sk 15189 had been placed in a tightly flexed position on its left side with its head to the east. Sk 15190 was even less well-preserved and appeared more as a 'jumble' of bones placed immediately to the west of the other individual; the lower part of its mandible was found close to the pelvis of Sk 15189. As discussed in more detail in Chapter 5.III, this might attest to two separate burial events and it is even possible that continued access to the bodies may have been facilitated by a timber burial chamber of the kind documented or inferred for other multiple Early Neolithic burials in the region. Both skeletons were sealed by a single fill of dark reddish-black organic silty sand with occasional inclusions of flint pebbles. A tiny sherd of intrusive Late Neolithic/Early Bronze Age pottery was recovered from this backfill, while environmental sampling produced only sparse charcoal.

Radiocarbon dating of samples of bone from each skeleton produced date ranges in the early 4th millennium BC, and were subsequently confirmed by a series of replicate measurements, with three dates acquired for Sk 15189 (OxA-30871, OxA-33462, OxA33463) and two for Sk 15190 (see Appendix 2). The dates for each skeleton are statistically consistent (Sk 15189, X2 df=2 T=0.2 (5% 6.0); Sk 15190, X2 df=1 T=0.5 (5% 3.8); Ward and Wilson 1978) and can justifiably be combined (weighted mean) to produce date ranges of 3700–3640 cal BC for Sk 15189 and 3720–3640 cal BC for Sk 15190 at 95% confidence.

Pits
Figs 2.4 and 2.6
Two sub-circular pits (15187 and 15193) of similar size were located adjacent and to the south of the grave described above; however, they contained no finds and remain undated. Any direct association with the burials seems unlikely. Pit 15187, positioned 3.5m to the south-west of the burial, was sub-circular in plan (1.2m long, by 0.96m wide and 0.31m deep) with steeply sloping sides and a concave base. Its single fill contained several possibly deliberately placed but unworked large sandstone cobbles.

Three pits found in a loose cluster in the central/ southern part of Area I have been tentatively attributed to the Early Neolithic on the basis of their associated flintwork (Pit Group 6: 5133, 5135 and 5304; Fig. 2.4). Unusually, one of these features (5135) was very large, measuring 3.75m long and up to 1.36m deep, with a complex sequence of eight fills, generally consisting

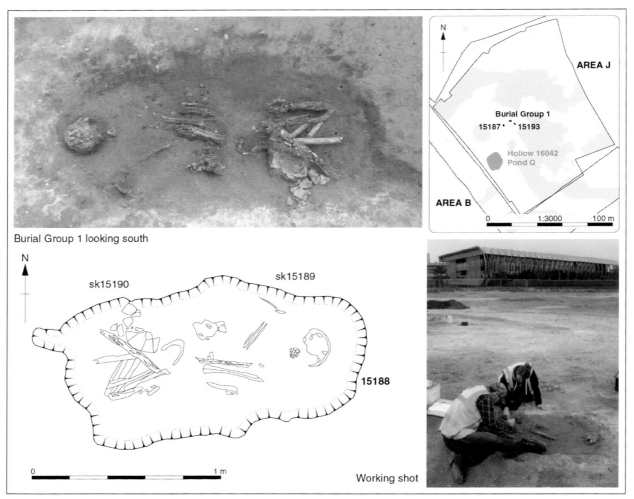

Burial Group 1 looking south

sk15190

sk15189

15188

Working shot

AREA J

Burial Group 1
15187 · ˙ ˙ 15193

Hollow 16042
Pond Q

AREA B

0   1:3000   100 m

Figure 2.6 Period 2.1: Area J, Early Neolithic double inhumation burial (Burial Group 1). Scale 1:20

of mid red/yellow brown sandy silts. Worked flint and scraps of animal bone were found in the upper fills. The small flint assemblage includes flakes, an end scraper and a multi-platform flake core. Immediately to the south-west was a smaller circular pit (5304; 1.07m in diameter by 0.35m deep) which contained a single mid brown silt sand deposit (5305), from which the largest single lithic assemblage from Area I (consisting of 98 pieces) was recovered, including a fine denticulated tool. To the west of these two features was a relatively small circular pit (5133; 0.78m diameter and 0.35m deep). It contained a single mid brown sand fill that yielded a small blade-based assemblage of Early Neolithic date including a serrate on a blade-like flake, a narrow blade, flakes with very parallel blade-like dorsal scars and a possible axehead thinning flake.

Middle to Late Neolithic
Fig. 2.4, 2.7
Five small groups of features (Pit Groups 16, 14, 17, 4 and 8, in order of their date) have been attributed to the Middle and Late Neolithic on the basis of diagnostic pottery, flintwork and/or radiocarbon dates. All were found within the main, southern/central parts of the site (Areas C, I and J).

Pit Group 16 (Area J)
Two pairs of small pits (15194 and 15196) were located *c.*40m to the north-east of Pond Q in Area J. Sub-circular in plan, they measured 0.5m and 0.6m wide and 0.19m and 0.25m deep respectively: both produced small flint assemblages (15 and 22 pieces respectively) – including a serrated blade from pit 15194 – but no pottery. Samples taken from the fills of both pits contained small quantities of hazelnut shell fragments, whilst that from pit 15194 produced a single charred cereal grain and a glume base. Whilst the crop remains may be intrusive, a fragment of charred hazelnut shell from this feature returned a result of 3110–2920 cal BC (72% confidence; SUERC-64624 2230±29 BP), indicating a date in the later part of the Middle Neolithic, consistent with the character of the flintwork recovered from both features.

Pit Group 14 (Area J)
In the north-east corner of Area J was a shallow pit and a possible posthole. The pit (15007; 0.8m wide and 0.2m deep) contained a single fill of dark red/black silt sand with inclusions of charcoal, burnt stone and flint pebbles. Finds were limited to three struck flints, which notably included a chisel arrowhead of Middle/Late Neolithic date. The adjacent posthole (15013) produced no finds.

20

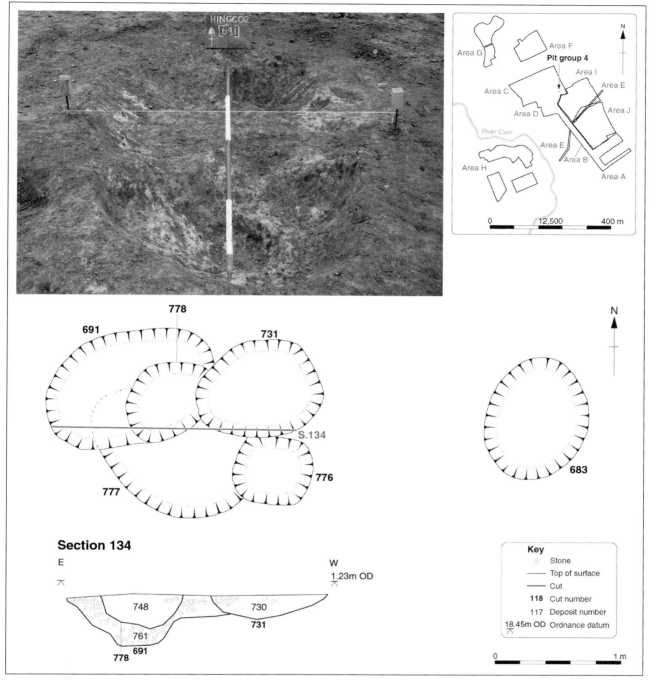

Figure 2.7 Period 2.1: Area C, Pit Group 4. Scale 1:30

Pit Group 17 (Area J)

A cluster of three small pits or tree throws (15325, 15237 and 15322) was identified in the northern part of Area J. The features measured between 0.4m and 1.1m wide and between 0.05m and 0.25m deep. Pit 15237 produced no finds, but worked flint was recovered from the other features, with a substantial assemblage of 85 flints coming from the fill of feature 15327, including a transverse (oblique) arrowhead and evidence for the use of a Levallois-like technology characteristic of the Middle/Late Neolithic. A smaller assemblage of six pieces was recovered from pit 15325, which included a transverse (chisel) arrowhead.

Pit Group 4 (Area C)

In the south-eastern part of Area C, a cluster of five intercutting pits (Fig. 2.7; 691, 731, 776, 777, 778) and an adjacent pit (683) were exposed (Pit Group 4), most of which produced quantities of Neolithic flintwork alongside a small assemblage of Late Neolithic, Grooved Ware, pottery. The pits were all circular or sub-oval in plan and ranged in size from 0.47m to 1.65m in diameter and between 0.10m and 0.44m deep. Their fills typically consisted of pale yellow brown or yellow brown sand silt, occasionally with high concentrations of charcoal and burnt stones. Pit 691 on the western edge was the most significant of these features, both because of its large size (1.65 x 0.44m in plan) and the fact that it contained a substantial flint assemblage

21

Plate 2.5 Middle to Late Neolithic pit 4908 (Pit Group 8, Area I), looking south-east

(109 pieces), including a number of scrapers, serrates and simple edge-trimmed pieces. A large naturally-shed red deer antler fragment was also found within this feature, alongside a single cattle bone which has been radiocarbon dated to 2880–2620 cal BC (92% confidence; SUERC-64619; 4138±33 BP). Pottery sherds belonging to a single vessel were spread over three of the fills (687, 690, 708), indicating the swift backfilling of this pit. The pottery assemblage also included a heavily abraded (and presumably intrusive) Beaker sherd.

Two subsequent intercutting pits (776 and 778) both contained similar dark blue-grey clay silt fills. Four Grooved Ware pottery sherds and nine struck flints were recovered from the fill of pit 776, whilst pit 778 contained twenty-five pieces of worked flint including two scrapers, one of which had been burnt. This deposit also produced a significant assemblage of pig remains consisting of nine bone and teeth fragments, including four mandibles (two of which articulated), three loose teeth and fragments of scapulae and tibia. At least two animals are represented, both identified as sows. A pig skull, radius and fibula fragments were also found (see Chapter 4.II).

Lying slightly to the east of the main cluster of pits was a further pit (683). It contained a single dark yellowish brown silt clay fill with charcoal and burnt stones. Only a tiny scrap of shell-tempered pottery was recovered from this fill, although it also contained a notable deposit of pig bone. The latter includes twenty-five bones or teeth fragments, all but one thoracic vertebra of which were from the head. Three pig skull fragments and a mandible fragment were also found. A minimum of three individuals is suggested, aged six to twelve months, one to two years, and over two years of age respectively. Two of these animals were again identified as sows (see Chapter 4.II). Also found within this deposit were twenty-seven struck

flints of very similar characteristics to the finds from the other pits, including single examples of a serrate and a scraper.

Pit Group 8 (Area I)
Pl. 2.5
Located in the eastern part of Area I was a cluster of four pits (4834, 4838, 4851, 4908; Pit Group 8). Three of these features were relatively small bowl-shaped pits (0.6–0.9m in diameter and up to 0.25m deep). However, pit 4908 was more substantial, measuring 1.3m in diameter and up to 0.6m deep with steeply sloping sides and a flat base (Pl. 2.5). The fills of these pits produced small quantities of pottery, alongside more substantial assemblages of worked flint. The pottery was in shell- and grog-tempered fabrics and the sherds from pits 4838 and 4851 have been tentatively identified as belonging to the Clacton sub-style of Grooved Ware (see Percival, Chapter 3.VII). A total of 136 worked flints came from these features; most notable was the assemblage of forty-three flints from pit 4834, which included an unusually high proportion of retouched tools including six scrapers (four on blanks struck from the same core), three serrates, a denticulate and a retouched flake (Bishop and Donnelly, Chapter 3.II).

Pit Groups 2 and 3 (Area F)
Within Area F, numerous pits dug into the periphery of the natural ponds were recorded. The pits lay in two separate clusters, some elements of which contained worked flint assemblages which may have been *in situ*. On the western side of one pond (3141/3176, Pond T) were two contemporary pits (Pit Group 2: 3174 and 3175): the larger pit (2.3 x 0.9m in plan) was kidney shaped, while the smaller one (0.6 x 0.2m) was of similar shape – neither pit was excavated. In the north-eastern part of Area F, to the south-east of Pond T,

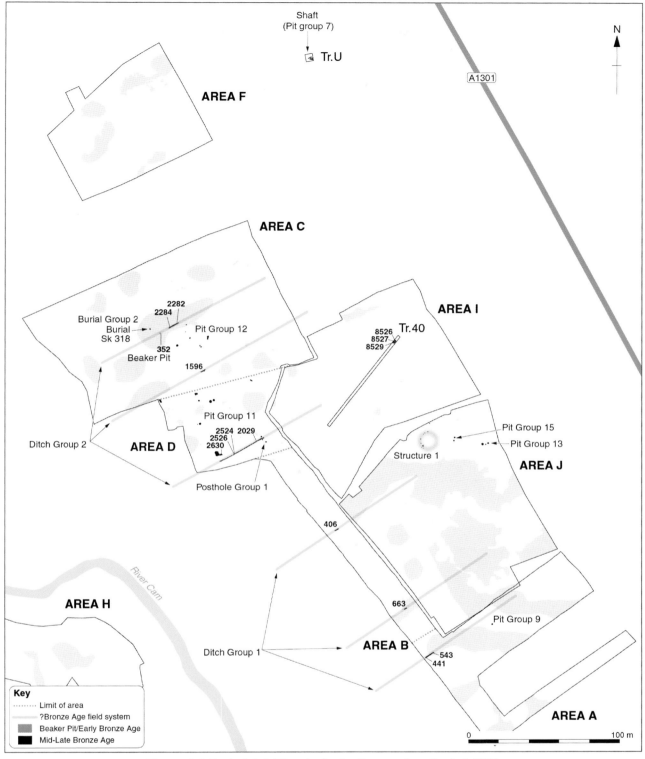

Figure 2.8 Period 2.2: The site in the Bronze Age. Scale 1:2500

were twenty-six circular and sub-circular intercutting shallow pits (Pit Group 3): these ranged in diameter between 1.15m and 2m and 0.14m to 0.35m in depth. The pits were filled with similar dark yellow brown silt sand deposits that produced quantities of worked flint possibly associated with seasonal domestic settlement, with pit 3063 containing flakes from a polished implement.

Flint scatters
A large proportion of the flint assemblage from the site was derived from the fills of later features and, as discussed by Bishop and Donnelly in Chapter 3.II, this included a major Neolithic component, with earlier Neolithic blade-based material being especially well-represented. Investigation of the deposits infilling the natural ponds generally produced very small and/or chronologically mixed assemblages of

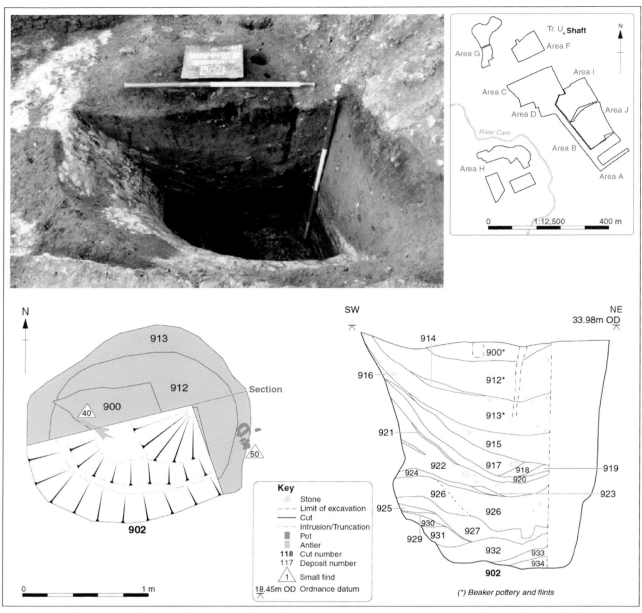

Figure 2.9 Period 2.2: Trench U, Late Neolithic/Early Bronze Age ritual shaft/pit 902 (Pit Group 7). Scale 1:30

Key

	Stone
- - -	Limit of excavation
——	Cut
- · -	Intrusion/Truncation
■	Pot
▨	Antler
118	Cut number
117	Deposit number
△1	Small find
18.45m OD ⊼	Ordnance datum

(*) Beaker pottery and flints

similar character to this residual material, although a somewhat more substantial quantity of Neolithic flint was recovered from Pond R (Area B), whilst a small but coherent Neolithic assemblage came from Pond H (Area C/I).

The flintwork from Pond R was recovered alongside a small quantity of Mesolithic material (see above), but the 243 flints deriving from test pitting of this feature appear largely to reflect Neolithic activity. The assemblage includes a number of axe thinning/finishing flakes, alongside blades and an unfinished leaf-shaped arrowhead – suggesting that this activity can be attributed to the Early Neolithic.

The assemblage of twenty flints from Pond H was much smaller, but this must at least partly reflect the lack of intensive sampling of this feature; the material was notable both for its fresh condition and in terms of appearing to derive from a small number of nodules. Dominated by narrow flakes and with a very high proportion of retouched pieces including scrapers, a

serrated flake and a chisel arrowhead, this material appears to represent a coherent Middle to Late Neolithic assemblage and it may have been associated (or contemporary) with Late Neolithic Pit Group 4, located less than 10m to the north of Pond H.

Period 2.2: Bronze Age (c.2200 to 800 BC)
Fig. 2.8

Introduction
The majority of the remains attributed to the Bronze Age were associated with Beaker pottery and date to the very beginning of this period. Most of the Beaker-associated remains appear to attest to settlement-type activity, with a substantial assemblage of domestic Beaker pottery coming from a midden-like deposit infilling a shaft-like feature in the northern part of the site (Trench U), alongside several small pit groups and a possible post-built structure in Area J. Evidence for contemporary funerary/ceremonial activity may

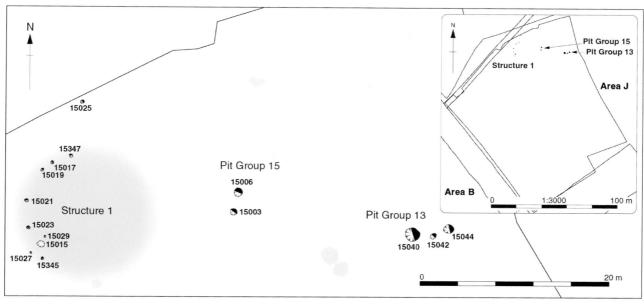

Figure 2.10 Period 2.2: Area J, Structure 1 and possibly associated pits (Pit Groups 13 and 15). Scale 1:400

be represented by a small pit containing a deliberate deposit of two Beaker vessels in Area C, found close to an inhumation burial radiocarbon dated to the Early/ Middle Bronze Age. Aside from this burial, the only possible evidence for substantive Middle Bronze Age activity consists of several poorly dated ditches which may represent the remains of a field system (Fig. 2.8).

Early Bronze Age/Beaker settlement

Shaft/pit (Pit Group 7)
Fig. 2.9
Geophysical survey of the northern part of the development area in 1993 had identified a large sub-circular anomaly, which was subsequently targeted by a small square trench (Trench U). This revealed a substantial 'shaft' (902) cut into the chalk bedrock and thin overlying deposits of brownish orange sand. Whether this feature had been deliberately cut or instead represented a natural geological feature (*i.e.* a solution hole) remains a matter for debate, but the upper part of its profile had been backfilled with a dark charcoal-rich deposit which produced a large assemblage of Beaker pottery and flintwork.

In plan, the shaft appeared as a regular, slightly oval, feature measuring 2 x 1.75m and was cut into the natural chalk to a depth of 1.95m, with near vertical sides and a broad flat base. Aside from the very dark upper fill (900), the shaft was filled by a sequence of yellow/brown sands and silty clays (912–915, 918, 922, 924-6, 929, 933–4) alternating with thinner layers of chalky silts/rubble (916–7, 919–21, 923, 930–1), all of which seem to be the result of natural weathering and silting. It seems likely that the profile of the shaft had stabilised, leaving a slight hollow, prior to the deposition of the finds-rich upper fill. The recovery of a few sherds of Beaker pottery and flints from the deposits immediately underlying the upper fill seems likely to reflect post-depositional downward movement due to bioturbation – a conclusion borne out by refitting fragments of burnt flint from fills 900

and 913. The only *possible* artefact from the lower fills is a quartzite cobble from fill 925, which had perhaps served as an anvil.

As is fully detailed in Chapter 3, a substantial finds assemblage was recovered from the upper part of the shaft's infill. The pottery consists of some 144 hand-excavated sherds forming parts of approximately thirty Beaker vessels, with an additional thirty small fragments recovered from bulk wet-sieving (Last with Percival, Chapter 3.VI). The majority of the pottery derives from 'fineware' comb-impressed Beakers but includes sherds from rusticated vessels and small abraded sherds, alongside several sets of fresher conjoining pieces representing substantial parts of individual vessels. The worked flint assemblage totalled 179 pieces, among which are twelve retouched forms, five utilised pieces and eight cores (Bishop and Donnelly, Chapter 3.II). The assemblage was found in mixed condition and a relatively high proportion had been burnt (14%), but it clearly represents a single period assemblage with the retouched tools including several distinctive Beaker or Early Bronze Age forms, such as a thumbnail scraper and an unfinished barbed-and-tanged arrowhead.

A small assemblage of faunal remains was recovered from the shaft, dominated by pig and including cattle and sheep/goat, and a red deer antler (see Bates, Chapter 4.II). Samples taken from one fill (900) were wet-sieved for plant and other organic remains, one of which produced cereal grains, including *Hordeum* (barley), as well as *Corylus* (hazel). Molluscan remains from the sample came from both woodland and open country species, perhaps implying that a mosaic of scrub/woodland and cleared areas surrounded the shaft at the time of the Beaker-associated activity.

Structure 1 and Clusters of Pits
Fig. 2.10, Pl. 2.6
Some 200m south of the shaft detailed above, a swathe of features associated with small quantities of Beaker pottery found across the northern part of Area J

Plate 2.6 Early Bronze Age pits (Pit Group 13) to the east of Structure 1 (Area J), looking north-east

appears to represent the ephemeral remains of a fairly extensive zone of Early Bronze Age activity. Close to the northern edge of excavation a group of small postholes and single pit may have been associated with a post-built structure (Structure 1; Fig. 2.10). Seven of these postholes (15017, 15019, 15021, 15023, 15027, 15345, 15347) formed an arc, perhaps creating the western side of sub/semi-circular building, with a more substantial pit (15015) and adjacent posthole (15029) located within its 'interior' and a further posthole lying isolated some 5m to the north (15025). Dating of this putative structure is tentative and rests on small quantities of Beaker pottery (14 sherds in total) recovered from posthole 15021 and pit 15015. Small quantities (1–2 pieces) of undiagnostic struck flint were also recovered from postholes 15025, 15023 and 15029, whilst a modest-sized but coherent assemblage of six flints including two small scrapers came from pit 15015.

Less than 20m to the east of the ?structure was a pair of pits (Pit Group 15), the deeper of which (pit 15003, 0.8 x 0.4m deep) contained a single dark red grey silt sand fill that produced a single sherd of Beaker pottery. An environmental sample from this fill yielded low levels of charred hazelnut shells, charcoal and crop-processing remains (chaff). An adjacent pit (15006) measured almost a metre long but was very shallow, at just 0.07m deep. Its single fill comprised soft dark brownish-grey clay sand which appeared slightly burnt in places, although the bulk sample produced only a single charred knotgrass seed.

Further to the east again, a cluster of three pits (Pit Group 13; Pl. 2.6) was found; all were roughly circular

in plan with diameters ranging between 0.6m and 1.6m and depths between 0.05m and 0.4m. The two easternmost pits were heavily truncated, with only shallow profiles surviving – both contained similar single silty sand backfills that produced no finds. However, pit 15040 – which was the most substantial feature in the group, with vertical sides and a flat base – contained a deliberate backfill of dark greyish brown sandy silt which produced two small sherds of Beaker pottery and five worked flints, including a flake core and several useable/blade-like flakes.

In addition to the pits detailed above, other pits (Pit Groups 9 and 11) found across the site produced no dating evidence aside from occasional abraded sherds of pottery in fabrics suggestive of a Bronze Age date.

Early to Middle Bronze Age ceremonial/funerary activity?
Fig. 2.11

In the central part of Area C, across and to the south of Pond D, was a scatter of small pits and postholes (2296, 2302, 2304, 2306, 2352, 2308, 2278, 2036, 352; Pit Group 12). These were mostly small in size, the majority measuring less than 1m along the longest axis and less than 0.5m deep. Finds were scarce and most of these features, although suspected to be prehistoric, are essentially undated. However, one small pit (352), measuring c.0.5m in length, contained a remarkable deposit of two poorly preserved semi-complete Beaker vessels laid on their side, one on top of the other, in the eastern half of the feature (Fig 2.11).

The formal deposition of complete vessels is very unusual in the context of Beaker-associated pit deposits and is a practice more normally associated with burials (see Chapter 5). Although not associated with any human remains, it seems possible that this feature was related to ceremonial/funerary activity quite distinct to that represented by the shaft's midden-like deposit, or the contemporary pit groups. This interpretation is supported by the presence of an adjacent inhumation burial – the tightly crouched skeleton of an adult female interred in an oval grave (319) less than 10m to the north-west (Burial Group 2; Sk 318; Fig. 2.11). Radiocarbon dated to 1750–1430 cal BC (95% confidence; Wk-12598; 3303±68 BP), this is likely to date to some centuries later than the deposition of the Beakers and implies that the area may have been marked in some way – perhaps even by a small turf-built barrow mound – and the location may have remained visible/marked into later prehistory, given the presence of an isolated Late Iron Age/Early Roman inhumation burial in the same area (see below, and Chapter 5.III for discussion).

A Bronze Age field system?
Fig. 2.8

Several short ditch remnants aligned south-west to north-east are interpreted the remains of a (Middle) Bronze Age field system, lying on the fairly flat ground of the valley terrace. Three such ditches survived in Area B (Ditch Group 1: 441/543, 663, 406 and possibly Evaluation Trench 40: 8526, 8529, 8527). The longest surviving section (ditch 406) was only 2.8m long and, as a group, they measured between 0.42 and 0.5m wide and between 0.05 and 0.12m deep. Their fills were all very similar, consisting of dark yellow brown sand silt,

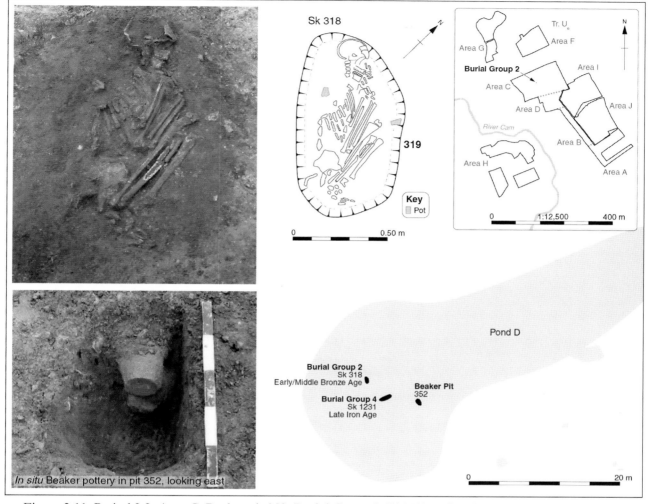

Figure 2.11 Period 2.2: Area C, Beaker pit 352, Burial Group 2 (Sk318) and Period 3.3 Burial Group 4 (Sk 1231). Scale 1:20 and Scale 1:500 (main plan)

mostly sterile, with small fragments of pottery, flint and animal bone. A similar group of ditches survived in Areas C and D, comprising three parallel north-east to south-west aligned narrow linear features (Ditch Group 2: 2029/2524/2526, 1596, 2282/2284). These ran on the same alignment as the other ditches with similar dimensions and fills, suggesting contemporaneity. The most southerly ditch (2029/2524/2526) was 33m long, 0.3–0.5m wide and 0.1m deep. In contrast, lengths of only 3m and 7m respectively survived of the other two features (1596, 2282/2284). The spacing between these three parallel boundaries was not identical, being 58m between the southern (2029/2524/2526) and central (1596) ditches and only 37m between the central and northern (2282/2284) ditches.

Scattered across the central part of Area D were various postholes (Posthole Group 1). All were sub-circular or circular in plan, 0.2–0.7m in diameter, with fills consisting of grey brown, brown or orange-brown sand silts. These postholes may have been associated with the ditch system, perhaps representing the remnants of fencing or gates.

V. Period 3: Iron Age to Romano-British (*c.*800 BC to AD 410)

Period 3.1: Middle to Late Iron Age (*c.*350 BC to AD 50)
Figs 2.12–2.14

Introduction
The most significant Iron Age remains found at the Genome Campus site evidently relate to activity during the very final part of the period and include a major multi-phase sub-square enclosure (Enclosures 1 and 2, and 'annex' Enclosure 3) which was probably first constructed and used during the last decades of the 1st century AD or sometime in the first half of the 1st century AD. There are, however, some indications of earlier, Middle Iron Age activity in the form of several small groups of pits exposed in Area J. It should also be noted that current understanding of the origins and development of Iron Age (and later) activity at the site is hampered by a lack of substantial investigations in the areas directly to the east of the River Cam and its floodplain, where cropmarks and the results of trenching hint at fairly extensive Iron Age activity to the south and east of the major areas of excavation. These difficulties aside, this phase of

27

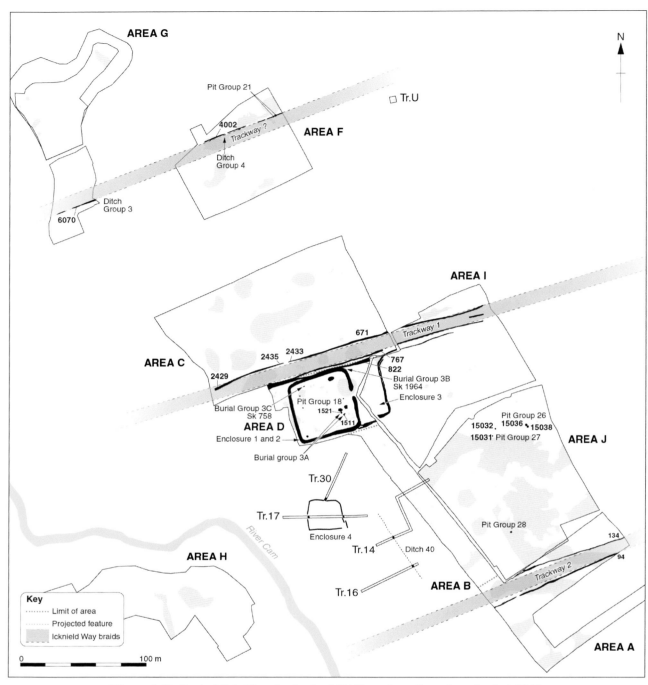

Figure 2.12 Period 3.1: The site in the Middle to Late Iron Age. Scale 1:3000

activity, preceding the Roman Conquest of AD 43, appears to have seen the establishment of a series of east to west aligned ditched trackways, broadly equating to the suggested 'southern' route of the Icknield Way (see Chapter 1.III). Slightly later, the sub-square enclosure referred to above was set out adjacent to one of the ditched trackways and was associated with major finds assemblages and evidence for funerary activity, including several inhumation burials and the deposition of disarticulated human remains. Other features attributed to this phase, albeit poorly understood, were investigated during trial trenching to the east of Area B and included a further sub-square enclosure (Enclosure 4) and a ditch aligned perpendicular to the trackways.

Middle Iron Age pits

At sites with a major Late Iron Age presence such as at the Genome Campus, isolating an earlier phase of Middle Iron Age activity can be difficult, given that handmade pottery in the 'Middle Iron tradition' continued in use alongside later forms during the Late Iron Age at many sites in this part of the region (see Hill 2002). Nonetheless, the ubiquity of diagnostically Late Iron Age pottery in most of the major assemblages suggests that Middle Iron Age activity may have been very limited, at least in the investigated areas, at the Genome Campus. The only features which have been confidently attributed to the Middle Iron Age, predating *c*.50 BC, were a small number of pits in Area J associated exclusively with Middle Iron Age pottery, one of which produced a radiocarbon date falling within the 4th or 3rd century BC.

Located in the northern part of Area J was a pair of very shallow circular pits (15036 and 15038, Pit Group 26; Fig. 2.12). The more northerly of these (pit 15036) measured 1.9m in diameter and 0.34m deep, with steeply sloping sides and a flat base. It contained two mixed silty sand fills, the lowest of which produced later prehistoric worked flints and a small quantity of pottery. An environmental sample contained very few remains, comprising a single indeterminate grain, small amounts of charcoal and an amphibian bone. Pit 15038, which measured 1.8m in diameter but was just 0.1m deep with gently sloping sides and a flat base, contained a single sterile fill of chalk-rich silty sand.

Two smaller roughly circular pits (15032 and 15031; Pit Group 27) were positioned approximately 24m to the west of Pit Group 26. The more northerly example (15032) measured 1.4m by 1.3m in plan and 0.93m deep with vertical sides and a flat base. This contained a single deliberate backfill of friable dark red-black sand silt with frequent inclusions of burnt clay (possibly daub) and burnt stones. Finds comprised animal bone, fired clay, flint and pottery, along with part of a possible saddlestone quern that may have been placed within the base of the pit. The second pit lay a few metres to the south-west and was heavily truncated: it measured 0.95m by 0.85m and was just 0.06m deep with a flat but slightly irregular base. It contained a mixed fill of soft dark brownish-grey to black sandy silt that produced a small quantity of pottery and worked flint. Environmental samples from both pits produced sparse remains, including single examples of cereal grains and a weed seed.

Positioned c. 80m to the south was another circular pit (15066; Pit Group 28) that had a diameter of 1.2m, with steep sides and a fairly flat base. This pit survived to a much greater depth (1.3m) and contained a single deliberately deposited backfill of dark brown-grey silt sand with chalk pebbles. Finds consisted of small amounts of animal bone, worked and burnt flint, fired clay and a collection of Iron Age pottery. An environmental sample produced a moderate amount of charcoal and a single barley grain; a radiocarbon date derived from the latter returned a date of 390–340 cal BC (22% confidence) or 330–200 cal BC (73% confidence) (SUERC-64620, 2230±29 BP; Appendix 2).

East to west aligned trackways

Trackway 1
Fig. 2.12; Pl. 2.7
A major development during this period was the establishment of a ditched trackway which ran west-south-west to east-north-east across the entire width of the excavated area (Areas C, D and I; Trackway 1). The ditches, which lay c.12m apart and bounded the trackway to the north and south, were dug in a series of overlapping shorter segments. In one place a gap was left between the segments of the northern ditch (between terminals 2435 and 2433), presumably to provide access onto the routeway. The ditches clearly showed evidence of long-standing maintenance as they were re-cut several times.

Plate 2.7 Handmade globular bowl of Middle Iron Age date, found unstratified. Scale 1:2

The northern ditch running across Areas C and I (671) varied in width (depending on levels of truncation) between 0.3m and 0.65m and was consistently shallow at between 0.07m and 0.42m deep, with a gently U-shaped profile. Its fills ranged from yellow-brown clay silt in the west to more light red-brown in the east. Finds were sparse, but this may be due – in part – to the severe truncation that had taken place. A possible re-cut of this ditch (2429) was found at the western end of the excavated area (Area C). It was very similar in its dimensions to the original ditch, at 0.45m wide and 0.12m deep, with a very dark grey-brown clay sand silt fill that contained no finds.

To the south, the first southern trackway ditch also extended across Areas C and I (822). This ditch was generally more substantial than its northern counterpart, varying in width between 1m and 3.3m and surviving to a maximum depth of 1m. As with the northern example, its infilling ranged from yellow-brown clay silt in the west to more light red-brown in the east. Finds were equally sparse, although animal bone was found in one fill. The ditch was later recut to the north (767); this phase of the ditch was also substantial and ranged between 0.56m and 1.05m wide and 0.18m and 1.1m deep. It had a similar 'U'-shaped profile with a flat base. The fill was consistently dark yellow-brown sand silt clay with occasional finds of pottery and bone fragments. Sixty-five sherds of pottery were recovered from the various ditch fills and, although there were no sherds diagnostic of form, this material included a large proportion of handmade pottery in sandy fabrics, alongside a small number of grog-tempered sherds; the presence here of considerable quantities of pottery in a Middle Iron Age tradition contrasts with the Late Iron Age assemblage from Enclosure 1/2 to the south (see below), suggesting that the trackway may have had its origins in the Middle Iron Age or at least the earlier part of the Late Iron Age (Brown and Percival, Chapter 3.VII). Additionally, part of a Middle Iron Age handmade globular bowl with post-firing perforations (Pl. 2.7) was also found to the north of the trackway during surface cleaning. Few animal bones attributed to this period were found. Articulating remains of a cow astragalus, calcaneum and navicular-cuboid (of the ankle joint) were found in the recut of the southern ditch. A bone tool, a small pointed blade fashioned from a sheep or goat tibia (SF 216), found in a fill of the southern ditch recut close to the western edge of Area C is suggested to be of earlier Iron Age date (see Riddler and Trzaska-Nartowski, Chapter 3.XI) and is hence probably residual.

Trackway 2
Some 200m to the south of Trackway 1, in Area A, ran another ditched trackway (Trackway 2), on a similar east north-east to west-south-west alignment, bounded by narrow, slightly divergent ditches. Its northern ditch (134) either terminated or turned to the north-west beneath the baulk at the junction of Areas A and B. Within the excavated area, the gap between the northern and southern trackway ditches narrowed from 16m at the west to only 10m at the east. Whilst the northern trackway boundary was uninterrupted within Area A, the southern side had a gap of less than 2.75m approximately 20m from the western baulk; the western terminal was removed by a later ditch, although the eastern terminal survived. The southern ditch (94) appeared to continue beyond the western baulk of Area A. Three postholes related to the northernmost ditch, while two others may have been associated with the butt end of the southern side (not illustrated). Deposits associated with this trackway yielded fourteen sherds (143g) of pottery. Although the track may have originated in the Late Iron Age, the pottery indicates that it remained in use during the 1st century AD or even later. Imported wares include a samian fragment of Les Martres-de-Veyre production, dated to AD 100–125 and a Spanish DR20 amphora sherd, a type circulating in Britain from the late 1st century to mid 3rd century AD. Native wares are all body sherds, mostly in sandy fabrics, some with a distinctly Romanised appearance.

Trackway or field boundaries?
In the northern part of the site (Areas F and G) were fragments of parallel ditches extending over a distance of 190m across Areas F and G (6070 and 804/4002; Ditch Groups 3 and 4; Fig. 2.12). These were aligned east-north-east to west-south-west, roughly equally spaced and broadly parallel to Trackways 1 and 2: combined they may have formed part of another trackway, or perhaps part of a field system (possibly both). The ditch cuts were a maximum of 0.5m wide by 0.34m deep but were more typically *c.*0.15m deep. The single fills comprised mid brown sand clay silt with occasional small stones. A flint scraper was recovered from one of the ditch fills during the evaluation phase, while a (residual) transverse arrowhead and flint debitage (in ditch 4002, Area F), a single sherd of undiagnostic pottery and a small number of animal bone fragments were retrieved during the main excavation.

A large mortuary or ceremonial enclosure (Enclosure 1/2)
Figs 2.12 and 2.13; Pl. 1.1
The sub-square enclosure laid out on the southern side of Trackway 1 represents the most significant element of the Late Iron Age remains investigated at the Genome Campus. The original enclosure ditch (Enclosure 1) had been subject to major phase of recutting (Enclosure 2), indicating a somewhat extended history – although the recut very closely followed the original layout of the ditch and faithfully preserved the original layout/morphology of the enclosure. Throughout its history, the enclosure's ditches defined an area measuring approximately 45m across internally; enclosing an area of some 0.2ha, with a 4m-wide entranceway on its eastern side leading into a ditched 'annex' (Enclosure 3, see below). The ditch defining the enclosure's northern side was cut through the earlier of the ditches making up the southern side of Trackway 1 and the remodelling of the trackway (represented by ditch 767; see above) seems likely to have taken place concurrently with the construction of the enclosure. Formal access to the enclosure appears only to have been possible from Trackway 1, being achieved by passing through the newly created gap in the southern side of the trackway ditch and through the annex represented by Enclosure 3 (Fig. 2.13).

Thirteen individual sections were cut through the enclosure ditches, varying from 1m to 4m in width, with particular attention paid to the entranceway and the corners of the enclosure. In the majority of these sections the full profile of the ditch and its recut was excavated (see Sections 304, 399, 598, Fig. 2.13), but along the southern side of the enclosure several additional sections were cut through the secondary and upper fills of the recut of the ditch (Enclosure 2, 3062 and 2557) in an area where particularly high concentrations of finds had been found in its fills.

The original cut of the ditch which formed Enclosure 1 (1572, 1762, 1541, 1906, 2567, 2589, 2685, 2390, 2146), was a fairly substantial feature and, although invariably heavily truncated by its later recut, it measured up to 1.2m deep and was probably originally up to 2m wide, with steeply sloping sides and a narrow concave base. Cut into the base of this feature in the north-eastern corner of the enclosure (2146) was an east to west aligned grave (2147), containing the skeleton of an (elderly) adult male (see below, Sk 1964; Burial Group 3B). This burial may have been cut through a thin primary fill of brown silty sand on the base of the ditch, but clearly occurred very soon after the original construction of the enclosure. The ditch was filled by a series of yellowish brown and brown silty sands and had infilled to an advanced stage when it was subject to a major phase of recutting. This recut ditch (Enclosure 2; 1569, 1509, 1777, 3034, 3062, 2539, 2392, 1931, 1903) was very similar in layout and morphology/size to the original cut. In places it had been cut almost exactly along the original line of the ditch (*e.g.* Section 598, Fig. 2.13), but elsewhere it was offset slightly towards the interior of the enclosure (Sections 304 and 399, Fig. 2.13). Although this shift of the ditch towards the interior of the enclosure may suggest the presence of an external bank which had slumped into the outer edge of the original ditch, the excavated sections through both ditches did not provide any clear evidence for the presence or location of a bank on either side of the ditch. That said, the location of features within the enclosure (see below), with a gap of a least 2m between these features and the internal edge of the ditch, may suggest that there was originally at least a low bank within the interior of the enclosure. The ditch of Enclosure 2 was filled

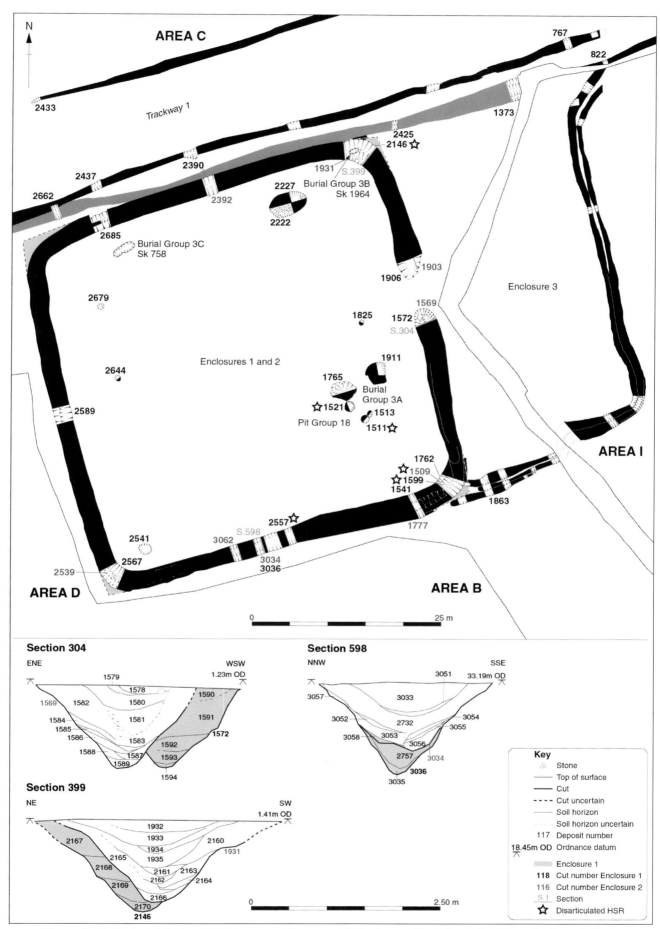

Figure 2.13 Period 3.1: Area D, Mortuary/Ceremonial Enclosure (1–3; Scale 1:500) and selected ditch sections. Scale 1:50

with a sequence of yellow-brown and brown silty sands similar in character to those of the earlier ditch, although localised deposits of darker brown silty sands were encountered in the ditch's upper profile.

Both the original ditch and its recut produced substantial finds assemblages dominated by Late Iron Age pottery and relatively large quantities of animal bone. Despite having been heavily truncated by the Enclosure 2 ditch, the fills of the ditch of Enclosure 1 produced 584 sherds of Late Iron Age pottery (9291g), dominated by grog- and sand- tempered sherds from wheel-thrown/-finished bowls and jars and including a single sherd of imported Roman amphora and sherds from locally produced copies of Gallo-Belgic beakers (see Brown, Chapter 3.VII). The animal bone included several groups of articulated elements from the upper fills of the ditch (including sheep/goat, dog and cattle), interpreted as butchery waste (see Bates, Chapter 4.II), while a single fragment of disarticulated human bone was recovered from the uppermost fill of the ditch in the north-east corner of the enclosure (2146, see below). Larger quantities of material were recovered from the ditch of Enclosure 2 – although this at least partly reflects both its better preservation and the more extensive targeted/selective excavation of its secondary and upper fills along the southern side of the enclosure. A total of 1003 sherds of pottery (18123g) came from the fills of this later cut, and is extremely similar in composition and character to that from the earlier ditch, with a range of Late Iron Age forms including copies of Gallo-Belgic forms and with at least one genuine, imported, Gallo-Belgic butt beaker and a sherd of 'salazon' amphora – produced in Cadiz, on the south-western coast of the Iberian peninsula. The animal bone was also of similar character to that of the earlier ditch, and again included several dumps of articulated butchery waste, including two groups of horse bone (Bates, Chapter 4.II, Table 4.6). At two locations on the enclosure's southern side, individual disarticulated human bones were recovered from the uppermost fills of the ditch (cuts 2557 and 1509; Burial Group 3A, see below). Other finds included a fragment of triangular clay loomweight and, more significantly, two fragmentary pieces of fired clay kiln structure and a cigar-shaped kiln bar came from the upper fill of the ditch along the southern side of the enclosure (2557 and 3062). These pieces almost certainly derive from an Early Roman, pre-Flavian, pottery kiln, and attest to the very latest episode of use or, more likely, the reuse of the enclosure in the later 1st century AD.

Pits within the enclosure
Fig. 2.13
As well as a single grave (see below, Burial Group 3C), eleven pits contemporary with the use of the larger mortuary enclosure were recorded (Pit Group 18), several of which were clustered in its south-east corner (1511, 1513, 1521, 1765, 1825, 1911). Two of these pits (1511 and 1521) contained the disarticulated bones of very young children (Burial Group 3A). The remainder of the pits were located at various points around the perimeter of the enclosure (2541, 2644, 2679, 2222/2227). The lack of discrete features within the central part of the enclosure's interior could indicate that this space was occupied by a structure which left no archaeological trace, or at least that the central part of the enclosure was set aside for activities which precluded disturbance of this area.

Of the cluster of pits in the south-east corner of the enclosure, sub-circular pit 1513 (0.95 x 0.7m and 0.09m deep) contained a yellow brown clay silt fill, which produced a small quantity of pottery. This feature was cut by a circular pit (1511, 1.15m in diameter and 0.2m deep) which contained a similar fill to the previous pit but which also contained disarticulated human bone and the articulated remains of a piglet. The human remains – a single, incomplete, right humerus – were of a young child, most probably an infant aged between 1 and 12 months old. The pig bones include the left mandible, both radii, left ulna and both fourth metacarpals, from a young animal less than one year of age.

A slightly larger circular pit (1521, 1.5m in diameter and 0.46m deep) which lay adjacent to the north-west contained a brown clay silt fill with fragments of pottery, human bone, stone and flint. The human remains derived from one individual and included eight rib fragments, a right ulna, right and left femora and tibiae, and a right fibula, all of which were incomplete. No age could be confidently obtained from the remains, but the bone morphology suggests they belonged to a young child, probably an infant of between 1 and 12 months (Anderson *et al.*, Chapter 4.I). Twenty-eight water vole bones were also recovered from this pit, deriving from a minimum of three individuals. Their presence suggests that the pit had been left open for a sufficient period of time to allow pit-falls to occur, possibly attesting to the exposure of the burial (Bates, Chapter 4.II).

A larger oval pit (1765, 1.48 x 1.47 and 0.49m deep) lay immediately to the north and had a single fill of stony sand silt clay from which fragments of pottery and bone were recovered. Adjacent to the southern ditch terminus of the entrance way into the enclosure was a small very shallow sub-circular pit (1825). It contained a sand silt clay deposit and a small amount of pottery. To the south of this pit was a larger rectangular pit (1911, 2.7 x 2.1 by 0.38m deep) with gently sloping sides and a flat base. Its primary fill of mid brown sand silt contained pottery, bone and flint; its upper fill was a grey-brown sand silt containing pottery, flint and bone.

In the south-west corner of the enclosure was a large shallow sub-rectangular pit (2541, 1.6 x 1.3m and 0.1m deep). Its primary fill contained yellow-brown clay silt and small quantities of pottery and worked flint, while its upper fill was brown clay silt containing residual worked flint. A circular pit (2644, 0.71m in diameter and 0.11m deep) was located to the west of the mortuary enclosure. Its fill comprised yellow-brown clay silt that contained a few fragments of pottery. Another circular pit (2679, 0.8m in diameter by 0.12m deep) was located in the north-west corner of the enclosure. It contained a dark olive brown clay silt fill and pottery and flint fragments. A large oval pit (2222/2227) lay in the north-east corner of the mortuary enclosure. It measured 5.25 x 3m and was 0.6m deep. It contained mid brown silt sand deposit and pottery.

Only four of the pits within the enclosure (1521, 2541, 2644 and 2679) produced very small quantities of pottery comprising 37 sherds (577g) representing

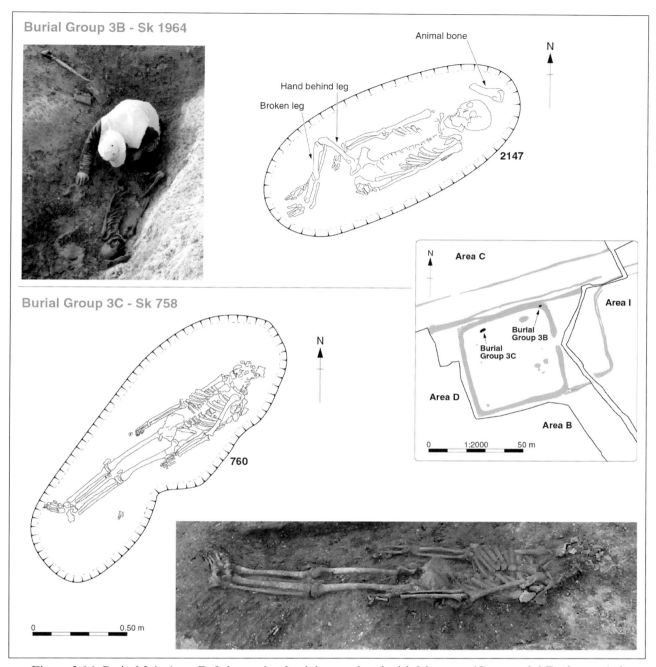

Figure 2.14 Period 3.1: Area D, Inhumation burials associated with Mortuary/Ceremonial Enclosure 1–2 (Burial Groups 3B and 3C). Scale 1:20

no more than twenty individual vessels. A globular handmade jar in a sandy fabric from pit 2679 is Middle Iron Age in style but need not be an early vessel as it was associated with comb-impressed grog-tempered sherds. A copy of a pedestal jar from pit 2644 resembles a Cam 202 of the same type from the Enclosure 2 ditch 3062 (Brown, Chapter 3.VII).

Burials and disarticulated human remains
Figs 2.13 and 2.14
As noted above, in addition to the disarticulated child burials from the pits within the enclosure, two burials and a small quantity of disarticulated bone (Burial Group 3B) were also found associated with the enclosures. These include the skeleton of an elderly male (Sk 1964) which lay within a shallow grave (2147)

cut into the base of the ditch of Enclosure 1 in the north-east corner of the enclosure. This individual was positioned in a slightly flexed east to west (head to east) position. The right leg of this individual showed signs of a healed fracture (Anderson *et al.*, Chapter 4.I) and a large fragment of cattle humerus lay above the skull and may have been a deliberate inclusion – although it is possible that it was disturbed from the general backfill of the ditch. A sample of bone from this skeleton has been radiocarbon dated to 120 cal BC – cal AD 60 at 94% confidence (OxA-29573; 2039±27 BP). The uppermost fill of this section of the ditch of Enclosure 1 (2146) also produced single fragment of adult tibia. Further disarticulated remains came from the upper fill of the later ditch of Enclosure 2: parts of an adult femur from ditch cut 2167 and the mandible of an adult male from ditch cut 1509.

The final human remains found associated with the mortuary enclosure (Burial Group 3C; Sk 758) belonged to an adolescent of unknown sex buried in a north-east to south-west aligned supine position within a shallow grave cut into a pit close to the north-west corner of the enclosure. The small collection of pottery associated with this burial consists of 57 sherds/296g, of which 28 sherds (102g) belong to a single vessel in Fabric S1. All are body sherds and only the presence of combing on one grog-tempered and eight sandy sherds is indicative of form – probably all jars. The grog-tempered vessel has burnt organic residue on the external surface, consistent with use as a cooking pot.

Enclosure 3 (Areas D and I)
Fig. 2.13
On the eastern side of Enclosures 1 and 2 was a series of narrow, shallow ditches (0.75m and 0.4m wide; between 0.1m and 0.2m deep) forming a c.50 x 25m 'entrance area' or annex (Enclosure 3) to the main enclosure. As noted above, a break in the modified southern ditch of Trackway 1, to the north, appears to have allowed direct access from the routeway into this area. The enclosure ditch was re-cut several times, different iterations of which both pre- and post-dated ditch of Enclosure 2. The fills of the Enclosure 3 ditches produced 207 sherds (1932g) of pottery, most of which came from a single grog-tempered comb-decorated storage jar from ditch 1863 (fill 1575). The remainder of the assemblage consists of body sherds in sandy and grog-tempered wares, two with combed decoration and only broadly datable to the Late Iron Age (Brown, Chapter 3.VII).

Small sub-square enclosure
Fig. 2.12; Pl. 1.1
A further sub-square enclosure (Enclosure 4) was identified from aerial photography (Pl. 1.1) and geophysical survey, located approximately 50m to the south of Enclosure 1/2. This was subject only to trial trenching, lying within an area where archaeological remains were to be preserved *in situ*. Based on the evidence of the cropmark/geophysics, it was less regular in plan and orientated slightly differently to its larger counterpart to the north; it was also considerably smaller, measuring approximately 25m north to south and 28m east to west and enclosing an area of some 700 sq. m (0.07ha). The ditch of the enclosure was exposed in two evaluation trenches in 1998 (Trenches 17 and 30) and was fully excavated on the western side of the enclosure (134; Trench 17), revealing a substantial ditch with a V-shaped profile (2.5m wide and 1.2m deep), which produced a small quantity of Late Iron Age pottery from its upper fills. The only other features found associated with the ditches were pits of Anglo-Saxon date and it seems likely that the earthworks of the enclosure became a focus of renewed activity during this period (see Part II; Clarke *et al.* forthcoming).

To the east of Enclosure 4, a c.80m length of a north-west to south-east aligned ditch, Ditch 40, was visible as a cropmark, and was exposed in Trenches 14 and 16. Aligned perpendicular to the trackways attributed to this period, excavation of this feature in Trench 14 revealed it to be up to 1.5m wide and 0.9m deep. It produced a substantial assemblage of pottery, dominated by handmade vessels with a small component of Late Iron Age material, which is likely to date to the early part of the Late Iron Age, probably in the second half of the 1st century BC.

Period 3.2: Early Roman/Conquest, Phase 1 (*c.*AD 40 to 100)

Introduction
In the period following the primary use of Enclosures 1 and 2, the site appears to have experienced a major reorganisation, with the route of Trackway 1 being slighted by a series of ditches associated with a major north to south aligned trackway, whilst various field/enclosure boundaries and pit groups across the southern part of the site have also been attributed to this phase, although at least some may have been contemporary with the enclosures of the preceding phase. Dating of the remains belonging to this period is imprecise, and in most cases features were associated with small quantities of Late Iron Age pottery similar to the material from Phase 3.1 Enclosure 1/2, but with some Romanised material which, together with stratigraphic/spatial relationships, suggests that much of the activity represented by these remains dated to the mid 1st century AD, in the years immediately following the Roman Conquest of AD 43.

Trackway 3
Figs 2.15 and 2.16
Crossing the central part of the site (Areas C and J), a north to south aligned 'spine' of parallel ditches demarcated a new track (Trackway 3). This lay to the east of the mortuary enclosures, which may still have been in use, possibly along with Trackway 2. Intriguingly, Trackway 3 was constructed at right angles to the earlier east to west running braid of the Icknield Way (Trackway 1) and cut across it. The trackway appears to have been dug initially in relatively short sections (some overlapping) with many gaps, presumably to provide access to the adjacent fields. These gaps may have been filled by portable fencing to allow for the movement of livestock. In the more southerly areas (A and B) the trackway ditches were difficult to trace, their line having been removed by a series of later ditches.

The trackside ditches measured between 0.34m and 0.8m wide, but were consistently shallow at between 0.08m and 0.5m in depth. They contained silt sands that varied in colour from mid grey-brown to mid red-brown. Most of the fills were sterile. The date of this track remains uncertain as only two ditches (717 and 2248; Fig. 2.16) yielded just three sherds (30g) of pottery in sandy fabrics, one of which is certainly of Roman type. As was the case with Trackway 2 to the south, this route probably continued in use, at least in part, well into the Roman period. The alignment was reiterated and the boundary ditches recut slightly to the east to form a substantial ditch (Ditch Group 12; see below) that was still extant in Saxo-Norman times and continued to form part of the route linking Great Chesterford and Hinxton into the medieval period (Part II; Clarke *et al.* forthcoming).

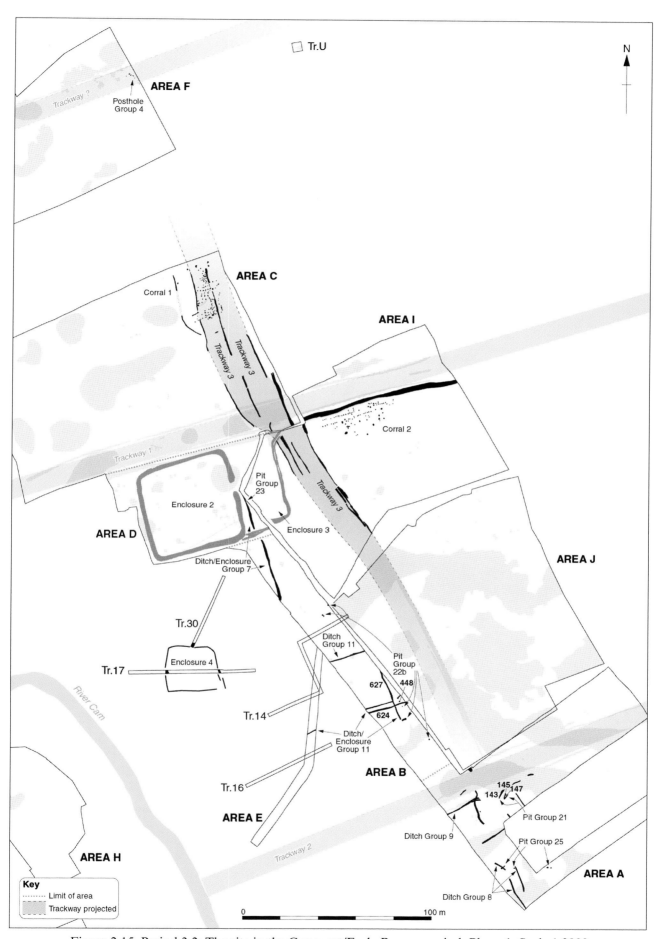

Figure 2.15 Period 3.2: The site in the Conquest/Early Roman period, Phase 1. Scale 1:2000

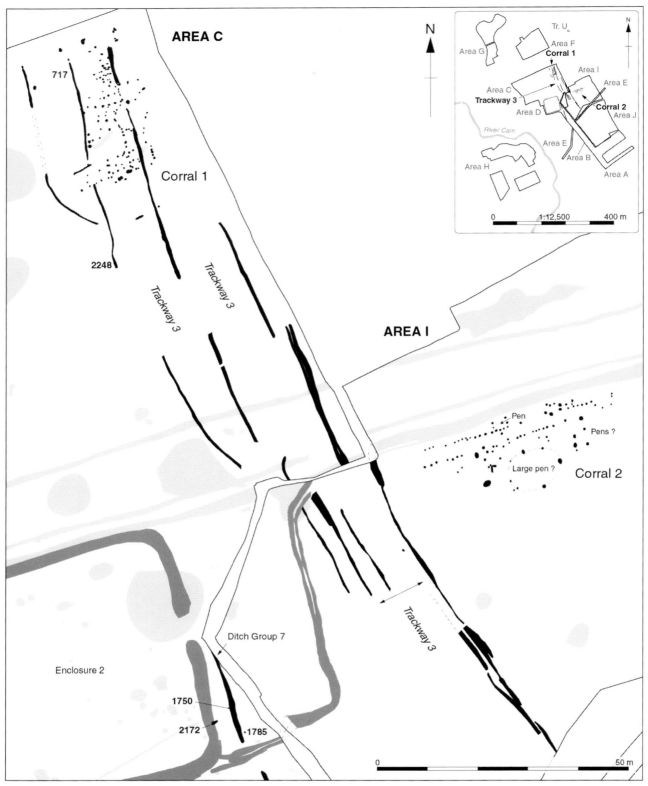

AREA C

717

Corral 1

2248

Trackway 3

Trackway 3

AREA I

N

Tr. U₅

Area G

Area F

Corral 1

Area C

Area I

Area E

Trackway 3

Area D

Corral 2

Area J

River Cam

Area E

Area H

Area B

Area A

0   1:12,500   400 m

Pen

Pens ?

Large pen ?

Corral 2

Trackway 3

Ditch Group 7

Enclosure 2

1750

2172   ·1785

0   50 m

Figure 2.16 Period 3.2: Detail of Trackway 3 and the related corrals. Scale 1:750

The corrals
Figs 2.15–2.17

Corral 1
Two groups of postholes interpreted as the remains of corrals or animal crushes were found, which would have been used to control large numbers of livestock. The northernmost example was set across the main course of Trackway 3, to which it was clearly related (Fig. 2.16). Here, at the limit of excavation in the north-east corner of Area C, lay more than 170 tightly grouped (although not evenly distributed) sub-circular postholes, probably made by the annual setting out of a system of livestock corrals and pens suitable for small animals such as sheep or goats. Many of these postholes were recorded only in plan, meaning that

no dating evidence could be recovered. Most of the postholes measured c.0.25–0.35m in diameter and, where excavated, survived to a depth of 0.2–0.4m.

The surviving remains suggest that Trackway 3 was adapted, with the area between its western and middle ditches being maintained to enhance the function of the corral. A narrow area defined by a curving ditch on the western edge of Trackway 3 was also probably associated with this livestock management system. The posts evidently created a complex system of pens, gates and funnels (Fig. 2.17), which directed animals into/from adjacent fields and holding areas. It is noteworthy that within the faunal assemblage, a sheep humerus showed evidence for trauma, or knocks, to the 'elbow' joint of a type created when the animals are put though corral systems (Bates, Chapter 4.II).

Environmental evidence from several of the postholes (notably feature 1355) associated with the corral comprises well-preserved charred barley grains in very large quantities. Barley is a cereal that was commonly used for animal fodder; however, the absence of chaff suggests this was prime barley grain more commonly used for human consumption (Chapter 4.III). Taken at face value, this might suggest that the postholes represent a concentrated area of granaries, although on balance it seems more likely that the barley represents an abnormally high quality animal feed, perhaps reflecting the specialisation of sheep breeding taking place at Hinxton.

Corral 2

To the east of Trackway 3 (in Area I) and adjacent to the (recut) southern line of Trackway 1, the presence of another possible corral is indicated by a further 102 postholes, many of which were set in regular lines (Fig. 2.16). These posts would have formed another system of animal pens and crushes, similar to Corral 1, although perhaps more substantial (typically the circular postholes measured 0.4m in diameter, with a depth of 0.25). This may have been a more permanent construction, since it did not appear to have been replaced seasonally, as may have been the case for Corral 1; this perhaps reflects the established nature of animal husbandry at the site at this time. The presence of what appears to have been a large roughly circular pen to the south of the lines of posts suggests that this corral may have been used for larger animals such as cattle or, more probably, horses.

Enclosures
Fig. 2.15
Associated with the new track and with Trackway 2 (which evidently remained in use from the previous phase) to the south were various boundaries and/or enclosures, some constructed using the same technique of numerous short discontinuous stretches of ditch – presumably to allow for movement between individual fields/paddocks. Many of these features respected the position of Middle to Late Iron Age features, such as the mortuary enclosure and the alignment of Trackway 2, and – as noted above – may have been at least partly contemporary. On the western side of Trackway 3 (in Areas D and B) was a series of narrow, approximately north to south aligned ditches (Ditch/ Enclosure Group 7), which respected the eastern side of the main mortuary enclosure and extended from

close to the southernmost (western) braid of Trackway 3. Two postholes and a pit were associated with the northern part of these ditches (1785, 1750 and 2172; not illustrated), one of which contained Late Iron Age pottery. An isolated pit (1999; Pit Group 23, c.0.63m by 0.35m and 0.25m deep) appears to have been cut by the northern extent of Ditch Group 7. It contained a single grey-brown silt clay fill from which fragments of animal bone were retrieved.

Further south, in Areas B and E, fragments of field boundaries (Ditch/Enclosure Group 11) ran on a similar east-north-east to west south-west orientation. Two of these ditches (624 and 657) were parallel and ran very close together suggesting the presence of another routeway, or perhaps a double-ditched and embanked/hedged boundary, the gap between them being around 1.7m. The more northerly of this pair terminated within the excavated area and there was no indication of continuation within the next 5.4m along the same alignment.

Other clusters of ditches lay in the southern part of the site (Area A), in the vicinity of Trackway 2. Of these, three narrow ditches aligned north-north-west and south-south-east (Ditch Group 8) may have formed the boundaries to a small and rather irregular trackway measuring 4.5m wide and at least 30m long, leading towards (or away from) a group of rectilinear ditches (Ditch Group 9) adjacent to the southern side of Trackway 2.

Pits and postholes
Fig. 2.15, Pl. 2.8
Several groups of small pits and postholes were scattered across the site. They generally lacked finds (and therefore dating) but may comprise the fragmentary remains of fence lines, temporary animal pens or pits with individual functions associated with the use of the site in the Late Iron Age/Conquest period.

A curving line of postholes/small pits found in Area F (Posthole Group 4) within the footprint of a possible earlier track (Period 3.1, Ditch Group 4) may have formed a fence line or partial stock enclosure, perhaps contemporary with the stock management systems described above.

Three shallow irregular oval intercutting pits (143, 145, 147; Pit Group 21) lay to the south of Trackway 2. Their exact dimensions remain unclear but they measured approximately 1m long by 0.55m wide and ranged between 0.15 and 0.22m in depth. Pit 143 contained a rim sherd of a globular vessel of Middle Iron Age style.

Further to the south, four pits lay on an east to west alignment in the southern part of Area A (239, 259, 261, 265; Pit Group 25). Sub-rectangular pit 239 (0.9 x 0.45m and 0.2m deep) contained a mid dark brown sand silt from which no finds were recovered. Another pit (259; 1.05 x 0.52m and 0.25m deep) of similar shape and fill contained fragments of animal bone and flint, while an adjacent pit (261) was sub-circular in plan (0.54 x 0.49m and 0.14m deep) and produced Late Iron Age pottery fragments. The final pit in the group (265) was more unusual as it was considerably larger than the other three examples and may have been a waterhole, although it was fairly steep-sided. The cut, which lay at the western extent

Figure 2.17 Period 3.2: Area C, Detail of Corral 1. Scale 1:200

Plate 2.8 Early Roman pit 265 (Area D, Pit Group 25), looking south-east

of the group, was oval in plan (2.83 x 1m with a depth of 0.68m), with a 'tear-drop' shaped base. Only one fill was present: a dark yellow-brown silt sand, that was notable for the number of large flint nodules and other (unworked) stones present (Pl. 2.8); it was relatively rich in finds including four sherds of Roman pottery, bone, stone and metalworking debris.

In the vicinity of Ditch/Enclosure Group 11 were three small circular features (Pit Group 22b) comprising a pit (448, 0.66m in diameter and 0.11m deep) and two postholes (492, 546; 0.35 in diameter and 0.12m in depth). These all lay on the eastern side of the trench on a north to south alignment and, although far apart, could possibly have formed the partial remains of a fence line. All three pits were filled with dark grey-brown sand clay silt; pit 448 contained fragments of Early Roman pottery and animal bone. At right angles to these pits, lying to the south, were three intercutting pits on an east–west axis. All three were circular and ranged between 0.42m and 0.94m in diameter and 0.38m and 0.46m deep. They each contained a single silt clay dark yellow-brown sterile fill.

Period 3.3: Early Roman/Conquest, Phase 2 (c.AD 40 to 150)
Figs 2.18–2.22

Introduction
Features attributed to this phase essentially relate to the same chronological period as those of Period 3.2 – the latest Iron Age and Conquest/Early Roman period – but in most cases are stratigraphically later than features belonging to the earlier phases of activity described above. Most significant was the establishment of a timber-built structure, interpreted as a shrine, within the footprint of Trackway 3, together with continued pitting and the reworking of ditched boundaries elsewhere on the site.

Shrine
Figs 2.18–2.19
Probably at some time after Corral 1 ceased to be utilised, a sub-square enclosure containing post-built divisions was created (in the south-eastern corner of Area C; Fig. 2.18). Aligned north-north-west to south-south-east, the enclosure lay to the north of Trackway 1 and Enclosures 1–3 of previous phases and it lay across and presumably blocked part of the wide routeway of Trackway 3. It is likely, however, that the trackway remained in use, perhaps immediately to the east of the structure, given that the route was in use in later periods (see below). This building has been interpreted as a shrine due to its distinctive design, which is similar to other nearby examples found at Duxford (Lyons 2011, 36–7, fig. 27) and Great Chesterford (Medlycott 2011a, 133–4, fig. 10.4).

The northern part of the enclosure and its internal structure were obscured by a later ditch forming part of a Middle to Late Roman trackway (Trackway 4; see Period 3.4, below). The surviving internal square enclosure (10.3 x 11.7m) of this structure (bounded by ditches 734/801/701, 699/886/864/754/814, 1487; Fig. 2.19) consisted of extremely shallow (truncated) ditches measuring between 0.27m and 0.8m wide, with concave or U-shaped bases and between 0.05m and 0.2m deep. The ditch fills were a consistent dark yellow-brown silt clay mix with occasional small flint pebbles and chalk flecks. Finds were scarce and comprised worked flint, along with animal bone fragments.

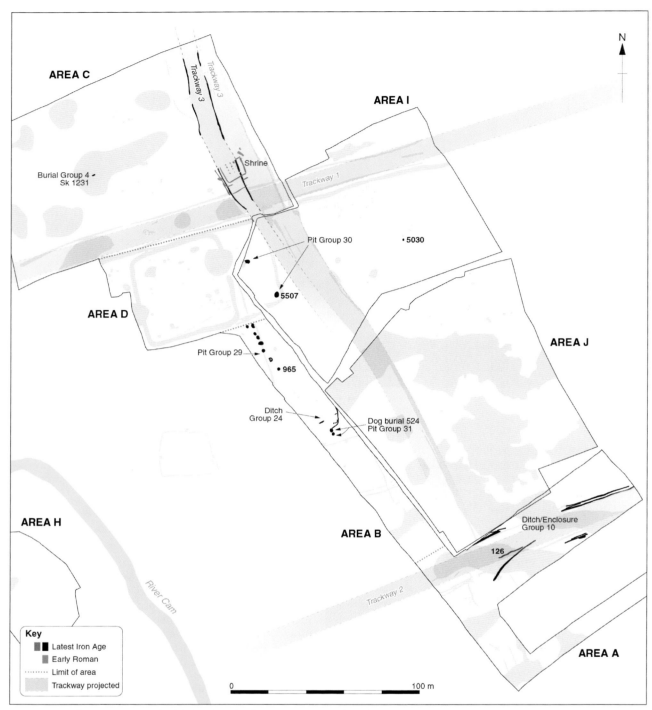

Figure 2.18 Period 3.3: The site in the Conquest/Early Roman period, Phase 2. Scale 1:3000

Surrounding the western and southern sides of this structure was another similar ditch (786/697, 775/862), positioned at a distance of c.2.5m from the inner ditch, with a c.5m-wide gap between the surviving ditch terminals. The outer ditch was between 0.2m and 0.33m wide and was severely truncated, surviving to depths of between 0.04m and 0.11m. It was filled with dark yellow-brown sand clay silt from which no finds were retrieved. It is possible that this is all that survived of a complete square outer ditch.

Applied to the south-west corner of the outer ditch, a further right-angled ditch fragment survived which may have provided an annexe or perhaps an entrance way (679, 681/704/1485/1483) for the shrine (similar to Mortuary Enclosure 3), although the possibility of an earlier (or later) phase of the shrine cannot be discounted since no dating evidence has survived. A posthole (677) was located at the east end of this ditch.

Within the central enclosed space were two parallel rows of unevenly spaced postholes, aligned with the enclosure and extending over a distance of 5.6–5.7m. These rows were spaced c.2m apart with six posts (833, 880, 835, 837, 868, 870, 882) in the western line and four in the eastern (831, 820, 818, 874). A further two postholes or pits (876, 878) survived to the east of these and may be the truncated remains of a third row.

Figure 2.19 Period 3.3: Area C, Late Iron Age to Early Roman shrine. Scale 1:125

All of the postholes were sub-circular, with diameters ranging between 0.17m and 0.66m, although most measured between 0.27m and 0.48m. One heavily truncated example (880) was only 0.05m deep, while the deepest (837) survived to a depth of 0.36m. Most had single fills that were consistently dark yellow-brown sandy silt. Finds were scarce, comprising only a few fragments of bone, pottery, flint and shell. No building material (such as daub, brick or tile) was recovered to provide an indication of the type of construction or appearance of the shrine. The lack of ceramic building material may point to a wooden (and thatched?) structure rather than anything more substantial. A scatter of pits and small postholes (799, 738 and 765)

lay around the eastern side of the structure, which are undated but may have been associated.

Inhumation burial (Burial Group 4)
Fig. 2.20
During the Late Iron Age/Early Roman period, an isolated burial (Burial Group 4; Sk. 1231, grave 1232) was placed above the same infilled pond (Pond D) as the Bronze Age skeleton (Burial Group 2) in Area C. As noted above, this burial may have been placed in reference to an earlier monument/grave marker (Fig. 2.11), but its location in relatively close proximity to the possible shrine may also be significant and, although it has been radiocarbon dated to a broad date range

41

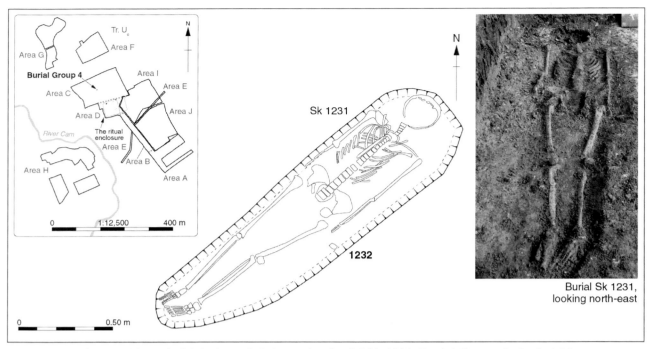

Figure 2.20 Period 3.3: Area C, Inhumation burial Sk 1231 (Burial Group 4). Scale 1:20

between 170 cal BC and cal AD 120 (95% confidence, Wk-12599; 2029±49 BP), it has been attributed to this specific phase on that basis. This individual, a middle/old adult male, was lying in a north-east to south-west orientated grave in an extended, supine position with his arms by his side and his head to the north-east.

Pits, postholes and a dog burial
Figs 2.18 and 2.21–2.22

In Area B, a north to south alignment of nine pits (965, 928, 931, 960, 966/968, 1250, 1117, 1368/1823/1865, 1370; Pit Group 29; Fig. 2.21), some 23m long, post-dated and followed the approximate course of an earlier ditch (Ditch Group 7; Period 3.2). These pits were generally irregular/sub-oval in plan (measuring between 0.58m and 2.8m wide and 0.4m to 0.99m deep), the exceptions being pits 960 and 965, which were circular. They also varied in depth and infill sequences, with the most northerly example (1823/1368/1865) being re-cut several times; this feature was not bottomed and was in excess of 1.6m deep with almost vertical sides, indicating that it may have been a well. The distance between the pits varied widely between 0.6m and 4.1m. Pit 928 (927) contained a small amount of iron smithing slag. A remarkable assemblage of butchered bone was recovered from a single fill (1007) within pit 966/968, which consisted largely of a maximum of seven sheep and sheep/goat carcasses (from animals between one and five years of age) and a small number of bones from other species. The sheep/goat remains include mainly elements of the head, with a small number of post-cranial bones. Butchery marks were found on all of the bones, associated with the dismemberment of animals. This may represent a secondary deposition of waste material. In addition, fourteen bones from one bird, a young domestic fowl, were excavated from fill 1919 in pit 1368, including parts of both wings and the right leg.

A number of pits or small quarries were scattered within and around Enclosure 1/2, which presumably survived as an earthwork. Located within the entranceway (Mortuary Enclosure 3) in Area I were two pits (4510 and 5507; Pit Group 30) that both produced latest Iron Age to Transitional Early Roman pottery: the largest of these (5507) measured 3m long and 0.85m deep. An isolated sub-circular pit (5030) found to the north-east in Area I was of medium size (1.05 x 0.80m) but shallow depth (0.25m). It contained two brown sand silt fills of different hues, but neither contained any finds, meaning that its attribution to this phase is uncertain..

Located some distance to the south of Pit Group 29 in Area B were two adjacent storage pits (Pit Group 31). Both were sub-circular in plan and steep-sided, pit 425 being the more ovoid of the two. Pit 461 was slightly larger, at 2.1 x 2m and 1.48m deep, while pit 425 measured 1.68 x 1.54m and 1.32m deep. Both features contained small quantities of Late Iron Age pottery and Roman tile, which may suggest that they both incorporated earlier material within their fills, perhaps from pre-existing features that were obliterated when these pits were dug. One interesting aspect of these features is that the processes of infill were markedly different between these pits. While the section through pit 425 shows three deposits of similar thickness, the infilling sequence of pit 461 was considerably more complex and includes one of the site's most curious contexts. When this pit was over half filled (by deposits 1337, 1312, 538 and 460), a smaller pit (712) was inserted fairly centrally within it and the remains of a dog carefully placed on the base of the new feature (Fig. 2.22). In the deposit immediately overlying the dog burial (486), numerous fragments of eggshell were found, their disposition indicating that they had originally been placed intact on top of the body or just above it in the backfill. Other bones from the same deposit include the left and right

42

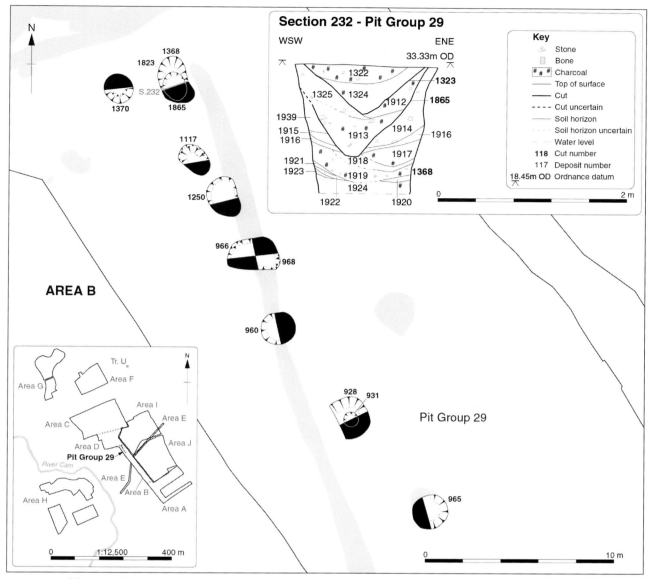

Figure 2.21 Period 3.3: Area B, Pit Group 29 (Scale 1:200) and selected section (Scale 1:40)

tarso-metatarsus of a young domestic fowl, possibly the foot (or feet) of a chicken. Three bulk samples taken from a deposit (486), directly above the dog burial, yielded significant quantities of charred grains of barley and rye along with charred pulses (probably peas) in addition to frequent fragments of eggshell and abundant amphibian bones and wood charcoal. A very large collection of amphibian bones was found in fill 538 within pit 461, consisting of at least 30 frogs, which combined with a further 62 frogs and a toad deriving from the dog burial, suggests that they may have been reworked 'pit fall' casualties from the earlier storage pit. Slag and hearth lining (associated with iron working) were also recovered from pit 712 (see Fosberry, Chapter 4.III).

Ditches associated with Trackway 2
Fig. 2.18
In the southern part of the site various narrow ditches cut across or possibly reiterated the line of Trackway 2 to the north and south of its route (Area A; Ditch Group 10). The common features of these 'subsidiary' ditch segments were their parallel alignments and their terminations at both ends, as well as the fact that they were recut several times. They varied widely in length between 6.5m and almost 35m long, while their widths were much more similar at 0.4–0.65m. A relatively large pottery assemblage was recovered from these ditches, which is notably different from the other ditched enclosures where finds were scarce. This could indicate the presence of domestic activity in the immediate area, which has left no other archaeological trace. Some 40 sherds of pottery (531g) were found in the fills of the various ditches (28, 30, 46, 48, 111, 126, 130, 181, and 183) making up this ditch group. The most interesting find was a necked bowl of Cam 214B in fabric S1 from the base of ditch 126 (see below, Fig. 3.18, No. 34); this type is not generally found until the 1st century AD. In the same deposit was a comb-decorated storage jar. Two residual earlier prehistoric flint-tempered sherds came from the fill of ditch 28, and (intrusive) medieval sherds were found in the fills of ditches 46, 48 and 130. A handful of wheel-thrown sandy and grog-tempered body sherds from ditches

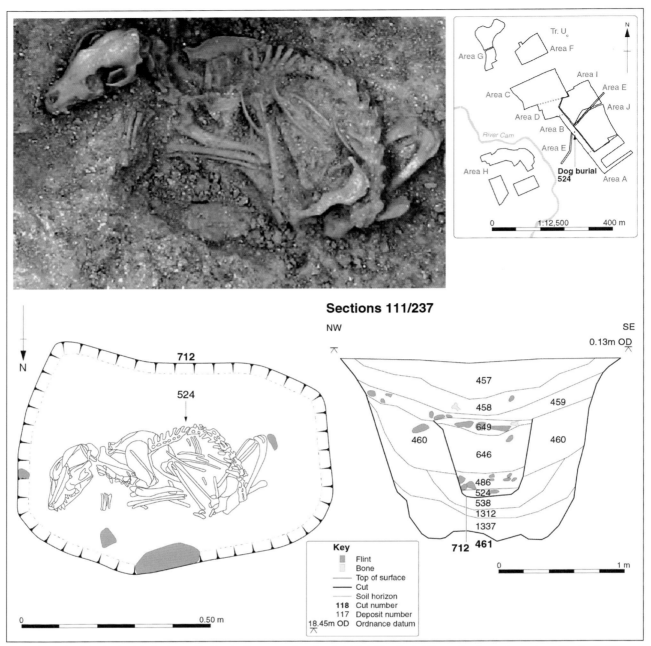

Figure 2.22 Period 3.3: Area B, Early Roman dog burial 524 (Scale 1:10) and selected section (Scale 1:30)

130 and 183 could belong to the post-Conquest period (Brown, Chapter 3.VII).

A narrow and shallow curving ditch (Ditch Group 24), which may have formed part of a larger enclosure, was also recorded to the north-west. Although undated, the terminal end of this ditch cut the two earlier storage pits, one of which contained the dog burial (Pit Group 31, see above). Adjacent to this were several small, elongated pits or ditch segments on the same alignment, none of which produced datable finds.

Period 3.4: Middle to Late Roman (AD 150 to 410)
Fig. 2.23

Trackway 4
A Middle Roman co-axial field system appears to have been laid out on both sides of the Cam Valley,

although associated dating evidence was relatively sparse. Extending over the footprint of the shrine in Area C were two parallel ditches (Ditch Group 14), possibly forming a track or droveway (Trackway 4), which were in turn cut across by a later north-north-west to south-south-east aligned boundary (Ditch Group 12; see below). The possible trackway was on a slightly different alignment than the earlier track (Trackway 1), but would presumably also have led down to a crossing point over the river, and/or joined with Trackway 5 (see below). The ditches were spaced between *c*.6m and 12m apart (narrowing to the east) and the ditch cuts ranged in width from *c*.0.4m to over 1m and from 0.15m to 0.6m in depth. Few finds were recovered from the sandy silt fills, apart from occasional pottery sherds of both prehistoric and Late Roman date. Other ditch fragments aligned parallel to Trackway 4 were present in the northern part of

Area C (Ditch Group 16), associated with which were numerous postholes (Posthole Group 8) which may represent fences or other temporary structures.

Trackway 5
Lower down the valley to the west was another trackway (Trackway 5) that followed a sinuous line along the contour close to the river: its route is still visible on modern aerial photographs (Pl. 1.1). It was observed in evaluation trenches 29, 17, 31, 32, 18, 33 and 34 and may have extended towards the enclosures and other ditches identified in Area G (see below); indeed, the eastern ditch of the more northerly enclosure (Ditch Group 17) may also have formed the western ditch of the track. No finds directly attributable to the trackway ditches were found, although the recovery of numerous Roman objects during metal detecting in the vicinity is suggestive of an origin in this period. During the evaluation in this area, cobbled surfaces and a chalk floor were found adjacent to the river, notably in Trench AA. Although undated, abraded fragments of Roman tile and burnt clay/daub were found on the surface of the cobbles. The location of the cobbled area in relation to the trackway suggests that it may represent the position of a ford linking Hinxton and Brookhampton hamlet in Ickleton (Taylor 1998, 40). This crossing point continued in use well into the post-Roman period (Clarke *et al.* forthcoming, Part II).

Associated ditches and enclosures
Various ditches also extended on the western bank of the river, in Ickleton (Area H; Ditch Group 15), forming enclosures or fields and presumably aiding drainage in this low-lying area adjacent to the river. Here, the remains of at least one dog appear to have been disposed of in one of the ditches (fill 4184 of ditch 4185), comprising a left jaw and humerus; a right radius, femur and tibia; a left metatarsal; and a lumbar vertebra. The humerus has a cut mark upon it suggesting that some of the meat had been removed from the animal. A single cow femur fragment was also recovered from this intervention (Bates, Chapter 4.II). The Area H ditches may have continued in use until the Late Saxon period (Clarke *et al.* forthcoming, Part II).

Remnants of possibly contemporary Roman fields and enclosures (on roughly the same alignment) extended into the northern part of the Hinxton landscape, on the eastern valley side. Traces survived in Areas F and G, where arguably the most tangible remains were present that subsequently appear to have influenced the development of the post-Roman landscape. In the northern part of Area G was a sub-rectangular enclosure (Ditch Group 17) measuring at least 44 by 27m internally and delineated by a 3.3m-wide and 0.7m-deep ditch (5066) which contained a single undated silty sand fill. At some point, this was recut by a narrower ditch (5069) that measured 2.5m wide and which in section appeared to represent three separate cuts: a central wider and deeper ditch (0.9 x 0.65m) flanked by two shallower ditches. The more easterly ditch may also have formed part of Trackway 5. A single deposit filled all three ditches and comprised a distinctive very dark, almost black, silty clay sand that contained small fragments of Roman tile and amphora along with abraded

Roman pottery, including sherds of possible Late Roman flagon. The southern part of the enclosure was cut by a narrow ditch (5071) that contained a mixed assemblage of finds including residual flints and several sherds from the same small Roman jar with combed decoration. The latter is datable to the 1st–2nd century which suggests that it was residual within this context, or that the ditch was infilled just prior to the Middle Roman period. A 3m-wide and 1.6m-deep ditch (5020) with a V-shaped profile cut the western arm of the enclosure and although undated, it had been recut at some point (5017), the lower fill of which contained a large amount of flint nodules, molluscs and two sherds of abraded Roman pottery. The upper fills were much more recent and relate to the landscaping of the Park in the mid-19th century (see Clarke *et al.* forthcoming; Part II).

To the west of, and extending at right angles to, the enclosure in Area G were two small parallel ditches (5052 and 5073; Ditch Group 18), set 5.8m apart and measuring approximately 1m wide and a maximum of 0.3m deep. Both had relatively flat bases and contained similar sandy silt clay fills. Associated finds comprise animal bone, flints and Late Roman pottery, along with fragments of amphora and five sherds from the same mortarium datable to the 3rd–4th century AD. To the south of these was a similar ditch aligned north-west to south-east that was not excavated, although sherds of amphora were noted on its surface. A number of the tree throws in this area also produced Roman pottery.

At least two ditches identified within the southern part of Area G also broadly date to the Roman period (Ditch Group 19). The largest of these was ditch 6066 and its recut (6098), which combined measured 4m wide and approximately 1.5m deep, extending on a north-east to south-west alignment, echoing that of an earlier possible trackway (Period 3.1 Ditch Groups 3 and 4). The two upper fills of the recut contained small quantities of animal bone, Roman tile and a mixed assemblage of abraded pottery, the latest of which dates to the 4th century AD. To the south of this was what appears to have been the north-western corner of a square or rectangular enclosure demarcated by a narrow ditch (6119). This was a maximum of 1.1m wide and 0.42m deep with steep sides and a rounded base. The ditch was cleaned out or recut along part of its length by a slightly narrower and shallower ditch (6076) that contained a single organic fill. This produced animal bone and tile along with Roman pottery, including fragments of storage jar datable to the 3rd to 4th centuries. Partly exposed in Area F and broadly following the same alignment as ditch 6119 was another ditch (1067) that produced a small quantity of Roman pottery in addition to pieces of animal bone and oyster shell. Other elements of field system may have been destroyed in this area by intensive activity associated with the Saxo-Norman settlement that was established here, detailed in Part II.

Pits and postholes
Fig. 2.23
Two pits lay immediately adjacent to, and possibly 'clipped', the western side of the earlier mortuary enclosure in Area D (2591, 2592; Pit Group 32). Pit 2591 contained ten fragments of undiagnostic

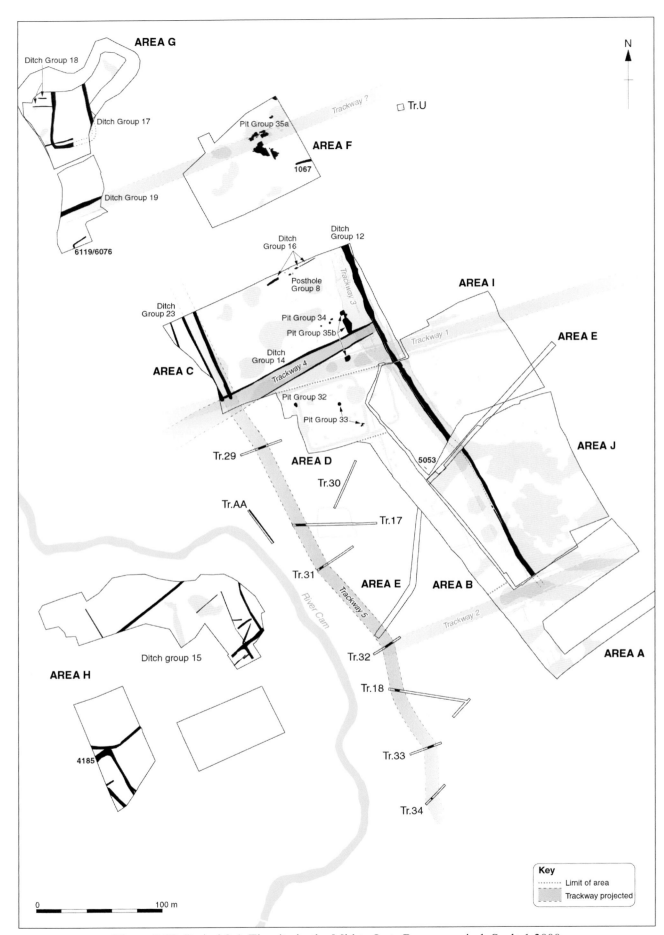

Figure 2.23 Period 3.4: The site in the Mid to Late Roman period. Scale 1:3000

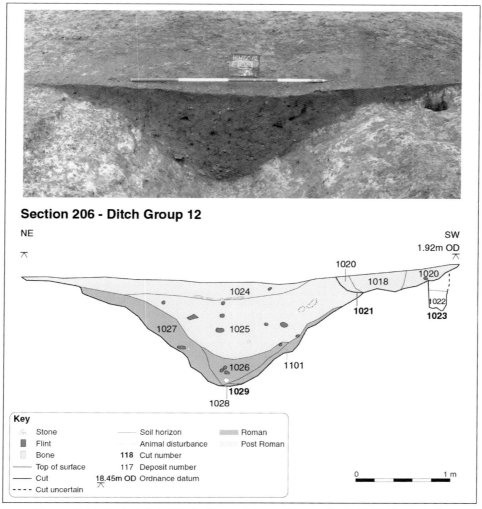

Section 206 - Ditch Group 12

NE

SW

1.92m OD

1020

1020

1018

1020

1024

1022

1021

1023

1027

1025

1026

1101

1029

1028

Key

⌀	Stone	—	Soil horizon	▨▨	Roman	
▪	Flint	∿	Animal disturbance	░	Post Roman	
▨	Bone	**118**	Cut number			
—	Top of surface	117	Deposit number			
—	Cut	**18.45m OD**	Ordnance datum			
- - -	Cut uncertain	⌐				

0   1 m

Figure 2.24 Period 3.4: Ditch Group 12, section of ditch 1029. Scale 1:40

ironworking debris, along with residual Late Iron Age pottery.

Several pits were located within the area formerly enclosed by the Late Iron Age ceremonial/mortuary enclosure (Pit Group 33), although by this time the ditches of the enclosure were backfilled. An isolated sub-oval pit (1962) was located (just off centre) within the enclosure. It measured 2.7m by 1.34m and 0.7m deep. Its primary fill of yellow-brown sandy clay contained pottery. Above this, a thick deposit of mid brown silt sand clay that contained a small but mixed assemblage of Late Iron Age and Roman pottery, animal bone and shell. An environmental sample retrieved a few cereal grains which may suggest that it had originally been a storage pit. In the south-eastern part of the enclosure were three contemporary pits (2025, 2027, 2157) which cut the terminal end of earlier Ditch Group 2. Pits 2025 and 2027 were similar circular examples (0.9m in diameter by 0.25m deep) that contained mid brown sand silt fills, but no finds. Between them lay a larger oval pit (2157: 1.25m in length and 0.33m deep) which contained two sand silt fills, a light orange-brown primary fill and a darker brown upper fill. Both fills contained a mixture of Late Iron Age and Roman pottery alongside animal bone, suggesting use as a rubbish pit.

To the north of Trackway 4 in Area C was a series of four circular pits (Pit Group 34) measuring between 0.8m and 1.78m wide and a maximum of 0.37m deep. Although probably broadly contemporary, one example (1773) was seen to cut (and therefore post-date) another (1775). This later pit produced a small assemblage of Roman pottery, along with tile and animal bone. A single small gully (5053) identified close to the western edge of Area I produced an Oxfordshire mortarium and a flanged bowl dated c.AD 250–410; no contemporary features were identified in the vicinity.

A major boundary
Figs 2.23 and 2.24
A very substantial north-west to south-east aligned boundary ditch (1029; Ditch Group 12), which is still visible on modern aerial photographs (Pl. 1.1), ran through Areas A, C, D, I and J. The ditch replaced the more sinuous Trackway 3 which had previously lain on the same alignment. It measured between 0.5m and 1.65m wide and was between 0.34m and 1.22m deep with a slightly rounded V-shaped profile. It was filled with a dark yellow-brown clay silt sand deposit. Although this boundary had its origins in the Roman period, it was recut many times and remained in use well into the post-Roman period (see Part II).

47

Quarry pits
Fig. 2.23
After the Middle Roman period, much of the farmland (apart perhaps from in the vicinity of Area G, see above) lay largely fallow: only sporadic quarrying on the gravel terraces above the river edge took place, perhaps to provide building materials for the Roman town at Great Chesterford or other more local projects. At least twenty features were identified as possible quarry pits (Pit Group 35) which were generally irregular in shape, sometimes stepped and measured a maximum of 4m by 3m in size and up to 1.52m deep. They were most prolific in the northern part of Area F (Pit Group 35a) and to the north of Trackway 4 in Area C (Pit Group 35b). Few finds were present, other than occasional sherds of residual Late Iron Age and Roman pottery.

Late Roman evidence from the ploughsoil
The presence of a small assemblage of Late Roman pottery, coinage (43 coins; mostly of later 3rd- and 4th-century date, as is common on rural Roman sites) and some personal objects including a Late Roman nail-cleaner type strap end reflects the fact that people were still passing through the local landscape at this time.

Chapter 3. The Finds

I. The Terminal Palaeolithic lithic assemblage
by Barry J. Bishop

Introduction, scope and methods

This report focuses exclusively on the substantial lithic assemblage recovered from Pond P (in Area J) and is based on the results of cataloguing carried out by the current author in 2016. Full versions of the catalogue are available in the archive and have been presented and summarised in an archival report (Bishop *et al.* 2016). Although of sufficient detail to provide a good characterisation of the assemblage and to enable comparisons with other contemporary industries, the reporting presented here is inevitably of a somewhat provisional nature, as there is a very high potential for further work, notably refitting and more extensive attribute/technological analyses, to provide further information on the organisation of flintworking technology, the nature of the occupation and the taphonomy of the scatter.

All of the lithics (overwhelmingly made up of struck flints, alongside a small quantity of unworked burnt flint and five sandstone artefacts) have been classified according to a simplified techno-typological scheme, whilst detailed descriptions and metrical and technological information of all retouched/utilised pieces and cores have been recorded. Details of the basic metric and technological traits of a small sample of unretouched flakes and blades has also been undertaken. The analysis followed standard technological and typological definitions (*e.g.* Inizan *et al.* 1999), adopting with some modifications the terminology used by Barton for the Hengistbury Head assemblages (Barton 1992). Measurements were taken following the methodology of Saville (1980) although, following Cooper (2006), some skewed blades were re-orientated to give a more accurate representation of their dimensions.

An initial pilot study of the suitability of the assemblage for microscopic use-wear analysis has determined that the material has a very high potential – with 87% of a sample of 100 implements submitted for assessment at the Leids Archeospecialistisch Bureau, Leiden, having been identified as being in a condition suitable for detailed analysis (García-Díaz and Verbaas 2014). No further analysis has been undertaken at this stage, but this clearly has implications for future work on the assemblage and its long-term curation. A small number of eleven specimens with macroscopically visible deposits/residues – thought possibly to represent use-related residues – were also submitted for provisional analysis as part of this sample. Microscopic inspection of these pieces confirmed that in four cases these did appear to represent residues. Further investigation of one of these residue deposits on the edge of an unretouched blade, carried out at Delft University under the auspices of the European Research Council funded *Ancient Adhesives* project, has identified it as pine tar (G. Langejans pers. comm.).

Distribution and condition of the struck flint

Distribution and density
Fig. 3.1

Virtually all of the 3,817 struck flints considered in this report came from the infilled hollow (16041) defined as Pond P. Nearly all of this material came from three main deposits; the upper 'colluvium' (15450), the middle 'silt layer' (15451) and lowest 'natural' (15452) (Table 3.1). A small amount of Late Glacial/Early Post-Glacial flintwork was recovered as residual material from later features that cut into the hollow's sediments and a large core comparable to others from the hollow is also included here, although it actually came from an adjacent feature. Of the material from the hollow, nearly all was contained within the upper two layers, these providing 98% of the assemblage in roughly equal proportions. There seems to be a paucity in the relative quantities of micro-debitage present within the assemblage. This is likely, at least partly, to reflect the sampling techniques undertaken on the site with only very limited wet sieving (*c.*2% of the deposits), but may also relate to post-depositional processes (*cf.* Barton 1992).

In terms of the total number of struck pieces from the hollow, it is clear that in respect of its horizontal distribution, the material was clustered and that the greatest densities occurred in the north-eastern quadrant, with the number of pieces diminishing to the south and west and being largely absent from the hollow's western side (Fig. 3.1). The highest quantities were found in the middle of the north-eastern edge of the hollow, with the densities quickly trailing off towards the north, south and west. However, the density distribution was often not gradual and often markedly different quantities were present in adjacent or nearby squares, which may indicate very localised episodes of flint manufacture and use. More specifically, the square with the highest concentration (K3) was located further to the south-east and appeared relatively isolated, being surrounded by squares with comparatively low densities of struck flint.

The horizontal distribution of the materials within the three stratigraphic horizons was very broadly comparable, with the greatest concentrations in all three layers occurring in the north-eastern quadrant. However, there were some differences: the distribution of flintwork was more diffuse within the colluvial layer 15450 and conversely showed a more marked concentration in the silt layer 15451, with the majority of the lithics from this layer being concentrated in the vicinity of square L8 and within square K3. This may suggest that the upper layer had experienced a higher, although still only limited, degree of post-depositional disturbance.

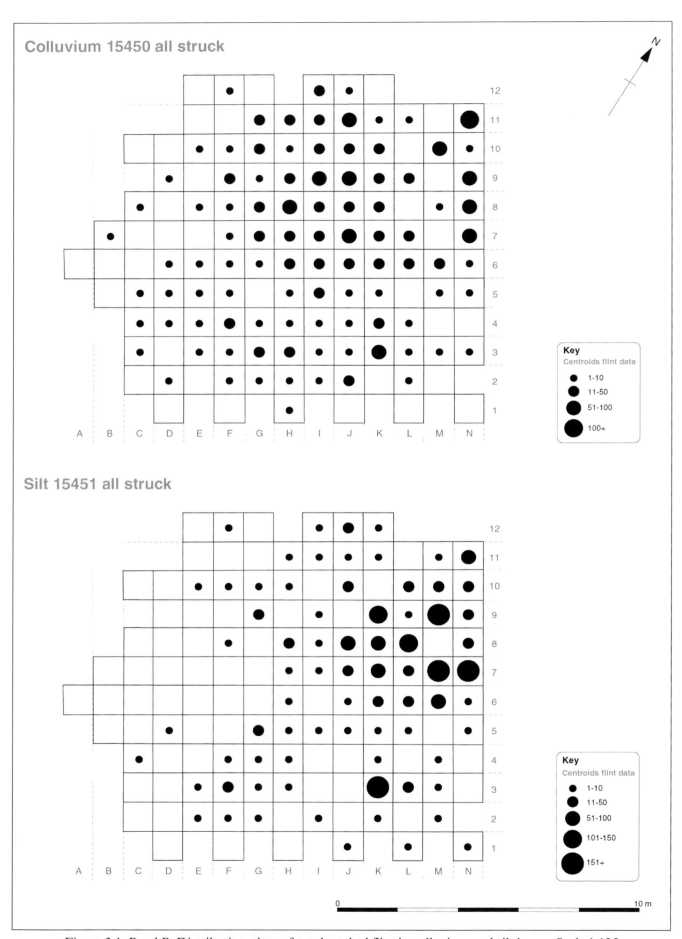

Figure 3.1 Pond P: Distribution plots of total worked flint in colluvium and silt layers. Scale 1:125

Spit	No. of squares containing flint	Total per spit	% of total	Ave. number / no. squares
15450 colluvium				
1	86	943	56.6	11.0
2	51	505	30.3	9.9
3	12	116	7.0	9.7
4	7	99	5.9	14.1
5	1	2	0.1	2.0
Total	*113*	*1665*	*100*	*14.7*
15451 silt layer				
1	72	832	45.4	11.6
2	42	572	31.2	13.6
3	24	265	14.5	11.0
4	7	127	6.9	18.1
5	1	35	1.9	35.0
Total	*105*	*1831*	*100*	*17.4*
15452 natural				
1	19	62	87.3	3.3
2	5	9	12.7	1.8
Total	*85*	*71*	*100*	*0.8*

Table 3.1 Vertical distribution of all struck flint within Pond P, recorded by spit

In order to understand the vertical density/ distribution of the flint assemblage, the three major stratigraphic units within the hollow were excavated in 50mm spits which, due to variations in the thickness of the deposits, varied in number from between one to five in the colluvium and silt layers and either one or two in the natural deposits (Table 3.1).

As noted, above, virtually all of the flint came from the upper two horizons, interpreted as colluvium and silt layers (15450 and 15451), whilst closer analysis of the vertical distribution of the flintwork in the hollow showed a general and gradual decrease in the overall quantity of flintwork with depth for both the colluvium and silt layer (see Table 3.1). However, this picture is slightly more complex if the density of the flintwork in terms of average number of pieces per square is taken into account. The colluvial layer contained the greatest densities of flint in spit 4, although otherwise showed a gradual decline with depth. The silt layer had the greatest concentrations in spit 5 but, as the fifth spit was only present in one of the squares, this should not be taken as representative. As with the colluvial layer, the next greatest densities were present in spit 4, with notably lower but roughly similar densities encountered in the overlying three spits. The 'natural' basal layer of the hollow, 15452, produced very little flint, amounting to less than 2% of the total, virtually all of which was found in the uppermost spit. It is likely that this material was intrusive, having worked its way into this deposit from the overlying layers.

Interpretation of the vertical distribution of the material within the two upper soil horizons is not simple. Nonetheless, although some later material was present in the colluvium, the vast majority of flintwork from both deposits shared an identical technological signature and similarities in the horizontal distribution of the two assemblages, combined with the presence of refits between pieces from the two layers (see below), would argue that they were both part of the same broad episode of occupation. The artefacts do appear to have moved vertically throughout both soil horizons, but that from the silt layer had clearly seen very little horizontal movement since discard, whilst the colluvial material had undoubtedly seen higher levels of disturbance, but its general distribution and the presence of further refits (see below) shows this to have been minimal and probably highly localised.

Refitting
Pl. 3.1

No formal attempts at refitting have been undertaken and this is an area where future work has the potential to make a major contribution to understanding the assemblage. However, it became clear during the cataloguing that many of the pieces did indeed refit, with ten separate refitting sequences involving a maximum of four sequential removals being identified (Table 3.2; Pl. 3.1). Half of these came from square K3 (Fig. 3.1) which provided the material selected for the detailed metrical and technological analyses (see below), no doubt due to these pieces having been examined in more detail. Refitting sequences were also found between pieces from the colluvial and silt layers. In addition, many broken pieces could be joined back together (break refits); although some of these breakages could have occurred during excavation it is clear from the presence of indicators such as differential wear or recortication that many of these had been broken in antiquity, some possibly intentionally (see below).

Together the refitting pieces provide good evidence for the very low levels of disturbance that much of the assemblage has experienced, and it is certain that far

Plate 3.1 Pond P: Sequence of refitting blades from grid square K3 (refit group E)

more refits, including pieces refitting from different squares, would be found if all of the material was examined in a similar level of detail.

Condition
A further indication of the taphonomic history of the assemblage is shown by the overall very good condition of the pieces, as confirmed by a preliminary assessment of microscopic use wear traces (see above). The great majority are in either a sharp or only slightly chipped condition, the latter probably accounted for by processes such as trampling and bioturbation, as well as glossing caused by settling within the sandy soils. Some of the material from the colluvial layer and particularly its uppermost spit is in a more chipped condition, sometimes quite markedly so. This, combined with obvious differences in raw materials, rates of recortication and possible variations in the technological attributes, would indicate that it contains a small component of 'intrusive' material originating from the later disturbance occurring on the surface of the hollow.

Despite the mainly low levels of post-depositional abrasion there is a high degree of breakage, with only 38% of the pieces being entirely complete. This almost certainly reflects the emphasis placed on the manufacture of often large but thin pieces and on long and fragile blades. Additionally, it is likely that some pieces may have been deliberately broken (see below).

Recortication is mostly absent but significant proportions show the first traces of surface 'milkiness' and a few pieces have become white or blue/white. There is no apparent chronological implication to the degree that this has occurred, however, and its intensity can vary even on individual pieces.

Of particular interest are the notably high proportions of flakes and blades that exhibit very slight internal changes indicative of having been heated. These show occasional cracking on the surface and

Sequence code	Context / spit	Square	Layer	Description
A	15976.1	K3	15451	Two almost completely cortical flakes struck from opposite directions with parts of their distal ends refitting
B	15976.1	K3	15451	Crested long blade refits onto a heavily bruised long blade
C	15975.4–15796.1	K3	15450–15451	Prismatic blade from 15976 refits to long blade from 15975 that was struck from the same direction
D	15976.1	K3	15451	Prismatic blade refits to another prismatic blade struck from the same direction, which in turn refit to the long blade from sequence C, which were struck from the opposite platform
E (Fig. 3.2)	15976.1	K3	15451	A sequence of four refits starting with a partially crested prismatic blade that refits to another partially crested non-prismatic blade which refit to two further non-prismatic blades, both of which have short stretches of edge crushing and abrasion
F	15525.2	K6	15450	Decortication flake refits to a cortical blade-like flake. The platform of the latter had been rejuvenated after the removal of the former
G	16016.2	E3	15451	Non-prismatic blade refits to a partially cortical prismatic blade struck from an opposite platform
H	15834.2	M9	15451	Large decortication flake refits to a large core modification flake
I	15834.2	M9	15451	Large and rather irregular prismatic blade refits to a large flake struck from an opposite platform
J	15538.0	J3	15450	Primary decortication blade refits to a partially cortical blade, both of which refit to a core although several other blades had been removed between the second blade and the core, one of which was a large plunged blade that removed the opposed platform

Table 3.2 Descriptions of refitting sequences associated with Pond P

52

Context		15450 colluvium	15451 silt layer	15452 natural deposits	Other features	Total no.	Total %
Total	No.	1804	1931	72	10	3817	
% of total	%	47.2	50.6	1.9	0.3	-	100
Flakes	No.	482	480	14	3	979	-
	%	26.7	24.8	19.4	30	-	25.6
Blades	No.	765	833	32	4	1634	-
	%	42.4	43.1	44.4	40	-	42.8
Unclassifiable flake / blade fragments	No.	270	275	13	1	559	-
	%	15	14.2	18.1	10	-	14.6
Micro-debitage (<15mm)	No.	192	260	9		461	-
	%	10.6	13.5	12.5		-	12.1
Core pieces	No.	25	21	1	1	48	-
	%	1.4	1.1	1.4	10	-	1.3
Secondarily worked / utilized implements	No.	68	62	3	1	134	-
	%	3.8	3.2	4.2	10	-	3.5
Hammerstone	No	2				2	0.1

Table 3.3 Basic composition of the struck flint assemblage from Pond P

incipient spalling and the formation of tiny circular or ovoid stress fractures that can be seen internally within the flint in the more transparent pieces, or as very fine 'hackling' type fracturing on breaks. It should also be noted that those pieces showing such traces are likely to be only a small proportion of pieces that might have been heated to some degree, as any less intense heating would not leave any macroscopic traces. The high proportion of pieces that display such evidence for very light heating can be contrasted with the very low numbers of pieces that show evidence of more intense burning, such as colour changes or 'fire crazing', which account for considerably less than 1% of the assemblage.

The pieces showing indications for having been lightly heated provide compelling evidence that at least some of the raw materials had been subjected to deliberate heat treatment in order to improve their flaking ability (e.g. Griffiths *et al.* 1987; Inizan *et al.* 1999, 23–4), but it is less certain how common this process may have been, or whether it was rarely or routinely undertaken. In recent years this has become a rather neglected aspect of research in lithic technology but the systematic macroscopic examination of this assemblage for such traces, combined with microscopic or chemical analysis of samples, has the potential to provide a better understanding of the extent to which this was practiced.

Summary
The condition, spatial distribution and the presence of refits indicates that the majority of the assemblage has witnessed only minor post-depositional movement, which can mostly be accounted for through processes such as trampling and bioturbation; it can essentially be regarded as having been found very close to where it was deposited when the site was abandoned. The technological similarities of the assemblages from the colluvium and the silt layer, combined with the distribution, condition and the presence of refitting pieces between the layers, would not appear to indicate more than one period of occupation.

Raw materials
The raw materials used for the struck assemblage comprise fine-grained translucent black flint with occasional opaque lighter grey patches. It is of a very good knapping quality and only very occasionally hindered by thermal (frost fracture) faults. Surviving cortex varies but the majority is creamy white, between 1mm and 7mm in thickness and relatively fresh. A minor but not insignificant proportion of the cortex is soft and retains very fine fossilised surface structures, demonstrating that these could not have experienced anything but the most minimal displacement from where they had formed in the chalk (cf. Bromley and Ekdale 1986). The cortex also demonstrates that the raw materials used consisted of nodular shaped cobbles of such a size that in one case refitting blades struck from opposed platforms demonstrated that, even after decortication and platform creation, the cores could measure in excess of 245mm.

The presence of occasional thermal faults indicates that the raw materials had been subjected to periglacial conditions and were probably gathered from mass wastage deposits as present on the surface of the chalk, in some cases directly from exposed flint seams (Gibbard 1986). Chalk outcrops prolifically in the area and at the site itself the bedrock geology comprises the Holywell Nodular Chalk of Turonian date, which includes many seams of good quality flint. Given the evidence for the preparation of raw materials at the site, it is likely that the flint was gathered very locally.

Technology and typology
Pl. 3.2
Of the 3,817 pieces of struck flint that form the basis of this report, the vast majority consist of flakes and blades which provide 78% of the assemblage with unclassifiable fragments making up most of the

Plate 3.2 Pond P: Selected long blades

remainder. Of this, 12% measures less than 15mm in maximum dimension (micro-debitage) and less than 4% has been retouched or shows convincing evidence for use. Cores provide just 0.6% of the total and two flaked hammerstones make up the remainder (Table 3.3).

Despite the colluvial layer having experienced some localised disturbance and containing small amounts of later intrusive flintwork, the basic distribution patterns and the typological composition of all of the assemblages from the hollow are extremely similar and the following analysis treats material from all deposits as a single assemblage.

Flakes and blades

The assemblage is clearly blade-based with an emphasis placed on the production of both large sturdy blades and more delicate prismatic types. The large size of many of the blades is a particularly notable feature of the assemblage, with over 150 being in excess of 120mm long and with the largest complete example measuring 193mm in length (Pl. 3.2).

The flakes and blades have been classified according to each piece's position within a simplified scheme broadly based on the concept of the chaîne opératoire: the sequences in which pieces of raw material are converted into useful implements which are used and eventually discarded (Table 3.4). This inevitably involves a degree of subjectivity but, by considering all of the material together, it is hoped that basic knapping trajectories can be established, and the bulk of the debitage is sufficiently technologically distinctive to allow confidence in assigning each piece's position within that reduction sequence.

Technological traits of the flakes and blades

As shown by Table 3.4, all stages in the reduction sequence are represented, from the decortication of raw materials to the production of useable flakes and blades which had then been used and discarded. The decortication flakes and blades all have at least 50% of their dorsal surfaces covered by cortex. These form

5% of the assemblage, just under a third being of blade dimensions. They certainly indicate that cores were being prepared at the site, but the quantities present are not excessive and only around 10% of the decortication flakes and blades are primary, in that their dorsal surfaces are entirely covered with cortex. This suggests the possibility that the raw materials may have been preliminarily dressed closer to where they were collected. However, the large size of the nodules and the extent to which they have been worked would also reduce the relative number of cortical flakes and blades.

Just over 2% of the assemblage comprises crested blades or, occasionally, flakes. These include pieces

Flake / blade type	Total no.	Total %
Core preparation and maintenance		
Decortication flake	135	3.5
Decortication blade	57	1.5
Crested flake	5	0.1
Crested blade	69	1.8
Core modification flake	39	1
Core modification blade	4	0.1
Core rejuvenation flake	61	1.6
Core rejuvenation blade	7	0.2
Chip (<15mm)	235	6.2
Flake and blade production		
Flake	629	16.5
Non-prismatic blade	382	10
Prismatic blade	1115	29.2
Blade-like flake	110	2.9
Unclassifiable flake / blade fragment >15mm	785	20.5
Use / discard		
Retouched / utilized flakes and blades	134	3.5

Table 3.4 Technological traits of the flakes and blades from Pond P

	Very narrow blades	Narrow blades	Blades	Narrow flakes	Flakes	Broad flakes
Breadth / Length Ratio	<0.2	0.21–0.4	0.41–0.6	0.61–0.8	0.81–1.0	1.0+
HINGEL14 L. UPal	**3.6**	**30.1**	**18.1**	**10.9**	**15.7**	**21.7**
Pitts 1978: E. Meso	2	43	27	13	6.5	9
Pitts 1978: L. Meso	0.5	15.5	30.5	22	14.5	17
Pitts and Jacobi 1979: E. Meso	1	34.5	26	15	9.5	14
Pitts and Jacobi 1979: L. Meso	0.5	13	27	22.5	14	23.5

Table 3.5 Complete flake breadth/length ratios of all complete flakes and blades (n = 83) from Pond P compared to Mesolithic assemblages recorded by Pitts (1978) and Pitts and Jacobi (1979)

created by knapping a vertical crest upon a core prior to and in order to facilitate the removal of further blades, but most appear to have been created in order to rejuvenate the faces of cores that were already in the process of being worked. Some of the former are very sturdy and have been utilised as 'bruised blades' (see below). The continual maintenance of 'ridges' on core faces to facilitate blade production seems to have been a commonly undertaken practice, with many other flakes and blades showing some evidence of orthogonal flaking on their dorsal surfaces.

The core modification flakes are not easy to classify but they are mostly large, bulky removals that have significantly altered the shape of the core, usually to form new core faces on cores that have already been partially reduced. Many probably represent the modification of very large cores that had produced long blades into smaller ones that were geared to produce relatively smaller prismatic blades.

The core rejuvenation flakes have all been struck to alter striking platforms and core faces in order to facilitate further flake and blade production. Those included here comprise true core tablets that removed the whole of the striking platform, as well as many flakes that removed only part of the platform and core-face edge. There are also plunged blades that have been struck from one platform but have also had all or part of an opposed platform removed, and many flakes struck transversely or longitudinally across the core face, most of which removed severe hinge or step fracture scars.

The pieces included here fall into easily recognised categories; in reality, the bulk of the flakes and probably many of the blades were probably removed as part of a continuous process of striking platform and core-face adjustment. In particular, the chips (small flakes measuring less than 15mm in any dimension), mostly derive from trimming the face of the core or facetting the striking platform.

The remaining flakes and blades are considered to represent the intended products of reduction and are either at least potentially useable or have been retouched to make formal tools. Potentially useable pieces account for just under 80% of the flakes and blades, although a quarter of these are fragmentary and it is unlikely that all were seen by the knapper as being suitable for use. These potentially useable pieces comprise flakes, blades and flakes that have blade-like traits such as parallel dorsal scars. They vary considerably in shape and size but there is a very clear preference for the manufacture of long and narrow

pieces, with nearly 43% of the total assemblage being of blade dimensions with potentially useable blades outnumbering flakes by 2:1. Of the potentially useable blades, almost three quarters can be regarded as prismatic, these having parallel sides and dorsal scars demonstrating that they were made by a systematic reduction strategy that resulted in the production of relatively standardised sized and shaped products. To these can be added the blade-like flakes, which although not of blade dimensions do have parallel sides and dorsal scars. The non-prismatic blades tend to be more irregular and thicker, but a high proportion should probably be regarded as systematically produced, just not truly prismatic as they have remnants of orthogonally aligned scars caused by earlier attempts at cresting.

In order to gain an impression of the metrical and technological characteristics of the assemblage, an analysis was conducted on a randomly chosen selection of 110 flakes and blades measuring in excess of 10mm taken from the first spit of the 'silt layer' of Grid Square K3. Of these, 83 were sufficiently complete to enable metrical analysis, revealing that in length they measured from 11mm to 172mm, averaging at 60.7mm. The breadths of the complete pieces ranged from 6mm to 97mm with an average of 35.4mm, and in thickness they varied from between 1mm and 18mm, at an average of 7.5mm. The strong propensity towards being thin and narrow is demonstrated by their breadth / length ratios, the distribution of which is presented in Table 3.5.

The complete pieces have an average breadth / length ratio of 0.77 with over 40% being at least twice as long as they are wide. The distribution of the shapes is closest to those of the Early Mesolithic assemblages examined by Pitts (1978) and Pitts and Jacobi (1979), although it does not necessarily conform in any straightforward way to the trend away from narrow to broader blade and flake production during the Early Holocene originally suggested by these authors.

Intact striking platforms on this sample of flakes and blades vary from 1mm to 23mm in width, with an average of 9.3mm, and from 1mm to 11mm at an average of 3.1mm in depth. Just over half are plain, with most of the remainder having been modified by fine flaking, resulting in faceted and dihedral examples (Table 3.6). Nine have been recorded as 'isolated'; these having resulted from attempts at using facetting to accentuate the desired point of percussion but there is no evidence for the deliberate or routine use of the en éperon technique (Barton 1990). Four had

Striking platform type	No.
Rubbed (ground)	4
Cortical	5
Dihedral	3
Facetted	17
Isolated	9
Missing	15
Plain flake scar	46
Shattered	11
Striking platform edge treatment	
Rubbed (ground)	10
Missing	15
Unmodified	36
Trimmed	23
Trimmed and rubbed	26

Table 3.6 Principal striking platform attributes of the selected flakes and blades from Pond P

Bulb of percussion type	No.
Diffuse	56
Discretely rounded	19
Missing	9
Pronounced	25
Thermal scar	1
Distal termination type	
Feathered	74
Hinged	21
Missing	9
Overshot / plunged	5
Stepped	1

Table 3.7 Principal technological attributes of the selected flakes and blades from Pond P

Dorsal scar pattern	No.
Fully Cortical	2
Orthogonal	11
Perpendicular	6
Uncertain/missing	5
Multi-directional	25
Opposed	15
Parallel – same direction	17
Unidirectional	29
Cortical dorsal surface	
None	55
1-30%	36
40-60%	14
70-99%	3
100%	2

Table 3.8 Principal dorsal surface attributes of the selected flakes and blades from Pond P

been rubbed smooth and eleven had shattered due the detaching blow falling very close to the platform's edge. Although the majority of pieces had plain platform surfaces, nearly three-quarters show evidence for the modification of the platform's edge, which was usually achieved through fine flaking and frequently grinding the edge.

Just over half of the flakes and blades have diffuse bulbs of percussion with a further 20% having a small and isolated hemispherical bulb, typical of the use of relatively 'soft' percussors (Table 3.7). The remaining pieces with extant proximal ends have pronounced bulbs and one flake has a ventral surface formed largely from the blow being diverted along a thermal (frost fractured) flaw. Complementing the bulb types, almost 70% of the flakes and blades have feathered terminations, whilst 20% are hinged. Five blades with plunged distal terminations are also present, some of which may have been deliberately struck in order to alter the opposed platform.

The dorsal scar patterns on the blades and flakes vary considerably (Table 3.8). Notable are the number of pieces with orthogonal or perpendicular dorsal scars. These typify the crested blades but also include many other flakes and blades which display remnant scars from earlier attempts at cresting and indicate that cresting was frequently undertaken throughout reduction. Perhaps more surprisingly, given the nature of the majority of the cores, only a relatively small proportion of pieces have opposed parallel scars. This is perhaps somewhat misleading, however, as it is likely that many of the pieces with multi-directional scars also came from opposed platformed cores, as would some of the pieces with uni-directional parallel scars but which do not retain the scars from the opposite platform.

True primary flakes make up less than 2% of the flakes and blades whilst only 10% have 50% or more of their dorsal surfaces covered. Tertiary flakes, retaining no cortex, account for over half of the flakes and blades. The low proportions of cortical flakes, particularly primary flakes, may indicate that the early stages in raw material processing occurred closer to the source, but those that are present show that cores were being prepared and that most of the reduction sequence is represented.

Cores
Fig. 3.2
Twenty-three complete cores were recovered, these representing a relatively low 0.6% of the total assemblage. A further 25 conchoidally fractured pieces, many of which are likely to be either cores that disintegrated during reduction or fragments of discarded 'tested' pieces, were also recorded, although even including these, the core pieces only amount to 1.3% of the total assemblage. The relative paucity of cores raises the possibility that some which were worked and perhaps even prepared at the site were taken away for use elsewhere, although the large size of the cores and the intensity of their reduction would also result in relatively low proportions.

All but three of the 23 complete cores comprise opposed platformed examples of relatively uniform morphology which had produced blades on their fronts and often side faces but with the backs remaining

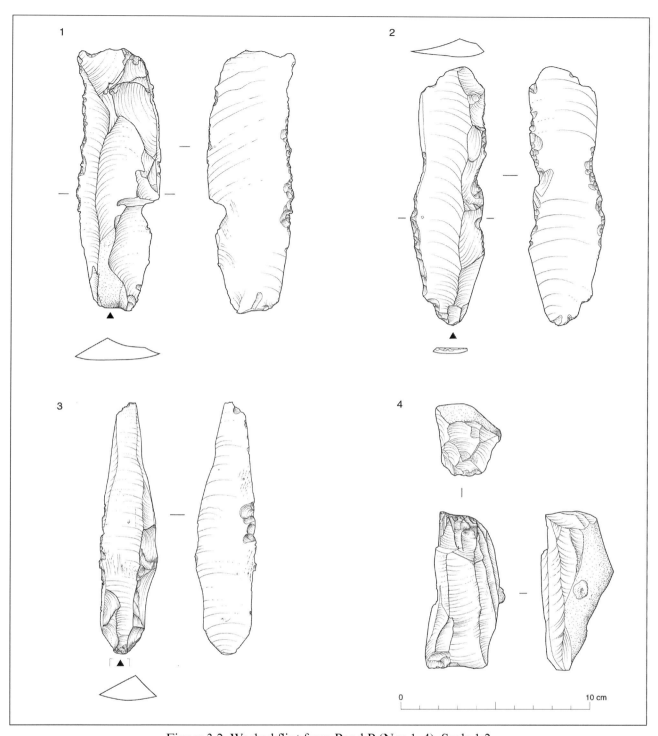

Figure 3.2 Worked flint from Pond P (Nos 1–4). Scale 1:2

either cortical or shaped by simple flaking (Fig. 3.2, No. 4). The platforms are mostly set at notably acute angles to the faces and frequently display evidence of platform rejuvenation. The rejuvenation of striking platforms by the complete or partial removal of core tablets appears to have been frequently undertaken. This has resulted in the cores rapidly diminishing in length during reduction; refitting has demonstrated that some of the cores used at the site were originally in excess of 245mm long, but the average size of the cores actually recovered was 75mm with the largest being only 90mm long. The cores' faces are also relatively

narrow; the widest is 70mm but on average they are a little under 40mm, showing that they tend towards being nearly twice as long as broad. Again, this is at odds with the width of many of the flakes and blades from the site, which must have been produced from much larger cores. The implications are that either the larger cores had been removed from the site or that they had started off being much larger and were extensively worked down before being abandoned.

Five of the twenty opposed platformed cores have had one of their striking platforms completely removed by rejuvenation before having been discarded,

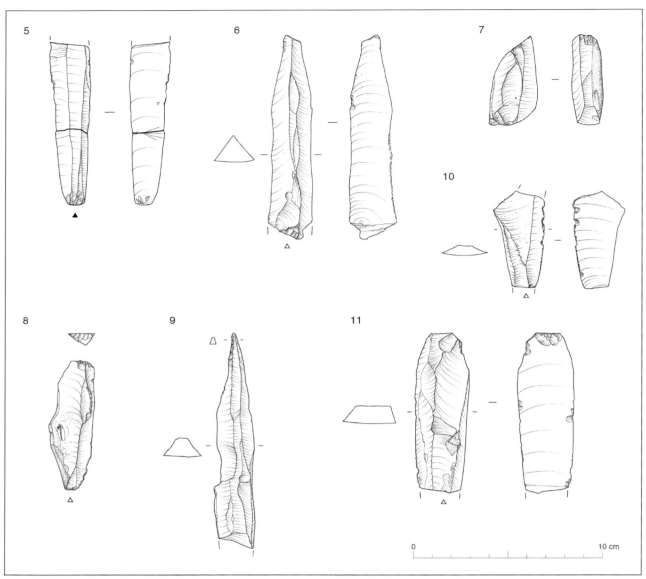

Figure 3.3 Worked flint from Pond P (Nos 5–11). Scale 1:2

leaving only bidirectional blade scars to indicate their original form. Of the remaining 35 striking platforms, the majority (24 or 69%) have plain flaked surfaces, nine are faceted and the remaining two, both on the same core, are keeled, with blades being removed from the front and partly down the back of the core. The striking platform / core face angles were nearly all prepared, with 25 being finely trimmed and seven rubbed smooth from grinding, leaving only three without any additional modification.

The remaining three cores are diverse examples that include a partially nodular cobble that appears to have been abandoned during the decortication stage, possibly due to the emergence of thermal flaws, and an elongated split nodule or large blade that has had a number of blades taken off one side but again was abandoned at an early stage. The remainder is an irregular piece that has a single platform but could be part of an opposed platformed core that has a severe 'plunge' fracture or alternatively has a beaked burin-like edge reminiscent of 'pseudo-burins' (*cf*. Rankine 1952, fig 6; Jacobi *et al*. 1978, 218).

Retouched and utilised implements
Figs 3.2–3.3
Altogether, 134 flakes and blades, representing 3.5% of the total assemblage, had been retouched or exhibited convincing damage caused through use (Table 3.9). One of these is a small bifacially and invasively worked piece that is almost certainly a fragment of a Neolithic or Early Bronze Age arrowhead. Although apparently recovered from the base of the silt layer, if this is indeed an arrowhead then it must be intrusive. The rest are variable in the nature of their secondary working and the shape of the blanks used, but there are no reasons to assume they are not part of the Late Upper Palaeolithic industry.

The majority of the implements, amounting to 108 pieces or just over 80% of the total, have macroscopic damage to their edge but have not necessarily been deliberately retouched. These have been roughly divided into three groups, largely based on the degree and form of the abrasion that has affected their edges.

Those with light edge damage have either very fine retouch or light spalling along parts of their edges.

Of the twenty examples so classified, all but three comprise blades with the majority being prismatic, the exceptions being a blade-like flake, a flake and one that is too fragmentary to classify. The blanks used varied considerably in shape and size; only eight are complete and these vary in maximum length from 35mm to 122mm. This probably suggests that they were used in a variety of ways on different materials. With a few of these, the edge modification is uneven and these may actually represent worn serrated implements.

The most common group are those with moderate edge damage that is often bifacial and includes chipping, crushing and rounding along parts of their edges (Fig. 3.3, No. 10). The blanks used vary, with 40 out of the 51 (78%) comprising blades, just over half of which are prismatic; also included are crested blades and decortication blades. Five flakes, a decortication flake, a core rejuvenation flake and five fragmented pieces also exhibit moderate edge damage. The blanks tend to be large, with the seventeen complete pieces averaging at 99mm in length but varying between 55mm and 192mm.

The nature of the damage, which includes crushing and rounding, suggests that they were used for cutting, scraping or chopping hard materials such as wood or bone. In at least two cases they also have visible striations running perpendicular from the edge suggestive of a whittling action. In a few cases the abrasion has begun to form small concavities along the edges, similar to those seen on the bruised blades and it is very likely that at least some of these are relatively lightly used bruised blades.

Pieces with heavy abrasion and what may be considered true 'bruising' account for over a quarter of all the identified implements. Whilst the edge modification on these items does vary in intensity, all of these pieces have heavy damage that has significantly affected parts of one or more edges. The blanks used also vary with 24 of the 37 pieces (65%) made using blades of which most comprise large, sturdy non-prismatic, crested or decortication blades (Fig. 3.2, Nos 1–3). A decortication flake, a core modification flake and three other flakes also have bruising on their edges. The remaining eight bruised pieces are all flake or blade fragments, their high proportions suggesting that, in whatever way they were actually used, it involved some force. The twelve complete implements varied in length from 54mm to 145mm with an average of 106mm.

The 'bruising' consists of edge abrasion and shallow scalar splintering that usually occurs bifacially, although is often heaviest on one, usually the ventral, face and sometimes forms concave or coarsely denticulated sides. The most extensively damaged pieces show a notable loss of mass from the repeated battering. The spalling can be quite invasive but the scars can also be deep and often have step terminations, and the actual edges of the implements are frequently crushed and even smooth-worn. The damage is consistent with the blades having been used in a repetitive chopping-like action against relatively hard and convex-sided objects such as bone, antler, hard wood or stone (cf. Barton 1986a; Froom 2005, 34–8).

Type	No.	%
Arrowhead	1	0.7
Burin	5	3.7
Edge modified – light	20	14.9
Edge modified – moderate	51	38.1
Edge modified – heavy / bruised	37	27.6
Serrated edge	1	0.7
Notch	8	6.0
Piercer	7	5.2
Scraper	1	0.7
Truncated blade	3	2.2
Total	**134**	**99.8**

Table 3.9 Classification of retouched and edge damaged implements from Pond P

Burins
Five burins were identified. Four of these are relatively simple and comprise blade segments with burin spalls removed longitudinally along their edges, two of the examples having the spalls removed from both ends forming double-ended types (Fig. 3.3, No. 7). The fifth is similar but has the burin spalls removed from an inversely retouched break. One of the cores also has a 'beaked' edge formed by the removal of a number of micro-blades, and this may also have been used as a burin-like tool.

Serrated blade
A large prismatic blade measuring at least 113mm in length has fine serrations of c.8 per cm cut along its left margin (Fig. 3.3, No. 6). Its proximal and distal end was broken off and had possibly been intentionally removed. As noted above, a few of the finely retouched blades may also be worn serrated implements.

Notches
Eight notched implements were identified, five made on blades, two on flakes and the remainder on a core rejuvenation flake. The notches are all shallow with the largest measuring 15mm across and 5mm deep. In some cases the notches might have been caused by accidental post-depositional damage, but many do show some evidence of wear and some have additional light retouch along their sides.

Piercers
Seven piercers were identified, all but one made using prismatic blades (Fig. 3.3, No. 9). The exception is a flake that has fine retouch removing its striking platform forming an awl-like point. All of the blades had been lightly retouched or notched to form fine sharp points, five at their distal ends and one at its proximal end. One of those worked at its distal end has a micro-burin like removal and additional fine retouch forming an awl-like edge, whilst another has an asymmetric spurred end, similar to those seen on 'Zinken-like' implements, which are argued to have been used as scrapers and borers for antler working (see Kufel-Diakowska 2011, 238 and references therein).

Scraper

A single scraper, consisting of a long end type made on a 71mm long prismatic blade, was identified (Fig 3.3, No. 8). This has steep scalar retouch forming a slightly convex working edge at its distal end.

Truncated blades

Three blades with straight transverse truncations were identified. Two of these are prismatic, the other a crested blade. The prismatic blades both have slightly invasive inverse retouch across their distal ends whilst the crested blade's distal end has bifacial retouch that has been heavy crushed (Fig. 3.3, No. 11). The wear on all three is perhaps most plausibly the result of their use as graving or chisel-like implements.

Intentional breaks

A high proportion of the assemblage is broken, which is perhaps not surprising given the large sizes and fragility of many of the flakes and blades. However, it is also likely than many of the pieces, particularly the blade segments, have been broken intentionally with many showing characteristic traits such as *Languette* breaks, wedge-shaped fracture lines and dorsal crushing (Fig. 3.3, No. 5). Particularly convincing as being deliberately broken are a small number that have snaps initiated by small notches (Bergman *et al.* 1987). Whilst none of these show unequivocal evidence for use, intentionally broken blade segments appear to have been used for a wide variety of purposes. Further and more detailed examination including microscopic analysis of the blade segments could reveal the extent that intentional breakage was practised and the possible roles the pieces served.

Burnt flint

A total of 129 pieces of otherwise unworked burnt flint weighing just under 0.5kg was recovered from the hollow. The pieces mostly comprise fragments of small, rounded pebbles and small cobbles such as are present in natural river terrace deposits at the site. The degree that these have been burnt varies; most are only moderately burnt but all have changed colour to some extent and become 'fire crazed'. The variability in the extent to which individual pieces have been burnt is most indicative of the incidental burning of flint clasts from ground-set fires.

The highest quantities were found in silt layer 15451 which produced 89 pieces weighing 254g, with the rest coming from the colluvial layer 15450 which contained 40 pieces weighing 180g. No evidence for *in situ* hearths was recognised but the density distribution of the burnt flint in the silt layer closely mirrored that of the struck flint, suggesting that hearth use and flintworking occurred close by. The distribution of the burnt flint in the colluvium also generally matched that of the struck flint.

Sandstone objects

Five sandstone cobbles were also recovered from the hollow. These are likely to have been found as erratics in the local glacial tills and, whilst none have unequivocally been worked, they all have patches of abrasion or smoothing suggesting they may have been used as percussors. One (from colluvial layer 15450) weighs 1108g and has a wide flat surface that has experienced heavy attrition, consistent with use as an anvil-type object. The other four all have abrasion around their widest edges or extremities suggesting possible use as hammerstones, pounding or grinding tools. Three are substantial, weighing between 436g and 746g, which might make them rather unwieldly for use as flintworking hammerstones, although they would be suitable for abrading the platform edges which was commonly undertaken (see above). The fourth has a smoothed side, also consistent with a use as a rubbing or grinding tool. Further microscopic analysis could help elucidate whether the abrasion had been caused through deliberate use or from natural processes.

Discussion: technological strategies and dating

The basic technological strategy evidenced in the assemblage involved the production of both large, heavy blades and smaller and more delicate prismatic blades. Some of the blades were converted into a range of retouched pieces but, differing from most other Late Glacial and Holocene flint assemblages, the main macroscopic evidence for the use of tools came from extensive edge damage seen on mainly thick, large and heavy blades. In consideration of the technological and typological attributes of the assemblage and the evidence presented by the refitting sequences, a basic understanding of the reduction sequence from the site can be proposed:

1. Raw materials were decorticated, although it is possible that some of the basic nodule preparation was done closer to the source.

2. The nodules were 'exfoliated', resulting in variably sized, wide and markedly curved thin flakes, often with remnants of cortex on their distal ends. These are morphologically similar to biface thinning flakes and there are certain technological similarities between the early stages of the production of these cores and axes.

3. Large mass reduction flakes were removed to 'pre-form' the nodules into relatively long and narrow cores, usually leaving the 'backs' either cortical or simply flaked. This may also indicate the 'quartering' of large nodules. The presence of many shattered striking platforms, distinct points of percussion and occasional undeveloped Hertzian cones indicates that a large proportion of the earlier stages of decortication and core shaping employed hard hammers.

4. Once the core had been shaped, opposed platforms were created.

5. The core faces were carefully shaped with the removal of more wide, thin and often curved 'thinning-like' flakes, cresting being employed to create ridges running down the face. The crests were 'struck', producing mostly large, long, thick and very sturdy crested blades, some of which were utilised as bruised blades.

6. The removal of long crested blades allowed for further large long blades to be produced, although many of these are not truly prismatic. The longest refitting sequence identified shows that at least four blades were struck from the same platform, but the cores were regularly rotated and the opposed platform used. This

was, on some occasions, done when hinged fracture scars started developing. It also had the effect of flattening the core face which would become increasingly bowed.

7   Some long blades, especially the thicker and heavier examples, were also used as bruised blades. Others may well have been intentionally broken.

8   Cresting, sometimes fully or just with short stretches, was employed throughout the production of the long blades, rectifying any problems developing on the core faces and facilitating the continued production of blades. This resulted in high proportions of the longer blades having orthogonal dorsal scars.

9   Throughout reduction, the edges of striking platforms were constantly being modified by fine flaking and abrasion, facetting was often used to alter the platform surfaces and core tableting was also frequently undertaken, all with the aim of maintaining the cores' ability to produce blades.

10 As cores reduced in size from reduction and rejuvenation, smaller and more delicate (generally <80mm long) prismatic blade production took precedence. However, as shown by the refitting sequences, the production of relatively small prismatic blades also occurred during the earlier stages of reduction, often alternating with the production of large non-prismatic blades.

Full discussion of the assemblage is deferred to Chapter 5.II, but the technology and typology of the flintwork, in particular the presence of numerous 'long blades' (defined as those measuring in excess of 120mm), as well as distinctive 'bruised blades' (*lames mâchurées*), strongly suggests that the assemblage belongs to the 'long-blade' industries characteristic of the Terminal Upper Palaeolithic. The apparent regular use of opposed platformed cores, platform faceting and the straightness of the blades in profile would also be consistent with 'long-blade' industries (Barton 1989 and 1998; Barton and Roberts 1996 and 2004; Cooper 2006; Lewis with Rackham 2011).

Illustration catalogue

Fig. 3.2
1   **Bruised blade**, 15975 (15450), Spit 4, Square K3
2   **Bruised blade**, 15976 (15451) Spit 1, Square K3
3   **Bruised blade**, 15834 (15451), Spit 2, Square M9
4   Opposed platform **core**, 16036 (15451), Spit 1, Square H4

Fig. 3.3
5   Conjoined **long blade** fragments with probable intentional break, 15449 (15451), Spit 1, Square N11
6   Distal portion of serrated **long blade**, 15514 (15450), Spit 1, Square L11
7   **Burin**, double ended, 15984 (15450), Spit 1, Square M3
8   **End scraper**, 15561(15450), Spit 2, Square H9
9   **Piercer**, 15528 (15450), Spit 1, Square J11
10 Edge modified **blade fragment**, 15883 (15450), Spit 1, Square N8
11 Truncated **blade** with inverse distal retouch, 15834 (15451), Spit 3, Square M9

II. Later prehistoric worked flint
by Barry J. Bishop and Michael Donnelly
Figs 3.4–3.7

Introduction
Excluding the assemblage of Upper Palaeolithic flintwork discussed above, a total of 6,211 struck flints was retrieved from the various areas excavated across the site. Much of the flint was recovered as residual material from later features or from remnant soil horizons, which suggests that a proportion of the assemblage originated in knapping floors, occupation horizons and shallow features that have since been truncated. A notable exception to this was a large assemblage (2,114 pieces) of Early Neolithic flints that was recovered from a further pond or hollow in Area J, a few metres to the south of that containing the Palaeolithic material detailed above.

This report incorporates and builds upon a number of separate reports that were written for the purposes of assessing the archaeological research potential of the material following the four major phases of excavations: the material from Hinxton Hall (Area F) was compiled by Tim Reynolds, that from the Genome Campus Extension (Areas A–E) by Barry Bishop, the material from the Genome Technical Hub excavations was carried out by Michael Donnelly and that from the Hinxton Genome (South Field; Area J) by Barry Bishop. A publication report was written by Barry Bishop in 2008 and was subsequently updated to include summary descriptions of the assemblages from Areas I and J.

For the purposes of this report, the lithic material from all phases of the excavations is considered together, as it represents a consistent assemblage representing the occupation of this riverside location from the Mesolithic period through to at least the Bronze Age. The basic overall characteristics of the combined assemblages are described below, with comment on the chronological framework for flint use at the site. This is followed by a consideration of the individual assemblages from certain key features in order to highlight the changing nature of flint use at Hinxton, and concludes with a discussion of that use within its broader context and in terms of understanding lithic assemblages from contemporary sites in the region.

Raw materials
The raw materials used for the struck flint assemblage consist predominantly of a fine-grained flint, dense black in colour but varying to brown and grey, with only the thinnest flakes attaining translucency. This flint contains occasional red streaks and large grey patches occurred towards the nodules' centres. A variety of flints of other colours and textures are also present but in limited numbers. The flints' cortices, where retained, vary from smooth rolled and battered to thick and rough, with the latter types being predominantly used. Many thermal faults and ancient heavily recorticated thermal scars are evident on the struck pieces, resulting in the abandonment and disintegration of many of the cores, although generally the flint is of good knapping quality. The principal limitation of the raw materials appears to be the relatively small size of the cores,

Type	No	%
Decortication flakes	1040	11.1
Micro-debitage	2110	22.5
Core rejuvenation flakes	86	0.9
Flakes	2258	24.0
Flake fragments	938	10.0
Blades	1365	14.5
Blade-like flakes	486	5.2
Cores	225	2.4
Conchoidal chunks	470	5.0
Micro-burins	8	0.1
Retouched implements	405	4.3
Total	**9391**	**100%**

Table 3.10 Composition of the struck flint assemblage

the majority of which weigh under 100g and this is reflected in the size of the struck pieces; none exceed 100mm in maximum dimension, few even approach this figure and the majority measure under 50mm.

The nature of the raw materials indicates that they were obtained from derived deposits situated close to the parent Upper Chalk, which outcrops a few kilometres to the south of Hinxton (Gibbard 1986). Some of the flint has unabraded cortex suggesting it had been found close to the chalk and this may have been brought to the site. The majority of pieces, however, appear to have experienced periglacial weathering along with some alluvial transportation and these would have been available at and close to the site. At Hinxton, the River Cam meanders towards the east, eroding and exposing Pleistocene terrace deposits containing flint nodules derived both directly from the chalk and as redeposited material from the local glacial tills. This use of locally available flint raw materials with only occasional use of better quality chalk flint is typical for assemblages spanning the Mesolithic to Bronze Age in the region (*e.g.* Edmonds *et al.* 1999; Edmonds 2006, 131).

Condition
The condition of the material, although locally variable, is predominantly sharp or only slightly edge damaged, indicating that the assemblage overall has experienced only limited post-depositional disturbance. However, the high levels of broken pieces, which comprise about one third of the flakes and blades, suggest that much of the assemblage may have suffered from a degree of trampling, perhaps having been exposed in midden deposits and indicating that much of it may be redeposited. The frequency of thin flakes and blades alongside many micro-blades would also lead to a higher incidence of breakage than with more robust later prehistoric material.

Recortication varies in its extent, ranging from being completely absent to quite heavy. Although pieces manufactured earlier during the prehistoric period may have been prone to increasing degrees of recortication, a simple chronological explanation could not be universally applied as diagnostically contemporary pieces have been affected to sometimes quite notably different degrees. It would appear that variations in the raw materials, combined with localised differences in soil conditions, were at least as important as the age of the piece in determining its degree of recortication, if not more so, and this process cannot be used to estimate the age of any specific piece.

Characterisation of the assemblage

Overview
The assemblage may be regarded as moderately large given the size of the areas investigated. It contains pieces representing all stages in the reduction sequence, from rejected 'tested' pieces and decortication flakes, to used and worn-out tools (see Table 3.10). It is evident that flint raw materials were procured and converted to tools which were being used and discarded at the site.

Considerations of both the technological and typological aspects of the assemblage indicate that it had been manufactured over a long period, from at least the Late Glacial period through to the Bronze Age, with the added possibility that flint use continued at the site into the Iron Age.

Blades and flakes
Despite chronological attribution being only occasionally possible, a very large proportion of the assemblage is the product of a blade-based reduction strategy, characteristic of Mesolithic and Early Neolithic industries. Struck flint continued to be made and used at the site throughout the later Neolithic and Bronze Age, but this material seems to form a less substantial proportion of the overall assemblage. Blades form over 15% of the overall assemblage and associated with these are the blade-like flakes, which contribute around an additional 5%. Approximately half of the blades are clearly systematically produced, being made with great skill and exhibiting features such as neatly trimmed striking platforms, parallel lateral margins and dorsal scars, which demonstrates that they were manufactured as part of a process that enabled the repeated production of standardised blades. Furthermore, around half of these could be termed micro-blades, being 12mm or less wide. Although these can be incidentally produced as part of routine blade production, their deliberate and repeated manufacture suggests a concern with the manufacture of microlithic equipment. Systematically produced blades, particularly micro-blades, are more likely to be associated with Mesolithic industries, whilst the more casually produced are more common within Neolithic industries (*e.g.* Thatcher 2007; OA East forthcoming). In general, blade-based industries can only be broadly assigned to the Mesolithic and Early Neolithic periods but the mix of systematic and more casually produced blades here suggests that both periods are well-represented amongst this material.

The flakes vary in shape, size and technological attributes. As is the case with most struck flint assemblages, individual pieces can only rarely be assigned to any specific period, although many were relatively narrow and thin, had been competently produced and were probably associated with the production of blades. Some of the broader and less systematically produced flakes are more likely to be associated with the Later Neolithic or Early Bronze Age industries otherwise represented by diagnostic forms and some coherent feature assemblages, whilst even more crudely produced, thicker and broader pieces may represent later prehistoric flintworking, dating to the latter parts of the Bronze Age or possibly the Iron Age.

Retouched implements

Diagnostic implements include a number of microliths, a truncated blade and a transverse axe or adze, all chronological markers for the Mesolithic period (Table 3.11). Pieces indicative of Early Neolithic activity include leaf-shaped arrowheads and laurel leaf points, whilst the Later Neolithic is attested by transverse arrowheads and the Early Bronze Age by barbed and tanged arrowheads.

Most of the other retouched pieces are less chronologically diagnostic, although it should be noted that many were made on blades or blade-like flakes and would be typical of the range found on Mesolithic and Early Neolithic sites. Most commonly represented are simple edge-trimmed implements, followed by scrapers and serrates, which together represent nearly two-thirds of the retouched inventory. These three tool-types frequently form the largest categories of tools at early settlement sites. Serrated pieces and scrapers dominated the retouched pieces at Hurst Fen (Clark *et al.* 1960, 214) and they formed 68% of all Neolithic implements at Broome Heath (Wainwright 1972, 68). At Kilverstone, simple edge-retouched pieces formed the largest category of implement with scrapers being the most common formally retouched type (Beadsmoore 2006).

The simple edge-retouched implements comprise the most common implement type and are mostly made using blades or narrow flakes. The extent of modification is variable although it nearly always focuses on the longer, lateral, margins. It ranges from being limited to short lengths of the edge to encompassing most of the perimeter of the flake, and from being straight, convex or concave to sinuous. In most cases the modification clearly consists of very fine retouching, which is either abrupt and lightly blunts the edge, allowing it to be safely handled or even hafted, or is slightly invasive and helps strengthen an already acute edge. A few may represent worn-down serrates and in most cases it is likely that the flakes and blades were used as fine cutting tools. With some, it is not clear whether the modification was deliberately executed or consists of micro-chipping formed through utilising the flake as a cutting implement (*e.g.* Tringham *et al.* 1974).

Although the total number of scrapers is too low to allow meaningful metrical or morphological comparisons, they are comparable with those from other assemblages in that they vary considerably in shape, size and in the extent and nature of their retouch, and many of the simple edge-retouched flakes may represent minimally worked scrapers. Pit 4834 (Period 2.1; Pit Group 8, Late Neolithic) contained a large assemblage of six scrapers, including four that probably originated from the same core and are of very similar lengths (44mm, 46mm, 49mm and 56mm); two actually refitted. The remaining two show the variety

Type	No.	%
Arrowhead	12	4.7
Axe	3	1.2
Burin	1	0.4
Denticulate	10	4
Edge trimmed flake / blade	72	28.5
Fabricator	2	0.8
Knife	6	2.4
Laurel leaf	3	1.2
Microlith	4	1.6
Notch	14	5.5
Piercer	13	5.1
Rod / pick	2	0.8
Scraper	57	22.5
Serrate	33	13
Truncated blade	1	0.4
Core tool	20	7.9
Total retouched	**253**	**100%**

Table 3.11 Retouched implements

in the scraper population with a side scraper on a small, square flake and a double end scraper on a long blade-like flake.

The serrates are mostly worked on one side only and almost exclusively made on blades. Often they retain some cortex, either on the side opposite the serrations or on their distal ends, to potentially aid in handling. Again, there are too few to allow statistical comparison but they are certainly very comparable to the large collection of serrates recovered from the Early Neolithic occupation sites at Parnwell or Stow-cum-Quy (Webley 2007; Thatcher 2007). Denticulates with notches/teeth larger than those on serrates are also present in small numbers and are generally quite crude, expedient tools (Fig. 3.5, No. 9); however, one particularly fine and extremely fresh example was recovered from Period 2.1 pit 5304 (Pit Group 6, Early Neolithic) and had been formed on a discoidal decortication flake. It would appear that this piece has never been used and was deposited alongside many serrates and a very large side and end scraper (Fig. 3.5, No. 11). Notches and piercers are also common, with fourteen and thirteen examples being identified respectively. These vary considerably; the piercers range from fine sharp needle-like points made on distally modified blades to thick and blunt points made on extensively retouched large flakes. The notches are of variable sizes and made on a variety of blades and different shaped and sized flakes.

Projectile points are represented by microliths and arrowheads. The four microliths are all probably of Later Mesolithic date and there are also four micro-burins present, these being by-products of microlith manufacture. Arrowheads form a relatively high proportion of the retouched component at 5%. At Kilverstone, for example, they only formed 0.3% of the implements and at Broome Heath, although larger numbers were recovered, they still contributed only 1.8% of the total retouched pieces (Beadsmoore

2006; Wainwright 1972, 68). The examples here cannot be simply compared to those sites, as they were manufactured over a considerable period, from the Early Neolithic until the Early Bronze Age, but the proportions present do suggest that the use of these implements, usually associated with hunting, was a recurring and important aspect of occupation along the river.

The retouched pieces and core tools were clearly produced over a long period but the majority are likely to have been manufactured during the Mesolithic and Early Neolithic. Overall, they form 4.1% of the lithic assemblage, which may be adjusted to 6–7% if the considerable quantities of micro-debitage are excluded. This would compare well to other Early Neolithic sites: at the settlement sites of Kilverstone and Broome Heath, retouched pieces formed 5% of the assemblages (Beadsmoore 2006; Wainwright 1972, 66), 5–6% were recovered at Hurst Fen (Clark *et al.* 1960, 214) and a similar proportion to that was recorded at Spong Hill (Healy 1988, 32, table 14). These sites are thought to represent occupation sites where a wide range of activities was undertaken and suggest that the overall lithic assemblage here may be broadly termed a 'domestic' assemblage, typical of those from settlement sites.

Cores
Cores form 2.4% of the overall assemblage, which compares well with the 2.7% recovered at Kilverstone (Beadsmoore 2006) but is slightly less than the 3.4% recorded at Hurst Fen (Clark *et al.* 1960, fig. 7). Further cores may be indicated by the conchoidally fractured chunks, many of which probably represent cores that disintegrated during reduction. They were reduced using a variety of different strategies – a few instances of structured preparation, involving the pre-shaping of the cores, were noted, but the majority were reduced simply with little effort expended on preparing idealised core forms. The sequence mostly involved the creation of a basic flaked platform on an otherwise largely unmodified pebble or 'quartered' nodule, and this was used to detach a series of flakes and blades. Once this platform became unproductive the core was either discarded or, more often, a new platform was created on a suitable but otherwise seemingly random part of the core. Most of the cores are therefore rather irregular and blocky in shape and have randomly aligned striking platforms, although there are some finely shaped and worked conical and cylindrical blade and bladelet cores that typify Mesolithic knapping, such as the residual example from an Anglo-Saxon context (5108; Area I). Two-platform and multi-platform cores are in the majority, between them contributing around 70% of all cores, whilst single-platform cores contribute only around 14%. The remaining 16% comprise cores that have been reduced centripetally, either unifacially or bifacially, forming discoidal-shaped pieces. Some, such as those residual finds from contexts 2555 (ditch 2539; Period 3.1 Enclosure 3) and 2382 (pit 2358 in Roman Quarry Pit Group 35) are comparable to the later Neolithic 'discoidal' examples from the Babraham Road Park and Ride site and may be of similar date (Bishop 2000).

Despite the apparent casualness in preparing cores and creating striking platforms, the cores were generally skilfully and successfully reduced, and the production of blades was frequently achieved. Over 60% show evidence that they had once produced blades or narrow flakes, although once blade production had ceased many continued to be used to make flakes. Commensurate with blade production, most cores show some evidence for platform-edge modification and a number have been formally rejuvenated by core-tablets that removed the striking platform, a number of which were recognised within the overall lithic assemblage. To these may be added a number of other flakes that had rejuvenated the cores by mass removal of the cores' face, either to rectify the striking platform/core face angle or to remove prominent step or hinge fractures. Most cores had been extensively worked, they range from 26g to 140g in weight, averaging at 60g, but with the majority falling within the 30–50g bracket. A number appear to have been made on large, thick flakes, probably reflecting practices of 'quartering' the nodules prior to sustained flake production. Many cores may have been abandoned due to step fracturing and the development of thermal flaws, whilst the quantities of conchoidal chunks, many of which represent shattered cores, show that disintegration during reduction was a common occurrence.

Micro-debitage
Also recovered in substantial numbers are pieces of micro-debitage, consisting of conchoidal and angular shatter, micro-flakes and flake fragments, all less than 10mm in maximum dimension. The quantity of this material varies greatly between excavation areas from a high of 46.8% at the Hinxton Hall sites to a low of 6.6% at the Genome Technical Hub excavations. This is probably a factor of sampling bias but could also indicate areas where knapping occurred as opposed to locations where flint was used, repaired and/or deposited. These pieces were largely produced as incidental waste from core reduction and, as they are unlikely to have been deliberately removed from where they were produced, their presence in quantity is indicative of core working having occurred in the vicinity. Although much of the micro-debitage could not be assigned to any particular modes of core working, a relatively high number consist of small platform-edge trimming flakes, originating from careful platform preparation and likely to be associated with blade production. Very few pieces could be identified that relate to microlith manufacture, although these are admittedly difficult to identify amongst the micro-debitage originating from general core reduction.

Distribution
Struck flint was recovered from across most of the areas investigated at Hinxton (see Table 3.12). Almost half of the total assemblage was recovered from Area J, the majority of this coming from Neolithic Pond Q (Period 2.1, 16042) and resulting in this area producing the highest densities of struck flint than any of the other areas. The other two major excavation areas, Hinxton Hall (Area F) and the initial Genome Campus Extension excavation (Areas A–D) produced the next highest quantities of struck flint, with lesser numbers coming from the Genome

	Hinxton Hall (HINHH93/4) Area F	Genome Campus (HINGC02/03) Areas A–E	Genome Technical Hub (HINGEC11) Area I	Hinxton South Field (HINGEL14) Area J	other
Area in hectares	0.75	3	1	1.25	1
Total struck flints	1691	968	441	3031	80
Density per hectare	2250	323	441	2424	80
Total non micro-debitage	900	877	412	2753	75
Density per hectare	1200	292	412	2202	75

Table 3.12 Density of struck flint from the main excavation areas

Technical Hub excavations (Area I) and noticeably smaller quantities coming from across the river at Ickleton (Area H) and the New Lakes site (Area G). This, at least in part, is likely to reflect the much lower densities of subsoil features within these latter areas. These would have been instrumental in preserving the evidence of previous lithic-based activities which, as is argued below, was largely present as a surface scatter, confined to ploughsoil horizons and only recovered where redeposited into later features.

Although the distribution of struck flint largely reflects the densities of the features present, it is also possible that these variations did genuinely reflect real preferences in the areas chosen for flint reduction and tool use. The four main excavated areas were located on slightly elevated ground, close to and overlooking the river, but at a sufficient distance and height to escape the dampness and prospect of flooding that may have made adjacent areas less desirable for settlement. The densities of struck flint recovered from the evaluation trenches in the Genome Campus Extension show the greatest concentrations being present to the west of Area D, dropping off quickly the nearer they were to the river, although overall the trenches produced very little struck flint.

Across the whole site, it is more difficult to discern any meaningful spatial patterning in the concentrations of struck flint present. There was a scattering in most places but the main concentrations relate to the presence of artefact-rich features (such as Pond R and Pond D, which are discussed in more detail below), the Early Neolithic knapping scatter in Pond Q, also Middle/Late Neolithic and Early Bronze Age Pit Groups 4, 7, 8, 16 and 17. The hollow and 'ponds' may have provided foci for lithic production and use but the pits appear to represent specific depositional practices that resulted in the high quantities of struck flint present, but do not necessarily indicate the actual locations where the flints were made or used. Equally, there is nothing to suggest that these were not located close by, or that they may have been associated with surface scatters from disturbed middens and knapping floors. The overall scatter appears to have accumulated as a series of individual occupation events, creating a palimpsest that resulted in the masking of specific episodes of flint use or chronological variations in its spatial distribution.

Chronology of flint use at Hinxton

Mesolithic and Early Neolithic

Activity at the site during the Mesolithic period is attested by the recovery of four microliths; an obliquely truncated point from Pond X (1583/2093, Area F), a rod or lanceolate type from colluvial deposits in Area J, a scalene triangle from Period 2.1 Pit Group 6 (pit 5304) and a probable residual microlith fragment from Anglo-Saxon pit 2113, context 2112, these all being of probable later Mesolithic date (Jacobi 1976; 1978). Another ventrally backed bladelet from Pond X may represent an unusual microlithic piece but is also clearly of Mesolithic date. In addition to microlith use, the presence of microburins in Pond R (675, fill 587, Area B), Pond X the Period 3.3 Shrine (ditch 1483) and a posthole (4018; ungrouped) suggests that microliths were also being manufactured here, this activity perhaps principally focusing around the 'ponds'. Also indicative of Mesolithic activity is a finely made tranchet axe or adze, recovered from the 'Neolithic hollow' in Area J (Pond Q, context 15749; Fig. 3.4, No. 1; Pl. 2.2). Additionally, the number of micro-blades and accompanying micro-blade cores (e.g. from Ditch Groups 7 (ditch 1111) and 9 (ditch 200), Pond X , may well reflect the manufacture of microlithic equipment. Nevertheless, and despite extensive sampling having been undertaken, no further microliths or microburins were recovered. This absence suggests that microlith use was not the distinguishing activity as has been recorded at some Mesolithic 'hunting camp' sites, and a more diverse range of activities might therefore be envisioned.

Microliths are usually associated with hunting equipment, although a number of other uses have been forwarded (Clarke 1976; Finlay 2000a; 2000b). Although it is likely that they may have fulfilled several roles, it still remains probable that many did serve as projectile points, a function that leaf-shaped arrowheads undoubtedly performed. In this context, it seems likely that one of the activities conducted at the site during the Mesolithic was hunting, an activity which appeared to continue during the Neolithic and Early Bronze Age. The presence of the river and the mosaic of wetlands within which the site was situated would have provided a wealth of resources for hunter-gather communities, including ample hunting opportunities.

The largest group from a single feature and accounting for a third of all the struck flint from the site came from the scatter contained within Neolithic Pond Q in Area J, which can be dated both by its technological traits and associated pottery to the Early Neolithic. Other diagnostic Early Neolithic implements include the leaf-shaped arrowheads from tree throw 3088 (deposit 3097) and from the upper deposits within the hollow (fill 15521 in Pond P; hollow 16041) containing Palaeolithic material in Area J. Arrowheads were also being manufactured at the site, as demonstrated by unfinished arrowheads and blanks from the pond or hollow (context 15703 in hollow 16042, Pond Q) containing Neolithic material in Area J and from evaluation contexts 7001, 7081 (HIN RIV 98) and Pond R (675). A laurel leaf point came from Pond Q in Area J and there is also some evidence that these were also being manufactured here. A large fragment from a flaked flint axe (Fig. 3.5, No. 8) of probable Neolithic date was recovered from colluvial layer 5399 in Area I (ungrouped). This piece looks more like a fractured preform than a finished item and could arguably be Mesolithic in date. Possible evidence for axe manufacture during the Early Neolithic was also noted in Pond R (675) and from Pit Group 3 (pit 3063).

The collection of scrapers associated with numerous serrates from Pit Group 6 (pit 5304) and Pit Group 8 (pits 4834/4851 and 4908) in Area I are almost certainly of Early Neolithic date (Fig. 3.5, No. 11). Overall, the assemblages from these features appear to indicate Early Neolithic activity rather than the admixture of Mesolithic and Early Neolithic flintwork that was common at Hinxton Hall (Area F) and the Genome Campus excavations (Areas A–D). Very fine, regular elongated horseshoe and discoidal style end scrapers are extremely rare on Mesolithic sites, and the only piece from this collection that is unequivocally of Mesolithic date is a worn, recorticated microlith amongst fresh uncorticated material.

Along with the projectile points, a number of other retouched pieces could be assigned to the Mesolithic or Early Neolithic, although further refinement of this suggestion, to one or other of these periods, is not possible. These include a wide range of tool types, including end truncated pieces and a burin, many made on blades or blade-like flakes (see above).

Later Neolithic and Early Bronze Age
Activity continued at the site into the later Neolithic, as testified by the assemblages from Pit Groups 4, 8, 14, 16 and 17 and from the deposits comprising Pond H (2253), which include a transverse arrowhead. Another, residual, transverse arrowhead was recovered from Period 3.1 Ditch Group 4 (ditch 4002, fill 4035). Further clear evidence of later Neolithic activity is suggested by the recovery of a few residual discoidal cores that were comparable to examples from other sites of this date found in Late Iron Age Enclosure 2 (Period 3.1 ditch 2539, deposit 2555) and Late Roman Pit Group 35 (Period 3.4 pit 2358, fill 2382) in Areas C and D.

The principal evidence for lithic use during the Early Bronze Age comprises the assemblage from shaft/pit 902 (Period 2.2, Pit Group 7), which produced an unfinished barbed and tanged arrowhead in addition to a burnt fragment from another, as well as a variety of bifacially flaked tools (Fig. 3.6, Nos 12, 13, 22 and 23), including a finely made blunted backed knife (Fig. 3.6, No. 14).

The extent of confidently attested activity during the later Neolithic and Early Bronze Age, beyond that represented by the assemblages from the pit groups and the loss of a few arrowheads and other chronologically diagnostic pieces, is difficult to evaluate. The features clearly suggest some form of settlement and, as many of the flakes and other pieces could not easily be assigned to any particular period, activity at the site may have been more extensive than these features alone suggest. Nevertheless, the lack of significant quantities or concentrations of debitage or tools suggests rather transient occupation, perhaps geared more towards resource acquisition than prolonged settlement.

Later prehistoric
Low-level but nevertheless persistent lithic use of probable later 2nd or 1st millennium BC date is suggested by crudely produced, thick and squat flakes with very obtuse striking platforms (cf. Martingell 1990), a few crude and often minimally worked cores and the presence of simple core tools, such as that from the upper horizons of Period 2.1 Pond Q in Area J, pit 3210 (fills 2731, 1533; ungrouped in Area F or Period 3.2 Ditch Group 7 (ditch 2001) in Area D.

There are none of the larger accumulations of later prehistoric flintwork, as were recorded close by at Hinxton Quarry (Pollard 1998) and at a few other sites in the area. In the absence of these, later prehistoric flintworking can be difficult to identify, particularly where there is a high potential for residuality from earlier periods. However, the assemblages from a few features (some associated with the later Iron Age occupation) may indicate the occasional use of flint during the later prehistoric periods. Period 3.2 Pit Group 19 (pit 136), for example, produced a small assemblage that was in a sharp condition and possibly represents the reduction of a single nodule, although none of these pieces actually refitted. This assemblage includes a few crude flakes and three chunks which can best be described as 'bashed lumps'. This represents a very crude means of producing flakes and would be typical of Middle Bronze Age or later industries.

A similar assemblage was recovered from later Iron Age Enclosure 2 (Period 3.1 ditch 3034) in Area D, which consists of a few crude flakes and some randomly struck chunks, again, all in sharp condition and probably from the same nodule. This material is similar to some of the pieces recovered from Enclosure 2 ditch 3064, slot 3063 through the same ditch, which includes a few squat flakes and a minimally reduced core, although in this slot there were clearly residual pieces, such as the flake from a polished implement and blades in a chipped and abraded condition. A few other contexts in the vicinity (in Area D) also produced some similar very crude flakes. The material from around this area is technologically most typical of Middle Bronze Age to Iron Age flintworking and therefore potentially relates to the period that the enclosure was in use. Unfortunately, as this ditch also contained quantities of residual material and there is a considerable quantity of evidently earlier material in the vicinity, relating the flintworking to the enclosure ditch and confidently establishing the occurrence of Late Iron Age flintworking at the site remains problematic. Flint nodules and traces of earlier flintworking would have been commonly encountered by the Late Iron Age inhabitants and it may be argued that they would, at least occasionally, exploit the ability of flint to have and maintain a sharp edge, even if the use of such implements was limited, expedient and of short duration.

Key contextual groups
The largest individual assemblage from Hinxton – with the exception of the Late Upper Palaeolithic material from Pond P (see above) – came from the Neolithic hollow or pond (Pond Q) in Area J, which produced over a third of all struck flint from the various excavations. Whilst much of the remainder was residual and recovered from later features, a few features did contain assemblages that could be associated with them. A few of the 'ponds' may also have produced assemblages that reflect flintworking occurring close by.

Neolithic Hollow (Pond Q)
Fig. 3.4, Pls 2.1, 2.3 and 2.4
This pond/hollow (16042) in Area J produced an assemblage of 2114 struck flints, a sandstone hammerstone and a small quantity of burnt flint: the largest assemblage from any individual 'feature' investigated across the site. The artefact scatter was initially identified as a flint-rich relict soil horizon (15513) that had been protected within a large hollow which was subsequently excavated in 1m² units. Three distinct soil horizons were identified within the hollow. The lowest 'natural' layer (assigned group number 15697) contained relatively little struck flint but notably did provide a tranchet axe in good condition (Fig. 3.4, No. 1). The assemblage from the lowest layer was concentrated within a single 1m² (context 15712) and contains a much higher proportion of prismatic blades than the other main fill and also two core tablets. These indicate a greater intensity of systematic blade production and it is possible that these actually represent a discrete and brief episode of Mesolithic flintworking. This involved the production of blades, one of which has fine edge retouch. The two cores present had only been minimally reduced and appear to have been abandoned due to thermal flaws. The cores producing the blades had presumably been removed for use elsewhere. The axe was found about 3m to the north of the main concentration of flint and is a characteristic Mesolithic implement with a transversely sharpened cutting edge. It is a finely produced example of its type and comparable to the one found further downstream in the Cam Valley at Sawston (Bishop 2016, figs 4.1–4.2). It shows very little evidence of either use-wear or post-depositional damage.

Overlying the 'natural' was deposit 15696, interpreted as a buried soil, which contained both struck flint and pottery that can be dated to the Early Neolithic period. This provided a much larger struck flint assemblage, amounting to 922 pieces or 44% of the struck assemblage from the hollow. Virtually all of these pieces are in a sharp condition, indicating minimal post-depositional movement, although around one in ten of the pieces has been burnt and there is a high degree of breakage. A few pieces could be refitted and the presence of micro-debitage in the samples suggests a series of broadly contemporary knapping events occurring in the vicinity. No evidence for actual *in situ* knapping was forthcoming, however, and the assemblage as a whole had evidently been disturbed to a limited extent.

Overlying the buried soil was a deposit interpreted as being of colluvial origin (context 15965) which produced just over half of the struck flint from the hollow. The condition of this material is notably poorer than that from the buried soils, but is still mostly good with the majority of pieces showing only very light post-depositional damage and some refits were also achieved. This would indicate that whilst it had seen greater disturbance, it had not experienced any significant colluvial displacement and is probably part of the same scatter as that found in the buried soil, having been reworked during later activity in the area and through processes such as ploughing. Evidence for the former includes a small proportion of the struck flint that comprises thick and crudely detached flakes and irregularly worked retouched implements and core tools, these hinting at episodes of flintworking during the later Bronze Age. However, with the exception of these few pieces and slight differences in condition, the material from the buried soil and colluvium are indistinguishable in terms of technology or raw material use and can therefore be considered together.

The raw materials comprise large nodules of fine-grained translucent black nodular flint with heavily recorticated thermal (frost shattered) facets. Similar materials had been used to make some of the other flintwork at Hinxton but its almost exclusivity here suggests it may have been gathered from a single location, perhaps even from the natural terrace deposits present in or around the hollow. The flint is of good knapping quality although thermal flawing has led to high proportions of shattered pieces, disintegrated cores and step-fractured flakes.

The assemblage from the hollow is remarkably large compared to other contemporary assemblages from Hinxton Genome or elsewhere along the Cam Valley. It represents all stages in the reduction sequence, from the initial processing of raw materials to the discard of worn tools. Other than the small quantity of possible later prehistoric flintwork mixed in the colluvial layer, it is technologically homogeneous and geared towards the production of both blades and flakes. Blades contribute just over 20% of the assemblage, of which over half can be regarded as prismatic; that is having parallel sides and dorsal scars and which have clearly been produced as part of a systematic reduction strategy designed repeatedly to produce blanks of a standard shape and size. Flakes with parallel dorsal scars contribute a further 5% of the assemblage and many of the 'useable' flakes are thin and narrow. Nevertheless, a high proportion of the flakes, around a third, were produced during the decortication of raw materials and a further quarter had been struck in order to shape, prepare or maintain the cores' productivity. However, few true core rejuvenation flakes, such as core tablets, were recovered and few cores had seen any extensive attempts at pre-shaping prior to flake and blade production.

Complete cores form a relatively low proportion (2%) of the assemblage but to these may be added a further 5% that comprise fragments of disintegrated

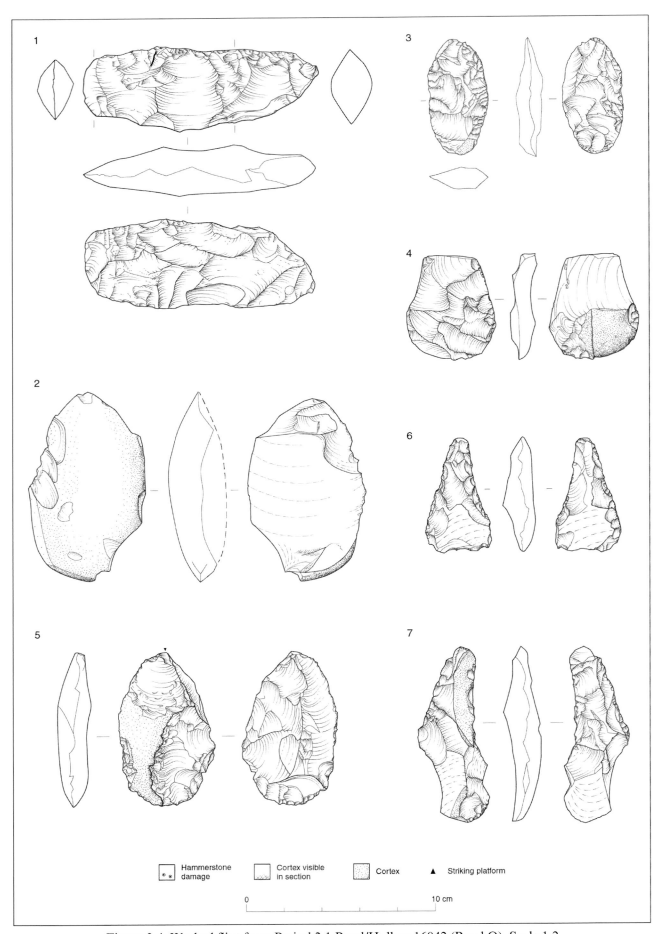

Figure 3.4 Worked flint from Period 2.1 Pond/Hollow 16042 (Pond Q). Scale 1:2

cores. Also present are a large number of shattered cobbles which comprise angular fragments with mostly thermally fractured surfaces but also retain at least some evidence of conchoidal fracture. Whilst some of these could have been created through natural means, it is likely that most represent the initial testing of raw materials which consequently failed, mostly due to thermal flawing. Of the 45 complete cores, nineteen had only been minimally worked, these having produced less than five flakes or blades before being discarded, again usually due to the development of thermal flaws. The more fully worked cores are variable in shape and size and reflect a number of different approaches to producing flakes and blades of a wide variety of shapes and sizes, with just over half of the cores having produced blades or narrow flakes. The most common type, with nine examples, has a single platform that had been worked only part way around. Six have two platforms, three of these with the platforms opposed on one face, the others having a platform on one face and the other set at a right angle on the back, or opposite side. The remainder have multiple platforms and include keeled types and bifacially worked examples, the latter possibly representing core tools. Complete cores vary in weight from 10g to 376g with an average of 83g, which is only slightly less than the minimally worked cores which weigh an average of 88g.

Retouched implements form a relatively low 2.6% of the assemblage. These include two axeheads; in addition to the tranchet axe, there is a large fragment of a finely polished axehead that, unlike the rest of the assemblage from the hollow, is made from a distinctive opaque grey flint (SF 533, context 15919, Fig. 3.4, No. 2; Pl. 2.4, No. 1). This retains part of a cutting edge and had fractured longitudinally, possibly during use. A few flakes have been removed after it broke although it does not seem to have been re-used as a core to any great extent. Other pieces of note include a laurel leaf; these are often regarded as points or projectiles, but this example has unifacial edge damage consistent with use as a knife (context 15964, Fig. 3.4, No. 3; Pl. 2.4, No. 2). A further bifacially worked flake was recovered from the hollow (context 15695, Fig. 3.4, No. 4; Pl. 2.4, No. 4) and another from colluvium in the western side of the site (context 15048, Fig. 3.4, No. 5; Pl. 2.4, No. 3), both of which may represent unfinished laurel leaves, suggesting that these otherwise relatively rare implements were being made at the site. Along with these are two bifacially worked large flakes and a core-tool that form rod-like implements (context 15719, Fig. 3.4, No. 6 and Pl. 2.4, No. 5; context 15895, Fig. 3.4, No. 7 and Pl. 2.4, No. 6). These are unusual implements, particularly within Early Neolithic assemblages, but are reminiscent of the 'picks' found at Grime's Graves which have been interpreted as digging implements (Saville 1981, 8). Other implements include an unfinished arrowhead, a fabricator or strike-a-light, four scrapers and two piercers, although the bulk of the retouched implements comprise flakes and blades with light edge blunting, fine denticulations or serrations along their edges, these comprising nearly three-quarters of the assemblage from the hollow.

Discussion of the Neolithic Hollow (Pond Q)

The assemblage from the lowest levels in this pond suggests a brief sojourn during the Mesolithic, during which an episode of blade production and use occurred. It is possible that the core responsible for the blades was made there, as two other, albeit failed, attempts at core manufacture had been made, and the successful one that had produced the blades was not recovered and may have been taken away to be further worked elsewhere. Close to this scatter was a tranchet axe which was in good condition and only exhibited faint traces of use; it is not clear why this had been left at the site.

The assemblage from the buried soils and overlying colluvial layer relates to much more intensive working of flint during the Early Neolithic period. It includes many minimally worked cores and shattered or 'tested' cobbles and there are high proportions of decortication and core shaping flakes, indicated that raw materials, presumably obtained locally, were being prepared and processed for further reduction, with many evidently being subsequently rejected. Retouched pieces form a low proportion of the assemblage and are dominated by simple cutting and scraping tools. They do demonstrate that a variety of activities were being undertaken but, in contrast to many Early Neolithic assemblages from the region, this has a much more of an 'industrial' feel and the assemblage is perhaps more comparable to those found at raw material sources, such as the quarries around Duxford or the Fordham Bypass site (Bishop 2012, 136–46; OA East forthcoming).

The condition of the material, particularly from the buried soil but also from the overlying colluvial layer, is very good and the presence of micro-debitage and refitting pieces demonstrates that the assemblage had seen little movement between production and deposition. However, neither is sufficiently abundant to indicate *in situ* knapping and it appears that the material has experienced some reworking and redeposition. Taking this evidence together with the distribution patterns of the struck flint in the hollow, it would suggest that the material had been collected shortly after having been knapped and gathered together or accumulated as a series of dumps, perhaps of midden-like material. In this respect, the assemblage is perhaps most similar to the deposits of flintwork recovered from a tree throw further north along the Cam Valley in Hinxton (Pollard 1996) and similar deposits have been recorded at other sites (*e.g.* Evans *et al.* 1999; Lamdin-Whymark 2008; Bishop and Proctor 2011; Tabor 2016). The identification of a possible midden is of considerable interest as the most prolific form of evidence for non-monumental Early Neolithic activity across Britain consists of groups of pits that often contain cultural material derived from secondary or intermediate contexts (*e.g.* Thomas 1999; Garrow 2006) and it may be that accumulations such as that in the hollow here provided the material to fill some of the pits recorded at Hinxton and elsewhere along the Cam Valley (*e.g.* see pits 15194 and 15196; also Mortimer and Evans 1996; Bishop 2016). Such middens are usually thought to have accumulated on the surface and therefore rarely survive later erosion and ploughing. They are generally only identifiable if protected, such as by later alluviation or within natural

Pond	Q		R		X		V	U	H	D		G
Feature	16042		675		1583/2093		4017	4100	2253	3203		3206
	No.	%	No.	%	No.	%	No.	No.	No.	No.	%	No.
Decortication flake	284	13.4	19	7.8	4	8.5	4	4	0	10	19.6	4
Micro-debitage	189	8.9	45	18.5	3	6.4	1	4	3	3	5.9	3
Core rejuvenation flakes	10	0.5	6	2.5	2	4.3		1	3	1	2	
Flakes	580	27.4	73	31.1	10	21.3	4	3	7	14	27.4	8
Flake fragments >10mm	157	7.4	27	11.1	4	8.5	4	7		6	11.8	4
Total blades	429	20.3	41	16.9	14	29.8	7	5		7	13.9	2
Blade-like flakes	117	5.5	23	9.5	2	4.3	3	1	1	4	8.9	
Cores	45	2.1	3	1.2	3	6.3	2	2		4	7.9	3
Chunks/core shatter	238	11.3	4	1.6	1	2.1		1	1			2
Arrowhead	1	0.1	1	0.4					1			
Axe	2	0.1										
Edge trimmed blade	31	1.5			1	2.1	1	1	1			
Denticulate	5	0.2										
Fabricator	1	0.1										
Knife	1	0.1										
Laurel leaf	2	0.1										
Micro-burin					1	2.1						
Microlith					1	2.1						
Notch	3	0.1										
Piercer	3	0.1										
Rod / pick	1	0.1										
Scraper	4	0.2								2		1
Serrate	2	0.1							1	2	1.9	
Truncated blade					1	2.1						
Core tool	9	0.4	1	0.4								
Context total	**2114**	**100**	**243**	**100**	**47**	**100**	**26**	**29**	**20**	**51**	**100**	**27**

Table 3.13 Quantification of lithics from ponds in Areas B, C, F and J

features such as tree throws, and the survival of this assemblage as a distinct entity rather than a surface scatter is probably only due to it being relatively protected within the hollow.

Other ponds
A further seven of the colluvium-filled hollows or 'ponds' produced quantities of struck flint, these comprising features designated as Pond X (Area F), Ponds U and V (Area F), Pond R (Area B), Pond H (Area C), Pond D (Area C) and Pond G (Area C) (Table 3.13). The other 'ponds' identified at the site produced either no or only very negligible quantities of struck lithic material.

Pond R (Area B)
Pond R (675) consisted of a hollow that had formed on the surface of an infilled palaeochannel. It contained a prolific assemblage comprising 243 pieces recovered from a series of 1m² squares dug across it. Most of this material is made from similar abraded and thermally shattered nodules as were used to manufacture the remainder of the assemblage at the site but, interestingly, a number of flakes retain cortex that indicates that they had been struck from a large nodule with a soft and friable chalky cortex. This must have been obtained directly from the Upper Chalk and imported to the site, possibly from the flint quarries that have been identified around the Heathfield area of Duxford to the north-west of Hinxton (Bishop 2012).

Overall, this assemblage was blade based and reasonably systematically produced, as evidenced by crested blades and core tablets. Blades form 17% of the assemblage, and blade-like flakes contribute a further 10%. Three cores were recovered, two had clearly produced blades and the other, technically a flake core, may have produced blades earlier in its productive life. The recovery of a later Mesolithic narrow blade micro-burin may suggest the manufacture of at least one microlith, although the only retouched implements consist of an unfinished leaf-shaped arrowhead and a large thermal spall, this having one finely trimmed edge that may have been intended for cutting or scraping but which might have represented initial attempts at preparing the spall for use as a core. A few flakes and blades were possibly utilised but even these are present in only very low numbers. The paucity of retouched pieces suggests that this assemblage primarily represents initial core reduction rather than tool use, presumably with the more useful pieces being removed for use elsewhere.

As well as a high number of blades, also present are a number of broad and often large and thin flakes with narrow and faceted striking platforms, a pronounced curvature and numerous opposed or multidirectional shallow dorsal scars. These appear to be shaping and thinning flakes from the manufacture of axes, probably of Neolithic form although similar flakes can be produced during the manufacture of Mesolithic tranchet axes. Some support for the manufacture of tranchet axes at Hinxton comes from the relatively freshly made example that was recovered from the base of the Neolithic hollow (Pond Q) in Area J and further evidence for their manufacture comes from further up the Cam Valley at Sawston (Bishop 2016). Whilst no complete Neolithic axes have been found at Hinxton, an axe fragment was recovered from layer 5399 (Fig. 3.5, No. 8) from the Genome Technical Hub excavations (Area I,

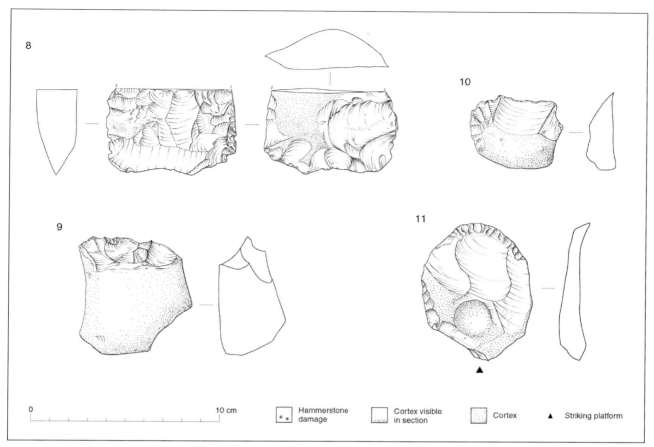

8

10

9

11

0   10 cm   ⊡ Hammerstone damage   ☐ Cortex visible in section   ☐ Cortex   ▲ Striking platform

Figure 3.5 Examples of Neolithic flint tools from other features and deposits. Scale 1:2

ungrouped). Further evidence of such objects comes in the form of a flake from a polished implement, of similar flint to the flakes here but recovered from Period 3.1 Enclosure 2 (ditch 3062). A large fragment of ground axe made from a non-local opaque grey flint was also recovered from the Neolithic hollow in Area J (Pond Q) and further flakes from polished implements of similar flint, were found in pit 97 (ungrouped) on the other (Ickleton) side of the Cam and from Period 2.1 Pit Groups 6 (pit 5304, fill 5305) and 8 (pit 4834, fill 4832) from the Genome Technical Hub excavations (Area I). Whatever the timing, this suggests that flint, possibly quarried from the surrounding chalklands, was being brought into the valley for making axes and perhaps other implements.

The distribution of the blades, the flakes with chalky cortex and the axe manufacturing flakes all show the same pattern and appear to represent a single episode of flintworking. Only a very small proportion of the waste, however, from either blade or axe production is present. Micro-debitage forms a reasonably high proportion of the assemblage but it is not present in sufficient quantities to indicate that any *in situ* flintworking occurred here; despite the fact that bulk samples were taken they still only contained a few pieces. The condition of the assemblage is good with very few pieces showing any evidence of attrition and it would appear that this material was either thrown or eroded into the feature from close by. The presence of a micro-burin, a type piece for the Mesolithic, and a leaf-shaped arrowhead blank of Early Neolithic date present some problems in dating this assemblage. They may represent separate and non-related knapping events, or a genuine transitional assemblage of the type suggested by Reynolds and Kaner (2000). The former is perhaps the least contentious explanation and suggests an episode of Mesolithic blade production and microlith manufacture followed some time later by Early Neolithic axe and arrowhead manufacture.

Pond X (Area F)

Of the 'ponds' within the main Hinxton Hall excavation site (Area F), Pond X (1583/2093) produced the largest assemblage, comprising 47 pieces. The material from this feature is generally in a good, sharp condition with only occasional pieces showing any edge abrasion, consistent with it having experienced some light trampling and/or

bioturbation, but being largely undisturbed. It is technologically homogeneous, being characteristic of Mesolithic industries, a date supported by the retouched implement and other pieces present. It demonstrates a careful and controlled approach to reduction; blades contributed a high 30% of the assemblage, nearly half of which were systematically produced, and these include a number of micro-blades. Three cores are present; one was a micro-blade core that would have been ideal for producing blanks for microliths (from context 1583), another had been prepared for blade production but had been abandoned at an early stage and the other a large thermal spall with a few large flakes removed. This latter example is not characteristic of Mesolithic industries and may even suggest some contamination from later industries, but it is also possible that it could represent a 'testing' nodule and therefore is potentially of a similar date to the others. Three retouched pieces are present, including a microlith and a truncated blade, both characteristically Mesolithic, together with an edge-trimmed blade. Microlith manufacture is also suggested by the recovery of a micro-burin. Complementing the probable use of many microliths as projectile points, it has been suggested that edge-trimmed and truncated blades may have been used in the manufacture of arrow shafts (R. Jacobi, pers. comm.). The assemblage would therefore seem to be related to the repair and manufacture of microlithic tool-kits. Interestingly, one of the two other microliths found at Hinxton was recovered from a pit that cut this feature and a further microburin was found in a gully that also cut it, raising the possibility that they may have been redeposited from the 'pond'. Thus, of the seven prime diagnostic pieces attributable to the Mesolithic that were found at Hinxton, five could be related to this feature.

Only a few pieces of micro-debitage were recovered, however, and most of the features cutting into the fill failed to produce any significant quantities of struck flint, although a number of micro-blades are present. Only one feature cutting this feature (pit 2113, ungrouped), produced any significant quantities of micro-debitage, this comprising waste from core trimming and blade-based reduction and indicative of knapping having occurred close by. This feature was located on the western side of the pond and similar micro-debitage in relatively large quantities was recovered from other features in its vicinity, including pits 2108, 2110 and 2149, possibly indicating that

71

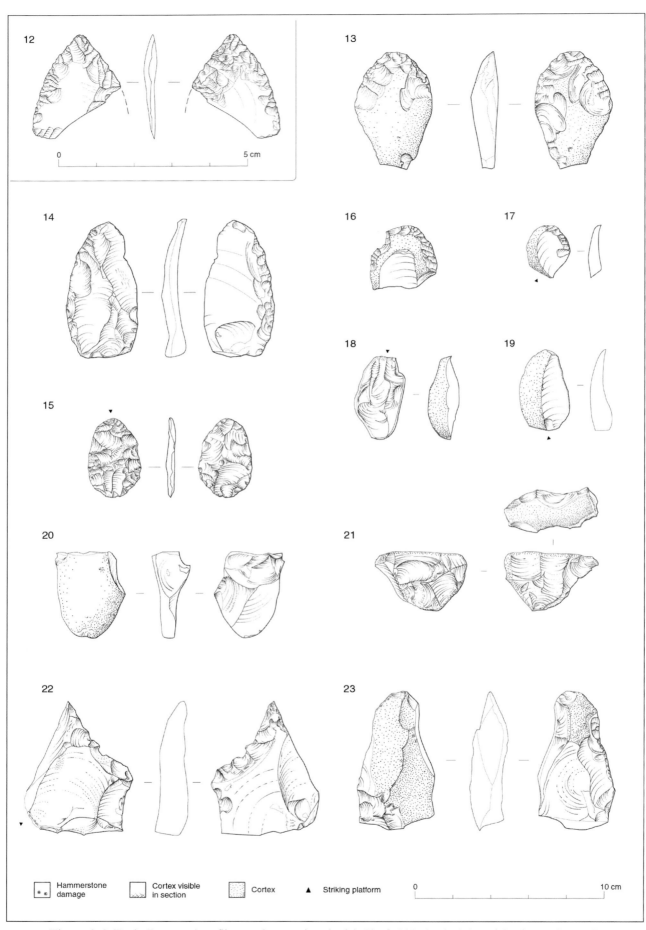

12

13

0   5 cm

14

16

17

15

18

19

20

21

22

23

| | Hammerstone damage | | Cortex visible in section | | Cortex | ▲ | Striking platform | 0 | | 10 cm |

Figure 3.6 Early Bronze Age flint tools associated with Shaft 902. Scale 1:2 and Scale 1:1 (No. 12)

actual reduction was being undertaken around the western margins of the pond. Nevertheless, other features containing relatively large quantities of micro-debitage and other struck flint could be found scattered to the north and the south-west, indicating that core reduction was a common occurrence across the area and need not have been directly related to this pond.

Pond V (Area F)
To the north-west of Pond X in Area F was Pond V (4017). This produced a similar but smaller assemblage of 26 pieces. The assemblage is in a sharp condition. None of the pieces actually refit but they probably resulted from the reduction of a limited number of nodules, perhaps only two or three different cores. Nearly a quarter of the group consists of blades, all of which were systematically produced and these include a number of micro-blades. The cores comprise a single-platformed narrow flake core and a two-platformed keeled blade core made on a small, rounded pebble. Only one retouched piece is present, comprising a burnt fragment from an edge-trimmed blade. None of the features that cut into this pond contained any significant quantities of struck flint but, perhaps significantly, ditch 4019 (ungrouped) did produce a micro-burin, indicative of microlith manufacture and of a similar form to those found in the vicinity of Pond X (1583/2093). Again, due to the small quantity of struck flint present and the limited area investigated it is difficult to suggest whether this represents a specific focus of activity or part of a more general spread of knapping waste fortuitously preserved by the hollow.

Pond U (Area F)
Pond U, represented by layers 4100, 4105, 4106 and 4107, produced a collection of 29 pieces. There is one micro-blade present but the other four blades were all unsystematically produced. The two cores both consist of single-platformed blade cores, one utilising a thermal facet as the striking platform. The only retouched piece comprises an edge-retouched blade. The material is in good condition however, and represents a limited number of knapping events, although no refittable pieces are present. Unlike 'Ponds' X and V (1583/2093 and 4017), the group contains few diagnostic pieces but there is nothing to suggest that this assemblage did not form in a similar manner and time to the Mesolithic knapping events suggested for these other features. The distribution of this material within the pond indicates a rapid drop off in quantity with depth and there are too few pieces to indicate whether there were any chronological or functional differences in the assemblages from the layers. Given the areas actually excavated within this feature, it is difficult to establish whether this material indicates a specific occupation focus or simply part of the general background of Mesolithic and Early Neolithic flintworking activity noted across the site.

Of the various features that truncated this 'pond', two produced relatively high quantities of knapping waste of similar technological characteristics, including two core rejuvenation flakes and a double-sided serrated blade from ditch 802 (ungrouped) and a later Neolithic oblique type transverse arrowhead from ditch 4002 (4035; Ditch Group 3). Quantities of micro-debitage were recovered from ditch 804 (Ditch Group 4), suggesting that actual knapping was occurring in the vicinity.

Pond H (Area C)
The material from Pond H (2253) in Area C is of a very different character to that from the other ponds, consisting of 20 fragments. It is mostly in good condition and the assemblage appears to have been struck from a limited number of cores, although no refitting pieces are present. It principally consists of hard-hammer struck narrow flakes, with no blades and only a single blade-like flake present. Cores or decortication flakes are also absent and, in notable contrast to the other ponds, this assemblage includes a very high retouched component, all of which appears used or broken. These include a side scraper and a short-end scraper, an edge-trimmed flake, a serrated flake and a chisel-type transverse arrowhead. Unlike the other assemblages from the ponds, this appears to represent a flake based, tool-dominated collection, perhaps even elements of a tool-kit, with the arrowhead confirming a later Neolithic date.

Pond D (Area C)
Pond D (3203) produced an assemblage of 51 pieces. These are mostly in a good and sharp condition but some are slightly edge chipped and abraded, indicating a small degree of post-depositional disturbance. As with much of the assemblage from the site, most pieces here are broadly of Mesolithic or Early Neolithic date but there are also a number of less carefully produced pieces, including thick and relatively irregularly struck flakes, which may be better placed in later, perhaps later Neolithic or Bronze Age, industries. The only retouched pieces consist of serrates, one made on a blade with a possible hafting notch and the other made on a blade-like flake with both margins roughly serrated, both being typical of Mesolithic or Early Neolithic industries. Four cores, a relatively high proportion, were recovered. Three of these consist of opposed platformed cores with carefully flaked flattened backs, typically Mesolithic or Early Neolithic types; the other was minimally and randomly reduced and this may be of later date. The cores are accompanied by a relatively high number of decortication and core maintenance flakes, and some small flakes and broken fragments are also present but not in sufficient quantities to indicate that *in situ* knapping had occurred, despite samples having been taken.

This assemblage represents the waste from the decortication and primary reduction of cores, along with some tool use, as represented by the serrated pieces. The material may have been deliberately thrown into the hollow but its condition and probable chronological admixing suggests it merely represents a part of the general scatter as recorded across the site that has been preserved within the hollow.

Pond G (Area C)
Pond G (3206) produced 27 struck flints which are in a variable condition. Four cores, a high proportion, are present. One consists of an irregularly shaped thermal chunk with small short flakes removed from around its margins. These flakes would have been too small to be of much use and it is possible that this represents a core tool. The three other cores are irregular in shape but at least one had produced blades and narrow flakes. The only retouched piece consists of an end-and-side scraper, although a flake struck from a bifacially flaked implement is also present; it is uncertain whether this represents a sharpening flake from a tranchet axe or an arrowhead that broke as it was being made. A few of the flakes and blades appear to have been utilised, although confident identification of these was hampered by the rather chipped and abraded condition of many of the pieces. The remainder of the assemblage represents knapping waste but there is little in the way of smaller flakes and fragmented pieces, despite samples being taken, to indicate that *in situ* knapping had occurred in the vicinity. As with Pond D, this assemblage appears to comprise part of the mixed period struck flint scatter as identified across the rest of the site.

Pits

Pit Group 1: Mesolithic Pit 3114 (Area F)
Pit Group 1 was cut into Pond S (1529/1530) in the northern part of Area F. Pond S itself produced a single struck piece, a small irregular core fragment that appears to have produced some blades. More notably, a feature that cut through it, pit 3114, contained a relatively substantial quantity of struck flint, including a high proportion of knapping waste (Table 3.14).

This material is comparable in composition and technology to the assemblages recovered from Ponds X and V in the same area. It appears to have originated from a limited number of cores and includes a particularly high proportion of systematically produced blades, including micro-blades, as well as a single retouched piece, a serrated blade. Largely absent from the ponds, but well represented here, are substantial quantities of micro-debitage, these pieces largely deriving from fine core trimming and micro-blade production.

Core reduction appears to have been the prime activity indicated by the struck flint, although only a single core is present, and there was some limited tool use, as indicated by the serrated blade. The relative scarcity of cores may indicate that these were removed for further reduction elsewhere. The numbers of micro-blades present suggest a Mesolithic date for this assemblage and, as it is in a good, sharp condition, there is nothing to indicate it had not been deliberately

Table 3.14 Lithic material from the pit groups

Group	PG1		PG6		PG4						PG8					PG7	
Feature	3114		5304		683	691	776	778	Total		4834	4851	4908	Total		902	
	No.	%	No.	%	No.	No.	No.	No.	No.	%	No.	No.	No.	No.	%	No.	%
Micro-debitage	57	42.9		0.0	3	5			8	4.7					0.0		0.0
Chunks/shatter	2	1.5	12	12.2	2				2	1.2	1	6	3	10	7.9	42	23.5
Decortication flake	7	5.3	4	4.1	1	13	1	2	17	10.0	3	1	5	9	7.1	32	17.9
Rejuvenation flake	1	0.8		0.0		1		1	2	1.2		1	1	2	1.6	2	1.1
Flake	9	6.8	34	34.7	6	32	6	11	55	32.4	23	8	25	56	44.4	42	23.5
Flake fragments	17	12.8	14	14.3	3	19		2	24	14.1	1	5	10	16	12.7	32	17.9
Blade	35	26.3	16	16.3	3	11	1	2	17	10.0	3		2	5	4.0	10	5.6
Broken blade		0.0		0.0	1	3			4	2.4					0.0		0.0
Blade-like flake	3	2.3	7	7.1	6	12		5	23	13.5	1	2	7	10	7.9	3	1.7
Core	1	0.8		0.0		1			1	0.6		2	1	3	2.4	4	2.2
Retouched	1	0.8	11	11.2	2	12	1	2	17	10.0	11	3	1	15	11.9	12	6.7
Context total	133	100.0	98	100.0	27	109	9	25	170	100.0	43	28	55	126	100.0	179	100.0
Burnt stone (No)	1															10	
Burnt stone (Wt g)	40															207	

dumped into the pit or knapped close by whilst the pit was open.

Pit Group 6: Early Neolithic Pit 5304
This feature contained the largest single assemblage from Area E, comprising 98 pieces (Table 3.14). The assemblage is generally in very good condition and displays distinctive cortex and internal patterning in the flints' inclusions indicative of the working of a limited number of cores. The cortex is very thin and weathered.

The assemblage clearly reflects a blade-based technology, albeit one less specialised in its production than any pure Mesolithic one and lacks very regular micro-blades. Blades and blade-like forms make up a considerable portion of the assemblage (23.4%) and include some micro-blades, one of which has been retouched down its right side, but in general the blades and blade-like flakes are quite large and are often not the product of systematic blade production; many display considerable portions of dorsal cortex indicating that they had been struck early on in a blade reduction sequence. Several microdenticulates/serrates are also present on blade forms as is a single scalene triangle microlith; however, this is in a noticeably poorer state than the assemblage as a whole, is partially recorticated and is certainly residual.

The feature contained a high incidence of retouched forms (11.2%) and had low levels of micro-debitage (12.2%) despite being sampled and despite containing a set of four refitting pieces alongside numerous near refits. Cores themselves are absent as is any form of rejuvenation. One flake from a polished implement is present as is a very large, regular end-and-side scraper and an extremely fresh denticulate. Other scrapers and retouched flakes round off the retouched tool inventory.

This feature was located around 35m south-west of the concentration of later Neolithic features including Pit Group 8 (described below) and other components of Pit Group 6 – immediately north of pit 5304 was a massive pit (pit 5135) while a smaller pit (pit 5133) was located around 12m to the north-west. Occasional postholes were also dotted within the vicinity. Pit 5135 contained a small assemblage including flakes, an end scraper and a multi-platform flake core, while pit 5133 contained a small blade-based assemblage including a serrate on a blade-like flake, a narrow blade, flakes with very parallel blade-like dorsal scars and a possible axe working flake.

Pit Group 16: Later Neolithic Pits 15194 and 15196 (Area J)
Near the centre of Area J were two adjacent and similar pits (15194 and 15196), both of which contained assemblages that can be dated to the Early Neolithic period. The assemblages are not large, at 15 and 22 pieces respectively, but they represent the full knapping sequence, from the decortication of raw materials to the production of useable flakes and tools. No cores are present but a core-tablet rejuvenation flake from pit 15196 testifies to core maintenance. The only retouched implement came from pit 15194 and comprises a finely serrated blade, although a few of the flakes from both pits show some evidence of utilisation. The condition of the pieces is variable and

although some pieces of micro-debitage are present, it appears the material had been selected from a larger accumulation, possibly even the nearby 'Neolithic hollow' (Pond Q).

Pit Group 17: Later Neolithic Pits 15325 and 15327 (Area J)
Fig. 3.7
Towards the northern edge of Area J were two adjacent features that contained later Neolithic flintwork, including a transverse arrowhead within each. The largest assemblage comprises 85 struck pieces and a small quantity of unworked burnt flint from pit 15327. The condition of the struck material is variable and there are few pieces of micro-debitage, suggesting that the assemblage had been selected prior to deposition. It represents a number of different knapping strategies, including the production of mostly non-prismatic blades along with wide but well struck flakes, many of which have faceted striking platforms. Some of these are likely to have been produced using the 'Levallois-like' techniques and one of the cores is bifacially worked with a plano-convex cross section, also suggesting the employment of this method (Fig. 3.7, No. 24). The other core from this feature has only been minimally worked but used a keeled platform. Four retouched implements are present which include a finely worked oblique type transverse arrowhead (Fig. 3.7, No. 25). The other implements comprise a bilaterally serrated blade and a large flake with coarse denticulations cut along one side (Fig. 3.7, Nos 26 and 27). The remaining piece is a fragmentary steeply retouched point, possibly a broken part of another transverse arrowhead. The pit also produced a core-tool, this comprising a large thermal spall with coarse denticulations not unlike those seen on the denticulated flake (Fig. 3.7, No. 28).

Pit 15325 contained a much smaller assemblage of just six pieces which includes a petit tranchet type transverse arrowhead (Fig. 3.7, No. 29) and a scraper, along with two flakes and two blades.

Pit Group 4: Later Neolithic Pits (Area C)
In the north of Area C, close to one of the ponds (Pond H) was a cluster of five intercutting pits, three of which (pits 691, 776 and 778) produced struck flint (Table 3.14). Close by was another pit (pit 683), which also contained struck flint of similar characteristics to the other pits in this group. With the exception of a small flake and a blade from a later ditch section 717 (Late Iron Age Trackway 3), none of the other features in the vicinity produced any struck flint. Indeed, although located adjacent to a pond (Pond H; Fig. 2.1), this feature – unlike others in the area – produced no struck flint and the relationship (if any) between it and the pits remains uncertain.

A total of 170 struck pieces were recovered from the four pits. This is mostly in good condition but does vary; some pieces have experienced a degree of edge chipping and abrasion and a few burnt pieces are present. Notably, however, it has all recorticated, unlike the rest of the material from the site where this had occurred only very occasionally. It is uncertain why this should have happened; recortication is a very variable process and is affected by factors such as

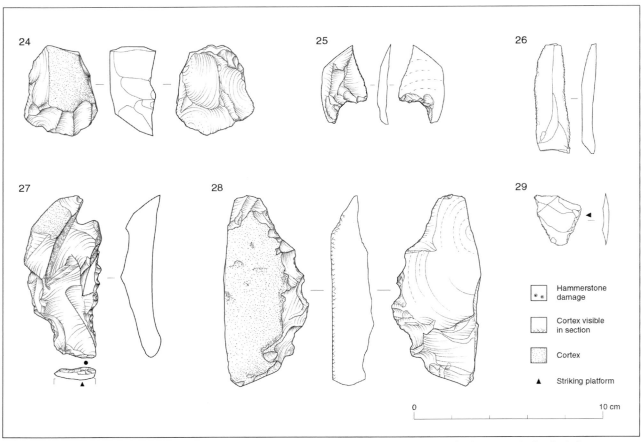

Hammerstone damage

Cortex visible in section

Cortex

Striking platform

0   10 cm

Figure 3.7 Worked flint from Later Neolithic pits 15325 and 15327 (Pit Group 17). Scale 1:2

localised soil conditions and the particular properties of the raw materials involved.

Pit 691 provided the greatest quantities of struck flint, at 109 pieces, most of it coming from fill 687. The retouched implements from this feature, which amount to twelve pieces, are limited to scrapers, serrates and simple edge-trimmed pieces. The scrapers include a long-end scraper, a concave scraper and a number of short-end scrapers, mostly made on thick flakes. Also present is a thick cortical flake with steep, rough and almost denticulated retouch along its side. This is perhaps an unfinished scraper or may have been intended for use as a saw. The serrates were mostly made on blades but with a few made using flakes and, possibly associated with these, are the edge-trimmed pieces, which were most probably used for cutting or light sawing.

Pit 683 produced the second largest assemblage from this pit group at 27 struck pieces and, although isolated from the other intercutting pits, is very similar in technology, typology and condition to their assemblages. The retouched implements are similarly limited and include a serrate and a scraper. The other two intercutting pits, 776 and 778, produced nine and twenty-five pieces respectively, each from a single fill, the retouched pieces consisting of two scrapers, one of which had been burnt, from pit 778 and a serrated blade from pit 776.

Overall, the assemblage from this group represents all stages in the reduction sequence, from the decortication of cores to the discard of used retouched pieces. It was clearly a blade-based technology, blades accounting for just under 13% of the assemblage, although few of these were systematically produced and there are very few micro-blades present. It has a high retouched component, at 10%, which is restricted to edge-trimmed flakes and flakes with smooth worn edges, serrates and scrapers. The flintwork indicates that cores were being reduced and tools manufactured; the restricted range of these suggesting fairly specialised activities were being pursued, these possibly being geared towards animal and plant processing. Most of these tools appear used, having worn edges, and some of the scrapers have been resharpened. A few serrates appear relatively fresh and may have only been used for a short period, although it is possible that some of the edge worn pieces may be worn down serrates. In contrast to the number of retouched pieces, only a single core is present. This consists of a single-platformed blade or narrow flake core from pit 10691. It is made on a quartered rounded nodule and has an extensively rejuvenated striking platform. It has not been exhausted but it was probably abandoned due to the development of step fractures.

Although the assemblage includes blades, very few of these were systematically produced and no other chronologically diagnostic pieces are present. It can be differentiated from Mesolithic and Early Neolithic assemblages, such as those from the 'Neolithic Hollow' (Area J, Pond Q) and 'Ponds' X and V (Area F), and suggests that a later Neolithic date is most likely, as confirmed by the small assemblage of Grooved Ware recovered from these features and by a radiocarbon determination from pit 691.

It appears to represent a 'complete' assemblage containing all stages from the decortication of raw materials to the production, use and discard of tools. Its rather variable condition and the paucity of pieces of micro-debitage that would have been produced in large numbers during knapping, combined with a lack of obvious refittable pieces, suggests that knapping was not occurring directly into the pits. Instead, the assemblage seems to be a selection of debris arising from a number of activities, including core reduction and tool use, which was gathered and deliberately placed into the pits. This suggests the material came from a primary source; perhaps a midden of accumulated residential waste material that included knapping debris from tool manufacture as well as used and discarded tools.

Pit Group 8: Later Neolithic pits
Fig. 3.5
Pit 4834 measured around 0.9m in diameter and was the most northerly of the four pits that comprised Pit Group 8, all of which contained relatively large quantities of struck flint. The assemblage from this feature amounts to 43 pieces but does not contain any micro-debitage or fine shatter, probably because the pit was not sampled (Table 3.14). The pieces exhibit a range of conditions and degrees of recortication; however, many of the tools recovered are very similarly recorticated and are near identical in size.

The assemblage is flake-based but includes several thin pieces with very parallel dorsal scars and many of the tools were fashioned on blades or blade-like flakes. The assemblage also includes a number of blades with significant amounts of dorsal cortex that were not systematically produced but did include one microblade. Amongst the flake assemblage, there is a mix of material from various stages of reduction including decortication flakes, but only one piece was broken. There are two groups of flakes that appear to originate from specific cores but no refits were identified. Also present are three flakes from ground flint implements of Neolithic date.

Of particular note is the tool assemblage as it amounts to over a quarter of all pieces within the feature and is easily the highest proportion of any single major assemblage from the site. It consists of six scrapers, three serrates, a denticulate and a retouched flake. The scrapers include four end scrapers, which appear to have originated from the same core with two that refitted, one double end scraper on a blade-like flake and one side scraper (Fig. 3.5, No. 10), on a squat irregular piece, a genuine oddity alongside five very fine examples. The two refitting pieces consist of an end of blade-like flake example with faceted platform and an end of regular flake example with a plain platform: both display very parallel dorsal blade scars. A near refit to these two is a standard end scraper on a fairly squat flake with a plain platform while the fourth is a discoidal scraper with faceted platform. All four are hard-hammer struck, none are broken or damaged in any way and three display very regular and highly skilled parallel abrupt retouch. The double end scraper is less well fashioned with a straight oblique zone of retouch at its left-proximal side and a fairly crude, narrow convex arc of retouch at its distal end.

Of the remaining tools, the retouched flake is heavily recorticated and edge damaged and may be residual, and the denticulate on a small squat flake is a quite crude example. The three serrated pieces include two single-edged examples on fine, soft-hammer struck systematically removed blades while the third is on a regular, hard-hammer struck flake.

The pit clearly did not contain simple waste disposal from midden material and the assemblage appears highly selective in nature. The exact reasons why such fine and functioning tools would be discarded are unclear and they may simply represent a cache, but they could also have been related to the act of imbuing the landscape with meaning, marking or laying claim to locations and connections with the past that may have been of utmost importance to the people moving through this landscape.

Pit 4851 lay around 2.1m south-west of pit 4834 and a short distance east of posthole/pit 4838 in this group. It contained a small assemblage of 28 pieces that includes a range of cores, flakes, blade-like flakes and three retouched tools (Table 3.14). The pieces vary in condition from fresh to moderately edge damaged and several display varying levels of recortication. Cortex is usually rough and thin but there are also two pieces with recorticated surfaces.

The cores consist of a single platform flake core on a large flake or thermally fractured chunk and a multi-platform flake core, quite heavily worked and weighing just 31g. There is also a possible core rejuvenation flake struck off a multi-platformed flake core, although this piece may also be a miss-hit off a flaked flint axe. It has a very curved profile but also a deep and slightly irregular faceted platform and displays multi-directional dorsal flake scars. The three tools consist of a fine double-edged serrated blade with traces of gloss, a retouched flake with a partially ground edge on its upper left shoulder and a probable dihedral burin on a secondary flake. As with pit 4834, above, it is likely that a selective mixing of placed tools alongside various stages of flint reduction occurred here.

Pit 4908 contained 55 flints (see Table 3.14), consisting primarily of material in good condition with only a very few more heavily edge damaged or recorticated pieces that are most likely to have been residual. Relatively substantial quantities of decortical material were found, together with a single platform core that had produced quite regular, almost blade-like flakes. Cortex is predominantly rough and thin but some slightly thicker, chalkier removals are apparent.

The assemblage is flake-based: some blades are present (3.6%) and blade-like flakes are common (12.7%) but very few were systematically produced and at least two appear to be residual as they display quite heavy edge damage and recortication. Many of the remaining blade-like forms are triangular in cross section and display multiple flaking directions on their dorsal surfaces and may relate to axe working. Faceted platforms are common, as are small flakes with curving or plunging profiles, again with multiple flaking directions in their dorsal scars. These all indicate that axe production may have occurred nearby. Fine knapping waste was very rare (1.8%) and indicated that knapping did not occur *in situ*, but that this material was brought to the pit for disposal.

No refits were observed which would also support a delay in deposition. Retouch consists solely of a single serrate/end scraper combination tool (1.8%) on a secondary flake.

Pit Group 7: Beaker Pit/Shaft
Fig. 3.6
This feature, a deep pit or shaft, produced the largest assemblage (179 pieces) from any single feature in Area C (Trench U), virtually all of it coming from upper fill 900 (Table 3.14).

A core, two core fragments and several edge-trimmed flakes (Fig. 3.6, Nos 17–21) were also found as unstratified material from close to the pit, and these may have originated from it. The condition of the material is generally very good and sharp. Although fairly high quantities of micro-debitage are present, there is no evidence that the material had been knapped directly into the pit but had probably been dumped into it, with the small pieces gathered along with the larger pieces.

The assemblage is the product of a flake-based reduction strategy. A relatively small proportion of the assemblage consists of blades although none of these were systematically produced, there are no micro-blades present and only three blade-like flakes were identified.

The flakes were competently produced and knapping was evidently skilful and accomplished, with many fine narrow flakes being present. The cores present are all small and extensively reduced and, in their final phases, produced small flakes from mostly unmodified striking platforms (Fig. 3.6, Nos 18, 20–21). There is a high proportion of retouched pieces present, most notable are two unfinished arrowheads. One had broken, apparently as a barb was being finished (Fig. 3.6, No. 12; SF 143) whilst another had broken and been burnt prior to being deposited within the pit (Fig. 3.6, No. 15). The arrowheads firmly suggest an Early Bronze Age date for the assemblage, which is backed up by the Beaker pottery found alongside it. Interestingly, four other pieces had also been bifacially worked which, excluding arrowheads, are the only bifacially worked tools found at the site. These include a finely made blunted backed knife, the only piece present in fill 913 (Fig. 3.6, No. 14; SF 42), two bifacially flaked cobbles (Fig. 3.6, Nos 13 and 23) and a rather crudely flaked denticulate or piercing-type tool, made on a large flake (Fig. 3.6, No. 22). The other pieces comprise simple edge-trimmed flakes and a scraper comparable to 'thumbnail' types, which has also been burnt (Fig. 3.6, No. 16). Possibly complementing the manufacture of the arrowheads are a number of small, very thin flakes with markedly curved profiles, which could have originated from thinning these implements. Compared to other features that contained quantities of micro-debitage, such as pit 3114 (Pit Group 1), there are few fine platform-trimming flakes, such as those with narrow striking platforms and numerous dorsal scars, compared to the simpler types with wider platforms and few dorsal scars. In addition to the struck flint, the pit also produced ten fragments of heavily and possibly deliberately burnt flint fragments, weighing 175g. A number of the flakes and blades have also been burnt, further indicating that these at least had experienced an hiatus between manufacture and deposition.

This material, virtually all from only one of the (upper) fills, is in a variable condition and some of it had been burnt. This, combined with the low number of refittable pieces, would suggest that it had been gathered from a variety of sources, perhaps accumulations arising from knapping and tool using events, which had witnessed differing degrees of weathering and burning. The presence of knapping waste, used tools and implements that may have broken during manufacture suggests that it is discarded refuse, but it appears to be refuse that had been accumulated before part of it was purposefully selected and intentionally deposited.

Although the flintwork was deposited much later than that in pit 691 and associated features (Pit Group 4) and is clearly datable to the Early Bronze Age, the sequence of activities surrounding the burial of this material was very similar and it may also be compared to the material from Early Neolithic pit sites, such as at Kilverstone (Beadsmoore 2006), or the Later Neolithic pits at Linton (Beadsmoore 2005; Dickson forthcoming). The selection of this material and the events surrounding its deposition suggest that it was part of a prescribed series of activities, or ceremonies, that held special meaning to those enacting them.

Discussion
The struck flint from the site can be regarded as a large assemblage which demonstrates that activity commenced here by the end of the last glacial period and continued into the Bronze Age and perhaps the Iron Age. It can generally be regarded as essentially 'domestic' in character, with the high proportion and wide variety of tool types suggesting that a range of different activities was being pursued. The flintwork from the 'Neolithic hollow' (Pond Q) in Area J does have more of an 'industrial' feel, however, and this may represent the exploitation and processing of raw materials along with other activities during the Early Neolithic. The flintwork concentrated around the slightly higher positions within the excavated areas, particularly within Areas F and J, and foreshadowed the areas later chosen for occupation during the Iron Age to Anglo-Saxon and later periods, most likely due to the suitability of those localities away from the low-lying and presumably wetter areas. These low-lying areas would still have seen activity related to flint use, as they would have been areas attractive to a wide range of animals and probably containing a diverse array of plant life.

With the exception of the large flintwork scatter preserved within the 'Neolithic hollow' (Pond Q) most of the struck flint was recovered from cut features. Some of the features were contemporary with their flintwork but most were later and the flintwork had been incorporated within them as residual material, probably from a palimpsest of surface scatters and midden deposits. It appears that the flint used at the site was predominantly disposed of on contemporary surfaces, perhaps within middens or shallow cut features, and incorporated into topsoil deposits through bioturbation and ploughing. This would be supported by the flintwork recovered from other sites excavated along this stretch of the Cam Valley. At

Hinxton Quarry to the north, fieldwalking identified that substantial quantities of struck flints were present within the ploughsoil (Evans 1993; Mortimer and Evans 1996; Austin and Sydes 1998; Pollard 1998). When the topsoil was removed a handful of features were revealed that also contained substantial assemblages, but this material would have only been a fraction of that contained within the ploughsoil. The quantity of fieldwalked material recovered at Hinxton Quarry was described as 'extraordinary' and attests to intensive activity along the riverine terraces of the River Cam from the Mesolithic through to the Bronze Age (Evans 1993, 7, 10). A similar picture may be envisioned here – the recovered struck flint assemblage is large and this must be further emphasised by the probability that the majority of what was originally produced may have remained in the topsoil and escaped recovery.

The presence of hollows within the site's natural topography, including the 'ponds', had also preserved remnants of struck flint scatters from incorporation into later ploughsoils. The 'Neolithic Hollow' is likely to represent raw material processing as well as other, perhaps more 'domestic', activities. Pond X probably represents an episode of blade manufacture and repair of microlithic tool kits, and it is possible that the assemblage from Pond V represents similar activities. This produced a number of systematically produced blades, which combined with a microburin recovered from a ditch that cut into it, strongly indicates that this assemblage could also be dated to the Mesolithic period. The material from Pond R would appear to represent Mesolithic blade and microlith manufacture, but additional Early Neolithic axe and arrowhead manufacture also seemed to have occurred there, although it is uncertain how these two episodes of activity related to each other. Unlike these features, Pond H contained a high proportion of retouched implements and relatively few waste flakes, indicating that this may represent a tool-using episode datable, by both the technology used to manufacture the assemblage and by the presence of a transverse arrowhead, to the later Neolithic period. These features appear to include material from specific knapping events, possibly deliberately discarded into extant ponds, whilst others contained remnants of larger scatters that the hollows fortuitously preserved.

Struck flint manufacture and use evidently did occur adjacent to these natural features during the Mesolithic and Neolithic periods, although as most of the struck flint from the site was only preserved where it was incorporated into later features, it is difficult to estimate the degree to which occupation genuinely focussed upon these, or whether they merely fortuitously preserved evidence for such activities that originally would have been more widespread across the site. Nevertheless, they reinforce the impression that in general the struck flint assemblage from the site represents a palimpsest of numerous knapping events, suggestive of a succession of short-term occupation episodes. This scenario would be typical for the Mesolithic and probably also for the great majority of Neolithic occupation sites. It is comparable to the evidence recorded at Duxford Mill, also within the Cam Valley floodplain and located just to the north of the site. Here, Mesolithic or Early Neolithic struck flint was identified, existing as a scatter on a contemporary surface and preserved as a discrete knapping event by later alluviation and peat formation (Schlee and Robinson 1995; Austin and Sydes 1998).

The presence of flint-filled pits, both here and at Hinxton Quarry, suggests that at least two quite different depositional practices were being followed. Whilst most of the struck material was informally disposed of on the surface, eventually to be incorporated into the topsoil, on occasion a portion of the accumulated struck flint waste was singled out and selected for deliberate deposition within pits or, in the case of the later Bronze Age material from Hinxton Quarry, within the ditches of a ring-ditch monument. At the current site, very few features were identified that could be confidently associated with their contained struck flint, but include the pit groups described above.

These features often received large quantities of knapping waste and/or tools, probably the accumulated debris from varied activities undertaken during a period of settlement at the site, and its deposition appears to have held some commemorative or ceremonial aspects. The digging of pits and their infilling appear as if intended to convey some specific meaning, information or story. As Thomas (1999, 69) suggests, the materials employed as pit deposits and the details of their arrangement and interment may have acted as a material language, albeit one that was highly localised in its meaning. This may relate to the marking out of a culturally or topographically significant place or period of occupation. It is also possible that the range and proportions of artefacts deposited within the pits could have reflected, however symbolically, the nature of the occupation and the range of activities that were undertaken (*e.g.* Garrow *et al.* 2005). In this sense, it is probable that the contents do indeed represent 'rubbish', but rubbish that had been curated, selected and deposited, with the intention of making statements or conveying information.

Similar depositional practices are widely attested during the prehistoric periods, particularly during the Neolithic, and the material from these pit complexes can be favourably compared to that from Early Neolithic 'pit sites', such as Hurst Fen, Broome Heath or Kilverstone, where large numbers of similar pits were recorded (Clark *et al.* 1960; Wainwright 1972; Garrow *et al.* 2006), as well as to that from local later Neolithic sites, such as at Linton (Beadsmoore 2005). The pits at these sites mostly contained knapping waste with varying proportions of used tools also being present, and their fills revealed a complex depositional history, with material being periodically selected from larger accumulations prior to being placed in the pits. Such practices involving the deposition of large quantities of occupational debris are not so frequently recorded for the Early Bronze Age, when the deposition of carefully selected and often prestigious items is perhaps more commonly encountered. The presence here of at least some Early Bronze Age material in the upper reaches of shaft/pit 902, including knapping debris, is therefore of interest. It is an unusually large assemblage that contains some specialised flintwork, such as the arrowheads and bifacially worked implements, but the upper part of the shaft was mostly filled with unremarkable knapping debris, which showed greater similarities to the earlier practices of infilling pits and may reflect a similar admixture of intentional Early Bronze Age material alongside dumps of Neolithic knapping waste. In light of the suggestion that the Hinxton stretch of the River Cam may have been regarded as a 'preferred location' for settlement (Pollard 1998, 67–8), it is interesting to note that not only did settlement persist here, but similar ceremonial practices may also have been maintained.

Although the pits are interesting and notwithstanding the degree of later disturbance to the site, it was clear that there could only ever have been present a few small clusters of features comparable to those recorded at the larger East Anglian 'pit sites', where hundreds of pits are sometimes recorded. At the Hinxton Genome site, a large proportion of the struck flint that would have accrued from settlement was left on the surface or, at best, placed into shallow features that did not survive later ploughing. This can be contrasted to the 'pit sites', where much of that type of material, including waste products and tools, was carefully accumulated and subsequently and purposefully placed into the pits that distinguish these sites. There are few typological differences between the struck flint from this site and the 'pit sites'; they both consisted of material from all stages in the reduction process and included a high proportion and wide range of retouched implements, indicative of diverse settlement-type activities. Similarly, locally obtained raw materials were procured and fully reduced, a range of tools was made and a multitude of tasks undertaken. Both types of site suggest the repeated return of communities, who undertook these tasks as a routine part of their lives, to what would appear to be preferred places within the landscape. What does appear to differ is that here most of the material was discarded on the surface whilst at the 'pit sites' the accumulating debris was middened and, when deemed appropriate, gathered up and carefully buried. Why this was routinely practiced in some locations but not in others is much harder to elucidate. The most obvious differences must remain the sites' topographical locations, most of the 'pit sites' are not situated immediately adjacent to the rivers but are located beyond the valley floors on relatively elevated positions that overlook them. The Hinxton Genome site, although on a gravel terrace, is low lying and appears to have been prone to sporadic flooding, as evidenced by the alluvium and colluvium-filled 'ponds' and other deposits recorded closer to the river. This may suggest that although comparable ranges of activities were undertaken at both types of site, the episodes of occupation at the site may have been more punctuated and expedient, perhaps being seasonally determined. Although repeatedly visited, individual episodes of occupation may have been of shorter duration and with fewer people involved. With less time and fewer people, there may perhaps have been less desire to mark the occasion or location with the formality afforded to the 'pit site' locations. There is also likely to be a chronological dimension to the differences between these types of site. The 'pit sites' are firmly placed in the Neolithic period, particularly its earlier parts, whilst at Hinxton an unquantifiable but probably substantial proportion of the assemblage was probably generated during the Mesolithic when there may have been no desire to mark occupation with the formality seen during the Neolithic. Whatever the explanation, it is certain that patterns of settlement and mobility during the Mesolithic to Bronze Age periods would have been both complex and diverse, with numerous differing strategies being followed at different times and different places (*e.g.* Brück 1999; Pollard 1999).

There is evidence that flintworking continued at the site after the Early Bronze Age, although quantifying its extent is difficult. There are few technological characteristics that can differentiate Middle Bronze Age through to Iron Age assemblages, and flint use during these periods is usually thought to have been of low intensity and opportunistically undertaken. There were no obvious worked flint accumulations comparable to those recorded at other sites in the area, such as at the nearby ring-ditch at Hinxton Quarry or the similar features at Pampisford and Thriplow, or that from the enclosures at Granta Park in Abington or Sawston Police Station (Trump 1956; Pollard 1996; 1998; 2002; Brudenell 2004; Mortimer 2006). This accords with the absence here of structural evidence of occupation from the Middle Bronze Age to Early Iron Age, despite a widely identified intensity of landscape exploitation and modification along the surrounding terraces of the Cam Valley and the chalklands bordering it. It may be that, although the river was unlikely to have been ignored, this particular area was perhaps too wet or otherwise regarded as inappropriate to permit actual occupation in its vicinity. It is interesting to note that at Hinxton Quarry, flintworking mainly focused on a ring-ditch, as it did at Bourn Bridge, and the creation of these assemblages was probably ceremonially inspired, rather than created through necessity (Pollard 1998, 68–9).

The presence of some evidence for crude flintworking in a few of the Late Iron Age features perhaps indicates the sporadic use of worked flint at the settlement. The evidence here is far from unambiguous but potentially contributes an interesting addition to the corpus of flintworking practices during this period. The reality and characteristics of flintworking during this time has been much discussed (Young and Humphrey 1999; Humphrey 2003) and Iron Age flintworking is now generally accepted and its further investigation even seen as a research priority (Haselgrove *et al.* 2001). The presence here of what is little more than a handful of 'bashed chunks' of flint and the production of a few flakes with sharp edges suggest that when the necessity arose, pieces of readily to hand raw materials were struck with little overall strategy or proficiency but until suitable edges were procured, these were then used and, once the task was completed, discarded with little formality.

Illustration catalogue

Worked flint from Pond/Hollow Q (16042, Area J)
Fig. 3.4
1   Mesolithic **transverse axe**. SF 529, 15749
2   **Polished axe** fragment. SF 533, 15915
3   **Laurel leaf**. SF 534, 15964
4   Bifacially worked **implement** - possible laurel leaf blank. 15965
5   Bifacially worked **implement** - possible laurel leaf blank. 15048

6   Rod-like **implement**. 15719
7   Rod-like **implement**. 15895

Examples of Neolithic flint tools from other features and deposits
Fig. 3.5
8   Broken **axe preform**, possibly reused as a core Neolithic. Colluvium 5399, Area I, unphased
9   Chopper **denticulate**, Neolithic? Unstratified
10   Side **scraper**, Neolithic. Fill 2000, ditch 2001, Ditch Group 7, Area D, Period 3.2
11   Side and end **scraper**, Early Neolithic. Fill 5305, pit 5304, Pit Group 6, Area I, Period 2.1

Early Bronze Age flint tools associated with Pit/Shaft 902 (Pit Group 7, Area C, Trench U)
Fig. 3.6
12   Unfinished **arrowhead**, broken barbed and tanged/triangular arrowhead. SF 143, 900
13   Bifacially flaked **cobble**. SF 142, upper fill 900
14   Backed **knife**. SF 42, fill 913
15   Unfinished **arrowhead**. Upper fill 900
16   Thumbnail **scraper**. Upper fill 900
17   Edge trimmed **flake**. Unstratified
18   Exhausted flake **core**. Unstratified
19   Edge trimmed **flake**. Unstratified
20   Heavily worked **flake core**. Unstratified
21   Exhausted flake **core**. Upper fill 900
22   Bifacially worked **piercer**. Upper fill 900
23   Bifacially flaked **cobble**. Upper fill 900

Worked flint from Bronze Age pits 15325 and 15327 (Area J, Pit Group 17)
Fig. 3.7
24   Levallois-like **core**. Fill 15326, pit 15327
25   Oblique type transverse **arrowhead**. SF 517, fill 15326, pit 15327
26   Serrated **blade**. SF 518, fill 15326, pit 15327
27   Denticulated **flake**. Fill 15326, pit 15327
28   Denticulated **core-tool**. Fill 15326, pit 15327
29   Petit tranchet type transverse **arrowhead**. SF 521, fill 15324, pit 15325

III. Metalwork
by Christine Howard-Davis
Figs 3.8–3.9

Introduction
In total, *c.*500 metal objects (excluding coins) were recovered from all phases of the project, the majority as a result of continuous metal detecting. Reflecting this method of retrieval, most of the assemblage (*c.*85%) came from unstratified topsoil or spoilheap deposits. A total of 295 metal objects came from Areas A to E. Most of the metal finds, including the majority of the iron objects, are post-Roman and are therefore described in Part II (Howard-Davis in Clarke *et al.* forthcoming).

A limited range of copper alloy objects (excluding coins, which are reported on separately below) of Roman or potentially Roman date were examined, coming from a succession of excavations, beginning with those at Hinxton Hall in 1993 (HINHH 93; Area F), with the latest being recovered from excavations in 2011 and 2014 (HINGEC 11 and HINGEL 14; Areas I and J). Their condition varies from very well preserved to fragmentary scraps: only those regarded as of unequivocally Iron Age or Roman date are discussed below. Very little ironwork that could definitively be assigned to the Iron Age and Roman periods was evident amongst the material collected and less still was identifiable or retained any chronologically diagnostic features.

Dress accessories and personal adornment
Fig. 3.8

Brooches
Brooches seem to have been worn by both men and women (often in pairs) throughout the Late Iron Age and Roman periods and several examples were found at Hinxton. A small corroded part of the spring and bow of a brooch (SF 192; not illus.) of Late Iron Age type (Nauheim derivative *c.*AD 25–100) was recovered from Area I (HINGC02) ditch 1541 (fill 1538); part of Enclosure 1. A residual Late La Tène III brooch (SF 61) was recovered from an Early Anglo-Saxon sunken-featured building (SFB) in Area F (Hinxton Hall), possibly present in the building as a curated item as has been noted elsewhere (White 1988). The type probably spans the period from the 1st century BC to the Flavian period, although such brooches are quite often found in later contexts (see the dating summarised by Mackreth 1996, 302–3). A brooch from the Genome Campus (HINGC02, unstratified), is of typical Langton Down form (SF 55). This form is more restricted in date than SF 61, spanning only the first few decades of the Roman period and probably falling out of fashion by the middle of the 1st century AD (Mackreth 2011, 34). The form was current in Gaul from the late 1st century BC, and some individual brooches probably reached Britain in pre-Conquest trade (Olivier 1996, 244), although it is likely that the type broadly arrived with the Roman army (Hattatt 1989) and fell from popularity within a few years. A well-preserved plate brooch from the Hinxton Hall site (Area F) is again unstratified (SF 39). It can be paralleled amongst the surface collection assemblage published from Stonea, Cambridgeshire; however, unlike this example which bears traces of blue enamel, there was no evidence that the Stonea brooch had been enamelled, albeit that it was, in part at least, coated with white metal (Mackreth 1996, 320, fig. 98.71). Brooches of this type can be placed, for the most part, in the 2nd century (*ibid.*, 304), when enamelling was reaching the height of its popularity (Bateson 1981), and like many plate brooches, this example cannot be dated with any more precision.

Bangle
Although brooches seem to have been worn by both men and women, some other items of adornment (for instance bangles, pins, and ear-rings) appear to have been more gender specific, worn, in most circumstances, by women (Swift 2011) and, in the case of bangles, to have had distinct periods of preference. A cast fragment from Hinxton Hall, Area F (SF 16) is probably part of a plain bangle with a D-shaped section. Bangles seem to have been at their most fashionable in the later 3rd and 4th century (Crummy 1983, 37), probably reaching the peak of their popularity in the 4th century (Swift 2011). They are, however, known in small numbers, from earlier sites, but – without supplementary dating evidence – it seems reasonable to assign the Hinxton example to their main period of popularity. A second small fragment from a relatively plain strip bangle (SF 313) with stamped S-motif decoration, came from a posthole at the Genome Campus site, where part of a rather more elaborate example (SF 143) was recovered unstratified.

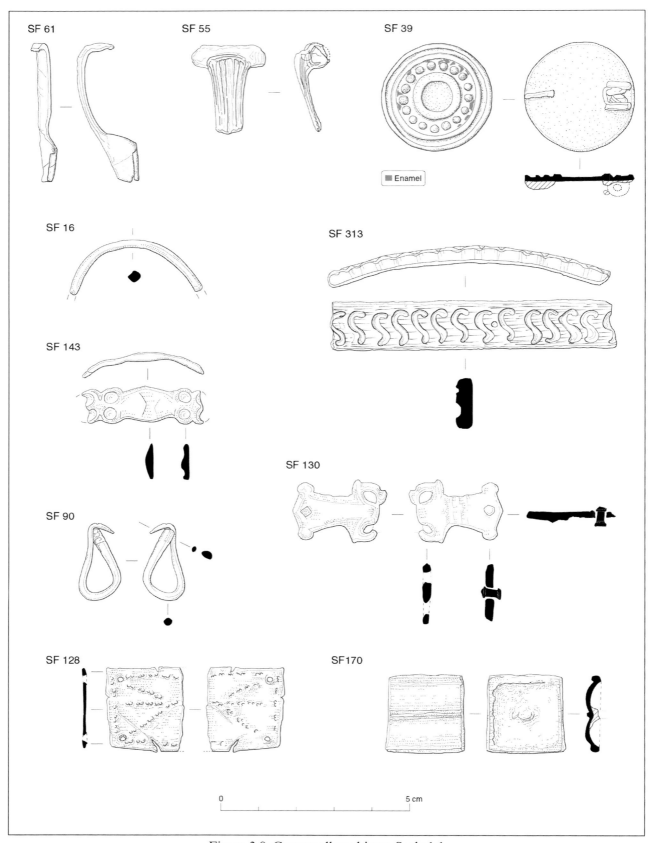

SF 61

SF 55

SF 39

■ Enamel

SF 16

SF 313

SF 143

SF 130

SF 90

SF 128

SF170

0　　　　　　　　　　　　　5 cm

Figure 3.8 Copper alloy objects. Scale 1:1

Earring

A long narrow triangular fragment of relatively thin sheet (SF 90), bent now into a rough triangle, but with a neat hooked end, has been tentatively identified as a simple earring, perhaps reminiscent of Allason-Jones type 9 (1989), but clearly lacking the spiral which characterises that early form.

Strap ends

A fragmentary strap end from the Genome Campus (SF 130) is probably of late 4th-century date, resembling examples from the Lankhills Cemetery (Clarke 1979, fig. 36.128) and reminiscent of that published by Bishop and Coulston (1993, fig. 125.12). Part of a poorly executed embossed buckle plate (SF128) found unstratified on the same part of the site could similarly be Late Roman in date (see for instance Clarke 1979, fig. 34.126), although embossed buckle plates also appear in the Early Anglo-Saxon period, at which time some wrist clasps also bear simple embossed decoration; see for example, several of the grave assemblages at Bergh Apton, in Norfolk (Green and Rogerson 1978). A second fragmentary buckle plate or strap terminal was recovered from a medieval ditch at the Genome Campus (SF 78, not illus.). The simple form of the latter makes it difficult to date with precision, but it is probably Roman.

Hairpin

A long, probably slender pin, possibly with a round head (SF 163; not illus.) came from HINGC 02 (Area B) pit 931 (fill 929). Its size suggests a hairpin, although iron hairpins are not common in the Roman period; a stylus is a possible alternative identification.

Buckle

There is the loop of a small D-shaped buckle (SF 197; not illus.), from Period 2 posthole HINGC02 2378 (fill 1965; ungrouped). It is likely that most small buckles derive from military equipment in this period, but this example is too poorly preserved for any more detailed identification. Two fragmentary hobnails (no SF; not illus.) were found unstratified on the same site. They probably derive from Roman footwear.

Illustration catalogue

SF 61   Bow and part of catchplate of La Tène III **brooch**, spring missing. L: 39mm; W: 10mm; Ht: 3mm. HIN HH 93 (Area F), Anglo-Saxon SFB 2674, fill 2672, Period 4, 1st century BC to mid-1st century AD

SF 55   Head and part of reeded bow of Langton Down **brooch** of convex curved head form (Olivier 1996, 244). Pin, spring, and lower part of bow and catchplate all missing. L: 25mm; W: 20mm; Ht: 9mm. HIN GC 02 (Areas A–D), unstratified, early to mid-1st century

SF 39   Round plate **brooch** with pin missing. Design consists of concentric rings framing embossed pellets; traces of light blue enamel between the rings. Pin does not survive, but seems to have been sprung. Diam: 29mm; Ht: 5mm. HIN HH 93 (Area F), unstratified 2001, 2nd century?

SF 16   Curving cast fragment with D-shaped section, perhaps a **bangle**. L:35mm; W: 3mm; Th: 2mm. HIN HH 93, unstratified 1111, later 3rd-century onwards

SF 313 Fragment of narrow **bangle** with stamped or punched S-motif decoration. Rectangular section. L: 19mm; W: 3.5mm; Th: 1mm. HIN GEC 11 (Area I), posthole 5100, Ctx 5099, Period 4, later 3rd century onwards

SF 143 **Bangle** fragment? L: 32mm; W: 9.5mm; Th: 2mm. HIN GC 02 (Areas A–D), unstratified, later 3rd century onwards

SF 90   Tapering fragment of **wire**, with a point at one end, and a rectangular section at the other. Now bent into a triangle, with the point forming a short hook. L: 20mm; W (overall): 12mm; Th (max): 1.5mm. HIN GC 02 (Areas A-D), unstratified

SF 130 **Strap end.** L: 25mm; W: 17mm; Th: 5mm. HIN GC 02 (Areas A–D), unstratified, late 4th century

SF 128 Half of an embossed **buckle plate**. L: 21mm; W: 23mm; Th: 1mm. HIN GC 02 (Areas A–D), unstratified, Late Roman or Early Anglo-Saxon

Item associated with religion
Fig. 3.9

The lower part of a small, solid-cast figurine (SF 144) was found unstratified at the Genome Campus (Areas A–D). It represents a fully draped, probably female, figure with one knee flexed, similar to that from Colchester (Crummy 1983, fig. 167) identified there as Fortuna or Abundantia. Minerva and Fortuna seem to be the most commonly represented female deities (see for instance Kaufmann-Heinimann 1998) and, although there is little else to help identify the deity represented at Hinxton, the flexed knee suggests Fortuna, often depicted carrying a *patera* and an over-flowing *cornucopia*. The goddess, representing good fortune, was a popular household deity amongst soldiers and civilians alike (Henig 1984, 77–8, 172), overseeing many of the more vulnerable aspects of daily life.

Illustration catalogue

SF 144 Lower part of substantial solid cast **figure**. The figure is fully draped and seems likely to be female. Ht: 30mm; W: 28mm; Th: 17mm. HIN GC 02 (Areas A–D), unstratified, Roman.

Domestic objects

Knife blades

The best preserved iron object from Period 1 is a small, slender blade (SF 205; not illus.) found in external surface 796 (HIN GC 02, Areas A–C, ungrouped). The blade is distinctive in having a tang almost as long as the slightly offset triangular blade. It conforms most closely to Manning's blade type 16 (1985, fig. 28), described by him as a long-lived form.

A large twisted fragment (SF 209; not illus.) from the Late Iron Age Enclosure 2 ditch in Area D (HIN GC 02 ditch 2557, fill 2556) is part of a draw knife (see, for instance Manning 1985, 19 and B19), but this cannot be stated with complete confidence. The same fill also produced a fragmentary nail (SF 208; not illus.).

A single knife blade (SF 183; not illus.) was recovered from Period 3.3 pit 1865 (fill 1325) in Pit Group 29 (HIN GC 02, Area B). Although incomplete, it clearly had a short whittle tang, and a slender, slightly offset blade, being of similar form to that from an Iron Age surface discussed above (SF 205; not illus.), suggesting that both are broadly contemporary. A second small blade (SF 178; not illus.), found unstratified, is also likely to be of Roman date, although its form is, like many Roman knives, long-lived and not particularly chronologically diagnostic.

Other domestic objects and tools

Two iron objects (SF 94, SF 80; not illus.), from ditches 114 (fill 121; part of Period 3.3 Ditch Group 10, Area A) and 194 (fill 193; Period 3.4 Ditch Group 12, Areas A–D and I)), have both been identified as small smith's

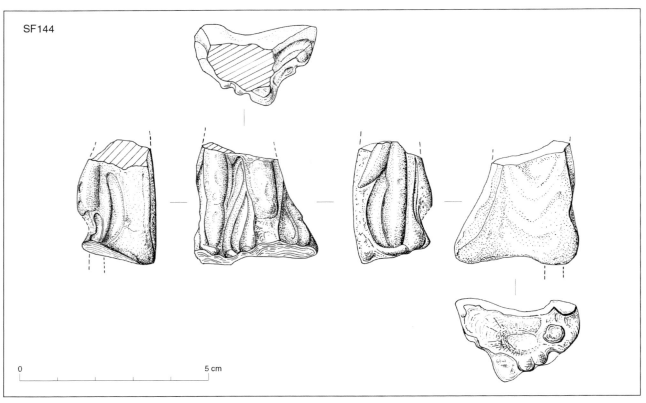

SF144

0   5 cm

Figure 3.9 Copper alloy figurine. Scale 1:1

punches, probably associated with metalworking, although in the absence of x-rays, this could not be confirmed. Both are square-sectioned bars, tapering to a point at one end. Broadly similar mid 1st-century examples from Hod Hill are illustrated by Manning (1985, 10; pl. 6 A31–2). He notes, however, that this was a common and widely-found type, used throughout the Roman period.

A large, L-sectioned iron fragment (SF 198; not illus.) from HIN GC 02 pit 1970 (fill 1969; Tree Throw Group 1; Area C), has been tentatively identified, from its potential size, as part of a spade shoe. It could, however, be from the socket of any large-socketed tool, but is most likely to be agricultural.

A substantial wrought hook or spiral (no SF; not illus.) was recovered from spoil, probably originating from Middle–Late Iron Age pit 350 (fill 348; Area B Pit Group 10, Period 2.2). It may have had a domestic function such as a cauldron suspension hook.

Studs and nails
Fig. 3.8
A number of studs and nails, often with large decorative heads, were recovered from the Genome Campus, since all are unstratified, most are not illustrated. A stud (SF 170), with a square hollow head, decorated with half-round mouldings, is of Roman date, and can be seen in both military and civilian contexts. The others (SF 65, SF 120 (two examples, not illus.), SF164, and unstratified with no SF number), all with flat or slightly domed round heads, seem most likely to be of Roman origin, probably used to decorate leatherwork or furniture. It must be noted, however, that such studs appear throughout the Roman and

later archaeological record, and without context, their dating cannot be confirmed.

A fragmentary nail was also recovered from the Late Iron Age Enclosure 2 ditch in Area D (HIN GC 02 ditch 2557, fill 2556; Period 3.1) (SF 208; not illus.).

Illustration catalogue

SF 170 Decorative **stud**, with robust square hollow-cast head. Shank missing. L: 20mm; W: 20mm; Ht: 3.5mm. HINGC02 (Areas A–D), unstratified

Discussion
The limited size and range of the assemblage of Late Iron Age and Romano-British metalwork from the site is perhaps surprising in view of the long period of occupation. It appears to confirm the other evidence from the site (in particular the general absence of roundhouses and other structures) that it did not lie at the focus of settlement at this time. It is clear, however, that most, if not all of the material suggests an entirely domestic *milieu*, with most objects associated with personal attire and probably reflecting occasional losses over an extended period. There is nothing to suggest a particularly elevated status, although this must remain subjective, and undoubtedly intrinsically valuable objects would have been more likely to have been carefully cared for, recycled, or scavenged at a later date. Similarly, there is no particular concentration or association of metalwork which might suggest specialist activity or any particular status.

It is possible that the earliest of the four brooches recovered predates the arrival of Rome and a third example dates to its earliest years. It is, however, clear that these early brooches do not predate the arrival of Roman influence and they are relatively frequent finds in immediately pre-Roman cemeteries in the region. It appears, as has been suggested by Eckhardt and Crummy (2008, 88), that the Late Iron Age inhabitants of Southern Britain were willing, in what seems to have been a period of political and social turmoil, to acquire novel and presumably culturally significant objects, and espouse the practices with which they were associated, from both their immediate neighbours and from further afield.

Although metalwork remains sparse on the site throughout the Roman period, it seems to reflect a continued, fairly comfortable level of domestic activity in the vicinity of the site, with the consistent appearance of personal items such as brooches, and in the 3rd/4th century, bangles, suggesting the acquisition of items intended not only to serve a practical purpose, but also to follow the general fashions of the day. In addition, a small statuette, possibly representing the goddess Fortuna, implies a personal interest in Romanised deities, at least at the individual level of seeking their protection for house and home: this item resonates with the presence of a shrine at the site. Studs and small nails hint at the presence of upholstered furniture, suggesting not only a desire for comfort but, to a limited extent, the means to achieve it. It must be noted, however, that an almost complete absence of evidence for some other sorts of 'luxury goods', for instance glass vessels, may suggest that this might not always have been the case.

IV. Coins
by Paul Booth

Introduction and methodology
Three Iron Age coins and 52 Roman coins were recovered in the excavations. One coin was found at Hinxton Hall (HIN HH 93, Area F), one Iron Age and seven Roman coins come from Ickleton (ICK GC 03, Area H), one Iron Age and one Roman coin from the Genome Campus found in 2014 (HINGEL 14, Area J) and the remainder are from the 2002 excavations (HIN GC 02, Areas A–D). Post-Roman coins and tokens are reported in Part II. The coins were scanned quite rapidly, although a fairly full record (based in part on English Heritage guidelines; Brickstock 2004) was made where possible. Only the coins from Area J had been cleaned before examination; rudimentary manual cleaning was carried out in some cases during the reporting process, but while a few coins would have benefitted from further formal treatment the generally unstratified nature of the assemblage meant that such work was not justified.

Summary of the assemblage
The Iron Age coin from Area D is a northern bronze unit of Cunobelin, with a horse and naked rider obverse and helmeted figure reverse (Hobbs 1996, nos 1961–1967; as Van Arsdell 1989, 2093) and is broadly datable to c.AD 10–40. The second Iron Age coin, a small bronze unit from Area H, is less securely identified as the reverse is completely encrusted. It appears to be of 'bearded head' type (cf. Hobbs 1996, nos 1714–1716) with a mid to late 1st-century BC date, but this is not certain. The two coins from Area J

Date	Reece Period	Total coins	Phase total
Phase A (–260)	uncertain	5	5
Phase B			15
260–275	13	4	
275–296	14	11 (8?)	
Phase C			3
296–317	15	1	
317–330	16	2	
Phase D			26
330–348	17	15	
348–364	18	-	
364–378	19	8	
378–388	20	-	
388–402	21	3	
3rd–4th century	uncertain		3
Total		**52**	

for Phase B, numbers of irregular issues are given in brackets

Table 3.15 Quantification of Roman coins by issue period and phase

comprise another example of the Cunobelin horse and rider type and a Victoria Auggg issue of AD 388–402.

The 43 Roman coins from Areas A–D cover most of the period, although no certain 1st-century pieces were identified. The majority are of later 3rd- and 4th-century date, as would be expected. The coins vary greatly in condition; a few are in good condition, while a relatively small number are badly eroded and completely illegible. The majority, however, are affected by varying degrees of corrosion or encrustation and as a result of these factors (and very variable amounts of wear) were only identified incompletely. The single coin from Area F is a Victoriae issue of AD 341–348.

The coins are tabulated (Table 3.15) in approximate chronological order of minting. In more general terms, however, the chronological profile of the coins can be summarised, using the period and broader coin-loss phase categories of Reece (e.g. 1991) as follows:

Four dupondii/asses are of probable 1st- or 2nd-century date. One (SF 127) is incomplete (a cut portion comprising about one third of the coin), and two of the others have female busts, one perhaps of Faustina II. The other Early Roman coin is a 2nd-century sestertius. Radiate coins are fairly well represented in the assemblage, although the division between periods 13 and 14 is slightly arbitrary, in part because the identification of irregular issues is not always certain as a result of the condition of the coins. All irregular or probably irregular issues (numbers in brackets in Table 3.15) have been assigned to period 14 here. Coins of period 13 were antoniniani of Gallienus (SF 122), a PM TRP VII type dated AD 266 (Bland and Burnett 1988, 124; contra RIC V, 170), Claudius (SF 166), Postumus (SF 51) and Tetricus I (SF 4101). A coin of Allectus (SF 172) was the only certain regular piece in period 14, while the condition of SF 30 and SF 33 assigned to this period meant that their character was uncertain. Irregular issues include two of Tetricus I.

Fourth-century coins make up the majority of the assemblage (58% of the coins assigned to phase), as might be expected. Perhaps as many as six of the fifteen period 17 coins are irregular issues. Since both periods 17 and 19 (AD 330–348 and 364–378 respectively) are well-represented, the absence of irregular coins of the intervening period (characteristically represented by imitations of Fel Temp Reparatio issues) is notable and not readily explained. It should be noted, however, that one of the 'uncertain' 3rd–4th-century pieces is a smooth disc 11mm in diameter. This is exactly the sort of size often used for such issues, but it has not been struck at all; while it is likely that it was intended to be used as a coin this cannot be certain. The latest 4th-century coins comprise two of Valentinian II dated AD 388–392. There is a reasonable distribution of mints amongst the identifiable 4th-century sources. London, Trier (5) and Lyon are represented in the first half of the century, the dominance of Trier being characteristic of the period. Later 4th- century mints identified are the standard western ones of Arles (2) and Lyon, but also Aquileia (2?) and Siscia.

Discussion
The assemblage is small and most of the coins are unstratified, many having been recovered with the aid of a metal detector. It is broadly characteristic of material from many rural settlements. The character of the small group from the area of Roman fields west of the Cam (site ICK GC 02-03; Area H) does not appear to be significantly different from that of the main assemblage. Although there is broad correspondence between the coin assemblage and overall site chronologies, it is not particularly likely that the Early Roman coins reflect contemporary coin use (as opposed to settlement) on the site – their condition is suggestive of circulation in the 3rd century. The predominance of later material regardless of the intensity of any Early Roman occupation is as would be expected. The size of the assemblage precludes detailed analysis, particularly based upon absence, although the lack of coin of the period AD 348–364 still appears worthy of comment. This apart, however, the coins indicate some activity on the site probably right up to the end of the Roman period. In broad terms, the ratio of coins of Reece's phase group B (c.AD 260–294) to phase group D (AD 330–402), 15:25, is consistent with the pattern seen widely in lower status rural settlements (Reece 1991, 102–3).

In view of the size of the assemblage wider comparison is not particularly meaningful, but Hobbs (2011) provides a useful summary of coinage from nearby Great Chesterford. Given the differences in nature between the two sites close similarity would not necessarily be expected, although coin assemblages from 'small towns' generally have a broadly rural character. This is seen in crude terms in the present case, although coinage of the later 3rd century is better represented at Great Chesterford than at Hinxton. One specific point of similarity is that the scarcity of coinage of Reece period 17 noted above at Hinxton is also seen at Great Chesterford, where it is more pronounced than in a group of eastern settlements used by Hobbs for comparison with Great Chesterford (*ibid.*, 259–60).

V. Metalworking debris
by Tom Eley and Sarah Percival

A small assemblage (1.639kg) of iron smithing slag was recovered during the excavations at the Genome Campus (Areas A–D). It was primarily recovered from Iron Age and Roman deposits. Although no material was found undisturbed in its primary location, most seems to have been concentrated around the northern part of Area B which may indicate that smithing waste was dumped in this area, perhaps as hardcore or to aid drainage around enclosure ditches and their entrances. The limited quantity found does not necessarily suggest that ironworking was taking place in the immediate vicinity of the site. During further excavation in 2014 (Area J) a single undated and abraded, vesicular grey/brown lump of ferruginous metalworking debris weighing 4g was found as intrusive material within the colluvial fill of natural hollow 16042 (Pond Q).

VI. Early Bronze Age pottery from Pit/Shaft 902
by Jonathan Last, with Sarah Percival
Figs 3.10–3.12

Description
The pottery from the pit/'shaft' (902, Pit Group 7) found in Trench U (Area C) consists of 144 hand-excavated sherds forming parts of approximately 30 Beaker vessels. In addition, some 30 small fragments were recovered from bulk wet-sieving. The assemblage weighs 1.016kg. At the time of its excavation, the assemblage represented one of the largest and most significant assemblages of 'domestic' Beaker pottery from the county; it was analysed and reported on in detail during the early stages of the project's history by one of the authors (JL; with the reporting subsequently updated and edited by SP). Differences in the methods and level of analysis have necessitated that it is presented separately from the other prehistoric pottery from the excavations detailed below in Section VII.

The majority of the pottery derives from 'fineware' comb-impressed Beakers, although 26 sherds come from rusticated vessels and there are also 19 small undecorated fragments, most of which probably derive from decorated pots. Only two sherds may be non-Beaker types. A single rounded and slightly thickened flint-gritted rim, which may be everted and is anyway quite different in form from the Beaker rims, might represent a plain vessel, of uncertain type. A small fragment of an externally-thickened coarsely flint-gritted rim recovered from wet-sieving has a mixture of fingernail (internal) and cord-impressed (external) decoration, and may derive from a Mortlake ware vessel.

The majority of the comb-impressed sherds are 4–7mm thick, with red or yellow-brown surfaces. Many of the pieces are mottled in colour but external surfaces are generally red (5YR or redder: 64%) while dark faces are more common on the interiors. Firing was often uneven, therefore, and temperatures were presumably not very high since 68% of vessels have a grey core, at least in part. The pastes nearly all contain sparse to moderate fine quartz sand, generally well-sorted but with rare coarse quartz fragments. The sand was probably naturally included within the clay but where more abundant it could have been added as a filler. The principal added inclusions are coarse to very coarse angular crushed and burnt flint, and medium to very coarse grog or clay pellets. Flint and grog may occur in the same vessel, but one usually predominates. Of the comb-impressed Beakers, 46% of vessels are principally flint-gritted, 21% contain mainly grog and 29% mainly sand with rare to sparse flint or grog. The rusticated sherds, in contrast, are predominantly grog-tempered. The pottery was coil-built and has occasionally broken along the edge of a coil, *e.g.* one sherd of No. 8a.

At Hinxton the presence on the fineware vessels of impressed or finger-pinched punctates within comb-defined bands or diamonds (*e.g.* Figs 3.10–3.11, Nos 1, 2, 3, 8b–d, 11, 12, 907:1) is characteristic and shows the stylistic unity of the assemblage. While some of these are similar enough in terms of decoration to be from the same vessel, the variation in fabric (particularly surface colours) and wall thickness appears too great for these sherds to be entirely from one pot.

Within fill 900 lay a cluster or pile of sherds (SF 50) thought to represent a discrete deposit. It comprises vessel Nos 6 and 12, as well as a large part of No. 11. The size of the reconstructed fragments in SF 50 and the connections through No. 11 with the rest of the assemblage indicates that these finds were not residual or redeposited.

The initial impression of the group as a whole is that it represents a domestic assemblage akin to others in the region (see discussion below).

Interpretive catalogue of pottery

Note: fabric descriptions follow the guidelines of the Prehistoric Ceramics Research Group (PCRG 1995).

Comb-impressed vessels

Where there are no direct joins the division into vessels is based on visible similarity of paste and decoration. Given the possible variation across the body of a handmade, bonfire-fired pot, this may overestimate the number of vessels. For instance, vessel Nos 11 to 14 have similar decoration and inclusions but marked differences in surface colour. All pieces derive from fill 900 except No. 25, which came from fill 912. A selection of these is illustrated with single numbers reflecting individual vessels and sub-divisions (a, b, c) of multiple vessels.

Fig. 3.10

1   5 sherds (82g). **Fabric**: thickness – 3.5–4mm; colours – exterior 7.5YR6/6–10YR5/4, interior grey at base, as ext. at rim, core grey; fabric soft; inclusions are moderate fine/medium quartz sand, sparse coarse/very coarse angular flint to 6mm. **Form**: rim with funnel–necked profile, flat–topped, diam. 90mm, 10% preserved; base simple with slight internal thickening, angle 60°; diam. 50mm, 100% preserved; waist inflexion slack. **Decoration**: Base – irregularly applied double (occasionally single) row of comb impressions above base and further rows above that at intervals of *c.*15mm. Between first and second lines a double band of crude, elongated, irregularly arranged impressed punctates *c.*5.5x3.5mm. Waist – similar bands of punctates within double rows of comb impressions framing an undecorated waist zone 12mm high. Rim – similar bands framing an undecorated band 7–8mm high. **Comments**: this vessel is characterised by the careless application of the decoration, particularly the discontinuous and rather indistinct lines of comb impression. The flared rim may be an early form, *cf.* Clarke's (1970) no. 66 (S1, Doddington, Cambs). The zoned

bands of elongated impressions recall a similar band on Clarke's no. 145 (S2, Rusden Low, Derbys).

2   2 joining sherds (53g). **Fabric**: 6mm; ext. & int. 7.5YR 6/6–5/4; partial light grey core; soft; moderate very fine/fine sand, rare coarse/very coarse flint to 2mm. **Form**: lower belly. **Decoration**: double or triple rows of broad comb impression (4 teeth/cm) framing single bands 9–10mm high of finger-pinched rustication and an undecorated zone 16mm high. **Comments**: the unusual combination of rusticated elements within comb-defined bands was noted by Leaf as rare but is paralleled at Chippenham Barrow 5, Cambs and Goodmanham, Yorks (Leaf 1940, figs 15, 19; Clarke 1970, no. 64, S2) as well as at Lakenheath, Suffolk (Briscoe 1949, fig. 6d) and Hockwold, Norfolk (Bamford 1982, fig. 5 – P93.028).

3   2 joining sherds (13g). **Fabric**: 6–7mm; ext. & int. 2.5YR6/6–7.5YR6/4, grey core; medium; moderate fine sand, sparse coarse/very coarse grog to 2mm, rare coarse sand, rare coarse flint. **Decoration**: triple row of deep comb impressions with only low narrow ridges between teeth, framing single band 8mm high of cuneiform impressions and another possibly with finger-pinched rustication. **Comments**: the distinctive impressions suggest a shallowly notched tool for the comb rows. The cuneiform marks are similar to those depicted on the rim of a vessel from Fengate, Cambs (Gibson 1982, 384, no. 7).

4   2 sherds (12g). **Fabric**: 4–5mm; ext. *c.*5YR5/6, int. & core grey; soft; moderate fine/medium sand. **Decoration**: double rows of broad-toothed comb impressions framing (a) comb-impressed lozenge, perhaps filled; (b) band 19mm high of diagonal comb-impressed lines (9 teeth). **Comments**: common motifs of S1–2.

5   1 sherd (13g). **Fabric**: 5–6mm; ext. 7.5YR6/4–6, lightly burnished, int. 10YR 5/3–4, core light grey; medium; moderate fine sand, rare coarse flint. **Decoration**: triple band of bar chevrons *c.*10mm high filled by vertical comb-impressed strokes (5–6 teeth). **Comments**: parallels for the decoration include Clarke's nos 445 (S1, Denton, Lincs), 64 (S2, Chippenham Barrow 5: Leaf 1940, fig. 16, no. 18), 894 (S2, Gravel, Suffolk), 366 (S2, Houghton, Hunts – filled with fingernail impressions), 1355 (S3, Painsthorpe, Yorks). By analogy this sherd is probably part of the neck.

6   10 joining sherds (136g). **Fabric**: 6–7mm; ext. 7.5YR5/6–2.5YR5/6, int. 10YR5/4–6/4, core grey; medium; moderate fine sand, sparse very coarse flint to 4mm, rare very coarse grog to 2mm. **Form**: base slightly pedestalled with internal thickening, angle 55°, diam. 80mm, 100%. **Decoration**: single comb-impressed rows framing bands 8–10mm high of 'maggot' impressions made with notched tool, separated by undecorated bands 5–7mm high. **Comments**: although technically comb-impressed, the 'maggots' resemble the elongated punctates found on other vessels. The elaborate base is more likely to be early, *cf.* Clarke's no. 1190 (S1, Winterbourne Stoke, Wilts). The multiple equal-zone style is paralleled at another Winterbourne Stoke barrow, Clarke's no. 1195 (S2).

7   3 joining sherds (53g). **Fabric**: 4mm; ext. mottled *c.*5YR5/4 and 10YR4/2, int. similar but less red, core grey; medium; moderate fine/medium sand, sparse coarse/very coarse flint to 2mm, rare (locally sparse) very coarse grog to 3mm. **Form**: base simple but thickened (7.5mm), angle 55°, diam. 50mm, 100% preserved. **Decoration**: triple row of comb impressions above broad field 31–36mm high of comb-impressed lattice. **Comments**: the lattice pattern is rather irregular and was clearly put together as individual lozenges rather than broad criss-cross lines. Hence the lowest line above the base approximates to horizontal but is rather irregular, *cf.* a vessel from Fengate (Gibson 1982, 386, no. 11). This is unlike the horizontal border at the base of a vessel from Chippenham 5 (Leaf 1940, fig. 20, no. 25) or where the lattice just runs out at the base, *e.g.* Clarke's no. 10 (S1, Turvey Abbey, Beds).

8   28 sherds with some joins, similar but not necessarily of same vessel, subdivided into five groups.

8a   (35g) **Fabric**: 5–6.5mm; ext. 7.5YR6/4–2.5YR5/6, int. 7.5YR6/4 and grey mottles, core grey; medium; moderate coarse/very coarse flint to 2mm, sparse very fine sand. **Decoration**: double row of comb impressions bordering broad lattice field at least 45mm high. **Comments**: lattice fields are common from S1–S3. A local parallel is Clarke's

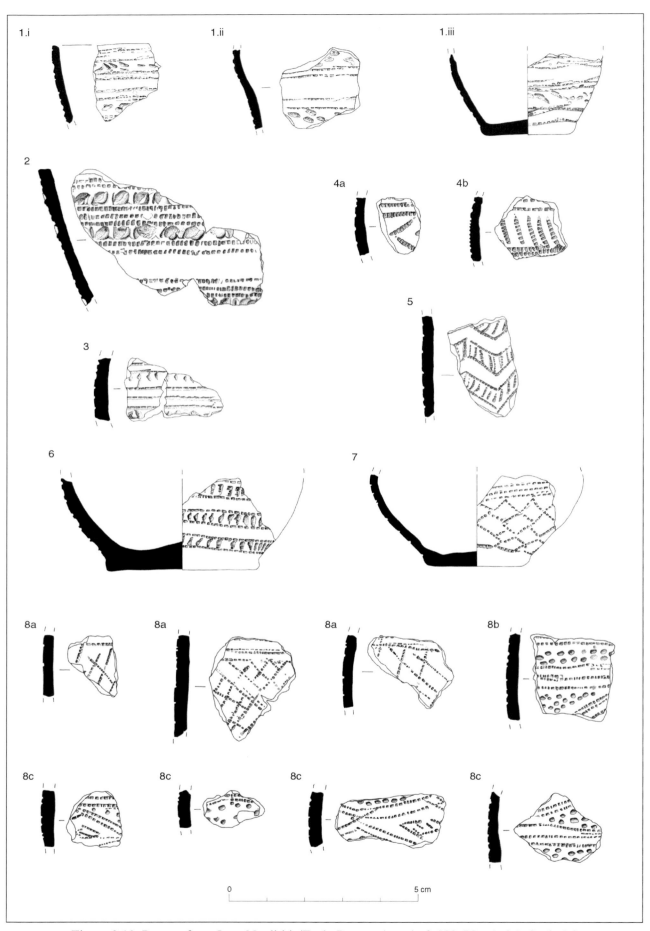

Figure 3.10 Pottery from Late Neolithic/Early Bronze Age shaft 902 (Nos 1–8c). Scale 1:2

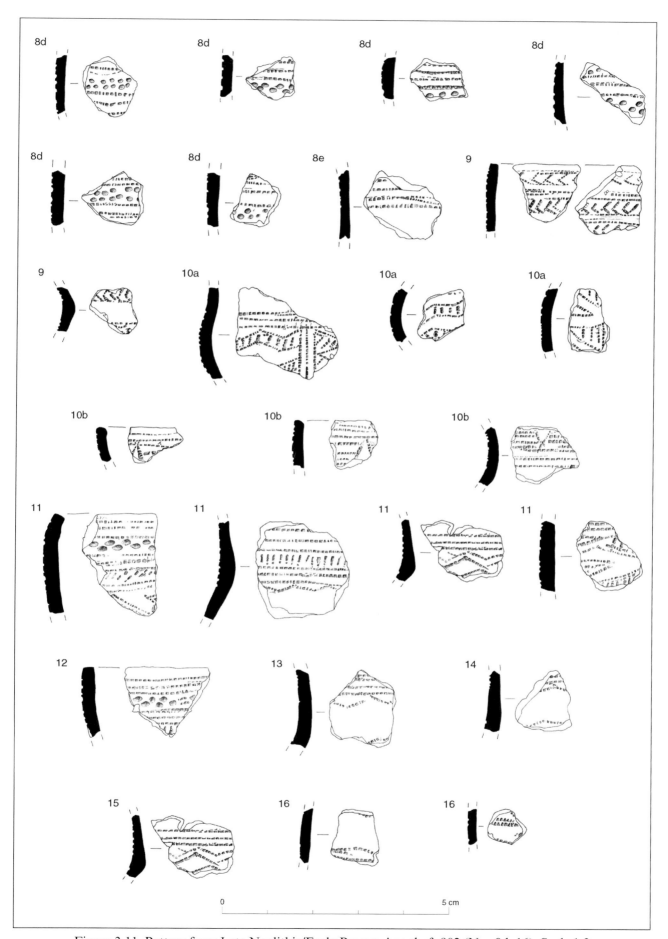

Figure 3.11 Pottery from Late Neolithic/Early Bronze Age shaft 902 (Nos 8d–16). Scale 1:2

no. 953 (S3, Great Chesterford, Essex).

8b (16g) **Fabric**: as 8a. **Decoration**: double row of comb impressions bordering double band 14mm high of impressed punctates and probable row of pendant chevrons filled with punctates.

8c (33g) **Fabric**: as 8a but with dark mottled int. and no grey core. **Decoration**: at least one row of comb-impressed lozenges filled with concentric lines of comb impressions or punctates.

Fig. 3.11

8d (29g) **Fabric**: as 8c but with partial grey cores. **Decoration**: double or triple row of comb impressions bordering double band 10mm high of impressed punctates.

8e (9g) **Fabric**: as 8d. **Decoration**: triple or quadruple row of comb impressions above undecorated zone at least 15mm high. **Comments**: some parallels include Clarke's no. 819 (S2, Brassington, Derbys) with a row of lozenges filled in this case by fingernail impressions, 904 (S2, Ipswich, Suffolk) with a row of punctate- or 'maggot'-filled lozenges, a vessel from Fengate (Wyman Abbott and Smith 1910, fig. 5, lower right), and a large Beaker from Lakenheath (Briscoe 1960, fig. 2a), both with filled lozenges. The form of the punctates on the present sherds seems to define this particular assemblage, with few parallels elsewhere in the region, although they do resemble a single sherd from Lakenheath with a double row of 'shallow oblong depressions' framed by comb-impressed lines (Briscoe 1949, fig. 6g). Such jabbed impressions are generally more common in the free designs of S3–4, *e.g.* Clarke's no. 550 (S4, Hilgay, Norfolk).

9 3 sherds (16g). **Fabric**: 5mm; ext. 10YR5/2–3 to 7.5YR5/4–6; int. 10YR5/2–3; core as ext.; soft; sparse fine sand, sparse very coarse off-white grog/clay pellets to 5mm; rare very coarse flint to 3.5mm. **Form**: rim with straight profile, flat-topped, diam. 160mm, 7%; waist inflexion sharp. **Decoration**: single or double comb-impressed rows bordering bands of comb-impressed chevrons 7–8mm high. Empty zone on waist 10mm high. **Comments**: the arrows are impressed with notched tools of three and four teeth. For the multiple equal-zone style *cf.* no. 6. Parallels for the decoration are also generally S1–2, *e.g.* Clarke's nos. 827 (S1, Deepdale, Staffs) and 813 (S2, Rusden Low, Derbys).

10a 3 sherds (30g). **Fabric**: 5mm; ext. as 8a, int. 2.5YR5/6, core grey; medium; moderate and locally common poorly sorted medium to very coarse flint to 4mm, sparse very fine sand, rare other coarse/very coarse minerals to 2mm, rare coarse/very coarse grog to 1.5mm. **Form**: waist inflexion moderately slack. **Decoration**: below empty zone on waist (at least 12mm high) three comb-impressed rows above panelled decoration divided by three vertical comb-impressed rows. To one side parallel 'maggot'-filled bar chevrons, to other horizontally projecting 'maggot'-filled triangles. **Comments**: relatively rare oxidised (red) interior surface. Panel motifs begin in Clarke's S2. Parallels for this decoration include no. 822 (S2, Bradwell, Derbys), although this is on neck not belly; panels of different type are found on the belly of nos 856 (S2, Fengate) and 877 (S3, Eriswell, Suffolk).

10b 3 sherds (15g). **Fabric**: as 10a, but with sparse grog. **Form**: rim with ?funnel-necked profile, top flattish, diam. 120–130mm, 11%; waist inflexion moderately slack. **Decoration**: on rim three comb-impressed rows above ?pendant triangles, empty or filled with horizontal comb impressions. On waist unfilled ?pendant triangle breaking up zone of comb-impressed rows (at least 5). **Comments**: decorative scheme incomplete but regional parallels for empty triangles/lozenges within a filled field include vessels from Fengate (Wyman Abbott and Smith 1910, fig. 5, top left) and Lakenheath (Briscoe 1960, fig. 3f–g).

11 16 sherds (several joins) (59g). **Fabric**: 6.5–9mm; ext 10YR5/3 to 7.5YR6/4 to 2.5YR5/6, int. 7.5YR4/3–5/3 and greyer, core grey; medium; moderate/common medium to very coarse flint to 4mm, sparse/moderate fine sand, rare coarse/very coarse grog to 1.5mm, rare small organic voids. **Form**: rim with slightly in turned profile, top flattish, diam. ?200mm, 5%; waist inflexion moderately sharp. **Decoration**: complex pattern of filled triangles and lozenges above bands filled with punctates and vertical 'maggot' impressions bordered by three or four comb-impressed rows. A row of shallow pendant triangles on waist above empty zone at least 13mm high. **Comments**: the shallow unfilled pendant

triangles just below the waist are paralleled on vessels of Clarke's N3 tradition (*e.g.* no. 650 from Hempholme, Yorks) and others, *e.g.* no. 1298 (S1, Garton Slack, Yorks). In shape it appears that the belly diameter is greater than the neck diameter, which would be a typologically late trait. The apparently large diameter, albeit estimated from small sherds, might put this vessel in the 'giant Beaker' category (*cf.* Briscoe 1960). Similar to Nos 12 and 13.

12 1 sherd (13g). **Fabric**: 7mm; surfaces *c.*5YR5/4, core *c.*10YR5/3; hard; moderate/common medium to very coarse flint to 5mm, moderate fine sand, rare to sparse coarse grog. **Form**: rim with funnel-necked profile, top flattish, diam. 200–240mm, *c.*6%. **Decoration**: triple comb-impressed rows framing bands of punctates and comb-impressed 'maggots'. **Comments**: similar to No. 11 in form, layout of decoration and estimated diameter, so may well be same vessel, although surface colours and details of decoration vary slightly.

13 1 sherd (12g). **Fabric**: 7–8mm; surfaces and core *c.*7.5YR5/6–6/4; medium; moderate coarse/very coarse flint to 2mm, sparse or rare coarse/very coarse grog or clay pellets to 3mm, rare very fine sand. **Form**: waist inflexion moderately slack. **Decoration**: empty zone *c.*17mm high bordered by shallow unfilled pendant triangles. **Comments**: similar to Nos 11 and 14.

14 2 sherds (8g). **Fabric**: 6–8mm; ext. *c.*2.5YR5/6, int. *c.*5YR5/4, core partially grey; hard; moderate coarse/very coarse flint to 2mm, sparse very fine sand. **Form**: waist inflexion moderately slack. **Decoration**: as No. 13. **Comments**: similar to No. 13 in decoration and inclusions, but strongly oxidised surfaces.

15 2 joining sherds (8g). **Fabric**: 4–5.5mm; ext. 5YR4/3–5/4, int. 7.5YR5/4 mottled grey, core grey; medium; moderate fine/medium sand, sparse coarse flint, sparse coarse/very coarse grog to 3mm. **Form**: waist inflexion moderately sharp. **Decoration**: three rows of comb impressions above band of pendant triangles framing row of conjoined lozenges. **Comments**: parallels include Clarke's nos 904 (S2, Ipswich, Suffolk) and 1875 (S2, Llanelltyd, Wales), both with filled shapes, and *cf.* No. 8c.

16 4 sherds (8g). **Fabric**: 5mm; ext. 10YR4/2 to 5YR5/4, int. grey, core 10YR4/2; hard; moderate fine sand, rare very coarse grog to 2.5mm. **Decoration**: probably similar to No. 14.

Fig. 3.12

17 3 sherds (5g). **Fabric**: 5mm; ext. 7.5YR6/4–2.5YR5/6, int. 7.5YR6/6 thinly over grey core; medium; sparse very fine sand, sparse medium/coarse flint, sparse very coarse grog to 4mm. **Decoration**: seven parallel comb-impressed rows, unfilled. **Comments**: simple banded decoration of this type occurs locally on Clarke's nos. 365 (S1, Eynesbury, Hunts) and 504 (S1, Barton Bendish, Norfolk) as well as at Lakenheath (Briscoe 1960, fig. 2b), all with incised lines or grooves, and with comb impression on Clarke's no. 1324 (S2, Hanging Grimston, Yorks) and at Hockwold (Bamford 1982, fig. 1, P93.001–2).

18 2 sherds (3g). **Fabric**: 4–5mm; ext. 10YR4/2–5/2, int. 10YR4/1–2, core grey; hard; moderate coarse/very coarse grog to 3mm, sparse very fine sand, rare medium/coarse flint. **Decoration**: ?pendant unfilled triangles beneath two rows of comb impressions.

19 2 sherds (2g). **Fabric**: 4–5mm; surfaces *c.*2.5YR5/6, thin grey core; soft; moderate coarse/very coarse grog to 3mm, moderate fine sand. **Decoration**: comb-impressed rows or shapes partly filled by vertical incised strokes. **Comments**: rare examples of incision at Hinxton, similar in principle, perhaps, to a sherd from Lakenheath with incised strokes framed by comb-impressed lines (Briscoe 1949, fig. 8e).

20 2 sherds (11g). **Fabric**: 4–5mm; ext. 7.5YR5/4–2.5Y5/6, int. 7.5YR5/4 and greyer, core grey; hard; moderate fine sand, sparse/moderate very coarse grog to 3mm. **Decoration**: comb-impressed rows framing bands or shapes filled by diagonal comb-impressed lines. **Comments**: decoration impressed by a notched tool with large teeth up to 2 x 2mm (4 teeth/cm).

21 2 sherds (81g). **Fabric**: 7mm; surfaces and core *c.*7.5YR6/4; hard; common medium to very coarse flint to 3mm, sparse fine sand, rare coarse/very coarse grog or clay pellets to 2mm. **Decoration**: comb-impressed rows bordering ?band

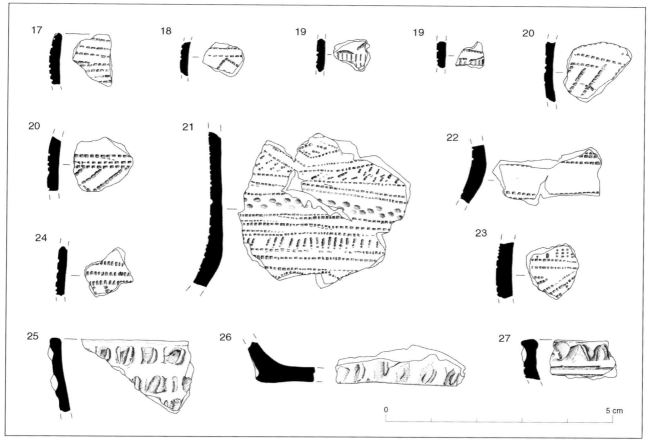

Figure 3.12 Pottery from Late Neolithic/Early Bronze Age shaft 902 (Nos 17–27). Scale 1:2

filled with vertical comb impressions and ?field of pendant triangles or lozenges.

22 3 sherds (2 join) (13g). **Fabric**: 5–7mm; ext. 2.5Y5/4–6, int. 7.5YR4/3–5/4, core grey; hard; moderate very coarse yellowish grog to 3mm, sparse fine quartz sand, rare coarse flint. **Form**: waist inflexion slack. **Decoration**: comb-impressed rows bordering empty zone 18mm high.

23 1 sherd (3g). **Fabric**: 4.5mm; ext. 7.5YR6/4–2.5YR5/6, int. 5YR5/3–4, core c.10YR6/4; medium; moderate fine/medium sand, sparse moderate to very coarse grog to 2mm. **Decoration**: two comb-impressed rows above ?lozenge filled with diagonal comb impressions.

24 1 sherd (2g). **Fabric**: 5mm; ext. 7.5YR6/4–6, int. 7.5YR6/4–2.5YR5/6, core grey; moderate medium to very coarse flint to 2mm, sparse coarse grog, sparse fine sand. **Decoration**: three comb-impressed rows below empty zone and above probable panel motif.

Rusticated vessels

Since the decoration is less variable, assigning non-joining sherds to the same vessel is necessarily more tentative.

25 1 sherd (14g). **Fabric**: 6mm; 7.5YR6/4 to 10YR6/4; int. and core with darker mottling; medium; sparse very fine/fine sand, rare coarse flint, rare coarse/very coarse grog to 2mm. **Form**: rim with slightly funnel-necked profile, flat-topped, diam. 200–240mm, c.8%. **Decoration**: rows of finger-pinched impressions. **Comments**: in shape this pot may be similar to two vessels from Hockwold (Bamford 1982, fig. 22, P63.145; fig. 25, P63.177).

26 1 sherd (9g). **Fabric**: 6mm; ext. and int. grey, core 7.5YR6/3–4; hard; moderate coarse/very coarse grog to 4mm, moderate fine/medium sand. **Form**: base slightly footed, angle 60°, diam. 90mm, ?%. **Decoration**: rows of finger-pinched impressions, running right down to base.

27 1 sherd (10g). **Fabric**: 6–7mm; ext. and int. 7.5YR4/1–2, core 7.5YR5/3; medium; sparse/moderate medium to very coarse grog to 1.5mm, rare coarse flint. **Form**: rim with

straight profile, flat-topped, slightly rolled over internally, diam. 100–140mm, c.7%. **Decoration**: row of double finger-pinched impressions (i.e. pinched up from either side) above horizontal groove. **Comments**: the combination of rustication and incision is unusual here. The sherd may be part of a 'fineware' vessel like Nos 2–3 but the broad rim form is reminiscent of rusticated pots from Hockwold (e.g. Bamford 1982, fig. 7, P93.038; fig. 8, P93.048). Additional 14 body sherds with finger-pinched rustication (generally oxidised exteriors, grog and sand inclusions).

Undecorated sherds (Not illustrated)

28 1 sherd (26g). **Fabric**: 7–8mm; ext. 7.5YR5/4–2.5YR5/4, int. 7.5YR4/3, core grey; moderate very coarse flint to 4mm. **Form**: rounded and thickened rim, perhaps everted, diameter uncertain.

29 1 sherd (30g). **Fabric**: 4mm; surfaces and core 7.5YR6/6; moderate fine sand, rare coarse flint. **Form**: rim with straight profile, top flattish, diameter uncertain. **Comments**: probably from a Beaker vessel.

Additional 11 body sherds, 9 flint-tempered and 2 grog-tempered, as well as 3 small fragments.

Sherds from bulk wet sieving

The majority of deposit 900 was wet-sieved as two samples (301 and 311). These produced around 30 fragments of pottery, most of them tiny. The list below summarises these finds:

301 12 sherds (52g) of comb-decorated Beaker: 6 flint-gritted, 5 with grog and a little flint, 2 with grog and sand. Decoration includes one sherd with probable filled lozenges, and one with a horizontal band of punctates. One rim-sherd (grog-tempered) with horizontal rows of comb impressions.

4 undecorated fragments, probably from comb-impressed vessels: one flint-gritted, one with grog and flint, one with grog and sand, one with sparse sand only.

8 sherds of rusticated Beaker with finger pinching, one

91

with grog and flint, 7 with grog and sand. One sherd has thickening perhaps indicative of raised shoulder/cordon.

311   2 sherds (9g) of comb-decorated Beaker: one flint-gritted, one with no visible inclusions. One plain sherd with grog and sand.
1 flattened rim with rusticated decoration, grog and sand temper.
1 externally thickened rim with oxidised surfaces and greyish core; moderate medium to very coarse flint and moderate fine/medium sand. Internal rim zone decorated with fingernail impressions; external rim ledge decorated with diagonal rows of shallow ?twisted cord impressions. ?Mortlake ware.

Sherds from context 907

Deposit 907 represents the fill of a later (post-medieval) feature (908) which appears to have disturbed the upper fill of 902 and incorporates a few Beaker sherds of similar type which almost certainly derive from the earlier feature.

907   5 sherds (20g), probably of same vessel. **Fabric:** 7mm; ext. 7.5YR6/4, int. 7.5YR5/3, partial grey core; moderate very coarse flint to 4mm, sparse coarse grog. **Form:** rim with straight profile, top flattish, diam. *c.*150mm, 5%. **Decoration:** three rows of comb impressions below rim, above band of impressed punctates. Body sherds include punctates, comb-impressed lozenges (*cf.* No. 8c), and 'maggots' (*cf.* 11).

Discussion

by Sarah Percival

Since excavation and original analysis of the Hinxton Beaker assemblage, significant programmes of research have been undertaken to refine Beaker typology and clarify dating (Needham 2005 and 2012; Healy 2012b; Woodward 2002; Garrow 2006). In addition, several important domestic Beaker assemblages have been published from the region (Gibson 2005; Allen 2008). The following discussion considers the domestic Beaker assemblage from pit/shaft 902 with reference to relevant recent research.

Dating of non-funerary Beaker assemblages is problematic (Healy 2012b, 157). Beaker derived from occupation sites frequently displays stylistically late decorative motifs especially the use of rustication, non-combed stamped motifs and combed infilled lozenges and triangles surrounded by reserve bands associated with long-necked forms (Needham 2005, fig. 9, 10–13; Healy 2012b, 158). Using radiocarbon dates derived from fourteen English sites, Healy suggests that Beaker began to be used in non-funerary contexts around 2490–2200 cal BC (at 95% probability) or 2350–2230 cal BC (at 68% probability).

Radiocarbon dates from recent excavations of non-funerary Beaker in East Anglia generally fall around the date range suggested by Healy. These include dates obtained for various pit sites, including two Beaker pits at Fenstanton where radiocarbon dating of charcoal suggested the pits were excavated around 2279–2030 cal BC (68% Wk-10430, Chapman *et al.* 2005); three Beaker pits at Harford Park and Ride, Norfolk which calibrate to 2460–2200 cal BC (95.4% Wk 17711), 2300–2030 BC (95.4% Wk 17706) and 2280–1980 BC (95.4% Wk 17712; G. Trimble pers. comm.); Bowthorpe, Norfolk, 2500–1950 cal BC, (Wk-8870; Percival 2002, 69); Worlingham, Suffolk, 2400–1900 cal BC (Gibson forthcoming) and Lakenheath, Suffolk (2200–1900 cal BC, GU13110-112, ERL 120; J. Caruth, pers. comm.). Also within this range is Northwold burnt mound which was created between

2265–2165 and 2140–2065 cal BC (95%; Bayliss *et al.* 2004).

The fine Beakers from pit/shaft 902 belong to Needham's 'long-necked' group (LN) defined as having an abrupt break of angle at the waist (Fig. 3.11, No. 11; Fig. 3.12, Nos 21, 22), long neck which represents 35% or more of the Beaker's total height (Fig. 3.10, Nos 2, 6, 8a), a well-rounded or bulbous body and late decorative motifs (Needham 2005, 195; Fig. 3.10, Nos 6 and 7; Fig. 3.11, No. 10). Needham suggests a date range for LN Beakers in burials, based on radiocarbon dates and artefact associations, focussing around 2200–2000BC (Needham 2012, 9). Form and decoration suggest therefore that the shaft assemblage was deposited towards the beginning of the period when Beaker began to be used in non-funerary contexts (Healy 2012b).

The mix of fingertip-rusticated and comb-impressed Beaker found in pit/shaft 902 compares well with large domestic deposits found on the fen-edge, notably at Hockwold cum Wilton and Fifty Farm, Nordelph, Norfolk (Gibson 1982; Bamford 1982; Healy 1988). The absence of incised decorated sherds found at many 'domestic' sites is of interest and may reflect the chronology of the assemblage or a local trend similar to the putative stylistic foci identified by Healy on the eastern fen-edge, the Sandlings around Colchester (Healy 1996, 117) and within unusual Beaker pits deposits within Biddenham Loop, Bedfordshire (Allen 2008, 113). Long-necked Beakers displaying a similar decoration have been found in Cambridgeshire at Church Farm, Fenstanton (Gibson 2005) and Bottisham (Gibson 1982, 360) and to the west at Biddenham Loop, west of Bedford (Allen 2008). Chippenham Barrow 5 may be typologically the closest domestic assemblage in the region (Martin and Denston 1976).

VII. Prehistoric and Roman pottery
by Lisa Brown with Sarah Percival
Figs 3.13–3.16

Introduction

A total of 4,490 sherds of multi-period pottery, weighing 58,209g, was recovered during the various phases of investigation (Table 3.16). Whilst a few Neolithic sherds were retrieved from pits and tree holes mostly concentrated in Areas F and I, a significant assemblage of 667 earlier Neolithic sherds (3,026g) was recovered during the most recent excavations in 2014 (Area J), mostly from buried soil and colluvium deposits associated with a large hollow or pond (Pond Q, 16042). In addition to the Beaker pottery recovered from pit/shaft 902, described separately above, scarce Bronze Age pottery fragments were found scattered across the excavation areas with a further 30 Beaker sherds and three Early Bronze Age sherds found in 2014 (Area J). The largest component of the Hinxton assemblage dates to the later part of the Iron Age and the Early Roman period, including freshly broken pottery of Aylesford-Swarling 'Belgic' type. Such pottery is, for the most part, grog-tempered and wheel-thrown and is directly related to developments in Southern Britain. Imported Roman pottery present in pre-Conquest contexts at Hinxton includes amphorae from Spain and Gallo-Belgic table crockery from Gaul, sufficient to suggest that this was a community of relatively high (or 'special') status at that time.

Methodology

The entire pottery assemblage (with the exception of the shaft material which was analysed separately) was recorded on *pro formae* devised by Paul Sealey and subsequently digitised within the following data fields: context; stratigraphic group; Small Find no.; fabric; count by rim, body and basal sherd, total count; weight; conjoins; manufacture technique; decoration; residue type; date; illustration number. Fabrics were defined by principal inclusion type and further subdivided, where relevant, by inclusion size. Inclusions are defined here as temper whether or not there is reason to regard them as deliberate additions to the clay.

Dating

Dating of the pottery was undertaken with close reference to firing techniques. The group includes many sherds with black cores caused by the incomplete combustion of carbonaceous matter that occurs naturally in the clay. Black cores are present in pottery that has been fired for shorter, rather than longer periods. They are indicative of vessels that have been fired in a bonfire, as opposed to a kiln (Gibson and Woods 1990, 54, 113–14). Although not all prehistoric pottery has a black core, its absence from contexts that span the divide between prehistory and the Roman period is a pointer towards the growing use of pottery fired in kilns. At Hinxton this feature helped distinguish between wares that are Late Iron Age or Roman in technique, although care had to be taken not to confuse it with the black cores occasionally found in kiln products (*ibid.*, 106).

Earlier prehistoric pottery

Earlier Neolithic (Period 2.1)

The earlier Neolithic assemblage from the 2014 excavations (Area J) comprises 667 sherds weighing 3,026g including rims from 24 vessels. Almost all the sherds are flint-tempered with smaller quantities in sandy and shell-tempered fabrics.

Flint-tempered fabrics form 88% of the total earlier Neolithic assemblage. Three flint fabrics are present, with fine, medium and coarse flint inclusions within a silty clay matrix, the largest flint inclusion being up to 5mm, the median size being 3mm. A further 8% of the sherds are made of sandy fabrics, most containing sparse fine flint pieces and a few are micaceous. The smallest fabric component is the shell-tempered group which contains fine to moderate shell inclusions up to 3mm in a fine clay matrix. The high proportion of flint fabrics is typical of contemporary assemblages from the region being found for example at Haddenham and Eynesbury in Cambridgeshire (Pollard 2006, 63; Mepham 2004, 29) and Hurst Fen, Mildenhall (Clark *et al.* 1960, 228). Shell-tempered Neolithic Bowl has been found at Eynesbury (Mepham 2004, 29).

Rims from 23 bowls and one small, fine cup were found. The undecorated, round-based bowls are a mix of forms, some with ledge-like shoulders, sixteen with

Ceramic date	No. sherds	Weight (g)	% Weight
Undated	124	719	1.2
Neolithic	697	3153	5.4
Early Bronze Age	86	644	1.1
Later prehistoric unspecified	98	459	0.8
Middle Iron Age	88	1015	1.7
Middle or Late Iron Age	287	3719	6.4
Late Iron Age	2573	41213	70.8
Late Iron Age or Early Roman	91	1071	1.8
Roman unspecified	384	5661	9.7
Roman 1st–3rd c.	51	410	0.7
Late Roman	11	145	0.2
Total	**4490**	**58209**	**100.0**

Table 3.16 The entire pottery assemblage, quantified by ceramic date

rolled or folded rims and six with simple, direct round, pointed or flat rims. One example has a thickened rim. The cup is fine, with burnished surfaces and a direct pointed rim. The predominance of unthickened simple or folded rims is similar to the large assemblage from Broome Heath, Norfolk (Wainwright 1972) and comparable to examples found more locally at Eynesbury (Mepham 2004, 30). Vessel form and the absence of decorated Mildenhall pottery suggests a date earlier in the Plain Bowl tradition (Cleal 1992).

The earlier Neolithic pottery was almost all recovered from colluvial layers and buried soils forming the fill of natural hollow 16042 (Pond Q) which produced 91% of the total assemblage by weight, a total of 643 sherds weighing 2,898g including 21 rims.

Late Neolithic to Early Bronze Age (Periods 2.1–2.2)
Fig. 3.13
Aside from the Beaker pottery from pit/shaft 902 (Pit Group 7; detailed by Last, above) relatively little Later Neolithic or Bronze Age pottery was recovered from the site, with the benefit that there is only limited contamination to Middle to Late Iron Age assemblages. Some small coarseware fragments are impossible to date to a particular period but it is assumed that very coarse, poorly fired flint-tempered sherds present in Middle to Late Iron Age deposits were residual, deriving from the limited general Neolithic or Bronze Age activity in the vicinity.

Later Neolithic pottery was found in three Pit Group 4 features (683, 691 and 776) in Area C and three Pit Group 8 features in Area I (4838, 4851 and 5369). Quantities from Pit Group 4 are meagre (24 sherds) and the material is abraded, with an average sherd weight of only 4g. Sherds belonging to a sand-tempered (S1) vessel with an oxidised outer surface were spread within three fills of pit 691; 687, 690, 708. The fabric is friable and poorly-fired and shallow furrows run across the surface in parallel lines. The four sherds in pit 776 (747) came from a pot with a flat base in a fabric tempered with shell, sand and chalk (SHCS). Pit 683 (682) produced a 1g scrap of shell-tempered pottery. Bearing in mind that the

Fabric	Components	Description
C	chalk	
F1	fine flint <1mm	
F2	flint <2mm	
F2I	flint <2mm and ironstone	Type sherd has abundant poorly sorted angular flint grains <2mm, sparse poorly-sorted dark brown rounded ironstone pellets <4mm across, and fine silver mica.
F3	flint <4mm	Type sherd has abundant poorly-sorted angular flint grains <4mm set in a clean clay and readily visible on the surface, with fine silver mica.
F1S	fine flint <1mm + sand	
F2S	flint <2mm + sand	Type sherd has sparse poorly-sorted angular flint grains <2mm and abundant well sorted grey to light brown fine sand inclusions <0.25mm, with fine silver mica.
F3S	flint <4mm + sand	Type sherd contains sparse poorly-sorted angular flint grains <4mm and well-sorted abundant sand inclusions <0.25mm; sometimes sparse rounded light brown grog pellets <0.25mm are present. Surfaces oxidised.
FG	flint + grog	Type sherd contains sparse poorly-sorted angular flint grains <4mm and angular light brown grog pellets <4mm; sometimes sparse rounded and well-sorted sand grains <0.25mm across also present. The fabric is friable and soft with oxidised surfaces.
FSV	flint + sand + vegetable temper	
G1	grog <1mm	Type sherd has fine silver mica and abundant poorly-sorted angular black grog with a few red grog pellets. Rough feel.
G2	grog <2mm	Type sherd has fine silver mica and abundant poorly-sorted angular to rounded light brown to red grog pellets. Soapy feel.
G3	grog pellets ranging from light brown-red-black <3mm	Type sherd has soapy feel with abundant sub-rounded to angular poorly-sorted brown, red and black grog pellets 1.5-3mm in a sand-free clay matrix. Some examples have fine silver mica.
G4	grog + oxidised surfaces	Type sherd is a local copy of an imported beaker from context 2556, has abundant angular to rounded grog in a sand-free matrix. The grog is <1mm across. Even light brown surfaces, grey core. The sherd demonstrates that the potters supplying Hinxton tried to copy oxidised Roman fabrics.
GS1	grog + sand <0.25mm	Type sherd has fine silver mica present, common poorly-sorted angular to rounded red and light grey grog, matrix dominated by rounded sand. More sand than grog. Soapy texture.
GS2	grog + sand <1mm	Type sherd has fine silver mica and well-rounded to rounded sand grains with common rounded grey and brown grog pellets.
GS3	grog + sand <2mm	
GS4	grog + sand + oxidised surfaces	Type sherd has a soapy fracture with sparse black grog <0.25mm across and some rounded grey grog <1mm across in a clay matrix with abundant rounded sand grains <0.25mm across. Surfaces are light brown and there is fine silver mica.
GC	grog + chalk	
GSC	grog + sand + chalk	
GSCI	grog + sand + chalk + ironstone	Type sherd is wheel-thrown and fabric dominated by abundant well-sorted rounded fine sand grains <0.25mm across. Angular and well-sorted black grog pellets <1mm across are sparse to common. Rounded ironstone inclusions and chalk pellets <2mm across scattered sparsely throughout.
GI	grog + ironstone	Type sherd is a Cam.202 wheel-thrown pedestal urn base. A light grey clay matrix with much fine silver mica is dominated by abundant well-sorted angular black grog grains <1mm across, with occasional well-rounded poorly-sorted dark brown to red ironstone pellets <3mm across. The fracture is smooth to soapy.
GSI	grog + sand + ironstone	
S1	sand <0.25mm	Type sherd contains abundant well-sorted rounded grey and brown sand grains <0.25mm across, but no fine mica.
S2	sand <1mm	
S3	sand <2mm	
S4	sand with oxidised surfaces	
SC	sand + chalk	
SCF	sand + chalk + flint	
SCV	sand + chalk + vegetable temper	
SFVI	sand + flint + vegetable temper + ironstone	
SH	shell	
SHS	shell + sand	

Fabric	Components	Description
SHCS	shell + chalk + sand	
SI	sand + ironstone	Homogenous fabric with well-sorted, rounded light grey and light brown sand grains <0.25mm with sparse ironstone pellets <2mm and abundant fine silver mica.
SIC	sand + ironstone + chalk	
SV	sand + vegetable temper	

Table 3.17 Iron Age pottery fabrics

worked flint associated with all of this pottery is Late Neolithic, it is reasonable to classify them broadly as Grooved Ware, although allocation to one of the sub-styles of Grooved Ware is not possible. A slightly more substantial assemblage of 43 sherds was recovered from Pit Group 8, although this displayed an even lower mean sherd weight (2.6g) and was similarly abraded. Unlike the sand-tempered vessels from Pit Group 4 they are made of coarse grog and shell-tempered fabric with numerous voids representing leached out shell inclusions. Several sherds are decorated with shallow incised channels, perhaps suggesting that they belong to the Clacton substyle (Longworth 1971, 237).

A semi-complete but fragmentary Beaker from pit 352 (Area C, Pit Group 12) has a flat base from which a plain (undecorated) wall rises steeply in a straight line. There is a broad mouth to the vessel with a rounded protruding rim; two prominent moulded cordons below are separated by deep grooves stamped obliquely with short parallel impressions (Fig. 3.13, No. 1). Some of the body sherds are rusticated. Although not all of the pot was retrieved, the likelihood is that the pit was a grave, or associated with a grave. A sherd with similar decoration was recovered from fill 708 of pit 691 (Area C, Pit Group 4) (Fig. 3.13, No. 2). Although still in the Beaker tradition and contemporary with the shaft 902 assemblage, these vessels are of interest as rusticated vessels are more commonly associated with domestic deposits such as those found at Hockwold (Bamford 1982, fig. 24, P63.169). While a domestic context may be accepted for the sherd recovered from pit 691 it is unlikely to be the case for the complete Beaker. It is worthy of note that a similar Beaker, with no evidence for cremated remains, was found in a pit (G522) at Biddenham, Bedfordshire (Luke 2008, fig. 6.13) where a ritual deposition has been proposed. In broader terms vessels of this type, decorated with multiple cordons and grooves, are well attested in the Beaker repertoire. In Eastern England, parallels are found from Barham (Kent), Narford (Norfolk), Risby Warren and Stainsby (both Lincolnshire) (Clarke 1970, 291 no.92; Gibson 1982, fig. MET.3 no.12, fig. R.W.18 no.1, and fig. STA.2 no.7). Examples from further afield include vessels from Oxfordshire, Yorkshire, Northumberland, Wales and the Channel Islands (Clarke 1970, 311 no. 240; 316 nos 284 and 288; 317 no. 299, 321 no. 334; 324 no. 355; 342 nos 507–8 and 511; and 343 no. 517).

Three sherds decorated with fingernail or fingertip decoration appear to belong to the earlier prehistoric period, although this decorative technique survived into the Middle Iron Age in Cambridgeshire. A fingernail impressed sherd in fabric F2I found in association with the Beaker from pit 352 may have belonged to a rusticated Beaker and another fingernail-impressed sherd in fabric SI came from Pond G (3206 in Area C). The only fingertip-impressed vessel is represented by seventeen sherds (110g) in coarse flint-tempered ware fabric F3, recovered from layer 838.

A further 30 Beaker sherds (192g) including two rims were recovered during the 2014 excavations (Area J). The majority of these sherds came from pits 15003, 15006, 15040 and 15015 (Structure 1; Pit Groups 15 and 13); the latter producing fourteen sherds (139g) from at least four vessels. The remainder of the Beaker sherds were residual in later features. The Beaker sherds found in Area J mimic those recovered during previous phases and include comb-impressed, tool-impressed and fingertip-impressed decorated examples. The two rims are both direct and rounded and the fabrics sandy with grog and/or flint inclusions. The mix of comb-impressed and fingertip/nail-impressed decorated vessels is typical of non-funerary domestic assemblages found locally at Linton Village College (Percival 2005).

Later prehistoric pottery
Of the pottery assigned to the Iron Age, some 88 sherds (1015g) are of Middle Iron Age character, while a further 287 sherds (3719g) are of Middle or Late Iron Age date. In addition, 2,573 sherds (41,213g) are of Late Iron Age date, while 91 sherds (1071g) are of the Late Iron Age or Early Roman period.

Middle or Late Iron Age

Fabrics
Thirty-seven Iron Age fabrics were recognised amongst the relevant group. Very few of the fabrics are homogenous but the majority incorporate some quantity of fine silver mica, which is rarely altogether absent. The sands in the Hinxton fabrics are generally rounded and appear to be natural (water-worn) components of the clays. Seven fabrics include ironstone, rounded red-brown to red rusty pellets that responded to a magnet.

The only inclusions that might be described as temper in the technical sense are those which do not occur naturally: crushed burnt flint (angular white grains), chopped vegetable matter and grog. Even some of these might have been accidentally introduced by the conditions in which the potter worked (Woudhuysen 1998, 33). Scientific analysis of structural fired clay and loomweights at Iron Age Haddenham showed that bone, grog and flint had been incorporated into the clays as an inadvertent result of preparing them in a domestic setting (Evans and Hodder 2006a, 136–7).

Fabric	Sherd count	Weight (g)
G1	111	1813
G2	36	914
G3	44	2091
G4	207	2062
GC	1	4
GI	27	1873
GS1	173	4015
GS2	42	390
GS3	2	1
GS4	40	774
GSC	2	41
GSCI	4	28
GSI	128	2279
Total grog-tempered	**817**	**16285**
S1	836	11786
S2	282	5287
S3	7	175
S4	195	2024
SC	21	191
SI	332	4636
SIC	19	298
SV	12	123
SH	6	18
SHCS	1	14
Total sand-tempered	**1711**	**24552**

Table 3.18 Middle to Late Iron Age fabric proportions

The fabrics are detailed in Table 3.17. Inclusions are described as sparse if there are fewer than six grains per cm², common if there are six–ten inclusions per cm², and abundant if there are more than ten per cm². Where particular fabrics encompass some variation across individual vessels (or sherds) the description is based on a selected 'type sherd'.

Middle Iron Age pottery in the Cambridgeshire region belongs to a tradition of handmade vessels typically made in sand-tempered fabrics. At Hinxton, some use of flint-tempered potting clay recipes may also have persisted from the earlier prehistoric period. The fabric range of the Hinxton Aylesford-Swarling assemblage tradition is varied but is also dominated by sandy wares. Although grog is the standard 'Belgic' temper in South-Eastern Britain (Thompson 1982, 4, 20) it has been proposed that much of the Cambridgeshire 'Belgic' pottery is sand-tempered instead (Thompson 1982, 17). Resent research has, however, demonstrated that fine grog temper is commonly present although not always visible without thin section analysis (Lyons 2009).

Some 1,711 sherds/24552g (67% by count/60% by weight) of the Late Iron Age pottery is sand-tempered as opposed to grog-tempered, which accounts for only 817 sherds/16285g (32% by count/39% by weight; Table 3.18). The relatively high weight proportion of grog-tempered wares reflects a bias linked to heavy, thick-walled storage jars in this fabric.

Form and decoration

In addition to being handmade in sand-tempered fabrics, Middle Iron Age pottery in the Hinxton and broader Cambridgeshire region is generally largely undecorated. Forms are dominated by round shouldered S-profiled jars and bowls, while rare decoration is largely confined to combing or scoring and finger-impressed zones on the rim or shoulder, the latter treatment ceasing sometime before the Late Iron Age. This type of pottery is found widely across East Anglia, Essex and Hertfordshire, and dates from the end of the 4th century BC (Sealey 1996, 46, 50). In East Anglia and north-east Essex, pottery of Middle Iron Age type remained in use on some settlements until the Roman invasion and beyond (Willis *et al.* 2008, 61). This was the case at Wardy Hill, Cambridgeshire (Hill and Horne 2003, 166), Wendens Ambo, Essex (Hodder 1982, 25), West Stow, Suffolk (West 1990, 63, 68) and Snettisham, Norfolk (Flitcroft 2001, 66).

A protracted overlapping of Middle and Late Iron Age ceramic traditions at the banjo enclosure and settlement site at Caldecote posed just such a problem in framing an Iron Age ceramic chronology for the site (Kenney and Lyons 2011). In fact, the pottery chronology was further confused by the vagaries of a site '...where, after an initial adoption of Aylesford-Swarling pottery, the vogue for this new pottery passed, and an existing Middle Iron Age tradition reasserted itself' (Sealey 2011, 28). Although there is no explicit evidence for a similar stylistic reassertion at Hinxton, the case for a partial retention of conservative, handmade forms at the site seems clear.

Sherds of Middle Iron Age style at Hinxton certainly occur in association with Late Iron Age material, usually as a minor component. Some of this may be residual but it is equally likely that this material is contemporary with the Late Iron Age pottery as it is often represented by large, unabraded sherds with fresh breaks. This suggests an overlap in stylistic and functional preference during a transitional phase from the end of the Middle Iron Age to the early part of the Late Iron Age. The Middle Iron Age style continued in use until it was displaced in the Late Iron Age by Aylesford-Swarling 'Belgic' pottery, but this gradual transition took place at different times in different places.

The three examples of finger-impressed vessels from Hinxton are clearly of earlier prehistoric rather than Early or Middle Iron Age date. Conversely, combing/scoring – a decorative technique which also persisted from the Middle Iron Age well into the Late Iron Age and Early Roman periods – is prolific at the site. An absence of correlation between the finger-impressed and combed decorative traditions may signify that the entire Iron Age assemblage, including the undecorated vessels, is broadly contemporary and that the ceramic sequence represents a relatively brief period dating from the earliest part of the Late Iron Age to the Early Roman period.

Most of the Middle Iron Age style pottery is sand-tempered, suggesting a date towards the end of the period, bearing in mind the generally gradual progression from flint to sand (and other tempers like shell) from the Late Bronze Age through the Iron Age (Rigby 1988, 103). Although there are context groups at Hinxton that consist exclusively of pottery of Middle Iron Age type, some of those groups are likely to have been contemporary with Late Iron Age Aylesford-Swarling 'Belgic' type pottery. It is, on balance, likely that the Middle Iron Age pottery at the settlement does not pre-date the appearance of the first 'Belgic' pottery on the site by a significant margin.

Some evidence gleaned by a correlation of stylistic and stratigraphic factors, however, might arguably allow for a Middle Iron Age settlement inception. Some 297 sherds of pottery weighing 3850g were classified as Middle Iron Age or Middle/Late Iron Age in style. Most were recovered as a residual component in later deposits and represent only 7% by weight of the total prehistoric and Roman assemblage from the site. The ceramic evidence could date the inception of Period 3.1 Trackway 1 to the Middle Iron Age. The total quantity of pottery collected from contexts associated with this feature, which transected Areas C and I, was only 65 sherds (757g), and included no fragments diagnostic of form. However, a considerable element of this group (from ditches 2662, 2437 and 2425) is handmade and in sandy fabrics, several sherds bearing combed grooved or scored decoration. This type of decoration is typically found on jars. Four undecorated sherds in different fabrics (S1, SCV, SV and SC) have burnt organic residues on the sherd interiors, indicating use as cooking vessels. Although some of the pottery from the fills of Trackway 1 ditches, including seven grog-tempered sherds, is consistent with a later Iron Age date, a preponderance of Middle Iron Age traits in this assemblage is interesting.

A sizeable collection of pottery with Middle Iron Age characteristics was recovered from the fills of two tree throws located on the west of the river in the parish of Ickleton (tree throws 18 and 20 in Area H; not illus.). Fill 19 of feature 20 yielded some 125 sherds of pottery (1,423g), of which the great majority (18 sherds/1,362g) are in sandy ware S1 and another sherd (3g) in S4. Fragments of a jar/bowl with gently everted rim and a globular jar, both in fabric S1, are Middle Iron Age in tradition. Single sherds in vegetable-tempered ware (SV) and chalk-tempered ware (C) could also be Middle Iron Age, and the few remaining grog-tempered sherds possibly intrusive. This context assemblage may, therefore, represent a secure Middle Iron Age deposit. Feature 18 also produced a notable number of body sherds in sandy fabrics, some with combed decoration, but these represent only about 10% of the feature group, which is dominated by grog-tempered wares, suggesting that they may have been residual.

Vessel fragments of Middle Iron Age style in relatively good condition were found in superficial deposits in Area C, perhaps indicating recent displacement from their original provenance. Surface cleaning of context 732 yielded two globular vessels in fabric S1, both of which had been modified by drilling perforations (Fig. 3.13, No. 3). Surface layer 796 produced a cordoned jar that is probably pre-Belgic along with an S-profile jar in sandy ware S2, also of typical Middle Iron Age type (Fig. 3.13, Nos 4 and 5).

One pottery group from ditch 40, Trench 14 (1998 evaluation) contained a potentially important group of Middle to Late Transitional Iron Age pottery. The lowest fill of the ditch (19) contained handmade pottery only including two rims – one of them joins

with a sherd from the top fill 17, showing that the three contexts in the ditch accumulated over a short space of time. Two large combed S1 sherds have burnt residues on the interior. The combing is shallow and irregular, reminiscent of the style of combing found in another assemblage transitional between the Middle and Late Iron Age, from Gatesbury Track, Hertfordshire (Partridge 1980, fig. 36 no. 1, fig. 37, no. 6). Very little grog is present in the pottery fabrics found. A vessel base in Fabric S1 has four perforations up to 10mm in diameter cut before firing. Another S1 sherd has a lattice pattern marked on the surface by burnishing.

The middle fill (18) contained many sherds of the combed storage jar in a grog-tempered fabric with oxidised surface; sherds from the same vessel were also present in the upper fill (17). The latter contained significant quantities of grog-tempered pottery, most of which came from two large storage jars. One is plain; the other has a combed outer surface with a red (oxidised finish). The context is early, earlier than those with imported table crockery and so in this instance the taste for oxidised surfaces cannot clearly be related to Roman influence, however much that might have been a factor in later contexts. Late Iron Age storage jars with oxidised surfaces have also been reported from Cambridge. Looking at the assemblage in its entirety, there is only one sherd that shows definite signs of production of a wheel. A sherd with a thick burnt residue on the interior comes from the same pot as the S1 sherds with burnt residues from the bottom fill (19). A rim from this top fill joins a rim from bottom fill.

The 2014 excavations (Area J) produced a further 71 sherds (702g) of pottery dating to the later Iron Age (350 BC onwards). The small assemblage includes rims from three vessels, all jars with direct, rounded rim endings, upright necks and slack-shoulders above ovoid bodies. All the sherds are in sandy fabrics, some with sparse shell or mica inclusions. The sherds were mostly recovered from the fills of four pits (15031, 15032, 15036 and 15066), the majority from pit 15066 (Pit Group 28) which contained 51 sherds weighing 554g including two rims and which was associated with a radiocarbon date indicating deposition during the 4th or 3rd century BC (Appendix 2; SUERC-64620). Later Iron Age sherds were also found during machine stripping of subsoil/colluvial layers in Area J, and from the uppermost deposit (15695) infilling Pond Q, whilst a single small sherd (3g) was found within the 'silt' deposit (15451) associated with the Terminal Palaeolithic flint scatter in Pond P.

Late Iron Age
Pottery of Late Iron Age type in the 'Belgic' tradition dominates the Hinxton assemblage, with 2,573 sherds (41,213g) accounting for 57.3% by sherd count and 70.8% by weight of the site total. Castle Hill in Cambridge is the only other Cambridgeshire site to have produced 'Belgic' pottery in comparable quantities, although the data on sherd counts and weights is not available in the published report (Farrar *et al.* 1999). This makes the Hinxton pottery all the more important because it provides an opportunity to quantify the incidence of Aylesford-Swarling type material on a Late Iron Age site in East Anglia where it was present in sizeable quantities.

The pottery from Late Iron Age Enclosures 1 and 2
by Lisa Brown
Fig. 3.14

Combined, the ditches making up Enclosure 1 in Area D, despite being heavily truncated by the recut of Enclosure 2, yielded a moderately large assemblage of 584 sherds weighing 9,291g. This group includes only a single import, a 10g sherd of Campanian 'black sand' amphora (CAT AM; Tomber and Dore 1998, 91, 230 no. 67), a type imported into Britain between the late 1st century BC and the late 2nd century AD. It came from high up in the fill sequence, from context 1538 of cut 1541, forming part of the south-east corner of the enclosure. A single freshly broken, large fragment (151g) of Nene Valley colour-coated ware came from the northern arm of the enclosure (ditch 2685): this can be no earlier in date than mid-2nd century AD and may be intrusive. A small fragment of East Midlands Scored Ware in fabric SV (Fig. 3.14, No. 13) from ditch 2589 is an import from the west of the county, a type that reached as far west as Shropshire, perhaps serving as specialist containers for cheese (Elsdon 1992, 84).

Otherwise, the pottery from Enclosure 1 is essentially Late Iron Age (or 'Belgic') in style, but produced in native wares. Sandy wares dominate this group, accounting for 69% by count and 59% by weight of the Enclosure 1 total, in contrast to 29%/39% grog-tempered wares. A few sherds specifically diagnostic of form were present, and amongst the classifiable vessels from ditch 1541 (fill 1538) is a necked storage jar in fabric SI, another storage jar sherd in G1 (Fig. 3.13, No. 7); two native copies of Gallo-Belgic beakers in fabric S4, one just the base (Fig. 3.13, No. 9), one with combed decoration (Fig. 3.13, No. 6); a pedestal base fragment in fabric G1; a highly burnished necked jar in fabric S4 (Fig. 3.13, No. 8); and a quoit-shaped base of Cam 203 form (type A4, Thompson 1984, 53) in fabric S1.

Fill 2682 of ditch 2589 yielded a narrow-necked, cordoned storage jar in fabric GS1 (Fig. 3.13, No. 10); a necked, cordoned bowl in fabric GS1 (Fig. 3.13, No. 11) and a cordoned jar in the same fabric (Fig. 3.13, No. 12), as well as the East Midlands sherd.

Ditch 2685 also contained a few diagnostic sherds, including two quoit-shaped bases from pedestal jars in fabrics G4 resembling Cam 202 forms (type A1, Thompson 1984, 35) and another in fabric S1; the base of a Belgic beaker copy in fabric S1 and a comb-decorated beaker sherd in fabric GS4; a necked bowl or jar with cordon at base of neck in fabric S1 (Fig. 3.14, No. 14); and a burnished quoit-shaped pedestal base in fabric SV.

A considerable quantity of pottery was found in features relating to the recut of the enclosure (Enclosure 2); some 1003 sherds (18,123g), representing 27% by count/33% by weight of the site total and 40%/44% of the total of Late Iron Age pottery. Only two imported vessels were identified. A small body sherd of a DR7-11 'salazon' amphora (Cam 186), manufactured in Cadiz (Tomber and Dore 1998, CADAM, 87), recovered from ditch 2557 (fill 2556), is a type manufactured from the late 1st century BC to the early 2nd century AD. It may have been in limited circulation in Britain in the pre-Conquest period (Tyers 1999, 99). The only other obvious import is a Cam 113 butt beaker of Neronian to early Flavian type from fill 3065 of ditch

3062. The ditch was not excavated to the base in this area, meaning that no datable material was available from the earlier sequence.

Two Braughing jars came from some of the higher fills of Enclosure 2 ditches, one in fabric S1 from fill 3065 (ditch 3062) (Fig. 3.15, No. 25), the other in fabric S2 from fill 1935 (ditch 1931). Elsewhere Braughing jars have been found in both funerary and domestic contexts. In the King Harry Lane cemetery there were twenty pots with horizontal combed decoration, from nineteen graves (Stead and Rigby 1989, Graves 14, 19, 21, 47, 55, 104, 106, 118, 1221, 127, 154, 202, 224, 287, 289, 317, 427, 459 and 471) – none of them combed all the way from shoulder to base. It seems that Braughing jars in particular (which are combed from shoulder to base) were deliberately not selected for inclusion in Late Iron Age graves there. Much the same was the case at Stansted Airport, where on the LTCP site 15 Braughing jars were present in settlement contexts but only one from a cemetery context (Cooke et al. 2008, 100). Rigby (1989, 187) also notes that what she describes as 'combed cooking pots' are rare in Iron Age graves but established themselves as regular components of funerary assemblages by the early 2nd century AD in Hertfordshire.

The remainder of the Enclosure 2 assemblage consists of local pottery, including native copies of Gallo-Belgic vessels in sandy fabrics (85%/71% wt) and grog-tempered wares (30%/47% wt). The group includes cordoned bowls, Aylesford-Swarling jars, beakers and storage jars, a vessel composition typical of this part of the world.

The most common classifiable vessels from Enclosure 2 ditches are necked bowls/jars and storage jars. A dozen storage jars, most in grog-tempered fabrics, were represented by fragments scattered within the fills of ditches 3062, 2557, 1931, 1509 and 1569 (Figs 3.14–3.15, Nos 18, 21, 23). Some were enhanced with cordons and/or combed decoration. At least eleven necked bowls were identified, some of them with cordons at the juncture between the neck and shoulder and some with combed decoration (Figs 3.14–3.16, Nos 15, 17, 30, 33). Again, the fabric range was restricted to varieties of sandy and grog-tempered wares.

The Gallo-Belgic range includes several beakers, predominantly in sandy wares, although half a dozen grog-tempered examples were recovered. For the most part, beakers are represented only by body sherds, in some cases with cordons or rouletted and/or impressed decoration surviving. Fill 3068 of Enclosure 2 ditch 2557 produced a native copy of Gallo-Belgic rouletted beaker in Fabric SI (Fig. 3.15, No. 27). A Cam 212 copy in fabric S1 with prominent cordons (Fig. 3.15, No. 28) came from fill 2732 of ditch 3034 and a grog-tempered copy of a terra rubra beaker with unusual decoration mimicking rouletting, but applied with a comb, came from fill 3065 of ditch 3062 (Fig. 3.14, No. 16). A similar decorative treatment applied with a comb observed on a handmade cup or bowl from Caldecote is thought to be an import from Lincolnshire, where there are several parallels (Sealey 2011, 28, fig. 8, no. 18; Arthur 2004, 160, fig. 108; Gregory and Elsdon 1996, 509). Iron Age potters were quite capable of applying rouletted decoration: square-tooth rouletting (for instance) is found on a native handmade pot in

98

Form	Fabric	Decoration	No.
Beaker	S1	Cordons	1
Beaker	S4		4
Beaker	S4	Roulette	1
Beaker	S4	Roulette/impressed	2
Beaker	SI	Cordon	1
Beaker	SI	Roulette	1
Beaker	GSI		2
Beaker	GS4	Roulette	4
Beaker	S1 red ware	Roulette	1
CAM 113 Butt beaker	X		1
Platter	S1		1
Puzzle pot	GS1		1
Pedestal urn base CAM 201	S1		1
Pedestal urn base CAM 202	G1		1
Pedestal urn base CAM 202	GS1		1
Pedestal urn base CAM 203	S1		1
Cordoned jar	GS1	Cordon	1
Cordoned jar	S1	Cordons	1
Cordoned jar	SI	Cordons	2
Cordoned jar	GS1	Cordons	1
Ovoid jar	S2	Combed/groove	1
Necked jar	S1	Cordons	1
Necked jar	S2		1
Necked jar	SI		2
Necked jar	SIC		1
Necked jar	GS1	Comb	1
Necked bowl	S1		3
Necked bowl	S1	Cordon	3
Necked bowl	S2	Cordon	2
Necked bowl	S4		3
Necked bowl	SI	Cordon	1
Necked bowl	G4		4
Necked bowl	GS1	Cordon	1
Necked jar/bowl	SI		2
Necked jar/bowl	SI		1
Necked jar/bowl	GS1		1
E Midlands Scored	SV	Scored	1
Braughing jar	S1	Combed	2
Braughing jar	S2	Comb/groove	1
Storage jar	S1		3
Storage jar	S1	Combed	1
Storage jar	S4		1
Storage jar	SI		1
Storage jar	G1		4
Storage jar	G2		2
Storage jar	G3	Combed	1
Storage jar	G4	Combed	2

Form	Fabric	Decoration	No.
Storage jar	GI	Combed/groove	2
Storage jar	GS1		1
Storage jar	GS1	Cordons	1
Storage jar	GS2		1
Storage jar	GS4		1

Table 3.19 Forms by fabric, decoration and number of vessels from Enclosure 2

the Henderson Collection from Skeleton Green in Hertfordshire (Partridge 1981, fig. 130, no. 52, 349).

Other native beaker copies came from fill 2732 of ditch 3034 (Fig. 3.15, No. 29) and fill 3063 of Ditch 3062 (Fig. 3.14, No. 22). Biddulph (2007, 224–5) drew attention to a small but important group of grog-tempered pottery with red surfaces from north Essex which includes butt beakers of forms Cam 115-15 and what appears to be imitation terra rubra. The only copy of a terra nigra platter from the site – conjoining fragments in fabric S1 – was recovered from fills 2556 and 3068, which were high up in the fill sequence on the south side of the ditch 2557 (Fig. 3.15, No. 29).

A quoit-shaped base of a native pedestal base copying CAM 202 in GS1, from fill 3065 of ditch 3062, resembles Thompson's type A1 (1984, 35) (Fig. 3.14, No. 20). Another pedestal base, this one sandy and from ditch 1509, may be a copy of a Cam 264 type jar. A neckless cordoned jar in fabric S1, possibly a pedestal jar minus its base, was found in the same fill (Fig. 3.14, No. 19).

Also from ditch 3062 is a very unusual vessel, a grog-tempered campaniforme pot with an open top and multiple small perforations (Fig. 3.15, No. 24). The perforations were cut pre-firing in this case, but some of the Hinxton vessels, necked bowls in particular, were perforated post-firing. Perforations cut in Late Iron Age pots post-firing are particularly common in Hertfordshire. The reason for this modification is unclear but Partridge (1989, 189 no. 113) suggested that the largest examples might have made the pot suitable for use as a bee skep (hive). A storage jar base in fabric GS4 from ditch 1569 and another smaller base in SI from ditch 2539 had multiple post-firing perforations.

In this region of England, the Late Iron Age pottery styles did not develop organically from the Middle Iron Age tradition that preceded them, but represent a radical new departure introduced from elsewhere. The tradition is dominated by the Aylesford-Swarling or 'Belgic' pottery widely found in north Kent, Essex, south Suffolk, Hertfordshire and parts of neighbouring counties. This distinctive typology includes pedestal urns, massive storage jars with thickened rims, Beakers and necked bowls and jars. Vessels are generally wheel-thrown, often enhanced with cordons, combed decoration or corrugated zones. Pedestal or foot-ring bases, sometimes of an exaggerated 'quoit-shape' are common. Vessel shapes are variable, with no apparent preference for either rounded or angular elements, but the necked bowls and jars, ovoid jars, beakers and cups and platters derive from ceramic traditions of Northern Gaul.

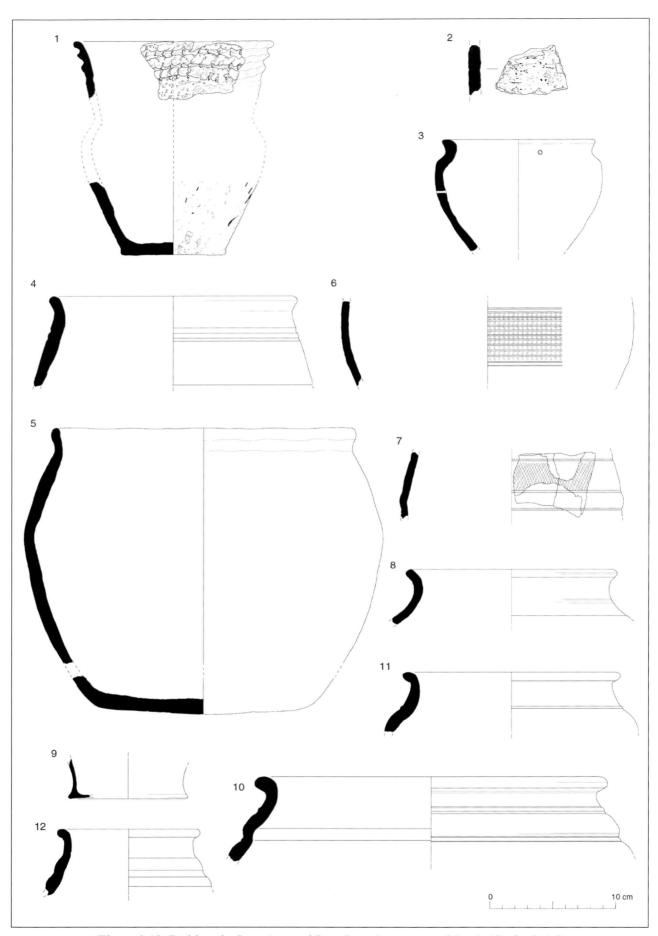

Figure 3.13 Prehistoric, Iron Age and Late Iron Age pottery (Nos 1–12). Scale 1:3

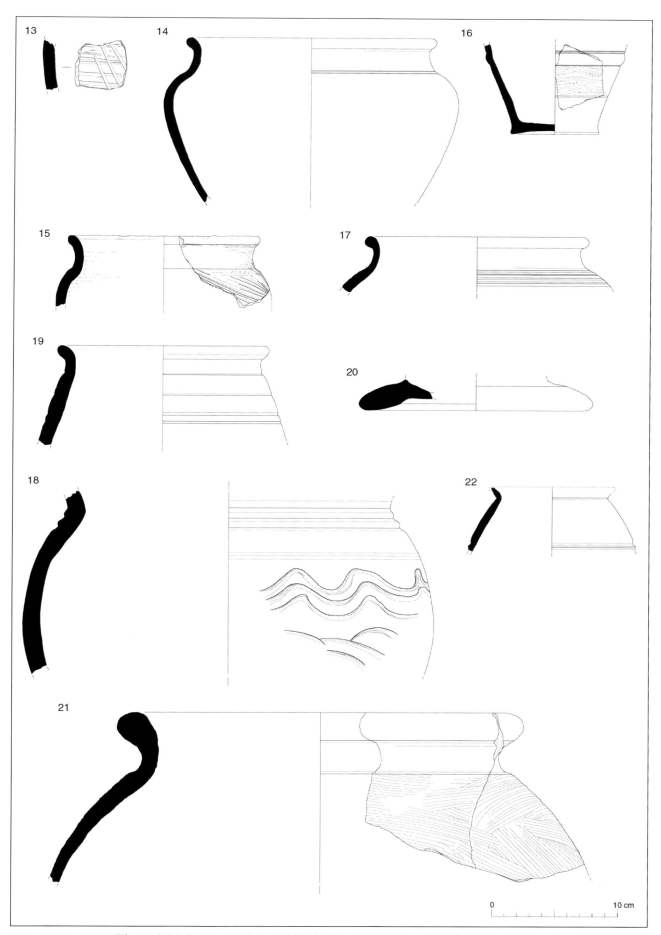

Figure 3.14 Late Iron Age and Early Roman pottery (Nos 13–22). Scale 1:3

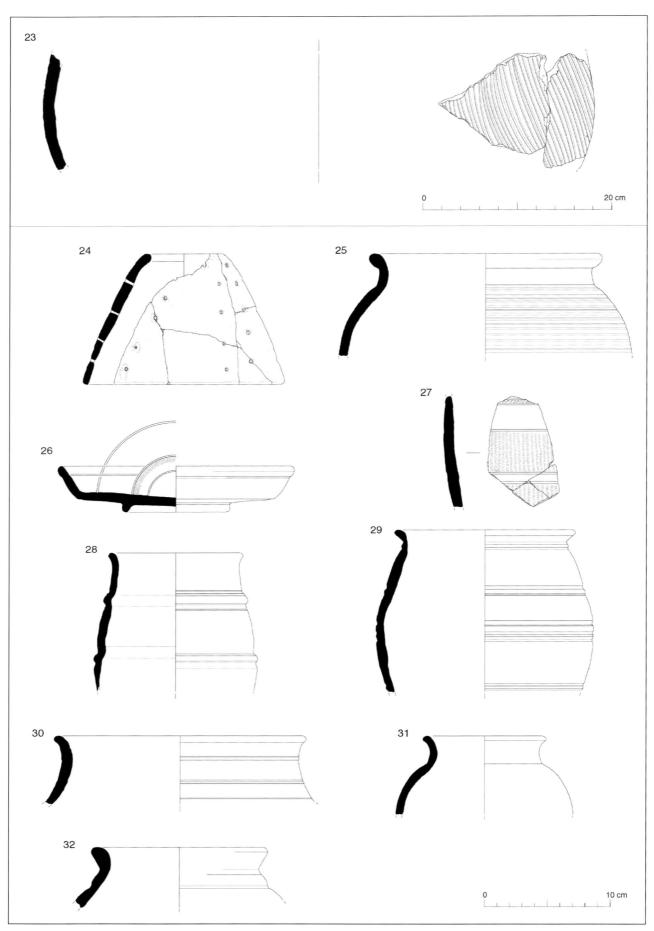

Figure 3.15 Late Iron Age and Early Roman pottery (Nos 23–32). Scale 1:3 and Scale 1:4 (No. 23)

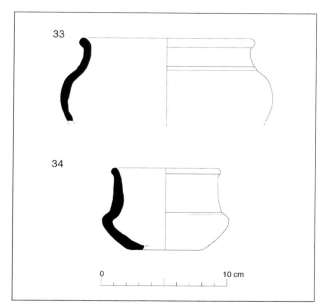

Figure 3.16 Late Iron Age and Early Roman pottery
(Nos 33–34). Scale 1:3

Form and decoration

The most commonly occurring forms in the Hinxton
Late Iron Age assemblage are necked bowls/jars (26
individual vessels) and storage jars (21 individual
vessels). Beakers are also very common (18 vessels).
The combing on Aylesford-Swarling pottery
sometimes has broad and shallow grooves separated
by the slightest of ridges. The grooves can be up to
4mm wide on storage jars. The 'Belgic' pottery at
Hinxton often has decoration formed by wiping the
exterior surface with a wide comb in overlapping,
curved, lines. This is a Hertfordshire, rather than
an Essex feature of Aylesford-Swarling pottery and
suggests that the Hinxton pottery and potters were
ultimately of Hertfordshire origin. Table 3.19 presents
each broad vessel class by fabric, decoration (where
present) and number of individual vessels.

Roman pottery

The quantities of Romano-British pottery recovered
from the site are modest. None of the groups is
large, and many consist of fewer than five sherds.
There are many contexts dated as Late Iron Age or
Early Roman that are difficult to date more precisely
because of the small numbers of Roman sherds within
an overwhelmingly native assemblage. In some of
these cases the Roman sherds were recovered from
the top fills of features. There is no indication in the
Roman pottery that the community using it was of
significant or exceptional status. It is difficult to date
the material with any precision because contexts are
small and many of the sherds consist of anonymous
sandy grey ware. There are some samian sherds and
a (very) few Nene Valley colour-coated scraps. Only
one Late Roman group could be identified, a small
assemblage of less than five sherds from gully 5053
in Area I, which produced an Oxfordshire mortarium
and a flanged bowl dated c.AD 250–410 +.

Illustration catalogue

Pits and deposits in Area C
Fig. 3.13
1   Late Neolithic/Early Bronze Age **Beaker** with slashed rim
     and moulded cordons. Fabric F3. Pit Group 12. Pit 352, fill
     351, Period 2.2.
2   Abraded Late Neolithic/Early Bronze Age **Beaker** sherd
     decorated with horizontal grooves. Fabric F3. Pit Group 4.
     Pit 691, fill 708, Period 2.1.
3   Handmade globular **bowl** with post-firing perforations near
     rim and on body. Fabric S1. Unstratified (surface cleaning
     732)
4   Handmade ovoid cordoned **jar**. Surface layer 796
     (ungrouped). Probably pre Belgic.
5   Handmade S-profile **jar** with short everted rim. Fabric S2.
     Surface layer 796 (ungrouped). Middle Iron Age type.

Enclosure 1 (Area D, Period 3.1)
Figs 3.13–3.15
Ditch 1541
6   Native copy of Gallo-Belgic **Beaker** with combed
     decoration. Fabric S4. Fill 1538.
7   Rim of wheel-thrown or wheel-finished storage **jar**. Fabric
     G1. Fill 1538.
8   Necked **jar**. Fabric S4, Burnished. Fill 1538.
9   Base of Gallo-Belgic **Beaker** copy. Fabric S4. Fill 1538.
Ditch 2589
10   Narrow-necked storage **jar** with a swollen everted rim
     and two prominent cordons on the shoulder. Fabric GS1.
     Wheel-thrown. Fill 2682.
11   Necked **bowl** with cordon at base of neck. Fabric GS1.
     Wheel-thrown. Fill 2682.
12   Cordoned, neckless **jar**. Fabric GS1. Wheel-thrown. Fill.
     2682.
13   Sherd of East Midlands Scored Ware with tramline
     decoration. Import. Fabric SV. Fill 2682.
Ditch 2685
14   Necked **bowl** or **jar** with cordon at base of neck. Fabric S1.
     Fill 2696.

Enclosure 2 (Area D, Period 3.1)
Figs. 3.14–3.16
Ditch 2557=3062
15   Wheel-thrown necked **jar** with expanded rim, decorated
     with oblique combing. Fabric GS1. Fill 2556=3065.
16   Native copy of terra rubra **beaker** with faux roulette
     decoration applied by two combs. Fabric GS4. Fill
     2556=3065
17   Necked **jar** with horizontal combing/rilling on shoulder.
     Fabric S2. Fill 2556=3065.
18   Storage **jar** with cordons at neck and combed and curvilinear
     grooved decoration. Fabric S1. Fill 2556=3065.
19   Neckless cordoned ovoid **jar** with short rounded rim. Fabric
     S1. Fill 2556=3065.
20   Quoit-shaped native **pedestal base** copying CAM 202
     form (Thompson Type A1, 1984, 35). Fabric GS1. Fill
     2556=3065.
Ditch 3062
21   Storage **jar** with combing on shoulder. Fabric G1. Fill 3063.
22   Native copy of imported **beaker**. Fabric GS1. Fill 3063.
23   Large storage **jar** with extensive combing. Fabric G3. Fill
     3065.
24   Campaniforne **vessel** with open top and multiple small
     perforations. Puzzle pot? Fabric GS1. Fill 3065.
25   Braughing **jar** with combed decoration. Wheel-thrown.
     Fabric S1. Fill 3065.

Ditch 2557
26   Native copy of imported terra nigra **platter**. Fabric S1. Fill
     3068 (conjoining sherds in Ditch 2557, fill 2556).
27   Native copy of Gallo-Belgic rouletted **beaker**. Fabric S1. Fill
     3068.
Ditch 3034
28   Native copy of an imported Gallo-Belgic **beaker** CAM 212
     with prominent cordons. Fabric S1. Fill 2732.
29   Native copy of Gallo-Belgic imported cordoned **beaker**.
     Fabric S1. Fill 2732.
30   Wheel-thrown cordoned **jar** with everted rim. Fabric S1. Fill
     2732.

31   Wheel-thrown necked **jar**. Fabric SIC. Fill 2732.
Ditch 1903
32   Wheel-thrown neckless **jar** with cordon below rim. Fabric GS1. Fill 1926.
33   Wheel-thrown necked **bowl** with cordon at base of neck. Fabric GS1. Fill 1928.
Ditch 126, Area A
34   Necked **bowl** with pronounced shoulder similar to CAM 214B (Thompson 1984, type E1–4). Complete profile. Fabric S1. Context 126 (=cut number)

VIII. Ceramic building material
by Phil Copleston, Carole Fletcher and Alice Lyons

Introduction
Ceramic building material (CBM) was recovered from most of the excavation areas, comprising a small, fragmentary and abraded assemblage of Roman and post-medieval material (weighing 46.117kg), the majority of which (*c.*64% by weight) is Roman. Its poor condition reflects the fact that the material was not directly associated with *in situ* buildings. It was consistently weighed but not all fragments were counted. The post-Roman material is discussed in Part II.

Fabrics and forms
All of the Roman fragments contain quartz sand and there are some shelly fabrics. A small quantity of non-local shell-tempered tile was found; this is not an uncommon find in the Midlands and is generally thought to originate from the Harrold industries in Bedfordshire (Zeepvat 1987, 118). This tile type dates from the Middle to Late Roman period (Hylton and Williams 1996, 154). Some of the CBM is also tempered with mica, typical of Essex-based production. A few fragments contain very coarse inclusions, such as flint, chalk and grog. The flint and chalk are typical inclusions in many Roman and later ceramics manufactured in the East Anglian region. The range of colours (orange, orange-brown, red and greys) and hardness all fall within the range anticipated of typical Roman fabrics.

The following forms were identified:
Tegula: flat roof tile, with upward facing side flanges and interlocks each end to secure the tile when overlapped;
Imbrex: cover-tile over tegulae flanges, curved and slightly tapered in section, and overlapped;
Roof ridge: similar to imbrex but generally larger in section and not tapered;
Pedalis: square shaped tile (1 Roman foot on each side), used for wall string courses, floor coverings and stacked for constructing hypocaust *pilae* (floor support columns);
Bipedalis: large, thick, square shaped tile (2 Roman feet on each side), used as floor coverings, particularly to span the gap between *pilae*;
Flat tile: flat tile fragments in Roman fabrics, but otherwise exact form unidentified.

No decorated tiles were found, although a few tally marks were observed on the upper surfaces of some *tegulae*. Such marks are very common in most assemblages. A few fragments show evidence for surface colour wash (dark grey-brown, dark grey, and cream) and some have accreted mortar. A single tile in a shelly fabric has a nail hole which was formed before firing, although the position of this in relation to the edge or corner of the tile is not known.

Discussion
This assemblage is typical of many redeposited Roman tile and brick assemblages. Although none of it can be dated precisely, the group is consistent with a Middle to Late Roman date. The majority of the material was almost certainly produced fairly locally, although the presence of mica in some fragments suggests that at least some was produced in Essex, while the shelly tile may have been imported from Bedfordshire.

No evidence for masonry buildings was identified at Hinxton and the small and fragmentary nature of the brick and tile assemblage suggests that this material may have been brought to the site (by the farming community) as hard core to be laid within muddy gateways or to repair trackways. The presence of the ceramic building material does, however, confirm that there were substantial Roman buildings in the surrounding area.

From the character of the assemblage, it can be stated that a building (or buildings) with a tiled roof and some areas of tiled floor was constructed nearby. The presence of *bipedalis* in association with *pedalis* and unidentified flat tile may also suggest a hypocaust (heated) floor. The *pedalis* or flat tile was commonly utilised to construct *pilae*, as well as generally being used as string courses within walls or for facing wall surfaces. There was no evidence for heated walls through the use of box flue tiles, although the small size of the assemblage may account for this. No other building materials (such as painted wall plaster or *tesserae*) were found. It is possible that the excavated assemblage originated from the Roman town of Great Chesterford which lies less than 1km to the southeast of Hinxton, although a villa is known to have existed in the parish of Ickleton and others (yet to be discovered) may also lie close by (see Chapter 1).

IX. Fired clay objects
by Alice Lyons, Sarah Percival and Ted Levermore

Loomweight
The remains of a triangular loomweight fragment (SF 913; nine pieces, weighing 184g) were found within the upper ditch fills in the south-east corner of Enclosure 2 (ditch recut 1509 (1752)). The clay is tempered with chalk and flint pieces and has smoothed surfaces, but no other diagnostic features remain. Triangular loomweights of this type were relatively common in the Late Iron Age in this region (Duncan and Mackreth 2005, 126; Etté and Lucas 2006, 197–201) and reflect wool processing and related production (Dawson 2005, 135).

Pottery kiln demolition debris
Three objects associated with pottery production were found in the southern ditch of Enclosure 2 (ditches 2557 and 3062), two of which are fragmentary pieces of kiln superstructure (one weighing 249g and the other 393g). The clay has been mixed with a chalk temper and has smoothed surfaces; one piece has two ?decorative incised lines. Produced in a similar fabric and therefore probably contemporary with the kiln material was a fragmentary (200g) square-sectioned 'cigar shaped' kiln bar (Swan 1984, 63–4; Lyons 2008, 57–9). Combined, these pieces were almost certainly

associated with an Early Roman pre-Flavian pottery kiln, of which no trace was found, which used portable kiln furniture (Swan 1984, 68–9, figs VIII and IX). This kiln type has been found elsewhere in Cambridgeshire (Willis *et al.* 2008, 72–3) and, although the corpus of known examples is growing, is still relatively scarce.

Oven debris
A fragment of possible oven superstructure in chalky fabric and a small fragment of possible hearth lining in dense sandy fabric with no visible inclusions were recovered from Iron Age pit 15032 (Pit Group 27) in Area J.

X. Worked stone
by Stephen Kemp, Alice Lyons, Sarah Percival and Christine Howard-Davis

Introduction
Twenty pre-Anglo-Saxon stone objects came from Areas A–E, with a further seven from Area H and thirty from Area J. The raw materials for most of the Iron Age and Roman objects (made from flint, sandstone or limestone) could have been sourced from the site's environs and probably came from the exposed alluvial terraces of the River Cam. Many of the items are unstratified, consisting of utilised pebbles or cobbles that were perhaps used in a domestic setting as rubbing stones or hearth surrounds (several are burnt). Others may have been used as surfacing or hard-core along the trackways and enclosure entrances. Much of the worked stone assemblage shows signs of reuse and secondary working.

Floor tile
Two fragments of sandstone fashioned into small tablet shapes were found on the eastern side of the river (Area H); one of the surfaces is smooth and the pieces resemble small floor tiles.

Hearth material
Worthy of note are the six large fragments of burnt sandstone, which probably originated from one or more hearths. These all derived from Enclosures 1 and 2; several were found in the (northern) terminal of the entrance into the enclosure, suggesting that they may have formed part of a deliberate deposit. No traces of working survived on the surfaces of these stones.

Hammerstones
Four sandstone hammerstones, found in both round and elongated forms, reflect the flint knapping that is known to have occurred in the vicinity (Bishop and Donnelly, above). Two of these objects came from the natural streams and ponds (*e.g.* Pond R, 675, in Area B) which were used in the Neolithic period as repositories for large quantities of flint-knapping waste. The remaining two hammerstones were found as residual objects in Late Iron Age and Roman deposits.

Millstones
A large fragment of a coarse Old Red Sandstone millstone from a small millstone with a diameter in excess of 600mm is probably part of an upper stone.

The rim survives, as does part of the grinding surface. The upper surface has two short but deep grooves running across the surface that may indicate it was reused as a sharpening stone after it had broken.

Quernstones
It is notable that, given the size and scope of the excavations, relatively few querns were found on the site. This must reflect the fact that little direct evidence for settlement (*e.g.* roundhouses) prior to the Anglo-Saxon occupation has yet been found at Hinxton and that cereal preparation was taking place elsewhere. Several examples, however, constructed of non-local stone (and showing signs of secondary use) were retrieved.

Vesicular lava
Two small fragments of lava were recovered, from separate contexts. One is fine textured, while the second has a more granular texture. The vesicular basalt is commonly given a Rhineland provenance (Kemp 2007, 69). Both pieces are obviously abraded, on the smoother fragment no dressed or worn surface could be identified – the piece is very worn and rounded. The second more granular fragment has a small area of flat surface that may be the remnants of a dressed surface. The small size of these fragments may suggest that at some stage they were (re)used as smaller rubbing stones.

Millstone Grit
Five fragments of Millstone Grit were recovered, of which two are very abraded and retain no traces of a dressed or polished surface, although two others retain a small area of polished surface, the remains of the grinding surface. All of these fragments are decayed and in poor condition. The final fragment, the largest surviving piece of gritstone is obviously part of a rotary quern and retains both its worn and polished grinding surface and its dressed upper surface. Part of the central spindle hole also survives.

Other stone
A large fragment of Basalt, glacially derived was excavated from Period 3.2 pit 312 (Pit Group 20) in Area A. The stone is irregular in shape but may have been worked in antiquity. The larger face appears somewhat curved as if used as a grinding surface, possibly as a saddle quern; the surface however is not particularly polished. The reverse of the stone also appears to have undergone some modification with some evidence of polishing.

Another possible saddle quern fragment, formed from a utilised quartzitic boulder, was collected from Period 3.2 pit 15032 (Pit Group 27) in Area J, which also contained Iron Age pottery. No grinding surface survives, although the dished profile and wear to the object's base suggest that it might be a quern. Similar improvised saddle querns, found at Bob's Wood, Hinchingbrooke, are of Early to Middle-Iron Age date (Sarah Percival, pers. obs.).

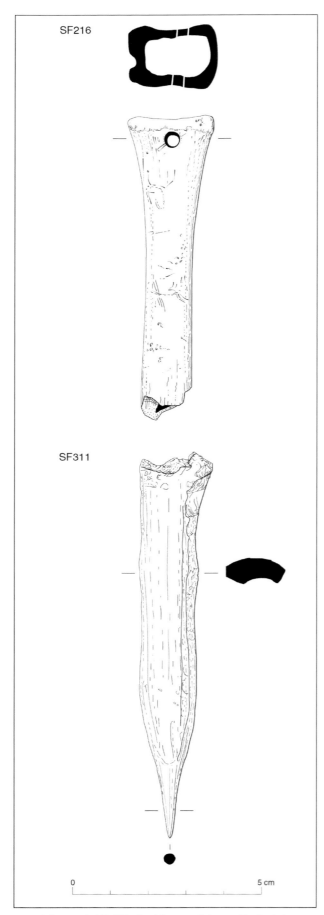

SF216

SF311

0   5 cm

Figure 3.17 Worked bone objects. Scale 1:1

XI. Worked bone
by Ian Riddler and Nicola Trzaska-Nartowski
Fig. 3.17

Awls

A bone awl recovered from a backfill of an Anglo-Saxon sunken-featured building (SFB) in Area I (see Clarke *et al.* forthcoming) is of later prehistoric date. It has been cut from a segment of the midshaft of a cattle-sized long bone, which has been trimmed at one end to provide a sharp point of circular section. There are traces of use-wear at the point, in the form of faint lateral lines forming a slightly corrugated and highly polished surface. Awls are defined by the presence of a sharp point, which is either indented from the main body of the implement, as here, or widens progressively from the tip. They are customarily separated into two groups by size, the larger form exceeding 75mm in length (Bulleid and Grey 1917, 430; Seager Smith 2000, 224 and fig. 89). This implement belongs to the larger group, which is the more common type. Earlier Bronze Age examples tend to retain the distal end of the bone, often including the condyles, whilst the particular form seen here belongs to the Iron Age type and falls into Danebury Class 3, defined as 'bone splinters which vary in size and character', each with a sharp, indented point (Sellwood 1984, 387; Poole 1991, fig 7.33). Sellwood (1984, 387–9) noted that awls of this type may have been used on textiles or leather, where the shape of the point would not create undue friction or leave a large hole. A bone awl from Eldon's Seat in Dorset forms a close parallel for the form of the object (Cunliffe and Phillipson 1968, pl. V).

Illustration catalogue

SF 311 Complete bone **awl**, cut from the midshaft area of a cattle-sized long bone, close to an articular end, and faceted to form a tapered, indented sharp point of circular section at one end. Point is highly polished. L: 105.9mm; W: 19.4mm. HINGEC11 (Area I), SFB 4630, fill 4660. Later prehistoric.

Small pointed blade

A fragmentary small pointed blade (SF 216) was found in the fill of Period 3.1 Trackway 1 ditch in Area C. It has been cut from the lower part of an ovicaprid tibia, with the distal end hollowed and perforated laterally. The upper section of the implement has fractured away but the presence of a lateral perforation close to the distal end, passing through the anterior and posterior faces, suggests that it was originally hafted. Implements of this type have often been described as 'gouges' but that is not considered to be their specific function and the neutral term 'small pointed blade', advocated by Britnell (2000, 183), forms a better descriptive term for them. The majority have been produced from ovicaprid bones, and frequently from the tibia.

Two forms of implement can be identified, depending on whether the base end has been cut from the proximal or the distal end of the bone. Wheeler noted a simple but significant chronological distinction between earlier Iron Age implements made from ovicaprid tibiae, for which the distal end of the bone formed the base end, and later Iron Age groups, where the proximal part of the bone was used as the base end (Wheeler 1943, 304 and pl. XXXIV; Cunnington

1923, 87). Subsequent work at Maiden Castle and Cadbury Castle endorsed this chronological division, albeit with an area of overlap between the two types (Laws 1981, 236; Britnell 2000, 186), but no obvious correlation was noted at Danebury (Sellwood 1984, 387). The distal end of the bone has been used as the base end in this case, suggesting that the implement belongs to the earlier part of the Iron Age. Objects of this type have previously been provided with a number of functional interpretations, most of which were eloquently summarised by Cunnington (1923, 86). Crowfoot interpreted them as possible weaving implements but recent texts have regarded them instead as hafted implements, utilised as spearheads (Crowfoot 1945; Olsen 2003, 107–11; Riddler 2007, 315–6; Mullins 2007, 36; Duncan and Riddler 2011, 66).

Illustration catalogue

SF 216 Fragmentary small pointed **blade**, cut from the lower midshaft of an ovicaprid tibia, with the distal end hollowed and perforated laterally on the anterior and posterior faces. The other end of the implement has fractured away. Faint traces of longitudinal smoothing lines on the shaft. Length: 82.1mm, Width: 21.8mm, HINGC02 (Area C), fill 3069, of ditch 3071, Period 3.1, Trackway 1.

Chapter 4. Zooarchaeological and Botanical Evidence, Geoarchaeological Studies and Scientific Dating

I. Human skeletal remains

by Sue Anderson, Zoë Uí Choileáin, Brian Dean, Louise Loe and Helen Webb

Introduction

The assemblage of human skeletal remains from the site comprises six articulated skeletons and five deposits of disarticulated human bone, spanning the Early Neolithic to the Late Iron Age/Early Roman periods (Table 4.1). The remains of two Early Neolithic skeletons (Burial Group 1, Sks 15189 and 15190) were recovered from a double burial in Area J, and a Middle Bronze Age inhumation was found in an infilled seasonal pond in Area C (Burial Group 2, Sk 318). The disarticulated remains (Burial Group 3A) were recovered from pit fills (pits 1511 and 1520) and ditch fills (contexts 1599, 2167 and 2556) dating to the Late Iron Age and forming part of the Enclosures 1 and 2 in Area D. Also associated with these enclosures were two articulated skeletons (Sk 1964, Burial Group 3B; and Sk 758, Burial Group 3C). An Iron Age or Early Roman inhumation (Sk 1231, Burial Group 4) was recovered from the infilled seasonal pond in Area C.

Methodology

Specialist examination was undertaken in three stages, each stage by a different osteologist, between 2007 and 2012 (Anderson 2007; Webb 2011; Dean 2012; Uí Choileáin 2014). This report integrates the results of these analyses. The work was undertaken in accordance with national guidelines (Brickley and McKinley 2004). Sexing and ageing techniques followed accepted standards (Buikstra and Ubelaker 1994; Brothwell 1981; Miles 1962 and 2001; Ferembach *et al.* 1980; Scheuer and Black 2000). In addition, some of the dental age estimations employed Bouts and Pot (1989). Statures were estimated by using the regression equations of Trotter and Gleser (Trotter 1970). Non-metric traits were scored with reference to Brothwell (1981), Berry and Berry (1967) and Finnegan (1978). Skeletal pathology was identified, described and diagnosed with reference to key texts (for example, Aufderheide and Rodriguez-Martin 1998; Ortner 2003; Resnick 1995).

The results are discussed below, alongside relevant archaeological information. Further details are given in the catalogue held in the project archive.

Burial Group 1: Early Neolithic

Skeletons 15189 and 15190 were buried within a single, shallow grave, both in a flexed position (Fig. 2.6). It is possible that these individuals were buried at the same time, although Sk 15189 was partially disarticulated and may have been moved aside for the later burial of Sk 15190. Both skeletons are very incomplete, with approximately 25% of each individual surviving. The bones are highly fragmented and have suffered moderate levels of surface erosion, consistent with McKinley's grade 2–3 (McKinley 2004, 16), meaning that parts of the surfaces are masked by erosive action.

Both skeletons are adult and, whilst there were no specific indicators of age in Sk 15190, the level of dental attrition in Sk 15189 is consistent with a 36–45 year old (Brothwell 1981; Miles 1962). However, age estimations based solely on dental attrition are not always reliable as a result of a number of factors, such as diet and occupational use of the teeth, which can increase the rate of wear. Sex could not be estimated for either skeleton. No non-metric traits or lesions of pathology were observed, undoubtedly due to the poor condition of the skeletons.

Burial Group 2: Middle Bronze Age

A Bronze Age skeleton (Sk 318; Fig. 2.11) was buried in a crouched position on their left side, in a north-west to south-east orientation. The grave was situated within an infilled seasonal pond. The remains are very incomplete (25–50%) and highly fragmented. The bone surface condition was scored as fair, with post-mortem erosion in places. The remains comprise the left side of the skull, left arm, right lower arm, hands, a few fragments of torso, left pelvis and fragments of lower legs and feet. Based on features of the skull and pelvis, it was determined that the remains are those of a female. Dental attrition suggests a young/middle adult.

Moderate deposits of calculus (or 'tartar') were observed on an incomplete dentition, but no other dental pathology was observed. Cribra orbitalia was evident on the left orbit, but the lesion is of mild expression only. The most popular and widely accepted causative factor of cribra orbitalia is iron deficiency anaemia, which may arise as a result of dietary deficiency, excessive blood loss through injury, chronic disease such as cancer and iron withholding in response to parasitic infections of the gut (Stuart Macadam 1991). There is also slight periostitis (non-specific reaction to inflammation or infection of the periosteum that covers the outer surfaces of bones) on the right tibia. Infection of soft tissue, trauma, neoplastic disease and haemorrhage may all cause periosteal new bone (Aufderheide and Rodriguez-Martin 1998, 172). Not surprisingly, given its proximity to the skin and its susceptibility to recurrent minor trauma, the tibia is often reported as the most frequently affected bone in archaeological populations (Roberts and Manchester 1995, 130).

Burial Group 3A: Late Iron Age – disarticulated bone

Deposit 1511
This deposit was found in a pit (1511) within Enclosure 1/2. The remains – a single, incomplete, right humerus – are of a young child, most probably an infant aged between 1 and 12 months old. The bone consists of proximal, middle and distal thirds of the diaphysis. The condition of the bone is fair (grade 2; McKinley 2004, 16).

Deposit 1520
The remains of another individual were deposited into an adjacent pit (1521): they include eight rib fragments, a right ulna, right and left femora and tibiae, and a right fibula, all incomplete. The bones have suffered post-mortem erosion to the extent that the detail of parts of the surfaces is obscured, but overall morphology has been maintained (consistent with grade 3, after McKinley 2004, 16). No age could be confidently assigned, but bone morphology suggests that the bones belong to a young child, probably an infant of between 1 and 12 months. No pathology or peri-mortem modification was observed.

Deposit 2167
Further remains came from the upper fill of the enclosure ditch in the north-eastern corner of Enclosure 1 (cut 2146). Bone from this context included a single fragment of the distal left tibia of an adult of unknown sex. Some surface degradation is visible in the form of slight, patchy erosion (consistent with grade 1; McKinley 2004, 16), but nothing to suggest any peri-mortem modification. No pathology was observed.

Deposit 2556
Two fragments of the distal shaft of the right femur came from the fill of the southern ditch of Enclosure 2 (cut 2557). The bone derives from an adult, but it was not possible to estimate a more precise age, or determine the sex of the individual (although the marked linea aspera on the back of the femur may suggest a male). Some post-mortem scratches and abrasions (consistent with the erosion grade 1; McKinley 2004, 16) were observed, as was a clean post-mortem break. No peri-mortem modification was apparent and no pathologies were observed.

Deposit 1599
Further remains came from the uppermost fill of the ditch of Enclosure 2 (cut 1509), in the south-east corner of the enclosure. The human bone from this context comprises a near complete adult male mandible with very flared gonions and a prominent chin. Only eight teeth have survived, the rest having been lost post-mortem. There is advanced alveolar resorption and medium calculus. Both deciduous canines had been retained (but lost post-mortem), with the adult canines impacted diagonally in the jaw.

Burial Group 3B: Late Iron Age
Pl. 4.1
An articulated Late Iron Age individual (Sk 1964) lay within a grave in the north-east corner of the ditch relating to Enclosure 2. The individual had been buried supine with their legs flexed, on an east to west alignment. The remains are 76–100% complete and, although fragmentary, the bone surfaces are in good condition, with little post-mortem erosion. The individual is estimated to be an older male, with a stature of 1.59m, which is within the normal range for the period (Roberts and Cox 2003). In addition, it was possible to calculate the cranial index, which indicates that the individual was dolichocranic (73.7), or had a relatively narrow skull.

Significant dental disease was observed in Sk 1964. The individual had periodontal disease (pitting and resorption of the alveolus), advanced caries involving their upper right canine and abscesses that involved eleven positions out of the nineteen that still had teeth at the time of death. In most cases these were caused by opening of the pulp cavity due to heavy wear, although the wear may have been accelerated by caries. The individual had also lost all molars and the lower right second premolar before death.

Non-dental pathology was also observed. This skeleton has a calcified xiphisternum, which may relate to a developmental condition. However, as this condition can also occur in mature individuals with a predisposition for 'bone forming' (Rogers and Waldron 1995), the diagnosis is unconfirmed. Bone formers are a subset of the skeletal population in which ossification of the entheses, fusion of the sacro-iliac joints, ossification of cartilage and large marginal osteophytes is common (ibid., 53). Osteophytes (new bone growth on or around joint margins) were also observed in this skeleton, affecting the mid to lower thoracic and lumbar vertebrae and acetabuli, and enthesophytes (new bone growth at ligament and tendon attachment sites) are present on the iliac crests. Some of the vertebrae appear osteoporotic with slight flattening of the bodies, particularly the second and fifth lumbars, and the pelvis may also have been affected.

Other pathological lesions observed include non-specific bone inflammation in the form of bilateral maxillary sinusitis. This was probably associated with the chronic dental disease described above. In addition, Sk 1964 has an oblique fracture of the right lower leg, which involved both the tibia and fibula (Pl. 4.1). The fracture line is oblique, crossing through the upper third of the fibula and the lower third of the tibia. Both bones are well-healed and are not noticeably shorter than their pairs. The callus is heavily remodelled, indicating that these were old wounds.

Burial Group 3C: Late Iron Age
Skeleton 758 lay in an extended supine position on a north–south alignment, in a grave located within the north-west corner of Enclosure 2. The skeleton is 76–100% complete and exhibits little post-mortem erosion, although the bones are fragmentary. The individual is suggested to be an adolescent, around 15 years of age and, whilst some of the features of the pelvis are in keeping with male morphology, the individual was too young to allow for a confident determination of sex.

Location	Skeleton no.	Burial context	Completeness	Condition	Sex	Age	Stature	Pathology and trauma
Early Neolithic								
Area J Burial Group 1	Sk 15189	Grave 15188. Double inhumation (with sk15190); crouched, lying on left side; NE–SW orientation, head at NE	0–25%	Poor, highly fragmented	?	Adult	-	None observed
	Sk 15190	Grave 15188. Double inhumation (with sk15189); ?crouched; NE–SW orientation, head at NE	0–25%	Poor, highly fragmented	?	Adult	-	None observed
Middle Bronze Age								
Area C Burial Group 2 Located in infilled seasonal pond (3203)	Sk 318	Grave 319. Crouched, lying on left side; NW–SE orientation, head at NW facing east	25–50%	Fair but very fragmented	F	Young/middle adult	-	Cribra orbitalia (L); probable periostitis, R. tibia; medium dental calculus
Middle/Late Iron Age								
Area D Burial Group 3A Disarticulated bone deposits associated with the ceremonial mortuary enclosure	1511 (disartic)	From pit 1510 located in SE part of enclosure. R humerus; mixed with animal bone		Fair	-	Young child	-	None observed
	1520 (disartic)	From pit 1521 located in SE part of enclosure. Disarticulated bones including eight rib fragments, a right ulna, right and left femora and tibiae, and a right fibula, all incomplete		Fair	-	Young child	-	None observed
	1599 (disartic)	From ditch 1509, SE corner of enclosure. Mandible.			Male	Adult	-	Advanced alveolar resorption; calculus; retention of deciduous canines with impaction of permanent canines
	2167 (disartic)	From ditch 2146, NE corner of enclosure. Fragment of L. tibia		Good	?	Adult	-	None observed
	2556 (disartic)	From ditch 2557, S enclosure. Two fragments of right femur		Good	?	Adult	-	None observed
Area D Burial Group 3B Skeleton associated with the ceremonial mortuary enclosure	Sk 1964	Grave 2147. N/E corner of enclosure ditch 2146; supine, legs flexed, arms straight by sides; E–W orientation, head at E facing north	76–100%	Good but fragmented	M	Old	159.0 cm	Maxillary sinusitis (bilateral); Schmorl's nodes TV6-9, LV1-2; osteophytosis TV7-12, LV2-4 and acetabuli; enthesophyte iliac crests. Lumbar vertebrae and pelvis appear osteoporotic; healed fracture R. tibia and fibula; advanced dental caries; AMTL; dental abscesses and periodontitis.

Location	Skeleton no.	Burial context	Completeness	Condition	Sex	Age	Stature	Pathology and trauma
Late Iron Age/Early Roman								
Area D Burial Group 3C Skeleton associated with the ceremonial mortuary enclosure	758	Grave 760. Within NW of enclosure; supine extended, arms by sides; N–S orientation, head at N	76-100%	Good	-	Adolescent (<16 yrs)	-	Lytic lesion **R**. clavicle, possibly secondary to trauma; slight dental calculus.
Iron Age/Early Roman								
Area C Burial Group 4 Located in infilled seasonal pond (3203)	1231	Grave 1232. Extended supine, arms by side; orientated NE–SW, head at NE	76-100%	Good	M	Middle/old adult	1.741 m	Calcified xiphisternum; Schmorl's nodes TV6-L5; maxillary sinusitis; osteophytosis TV3-LV5, acetabulae and SIJs; costo-vertebral and apophyseal joint OA (CV3, CV7–TV1, TV12); ankylosing hyperostosis; inflammation on ischial bursae; possible healed fracture, **R** scapula; Os acromiale; pronounced muscle sites; dental caries; dental calculus; AMTL; periodontitis; dental abscesses.

Key: **R**=right; **L**=left; CV – cervical vertebrae; TV=thoracic vertebra; LV=lumbar vertebra; OA=osteoarthritis; AMTL=ante=mortem tooth loss; SIJ=sacroiliac joint

Table 4.1 Overview of human skeletal remains

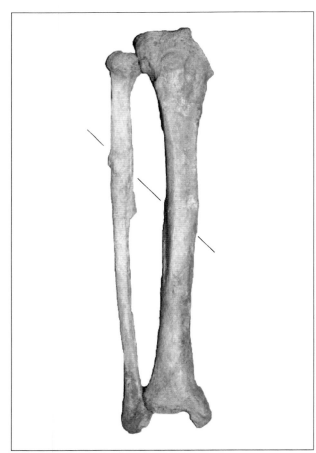

Plate 4.1 Late Iron Age Sk 1964, oblique fracture of the right lower leg, involving both bones

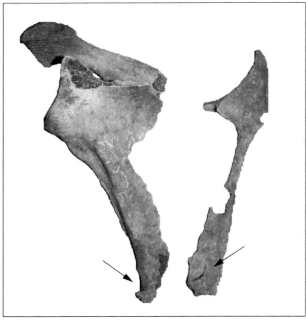

Plate 4.2 Late Iron Age/Early Roman Sk 1231, fractured scapula

This skeleton has an observable dentition and this exhibits slight calculus. The only other possible pathology observed is on the right clavicle, which is a cyst-like lytic lesion at the insertion of the costo-clavicular ligament. This may relate to torn muscle attachments as the result of trauma.

Burial Group 4: Iron Age/Early Roman
Pl. 4.2

During the Late Iron Age/Early Roman period, an isolated burial (Sk 1231, grave 1232) was placed above the same infilled pond (Pond D) as the Bronze Age skeleton (Burial Group 2) in Area C. Skeleton 1231 is 76–100% complete and in good condition with well-preserved bone surfaces. The individual is estimated to be a middle/old adult male, with a stature of 1.741m, which is in the normal range for the period (Roberts and Cox 2003).

This individual exhibits well marked muscle attachments, which may suggest that he had engaged in physically demanding activities from a young age (Knüsel 2000). Unfortunately, it was not possible to explore this further by metrical assessment to examine handedness and calculate robusticity indices (Bass 1981; Byers 2005). Bilateral detached acromial epiphyses (Os acromiale) were also observed. This trait, whilst it may be genetically or developmentally influenced, has been associated with archery as it was found to be common amongst the Tudor skeletons from the Mary Rose (Stirland 2000).

In keeping with his advanced age, Sk 1231 had suffered ante-mortem tooth loss (AMTL). A total of four maxillary teeth had been lost prior to death, although much of the mandible is missing meaning that the full extent of AMTL could not be ascertained. AMTL can result from a multitude of factors including trauma, severe periodontal disease secondary to calculus formation, and pulp exposure and abscess formation secondary to caries or severe attrition. Indeed, this skeleton exhibits advanced caries in the upper right first molar and upper left second premolar, and a small carious lesion at the cementum-enamel junction of the lower right second molar. In addition, abscesses are present at the sockets for the upper canine and first premolar.

Marginal osteophytes, growths of new bone extending from the margins of a joint, are present throughout the thoracic and lumbar vertebrae. In addition, osteoarthritis, diagnosed in accordance with Rogers and Waldron (1995, 44), is present on the apophyseal and costo-vertebral joints of a number of cervical and thoracic vertebrae. Whilst genetics, obesity, activity/lifestyle and environmental factors, such as climate, may all contribute to the development of osteoarthritis, prevalence rates generally show a positive correlation with increasing age (Rogers and Waldron 1995, 32–3; Roberts and Manchester 1995, 106) and it is likely that age was a significant factor in Sk 1231.

Schmorl's nodes, indentations on the vertebral end plates, are frequent in this individual. The lesions are particularly large on the tenth thoracic to first lumbar vertebra. They result from herniation of the intervertebral disc and subsequent pressure from the bulging of the nucleus pulposa, into the adjacent bone surface (Rogers and Waldron 1995, 27). Again, these are more common with advancing age, but are also seen in younger individuals as a result of activity or trauma (Jurmain 1999, 165).

Non-specific bone inflammation was observed in the form of maxillary sinusitis, identified as inflammatory new bone on the walls of the maxillary sinuses. Symptoms of this condition include nasal congestion, purulent nasal and pharyngeal discharges, facial and dental pain, oedema around the eye, earache and fever (K. Evans 1994, 1415–22). There are several factors that may lead to sinusitis, including dental abscesses, high levels of air pollution, poor ventilation and allergies (Roberts and Manchester 1995, 131). In the present skeleton, the sinusitis may have developed as a result of the abscess cavities observed in the maxillary dentition.

The distal end of the right scapula of Sk 1231 shows evidence for healed trauma, possibly a fracture, although it could have been the result of a piercing injury (Pl. 4.2). Unfortunately, this area of the bone is poorly preserved. The inferior angle has been pushed forwards, possibly with upward shifting of the medial border, and with rough new bone growth around a hole in this area close to the edge of the bone. None of the ribs appear to have been affected.

Discussion

The earliest human remains found at the site, dated to the Early Neolithic period, were articulated Sks 15189 and 15190, recovered from a single, shallow grave. Both skeletons were adult but, due to their poor condition, no other useful osteological information was deduced. Although burials of the Early Neolithic period in Britain are best known as elements of multiple, often disarticulated deposits in large monuments, inhumations in non-monumentalised contexts are not rare in this period, with a number of examples having been found in Southern Britain, and these also often consist of disarticulated and incomplete skeletons (Garwood and Barclay 1998, 275). The timing/sequence of the Genome Campus burials remains unclear. That one of the skeletons appeared to have been slightly disturbed was perhaps in keeping with the other burial having been added later, but the radiocarbon dates on both individuals are statistically indistinguishable and contemporary burial cannot be discounted.

A single burial of Bronze Age date was that of a young or middle-aged adult female, found in an oval grave that had been dug into the top of a silted-up pond. The individual was lying in a tightly crouched position, on her left hand side and with her head at the north-west end of the grave. The fragmentary nature of the skeleton precluded stature estimation, but the presence of cribra orbitalia and probable periostitis indicate that the woman had experienced physiological stresses in life.

The other human remains comprise three articulated skeletons (adolescent Sk 758, and adult males Sks 1964 and 1231) and five disarticulated bone deposits (two infants, Sks 1511, 1520, and three adults, Sks 1599, 2167, 2556), assigned to the Late Iron Age and Early Roman periods. Neither of the two articulated adult male skeletons were particularly young when they died. Older individuals were also common among the later 1st-century AD burials

excavated at the Hutchison site, Addenbrookes (Dodwell *et al.* 2008, 55) although there, a bias towards mature adult *females* was identified. Only one child, an infant, was found here. At Duxford, skeletons recovered from the Late Iron Age/Roman cemetery comprised ten juveniles (less than 18 years of age) and 25 adults. Among the latter, in contrast to the Genome Campus burials, young adults were common and the male to female ratio was 2:1 (Duhig 2011, 70). These patterns may refer to the differential selection of certain individuals for burial at these locations. However, small sample size, the extent of excavation and taphonomy, in particular the tendency for child burials to survive less well than adult burials, are other important factors that will have influenced these demographic trends.

Physically, metrical analysis (in particular, stature and skull shape) of the Iron Age/ Roman skeletons suggests that these individuals were within the normal range for the periods in which they lived (Roberts and Cox 2003; Brothwell 1981). A general lack of oral hygiene among the group is indicated by the deposits of calculus on their teeth and chronic dental disease, in the form of cavities, probable secondary maxillary sinusitis, periodontitis and ante-mortem tooth loss. The calculus may also suggest that the individuals ate relatively soft foods that required little chewing. Two of the individuals had sustained fractures, one of which, the possible scapula fracture (Sk 1231), may have been associated with direct violence and the other, a fracture of the lower leg (Sk 1964), could have been the result of a fall in which the leg had been twisted. In addition to these injuries, other lesions seen among the group (namely, Schmorl's nodes, lytic defects and marked muscle attachment sites), give the overall impression of individuals who had led physically demanding lives. Further, the presence of cribra orbitalia and maxillary sinusitis suggest individuals whose lives had not been free from physiological stress.

Associated with Enclosure 1/2 were adolescent Sk 758, older adult male Sk 1964, disarticulated bones, representing one or two infants from pits within the enclosure's boundaries, and disarticulated adult bones in the north-east corner of the enclosure ditch. Together, these burials may have formed part of a single dispersed cemetery, although no osteological indicators of familial relations were identified during the present analysis. Skeleton 758 was buried supine with their legs extended, whilst adult male Sk 1964 was flexed. Both had their arms by their sides. Adolescent Sk 758 was in a north to south orientation, whilst Sk 1964 was positioned east to west. This variety of burial rites is not unusual for rural Iron Age cemeteries and has been seen elsewhere in the locality, for example at Duxford (Lyons 2011). If the function of the enclosure found at the Genome Campus can be shown to have been mostly concerned with the processing and disposal of the dead, then it is a rare example from Britain. Perhaps the best known example from the country is that found at Folly Lane, on the outskirts of St Albans, Hertfordshire (Niblett 1999). Unlike Enclosure 1/2, a cremation was the focal burial, believed to be that of a male, possibly an aristocrat, but inhumations were found in the enclosure ditch.

Skeleton 1231 was buried in the same pond feature as the Bronze Age skeleton, some 1,250 years later, during the Late Iron Age/Early Roman period. The individual, a middle/old adult male, was lying in a north-east to south-west orientated grave in an extended, supine position with his arms by his side and his head in the north-east.

The burial of individuals in pits and enclosure boundaries is a typically Late Iron Age/Early Roman practice that has been encountered throughout central Southern England, including Cambridgeshire (Wait 1985; Gwilt and Haselgrove 1997; Whimster 1981). In addition to pits and enclosure ditches, burials have also been recovered from settlement ditches and hillfort ramparts. For example, at the Hutchison site, Addenbrookes, three inhumations were found in the boundary ditches of the adjacent settlement and at Clay Farm, Trumpington, bone fragments had been deposited in boundary ditches and pits during the Iron Age phases of the site's occupation (Phillips and Mortimer forthcoming). Folly Lane, St Albans (Niblett 1999), Spettisbury Rings, Dorset (Gresham 1939), Danebury, Hampshire (Cunliffe and Poole 1991) and Cadbury Castle, Somerset (Alcock 1971) are some of the better known sites, outside Cambridgeshire, where this practice has also been observed. The deposition of disarticulated bone fragments in these contexts may represent tokens of remembrance brought back from sites of excarnation, located some distance away (Lambrick 2009). However, no evidence for excarnation, such as scavenging and cut marks, was seen on the disarticulated bones from the Genome Campus. This may suggest that the remains had not been excarnated, or that excarnation had been performed by other methods (for example, defleshing by boiling and short term burial in the ground) (Carr and Knüsel 1997). At Folly Lane, a skull was recovered from a pit that had perforations, perhaps associated with blows at the time of death, and cut marks attributed to defleshing (Mays and Steele 1996). The treatment afforded to this skull may have been associated with a skull cult (Niblett 1999). The Hinxton assemblage is too small for any such conclusions to be drawn.

In general, the burial practices afforded to the Iron Age and Romano-British individuals found at the Genome Campus conform to a recognised pattern, typical of rural Iron Age communities with which small cemeteries, comprising poorly furnished graves that observed a mixture of rites and occupied a discrete area, were associated. They are also among a growing corpus of burials to be identified from East Anglia and south Cambridgeshire where inhumation was adopted as the primary rite, at a time when cremation was the main funerary rite elsewhere in South-Eastern England – as exemplified locally by the Hinxton Quarry cremation cemetery (Hill *et al.* 1999). Other local examples of Late Iron Age to Early Roman inhumations include those at Duxford (Lyons 2011), where a cemetery was found in association with a shrine, Linton (Clarke and Gilmour forthcoming), and the Hutchison site, Addenbrookes, where a cemetery and isolated burials were found immediately adjacent to a settlement (Evans *et al.* 2008). Unlike the Genome Campus, cremation burials were also found at Duxford and Addenbrookes, although they clearly represented a minority rite.

II. Faunal remains
by Andrew Bates
Figs 4.1–4.8

Introduction
A total of 5,626 (*c.*102kg) of animal bone and teeth fragments (number of individual specimens; NISP), were recovered, of which 1,122 (28%) were identified to a species level. The vast majority of the material was recovered by hand collection, although bone was also found within soil samples taken for charred remains. The minimal faunal assemblage recovered from the final phase of excavation (HINGEL14/Area J) has not been incorporated as its small sample size did not further augment the results of the previous stages, while some slight changes in phasing have also not been included for the same reasons.

Methodology
The material was identified using the reference collections held by the author and with reference to Halstead and Collins (1995) and Schmid (1972). All parts of the skeleton were identified where possible, including long bone shafts, skull fragments, all teeth and fairly complete vertebrae. Sheep/goat distinctions were made using reference material and published work by Boessneck (1969), Kratochvil (1969), Payne (1985) and Prummel and Frisch (1986). Red and fallow deer were separated following Lister (1996). Bird bones were identified with reference to Cohen and Serjeantson (1996), Bacher (1967) and Woelfle (1967). Frog and toad pelves were identified following Thomas (1996).

The assemblage was divided into countable 'A' bones and non-countable 'B' bones in line with the principals detailed in Dobney *et al.* (1999). For each 'A' bone, the following information was recorded where appropriate: context reference; species or species group; element; number of bones; side; the diagnostic zone as either more than or less than half present; fusion state; butchery; measurements; tooth wear development; and other comments. Pathology and other developmental or congenital anomalies were also noted. 'B' bones were recorded by species group and element only, unless they were measurable, displayed butchery marks, pathology or congenital traits, in which instance they were recorded in the same detail as 'A' bones.

The diagnostic zones used followed those described in Serjeantson (1996), although this excludes the mandible which was zoned as described in Worley (2011), fragments being recorded as 'A' bones when over 50% of a zone was present. Vertebrae (except axis and atlas) were recorded as 'A' bones when over 50% of the centrum was present.

The condition of the bone was recorded by context as ranked data. This included the state of bone preservation; angularity of archaeological breaks; the relative size of bone fragments; the proportion of the original complete bones present; the level of surface erosion; and the proportion of new breaks, butchered, burnt and gnawed bones.

The minimum number of elements (MNE) was calculated from the most frequently occurring diagnostic zone of each element. The minimum

Preservation category	Neolithic	Late Neolithic to Early Bronze Age	Bronze Age	Iron Age	Late Iron Age/ Early Romano-British	Romano-British
Surface erosion	0.4	0.4	0.6	0.5	0.6	0.6
Robustness	0.6	0.5	0.6	0.6	0.7	0.7
Fragmentation of 'A' bones (% of potential number of zones)	32.7	37.5	44.5	44.1	47.5	58.1
Butchered 'A' bones (%)	-	-	6.1	2.5	7.0	3.1
Gnawed 'A' bones (%)	-	-	3.1	0.8	4.0	1.3
'A' bones as a percentage of the total number of fragments	18.5	6.4	28.1	49.4	26.5	34.9

Table 4.2 Summary of animal bone preservation and other taphonomic agents by phase, presented as percentages and normalised values

number of individuals (MNI) equates to the highest MNE value, taking side into account. Estimating the numbers of principal stock animals within archaeozoological collections is problematic, as differential fragmentation and survival may affect the relative proportions of species and anatomical elements present. Percentage values derived from the MNI could be considered a minimum and those calculated from the NISP a maximum of the total estimated range of stock animals within the archaeozoological material (O'Connor 2003, 133–5).

The extent of mandibular tooth wear and the epiphysial fusion of long bones can be used to estimate the age at death of the principal stock animals. Wear stages were recorded for dP4s, P4s and lower permanent molars of the domestic species using Grant (1982) and grouped into age stages following the methods of Halstead (1985), Payne (1973) and Jones (2002). The fusion stage of post-cranial bones was recorded, with related age ranges taken from Silver (1969) and Getty (1975). Sexes were separated using morphological characteristics of the pelvis in sheep and cattle (Grigson 1982) and of the canines in pigs (Schmid 1972).

Measurements were taken on cattle, sheep/goat, pig and horse bones following von den Driesch (1976) and Davis (1992). Those taken on horse teeth followed Levine (1982).

Taphonomy
A number of factors may affect animal bone prior to inclusion into the archaeological record. These include the act of butchery, burning, gnawing, fragmentation before inclusion within an archaeological deposit, attack from acid roots, attack from acids within the soil or sediment and also the archaeological excavation process. An overview of the preservation, fragmentation and modification affecting the bone is presented in Table 4.2.

Very little Neolithic or Bronze Age animal bone was recovered, although the Neolithic material has suffered a higher degree of fragmentation and erosion than those of later deposits. The preservation of Late Iron Age/Early Romano-British and Romano-British bones varies somewhat, with bones of less than 50% of surface erosion, and over 50% surface erosion. Most bone fragments retain less than 50% of their

diagnostic zones, although a greater number of more complete bones were recorded from Romano-British deposits. This figure is somewhat influenced by a dog burial in pit 712. Excluding these remains results in a figure of 51.8% for the fragmentation of Romano-British 'A' bones.

Residual bone is inevitably an issue on multi-phase sites. Bone of a noticeably worse condition than other bone of the same deposit was recorded as 'Residual?' However, such material was recorded in very few instances, and is therefore thought to be a minor issue in this analysis.

Quantification and distribution
The majority of the animal bone is phased to the Late Iron Age/Early Romano-British or the Romano-British phases (Table 4.3). Of the sheep/goat category, where they could be assigned to one species or the other, the majority are of sheep, according with the national norm (Maltby 1996, 24, Maltby 1981, 159–60). Goats were evidently husbanded, but in smaller numbers. Few bones were excavated from soil samples, providing little information concerning any biases in the hand-collected sample.

Neolithic to Bronze Age (Period 2)
The Neolithic animal bone, detailed in Table 4.4, was recovered from seven pits and a treebole: of this c. 70% of the bone came from the pit/shaft in Trench U (Pit Group 7), with pig being the most frequently occurring animal.

Two groups of pig remains were noted, both from Pit Group 4 in Area C. Deposit 682, the only fill of pit 683, contained 25 pig bones or teeth fragments, all but one thoracic vertebra of which are of the head. In the non-countable 'B' bone category three pig skull fragments and a mandible fragment were also recorded. An MNI calculated from the mandible suggests a minimum of three individuals, aged six to twelve months, one to two years, and over two years of age. Two of these animals were identified as sows.

A possibly similar collection of pig remains was collected from fill 748 of pit 778 (also Pit Group 4). It contained nine bone and teeth fragments, including four mandibles (two of which articulated), three loose teeth, and fragments of scapulae and tibia. An MNI calculated from the mandible suggest a minimum of

Species	Neolithic	Late Neolithic to Early Bronze Age	Bronze Age	Iron Age	Late Iron Age/ Early Romano-British	Romano-British
Equus sp.			3	12	76	24
Cattle	7 (1)	2	16	41	192 (6)	98
Sheep/Goat	6		8 (1)	13	119 (4)	93 (2)
Sheep				1 (3)	4	33
Goat					2	2
Pig	39 (7)	1 (3)	9	3	65 (4)	28 (2)
Dog					16 (1)	28 (4)
Rabbit						16
Red Deer	1		3		2	1
Roe Deer	1				1	
Deer					4	
Water vole				25 (3)	1	(2)
Field vole						(5)
Vole				18 (1)	3 (1)	5 (32)
Mouse						(8)
Shrew				(3)		(6)
Total	**54 (8)**	**3 (3)**	**39 (1)**	**113 (10)**	**486 (16)**	**328 (61)**
Principal domestic stock animals (%)						
Cattle					50.5	25.8
Sheep/Goat					32.4	33.2
Pig					17.1	7.4

Numbers in brackets from soil samples

Table 4.3 The countable ('A') bones by species and phase collected by hand, bone of the same individual counted as 1 NISP

Fill of	Cattle	Sheep/goat	Pig	Red deer	Total
683	2	1	25		28
691	5	1	7	1	14
731			2		2
776			4		4
778	1		9		10

Table 4.4 Distribution of countable ('A') bones by feature from Neolithic Pit Group 4, counting bones of the same individual as 1 NISP

Species	Ditch	Pit	Other
Equus sp.	95.5	4.5	-
Cattle	89.1	4.6	6.3
Sheep/Goat	86.0	9.8	4.2
Pig	84.7	8.3	6.9

Table 4.5 Distribution of Period 3.1–3.2 species by feature type (%NISP). Sheep/goat and sheep have been totalled; bone of the same individual counted as 1 NISP

two individuals, both identified as sows. Within the non-countable ('B' bone) category a pig skull, radius and fibula fragments were also recorded. The pig remains within these two pits suggest some element of deliberate discarding of bone waste, or the inclusion of midden deposits.

Middle/Late Iron Age to Conquest period (Periods 3.1–3.2)

Few bones are attributed to possible Middle Iron Age contexts, with the majority of identifiable bones, some 85% excluding small mammals, being excavated from deposits associated with Trackway 1. The only articulating remains are those of a cow astragalus, calcaneum and navicular-cuboid (of the ankle joint) excavated from ditch fill 1372 (ditch 1373), the southern ditch associated with the trackway.

Cattle and sheep were the principal domestic stock animals at the site in the later Iron Age. Cattle bones were recovered in greater numbers. However, 85% to 95% of the bone from domestic stock animals came from ditches (Table 4.5), predominantly the ditches of the Late Iron Age Enclosures 1, 2 and 3.

It is likely that the numbers of cattle bones in the archaeozoological material are over-represented in comparison to the live flocks and herds. This may be an issue in an assemblage largely collected by hand, but in addition cattle bone from Iron Age and Romano-British sites is often recorded as more frequently occurring in ditches than those of sheep

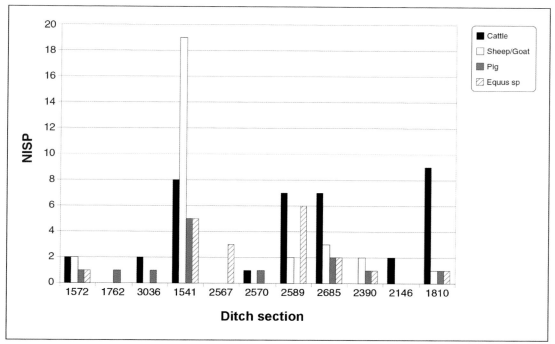

Figure 4.1 NISP of countable bones from Enclosure 1, by ditch section

(Wilson 1996; Bates *et al.* 2012, 269). The proportion of stock animals presented in Table 4.3 is, therefore, likely to be affected by this bias.

The general trend of deposition is of bones from domestic animals in low numbers per deposit, although some exceptions are detailed below.

Enclosures 1–3
Figs 4.1–4.2
In total, 23% of all the bones of the principal domestic stock animals were recovered from Enclosure 1, and 47% from Enclosure 2 in Area D. Most fills of these ditches produced low numbers of bones per species, although the exceptions are visible in Figures 4.1 and 4.2. In the case of the sheep/goat bones from ditch 1541 (Enclosure 1), and *Equus* sp. bones from ditch 1931 (Enclosure 2), higher counts of NISP are explained by articulating or potentially associated groups of bones (Table 4.6). A further four deposits contained articulating or paired bones of the same individuals.

The total sample size for each of the domestic stock animals from this enclosure is too small to permit a reliable analysis of the body parts represented, but most body parts appear to be represented. Overall, the impression is one of small numbers of bones from different individual animals deposited with a degree of frequency, with the inclusion of some bones of the same carcass. This is perhaps best interpreted as bone derived from nearby middens with occasional direct depositions such as the *Equus* sp vertebra from ditch 1931.

Within the enclosure, the remains of what was probably a single piglet came from the only fill (1510) of pit 1511 (Pit Group 18). They include the left mandible, both radii, left ulna and both fourth metacarpals, from a young animal less than one year of age. Further remains may have been located in the unexcavated half of the pit. This pit also contained one

Enclosure	Ditch cut	Deposit	Description
Enc 1	1541	1538	Seven bones from possibly two newborn or 'young' sheep/goats, and one neonatal sheep/goat fragment
Enc 1	1541	1539	Dog skull with articulating atlas (the first cervical vertebra)
Enc 1	2589	2682	Articulating cow astragalus and calcaneum
Enc 1	1931	2223	Three articulating groups of *Equus* sp. vertebra, probably all of the same animal. Including: articulating atlas and axis; five thoracic vertebra and 2 lumbar vertebra; and three further thoracic vertebra.
Enc 1/2	2557	2556	Two articulating Equus sp. lumbar vertebra. Articulating cow astragalus and calcaneum
Enc 1/2	1509	1753	Left and a right *Equus* sp. radii, probably of the same animal

Table 4.6 Articulating, paired and collection of newborn animal bone from Enclosures 1 and 2

bone of a young child (Sk 1511, detailed by Anderson *et al.,* above).

Associated or articulating bone groups

Grave 2147, Burial Group 3B
Grave 2147 contained an adult male (Sk 1964), interred in the north-east corner of Enclosure 1/2 in Area D. A single cow humerus was located above the head of the interred individual. No butchery marks were visible on the humerus, although this is probably the result of the level of erosion to the surface of the bone or the skill of the butcher. The humerus came from an

117

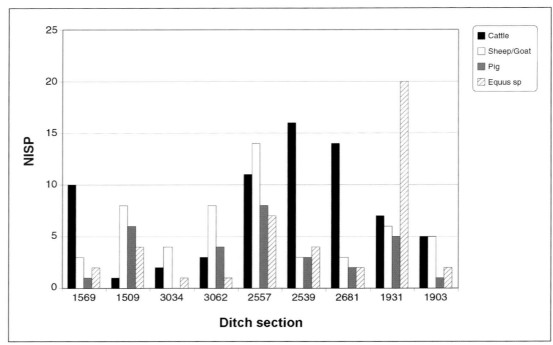

Figure 4.2 NISP of countable bones from Enclosure 2, by ditch section

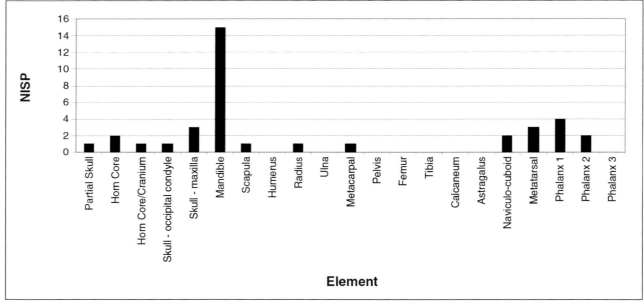

Figure 4.3 NISP counts of sheep/goat and sheep remains from fill 1007 of pit 966/968

animal over 18 months old. The meat from the top of the foreleg of a cow is tougher than that of the rear, and represents a more symbolic act, as opposed to a choice food offering.

Dog remains in ditch 40
Ditch 40 (ungrouped) in evaluation Trench 14 contained a number of bones from its three fills, predominantly representative of the low levels of deposition found in most features containing bone. The sacrum, all seven of the lumbar vertebrae, and eight of the thirteen thoracic vertebrae of a single dog were recovered from one fill (19). No other elements of dog, or rib fragments possibly associated with the

animal, were present. It seems likely that this animal had been dismembered, with the remainder of the carcass either being deposited elsewhere or dispersed along the length of the ditch.

Conquest period to Romano-British (Periods 3.3–3.4)
The Conquest period and Romano-British assemblage is characterised by low levels of deposition of the principal stock animals per deposit. The relative proportion of cattle and sheep presented in Table 4.3 suggests slightly higher numbers of sheep. However, 32% of all the sheep/goat and sheep bones of the latest Iron Age phase were excavated from pit 966/968 (Pit Group 29). Excluding this feature from the

118

Context	Sheep/Goat and Sheep		Cattle	Equus	Pig
	NISP	MNI	NISP	NISP	NISP
1007	32	5	2		2
1010	4	2			
1012	2	1	3	2	

Table 4.7 NISP of animal bones by species from pit 966/968 (Pit Group 29), with MNI provided for sheep/goat and sheep bones, bones of the same individual counted as 1 NISP

Wear Stage	Late Iron Age/Early Romano-British
A (neonatal)	-
B (0–6m)	0.5
C (5–18m)	3
D (16–28m)	1.75
E (26–36m)	1.25
F (34–43m)	0.25
G (40m–6.5y)	5
H (5–10y)	3.08
J (8–16y)	1.58
K (14–20y)	1.58

Table 4.8 Cattle mandibular wear stages; where a mandible could not be assigned to one wear stage it has been divided between wear stages

figures shown in Table 4.3 results in percentages of 42.5% cattle, 42.1% sheep/goat (including sheep) and 15.3% pig for the principal stock animals. Similarly, the contents of pit 966/969 have affected the overall results of species distribution by feature type for the site. Excluding this feature results in values of 54% of sheep/goat remains from pits and 42.5% from ditches. The rabbit bones listed in Table 4.3 are thought to be intrusive (from burrows in the archaeological features) and are therefore excluded from any further discussion.

Associated or articulated bone groups
Fig. 4.3

Pit 966/968 (Pit Group 29) (Period 3.3)
Pit 966/968 in Area B accounts for 32% of all the 'A' bones recorded for sheep/goat and sheep, the majority from fill 1007 (Table 4.7). They include mainly elements of the head, with a small number of post-cranial bones (Fig. 4.3). Of these bones, fourteen were identified as sheep. Bones of the same individual were found in three cases, including four of the five first and second phalanges identified as coming from the same foot and two pairs of articulating mandibles.

Butchery marks were found on mandibles, scapulae and a metatarsal, all associated with the dismemberment of animals. Ages estimated from the wear of mandibular teeth suggest one animal to be aged between one and two years old, two between two and four years, four between three and four years, and one between four and five years of age.

An MNI of five sheep was calculated from the mandibles, although taking wear stages into account suggests that the butchery waste of at least seven sheep is present in fill 1007, mixed with a small number of bones from other species. The quantity of waste material itself does not appear to be complete for this number of animals, although further remains may lie within the unexcavated part of the pit. Alternatively, this may be the result of secondary deposition of this waste material.

Dog skeleton in pit 712 (Period 3.3)
Pit 712 was cut into the infill of a much larger storage pit (461) in Area B, when it was half full. A complete adult male dog, excluding some of the phalanges, had been placed at its base (see Chapter 2, Fig. 2.22). No butchery marks were present upon the bones and the animal appears to have been deposited intact and with respect. Other bones from the same deposit include the left and right tarso-metatarsus of a young domestic fowl.

Dog remains in ditch 4185 (Period 3.4)
A group of dog bones from what was probably of the same animal were excavated from fill 4184 of Late Roman ditch 4185 in Area H. They comprise a left jaw and humerus; a right radius, femur and tibia; a left metatarsal; and a lumbar vertebra. The humerus has a cut mark, suggesting that some of the meat was removed from the animal. A single cow femur fragment was also recovered from this context.

Principal domestic stock animals

Age at death and sex

Cattle
In total, the age at death of 29 cattle was estimated from the wear of mandibular teeth, two being Bronze Age, two Iron Age, eighteen Late Iron Age/Early Romano-British and seven Romano-British in date. Overall, this comprises a small sample size from which to assess the husbandry strategy being implemented. Similarly, epiphysial fusion data which may also be used to estimate the mortality rate of the stock animals, was also scarce. However, some interpretative comments can be made based on the Late Iron Age/Early Romano-British data, as presented in Tables 4.8 and 4.9.

Generally speaking, the Iron Age mandibular tooth wear and epiphyseal fusion data agree. Tooth wear data suggests that around 62% of animals were culled after stage F, with significant drop in the age of the herd at stage G, 40 months to 6.5 years of age. Epiphyseal fusion data is more difficult to assess, since there are few specimens present in stages D and E. However, it is evident that few animals were culled until after stage C, with most bones in the fused category, whereas by stage F, nearly half of the animals have been culled. The majority of the cattle appear to have been slaughtered after three years of age, as adult animals, with possibly in the region of 40% of cattle slaughtered as younger animals. Of the cattle pelves,

Fusion Stage	Fused	Fusing	Unfused	Total
A (7–10m)	12	1	1	14
B (12–18m)	22	-	1	23
C (2–2.5/3y)	18	1	-	19
D (3–3.5y)	-	-	-	-
E (3.5–4y)	4	2	1	7
F (4.5–5y)	14	2	10	26

Table 4.9 Late Iron Age/Early Romano-British cattle epiphysial fusion data, incorporating large mammal vertebra for stage F

Wear Stage	Late Iron Age/Early Romano-British	Romano-British
A (0–2m)		0.5
B (2–6m)	1	0.5
C (6–12m)	2.5	
D (1–2y)	4.25	1.83
E (2–3y)	2.75	2.83
F (3–4y)	3.25	5.33
G (4–6y)	1.25	1.33
H (6–8y)		0.33
I (8–10y)		0.33
Total	**15**	**13**

Table 4.10 Sheep/goat and sheep mandibular wear stages; where a mandible could not be assigned to one wear stage it has divided between wear stages

Wear Stage	Neolithic	Bronze Age	Late Iron Age/Early Romano-British	Romano-British
A	1	0.33	1	0.5
B (<6m)	1	0.33	1	0.5
C (6–12m)	1.5	0.33	2.33	1
D (12–24m)	2.5		9.33	2.5
E (>24m)	2		3.33	0.5

Table 4.11 Pig mandibular wear stages; where a mandible could not be assigned to one wear stage it has divided between wear stages

Period	Range	Mean	SD	N
Iron Age	57.35–61.70	59.92	2.28	3
Late Iron Age/ Romano-British	58.50–61.15	59.49	1.18	4
Romano-British	58.5	-	-	1

SD - standard deviation

Table 4.12 Univariate statistics of cattle astragali

thirteen were attributed to a sex, most of which were identified as from female cattle.

It is likely that cattle husbandry of the Late Iron Age/Early Romano-British period involved a mixed strategy, probably with the majority of males being culled when they had gained meat weight after three years of age (stage G), with a population of older adult dairy cows and working animals being maintained. A small number of cattle were evidently slaughtered as very old animals at the end of their working life.

Sheep/Goat
Most of the sheep/goat or sheep mandibles from which an age of death could be estimated were excavated from Late Iron Age/Early Romano-British deposits, with smaller numbers from Romano-British deposits. Data from other periods are too scarce to be useful in analysis. Data from Late Iron Age/Early Romano-British and Romano-British phases are presented in Table 4.10. Epiphysial fusion data proved too limited for analysis.

The sample sizes presented in Table 4.10 are too small for over-interpretation, but there is a general trend towards most animals being culled before four years of age in the Late Iron Age/Early Romano-British and Romano-British phases. Significant numbers of older animals of a wool flock appear to be absent, and it is likely that meat was an important factor in the husbanding of sheep. Sexing data derived from pelves was too scarce to be useful; comprising a single pelvis of a Late Iron Age/Early Romano-British ewe.

Pig
The number of mandibles from deposits other than those of the Late Iron Age/Early Romano-British period were too small to be meaningful (Table 4.11). Most animals appear to have been slaughtered at young ages, as is typical in an animal exploited primarily for its meat and secondary products. Too few canines or mandibles were recovered to be useful in determining the male:female ratio of pigs.

Biometric data

Cattle
Fig. 4.4
Biometric data of cattle was more commonly recorded in Late Iron Age/Early Romano-British bones, with significantly less for Romano-British specimens, and was very rare for all other periods. This greatly hampers any attempt to investigate evidence of improved cattle of the Roman period in comparison to Iron Age stock, as apparent at Heybridge, Great Chesterford (Medlycott 2011a), Lincoln (Dobney *et al.* 1996) and Exeter (Maltby 1981).

Figure 4.4 presents the breadth of the distal humerus, proximal and distal radius, distal tibia, distal metatarsal and distal metacarpal in comparison to a standard Iron Age animal using a log ratio method suggested for sheep by Davis (1996). This is an attempt to increase the overall sample in analysis. The standard animal was calculated from average Iron Age cattle data from the south of England held by the Animal Bone Metrical Archive Project (ABMAP; University of Southampton 2003). Using archaeological data

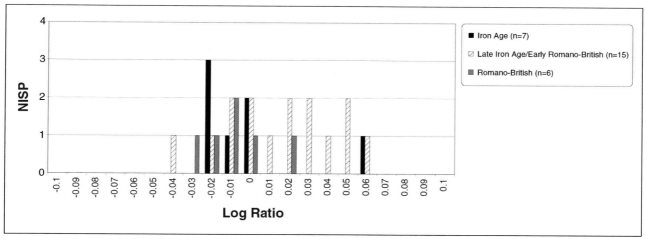

Figure 4.4 Comparison of Iron Age to Romano-British cattle limb bone greatest breadth

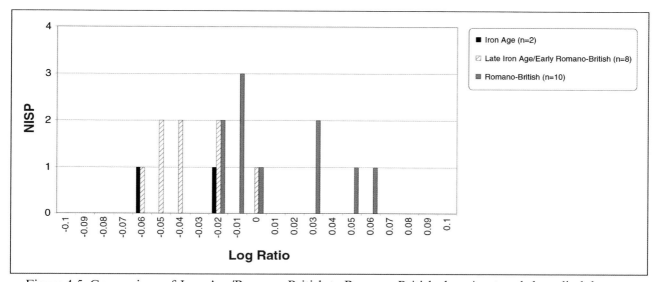

Figure 4.5 Comparison of Iron Age/Romano-British to Romano-British sheep/goat and sheep limb bone greatest breadth

in this way allows no control of the age or sex of the standard to be taken into account, but does give access to a wide range and number of measurements not easily obtainable from modern animals (Albarella 2002, 55). In addition, Table 4.12, presents the univariate statistics of the greatest lateral length of the astragalus. Figure 4.4 and Table 4.12 show no variance in the stock of cattle between the Iron Age and Roman periods.

Sheep
Figs 4.5–4.6
Biometric data are rare in sheep/goat and sheep records. As with cattle, in an attempt to increase the sample size, the breadth of long bones was compared to that of a standard sheep using a log ratio method (Fig. 4.5). The standard used was obtained from mean values of a group of Shetland ewes (Davis 1996). In addition, the width of the third molar was also examined (Fig. 4.6). These methods were chosen as they have been used with some success to identify the addition of new breeds to the Romano-British stock (Albarella 2002, 29).

The sample is limited, but variance between the Late Iron Age/Romano-British and Romano-British specimens is presented in Figure 4.5. The Late Iron Age/Romano-British specimens have statistically narrower breadths in comparison to the Romano-British specimens at the 99% confidence level (t=3.82, p=0.001). In contrast, the width of the third mandibular molar shows no variance (t=-0.65, p=0.53). However, all but one of the Romano-British third molars in Figure 4.6 were from pit 966/968, detailed above. Figure 4.6, therefore, includes the small number of individuals represented in this single butchery event, rather than a sample of the sheep population husbanded across the period.

Pig
Fig. 4.7
Biometric data from pig bones are rare on most anatomical parts. Figure 4.7 presents a combination of measurements compared to a standard wild boar using data and the log ratio method detailed by Payne and Bull (1988). Most of the measurements are of the length of teeth, although measurements of three

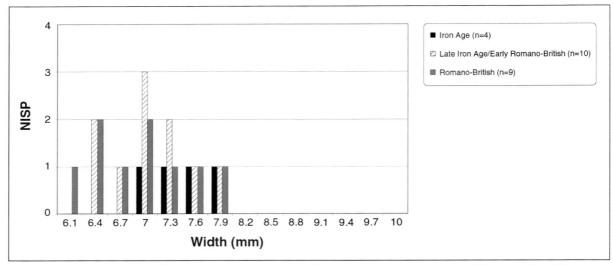

Figure 4.6 Comparison of Iron Age to Romano-British sheep/goat and sheep mandibular M3 widths (mm)

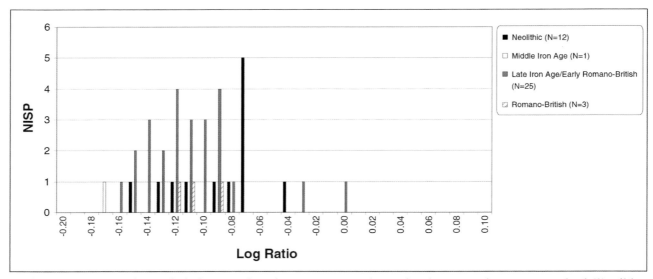

Figure 4.7 Comparison of pig bone and teeth measurements log ratios, in comparison to a standard (0) wild boar

scapulae, two ulnae and a humerus are also included. Only one measurement from one bone or tooth has been included, to avoid overpopulating the graph with data from the same bones or teeth.

One Late Iron Age/Early Romano-British wild boar mandible was identified using this method, excavated from the Late Iron Age enclosures (ditch 2685) in Area D.

Pathologies and congenital traits

Cattle

Eleven pathological specimens were recorded. A Late Iron Age/Early Romano-British pelvis acetabulum had evidently been fractured early in the life of the animal. This resulted in osteophytic growth between the pubis and ischium segments of the acetabulum, and deformation to the shape of the bone between the two. The pubis has set in a slightly closer position to the acetabulum than normal. The injury had healed

well before the death of the animal, with the new bone growth smoothed over.

A single set of Middle Iron Age tarsal bones shows evidence of a mild case of spavin. Exostoses between the navicular-cuboid and the external cuneiform resulted in the two bones being fused together. The calcaneum and astragalus of this same animal leg were also present, but with no signs of any pathology. The aetiology of spavin is undetermined, but it is considered to be caused by stresses placed on the joint. These stresses create inflammation of the soft tissues spreading to the periosteum, the membrane which lines all bones, stimulating new bone formation in the joint (Baker and Brothwell 1980, 118–23). Spavin is known to occur in draught animals, but would probably have only caused a mild lameness after which the animal would still have been useful for lighter work (*ibid.*, 119).

A single Late Iron Age/Early Romano-British metatarsal and a Romano-British metacarpal both had lateral extension of the distal lateral condyle,

Phase	Cattle		Sheep/Goat and Sheep		Pig		Total	
	Knife	Chop	Knife	Chop	Knife	Chop	Knife	Chop
Bronze Age	4	-	-	-	-	-	4	-
Iron Age	2	-	4		1		7	-
Late Iron Age/Early Romano-British	24	3	37	3	7	1	68	7
Romano-British	9	1	20	1	-	-	29	2

Table 4.13 NISP of the principal domestic stock with butchery marks by phase

termed a splayed metapodial. It is suggested that this asymmetry of cattle metapodials may be induced by excessive stresses placed on the limbs from utilising cattle as draught animals (Dobney *et al.* 1996, 39). Similarly, a Late Iron Age/Early Romano-British first phalanx has lateral extensions to the proximal, lateral, articular surfaces. This is the surface that would articulate to the splayed metapodial and the alteration of the phalanges in this manner presumably had the same cause.

A single instance of osteochrondritis dissecans was recorded, on the proximal articulation of a Middle Iron Age metacarpal. The condition is defined as the focal ischaemic necrosis of the growth cartilage initiated by necrosis of the cartilage canal blood vessel during growth of the bone (Ytrehus *et al.* 2007, 445), possibly resulting from sudden trauma or physical stress to the joint (Dobney *et al.* 1996, 38). Lastly, two Late Iron Age/Early Romano-British mandibles had shed the second premolar ante-mortem, with the alveolus in the process of healing over.

Congential traits include a single Late Iron Age/Early Romano-British mandible with an under- or overshot jaw, evident from the irregular wear on the premolar teeth and the third molar. Two Late Iron Age/Early Romano-British mandibles had additional foramina on the lingual (interior) side of the mandible, or 11.1% of the 18 Late Iron Age/Early Romano-British mandibles with this part of the bone present. Of the 22 mandibular third molars, only one has a reduced hypoconulid (Type 5), all the remainder being normal (Type 1).

Sheep/Goat
Pathologies were found upon three specimens. A Late Iron Age mandible had evidently suffered an internal infection (osteomyelitis), with bone swollen in the area of the deciduous premolars. Part of the bone was lost on the buccal side in the area of the second deciduous premolar, most likely where pus exited the bone, with osteoperiostitis evident on the surface of the mandible. The second and third deciduous premolars have been lost, probably due to the infection. The latter may have been caused by an oral injury, with the resulting infection making it difficult for the animal to eat and resulting in it being selected for slaughter.

Osteochrondritis dissecans was identified on a proximal articulation of a Late Iron Age/Early Romano-British metacarpal, probably of a sheep, possibly resulting from sudden stress to the joint early in the animal's life.

A Romano-British sheep humerus has an exostosis on the lateral side of the distal articulation. This is thought to be related to trauma, or knocks, to the 'elbow' joint where the animals are put though races or penned (Baker and Brothwell 1980, 127).

One congenital trait was identified on mandibles identified as sheep/goat and sheep. An additional foramen below the second or third premolar on the buccal side of the mandible was recorded in three out of thirteen Romano-British mandibles with this part of the bone present.

Butchery
Butchery marks were recorded on 117 specimens. Most of these are from the dismemberment and filleting of the limbs of the carcass using a knife (Table 4.13). Removal of the tongue and separation of the mandible from the skull was recorded on Bronze Age and Late Iron Age/Early Romano-British and Romano-British specimens. A single skinning mark was recorded on a Romano-British cattle metacarpal. Removal of a sheep horn by chopping through the horn core was evident in one Romano-British skull; the horn would then have been soaked off the bone core. The hide and horn, however, would have been utilised in all periods. A Late Iron Age/Early Romano-British atlas had been chopped during the decapitation of the animal. A Romano-British sheep skull has been chopped transversely and longitudinally, to remove the brain and possibly to fit the parts into a pot to be boiled. In addition, a Romano-British cattle or red deer thoracic vertebra had knife marks upon it from where the tenderloin had been removed.

Other mammals

Equids
Separating horse from ass (donkey) and the two hybrids of these animals (mules and hinneys) has proved problematic in the archaeozoological record. Prehistoric equids are unlikely to be ass or a hybrid, as the Romans are thought to have introduction the ass into Britain (Clutton-Brock 1992, 117). Most of the equid remains from Romano-British deposits are thought likely to be horse, although other equids may well be present in smaller numbers. None of the remains from Hinxton have been identified as of ass or a hybrid species, with three mandibles identified as probably horse. Age estimates were calculated for one Middle Iron Age and four Late Iron Age mandibles, none of which were below ten years of age. Only two unfused equid bones were recorded from bones: a Late Iron Age cervical vertebra, of an animal less than five years of age and a Roman distal tibia of an animal less than twenty to twenty-four months old. Most

Period	Bone	Wither Height (mm)	Wither Height (hh)
Iron Age	Tibia	1303.536	12.3
Late Iron Age/Early Romano-British	Radius	1222.312	12
Late Iron Age/Early Romano-British	Radius	1183.339	11.3
Late Iron Age/Early Romano-British	Metacarpal	1172.926	11.2
Late Iron Age/Early Romano-British	Tibia	1222.465	12
Late Iron Age/Early Romano-British	Tibia	1336.06	13.1
Late Iron Age/Early Romano-British	Tibia	1284.749	12.3
Romano-British	Radius	1299.108	12.3

Table 4.14 Calculated wither heights from equid long bones

horses were evidently mature animals, with potentially all horses rounded-up from wild herds (Moore-Colyer 1994, 5). There is no direct evidence of horse breeding, although it could be argued that the Roman unfused tibia may be of an animal domestically bred. Animals less than two years of age caught from wild stock would have to be maintained for at least another year before being sufficiently strong to use as a working animal.

Most of the articulating equid bones are described in Table 4.14. In addition, a Roman femur and both pelves of the same animal were excavated from fill 188 of Middle to Late Roman ditch 189 (Period 3.4 Ditch Group 12). There is no evidence to suggest the carcasses of equids were not treated in a similar manner to cattle, with equid bones normally found in association with cattle bones in Iron Age, Late Iron Age/Early Romano-British, and Romano-British phases. Butchery marks were recorded upon eight bones, almost all knife marks associated with the dismemberment and filleting of the limbs. In addition, a Late Iron Age/Early Romano-British metacarpal has skinning marks upon it, and a Romano-British radius has chop marks from the filleting of the forelimb. Wither heights of equids were calculated from eight specimens (Table 4.14), all within the size range of ponies.

Two equid bones were recorded with pathologies. A Middle Iron Age lumbar vertebra has exostoses forming lesions around the proximal articular surface, a degenerative disease of the spine. Although such pathologies to the spine may be associated with horse riding, the pathology is not overly severe and may simply be associated with age (Levine *et al.* 2005, 102). A Late Iron Age/Early Romano-British metapodial fragment has exostoses around its proximal articular surface. This is probably associated with spavin, as described for cattle above. Faulty shoeing, hereditary factors affecting the conformation of the foot, walking on hard surfaces or heavy work may also have been factors in its development (Baker and Brothwell 1980, 118).

Dog

Excluding the associated or articulated bone groups described above, dog bones only occurred in eighteen other features, usually as single occurrences. Nine dog bones were recovered from ditch 1931 associated with Enclosure 2 in Area D, with six of these recovered from deposit 1935. However, at least two individuals were present and there was no evidence that any of these bones were from the same animal.

Two dog bones have pathologies The skull of the animal buried in Early Roman pit 712 in Area B provides evidence of chronic infection, osteomyelitis, in the root cavity of the right canine. An abscess had formed in the root cavity, with the subsequent loss of the base of the root. The infection had discharged through a sinus in the side of the maxilla, resulting in infection (osteoperiostitis) around the area of the sinus hole. Presumably, the lower part of the root was dissolved by the pus, or ejected via the sinus. New bone growth has created a raised area around the sinus hole, but although the edges of the sinus hole are heavily pitted, much of the new bone is smoothed over suggesting the animal recovered from the infection. Non-specific infections are haematological in origin, carried through the bloodstream from the infected part of the body (Baker and Brothwell 1980, 64), but it seems likely this infection was caused by an injury to the root of the canine. A Romano-British dog tibia had an ossified haematoma on the shaft of the bone. This results from a wound causing bleeding at the sub-periosteal level, where the resulting swelling is replaced by smooth bone (Baker and Brothwell 1980, 83).

Deer

Red and roe deer bones or antler were recovered from Late Neolithic/Early Bronze Age and Iron Age deposits, but constitute a very small percentage of the mammal bone. Three fragments of antler were recovered. One red deer antler came from the Beaker-associated pit/'shaft' (SF 40, 902, Pit Group 7). This still has part of the pedicle present, demonstrating that it had been cut from the skull, presumably from a hunted animal, and is not a naturally shed antler. There is evidence of cutting around the pedicle, beneath the coronet; these cuts could have occurred either during animal skinning or removal of the antler.

A large antler fragment was recovered from deposit 687 of pit 691 (Pit Group 4) and comprises the coronet, lower part of the beam, and the very base of the first two tines, of a red deer antler that had been naturally shed from the animal. A small fragment also came from Late Iron Age ditch 4562 (Enclosure 3), with a chop mark upon it. No further butchery marks were recorded upon the deer bones.

Species	Bronze Age	Late Iron Age	Late Iron Age/Early Roman	Romano-British	Total Roman
Domestic fowl		1	2	3	5
Domestic/Greylag goose			2	2	4
Mallard		1			0
Crane		1			0
Crow	1		3		3
Domestic fowl/pheasant				2	2
Corvus sp.			1		1
Passerine			1		1
Unidentified bird	1	2	12	21	33
Total	**2**	**5**	**21**	**28**	**49**

Table 4.15 NISP of bird bones by phase, bones of the same individual counted as 1 NISP

Small mammals

A number of small mammal bones were recovered from both pits and ditches, including voles, shrews and stoats or weasels, from Iron Age to Romano-British deposits (Table 4.3). Each species would have been found locally in the area since earlier Mesolithic times (Yalden 1999, 72). All of the twenty-eight Middle Iron Age water vole bones were excavated from fill 1520 of pit 1521 (Pit Group 18), and represent a minimum of three individuals.

Bird bone

A few bird bones were recovered from the Late Iron Age/Early Romano-British and Romano-British phases (Table 4.15). Fourteen bones of the same young domestic fowl were excavated from deposit 1919 in Romano-British pit 1368 (Pit Group 29), including parts of both wings and the right leg. The Late Iron Age/Early Romano-British domestic fowl radius was recovered from fill 2666 of pit 2667 (ungrouped), while two tarso-metatarsals from a young possible domestic fowl were found in the fill associated with the Early Roman dog skeleton in pit 712, described above. Domestic fowl is an introduced bird to the British Isles. It was more abundant from the Roman period onwards (Parker 1988, 202), but small numbers of the bird are known from a number of Iron Age sites (Maltby 1981, 162).

Butchery marks were found on one bird bone; a Romano/British greylag or domestic goose tibio-tarsus has a knife mark from dismemberment for consumption. Wild fowl such as mallard would have been available from the nearby River Cam. Crows are commensal birds, and their inclusion in archaeological deposits is probably incidental.

The list of bird species presented in Table 4.15 is unlikely to represent the full range of birds consumed by the local population, but the meat of birds does not appear to have made a large input into the local diet.

Amphibians

A number of frog (*Rana* sp.) and toad (*Bufo* sp.) bones (503 in total) were recovered from deposits dating from Neolithic to the Romano-British phases, most of which were collected in small numbers from soil samples. Four features contained larger numbers of amphibian bones.

The single fill of a large Late Iron Age/Early Romano-British posthole contained a minimum of twenty-two frogs and one toad. A minimum of five frogs and one toad were recovered from Romano-British pit 1336. A very large collection of amphibian bones was excavated from fill 538 of the Romano-British storage pit 461, and fill 486 associated with dog burial 712 (both Pit Group 31) that was excavated into the fills of this pit. Deposit 538 contained a minimum of 30 frogs, and deposit 486 a minimum of 62 frogs and a toad. The amphibian remains from the dog burial may either have been reworked bones from the underlying storage pit, or may represent pit falls.

Discussion
Fig. 4.8
The majority of animal bones came from Late Iron Age/Early Romano-British features, with small quantities from earlier deposits also being found. A significant portion of the analysis detailed above discussed deliberately placed or rapidly formed bone deposits, as opposed to the incidental inclusions of bone within features.

Two clearly deliberately placed bone deposits included a cow humerus within Late Iron Age Burial Group 3B, grave 2147, and the internment of a dog within Early Roman storage pit 461 (Pit Group 31). The placement of single species as food offerings within graves has pre-Roman origins. Offerings of pork are more commonly found, with the bones of cattle and sheep being less frequent (Philpott 1991). In a Romano-British context, such offerings are more frequently found in rural settings, and may indicate a survival of this pre-Roman belief system (*ibid.*). The burial of a dog within Romano-British storage pit 461 may have as much to do with referencing the storage pit as with the burial of the dog, again reflecting pre-Roman ideas. Within Iron Age contexts, dog and horse were reported by Cunliffe (1992, 77) to be the most frequently occurring interred species as both whole and partial skeletons, possibly because they are closely associated with deities of the Celtic belief system. However, this probably has regional variation. Excavations on the A2 Pepperhill to Cobham road scheme in Kent found that pig remains were more frequently deposited within Iron Age storage pits. Placement of animal remains, and other objects,

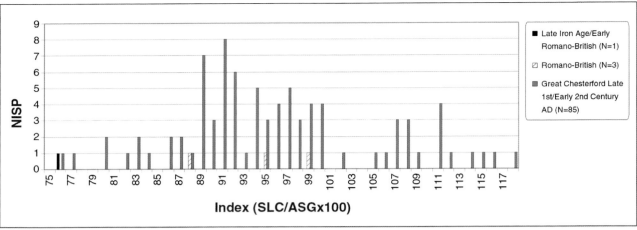

Figure 4.8 Sheep/Goat scapula neck measurements, incorporating data from Great Chesterford

throughout the depositional history of a storage pit may have been linked to a continued belief in chthonic deities and fertility (Cunliffe 1992, 79; Bates *et al.* 2012, 270).

The partial remains of carcasses were found in both pits and ditches. Two Neolithic pits (Pit Group 4; pits 683 and 778) contained a number of fragments of pig skulls, with smaller quantities of bone from other animals found in the same features. It is suggested that these deposits are the result of the direct accumulation or secondary deposition of midden deposits within these pits. A similar interpretation was offered for the sheep remains from a Period 3.3 pit (Pit Group 29; 966/968). In many ways, these features have similar depositional characteristics, albeit of different periods and involving different species.

A number of excavated sections across the ditches forming Enclosures 1/2 in Area D produced bones of the same individual, most notably in the remains of equids and dog. These animals appear to have been dismembered with the remains distributed along the lengths of the ditches. Parts of the carcass may have been utilised, although dog meat is unlikely to have been consumed. Bone of other species was also found in significant numbers, presumably from accumulations within the immediate vicinity, such as from middens within the enclosure.

Although the evidence proved too limited to make many comparisons between the Iron Age and Early Romano-British stock animals, some interpretations have been possible using data from the wider area. The relative proportion of stock animals suggested by Table 4.3 is probably misleading, as discussed above. Overall, the relative numbers of cattle and sheep may have been more equal in both the Late Iron Age and Early Romano-British periods. This does not take into account possible numbers of cattle or sheep removed from the site for slaughter at the nearby town of Great Chesterford. Pigs were husbanded in lower numbers during both periods.

When looking at the mortality data of the principal stock animals, sample sizes are generally too low for detailed interpretation. However, during the Late Iron Age/Early Romano-British period a mixed strategy appears to have been applied to the husbanding of cattle, with both dairy and meat being significant factors in the selection of animals for slaughter. Many

of them appear to have been maintained beyond their optimum meat weight. Sheep of the same period, by contrast, were normally slaughtered at an earlier age and the production of meat appears to have been a significant aim in the stock management of these animals. Pigs appear to have been typically slaughtered after reaching their optimum meat weight.

Although biometric data of sheep bones is limited, some interpretations are possible. Judging from the breadth of bones, they appear to have become stockier by the Romano-British period in comparison to their Late Iron Age counterparts. Comparing the shape of scapulae to those of short- and long-tailed breeds of sheep, and data from Great Chesterford (Fig. 4.8), there is evidence for the introduction of a long-tailed variety. Evidence from the wider region, including sites at Great Chesterford and Colchester, has demonstrated similar introductions in the Early and Middle Roman periods (Albarella *et al.* 2008; Baxter 2011; Luff 1985). In contrast, there was no such evidence for larger cattle. This has been observed elsewhere in cattle bones of the 1st century AD (Albarella *et al.* 2008), although it is quite possible that their absence here is due to the limitations of the data. At Hinxton, no cattle bones comparable in size to those recovered from Great Holts Farm, Boreham were found (Albarella 2003), which are thought to be first generation imported stock. It cannot be reliably assessed whether such animals did or did not have an influence on the stock at Hinxton.

Palaeopathological evidence is rare at the site, but demonstrates that care was taken of animals even after traumatic injuries. Pathologies thought to be associated with the use of animals for traction were found in Middle Iron Age, Late Iron Age/Early Romano-British and Romano-British cattle and a Romano-British equid.

Wild animals had little input into the diet, as is typical of both the Iron Age and Romano-British periods. One specimen of Late Iron Age/Early Romano-British wild boar was identified, as well as a small number of deer and wild fowl bones. Each species would have been locally hunted to supplement the diet.

III. Macrobotanical remains

by Val Fryer, with Rachel Fosberry

Introduction

Despite the extensive sampling that took place during the excavation of Areas A–E (240 samples) and a further 167 samples that were taken from Area J, a high percentage of the resultant macrobotanical assemblages contained insufficient material (*i.e.* <0.1 litres) to enable any accurate interpretation of the recovered plant macrofossils. The reason for this is not immediately apparent but it may have been due to the mainly pastoral regime which was being followed in the Iron Age and Early Roman periods, which left few traces in the archaeological record. Indeed, (pre-Saxon) evidence of domestic activity (both archaeologically and within the macrobotanical assemblage) on or near the site is very rare and, equally, cereals seem to have been largely grown and processed elsewhere. A possible reason for the largely negative results could be the changes in water levels that occurred over the millennia; this result is in direct contrast to the Anglo-Saxon and early medieval deposits that were sampled at Hinxton Hall (Area F; Fryer and Murphy in Clarke *et al.* forthcoming), at the Genome Extension excavations (Area I and Area J; Fosberry 2012 and 2015) and on the west bank of the river in the parish of Ickleton (Area H; Fryer 1993) where plant macrofossils were noticeably more abundant (producing evidence of abundant flax seeds and also of retting; see Clarke *et al.* forthcoming).

Evidence for the local environment, although equally scant, indicates that the excavated areas were primarily set in an area of dry, predominantly short grassland with possible nearby woodland or similar shaded areas. On the west of the River Cam (Area H) samples indicate that relatively dry conditions, with only intermittent flooding, were usual during the Iron Age and Early Roman periods.

Methodology

Samples for the extraction of the plant macrofossil assemblages were taken from across the main excavated areas (Areas A–D), and approximately 224 were submitted for assessment, which was undertaken by Val Fryer and forms the basis of this report. As preservation was poor only a few further samples were fully analysed; this work was undertaken by Rachel Fosberry. Of the samples from features in Area J, the majority were taken for the retrieval of flint debitage from the Palaeolithic and Neolithic hollows (Ponds P and Q) and assessment of the remainder indicated little potential for the survival of plant remains from pre-Anglo-Saxon deposits (Fosberry 2015); these are therefore not reported on here.

The soil samples were processed by tank flotation and the floating component (the flot) was collected in a 0.5mm nylon mesh and air dried. The flots were subsequently sorted using a binocular microscope at magnifications up to x60 and a complete list of the recorded remains compiled. Identification of plant remains is with reference to the *Digital Seed Atlas of the Netherlands* and the authors' own reference collections. Nomenclature is according to Stace (1997). Unless otherwise stated, all plant macrofossils were charred. Carbonised seeds and grains, by the process of burning and burial, become blackened and often distort and fragment leading to difficulty in identification. Plant remains have been identified to species where possible. Modern contaminants including fibrous roots, seeds and chaff were present throughout.

Sample volumes were estimated based on the original number of buckets of soil recorded. Individual cereal grains, chaff elements and seeds have been counted. Fragmented cereal grains have been counted when over half of the grain has survived (embryo ends only). Items that cannot be easily quantified such as charcoal, bones and eggshell have been scored for abundance according to the following criteria: + = rare, ++ = moderate, +++ = abundant.

Plant macrofossils

Cereal grains/chaff, seeds of common weeds and wetland plants and/or tree/shrub macrofossils were recorded at low to moderate densities from all but forty-six samples. Preservation is very variable; some cereal grains are very puffed and distorted (probably due to high temperatures during combustion), and many of the chaff elements are heavily fragmented.

Cereals

Cereal grains/chaff were recovered from 159 samples. Oat (*Avena* sp.), barley (*Hordeum* sp.), rye (*Secale cereale*) and wheat (*Triticum* sp.) grains were recorded, with wheat generally being predominant. Both 'drop form' grains typical of spelt wheat (*T. spelta*) and rounded forms of probable bread wheat (*T. aestivum/compactum*) or rivet wheat (*T. turgidum*) types were present throughout. An asymmetrical lateral grain of six-row barley (*H. vulgare*) was noted in Sample 188 from an Iron Age ditch fill in Enclosure 1 (Area D), which was possibly contaminated with intrusive Roman material. Chaff is generally rare, but emmer (*T. dicoccum*) and spelt glume bases were recorded along with rachis nodes of bread wheat and rivet wheat types, barley and rye. In the absence of the diagnostic floret bases, it was not possible to ascertain whether the oat grains derived from wild or cultivated types.

Wild flora

Seeds of common weed plants were recovered, generally at very low densities, from eighty-seven samples. Segetal taxa including corn cockle (*Agrostemma githago*), stinking mayweed (*Anthemis cotula*), brome (*Bromus* sp.), black bindweed (*Fallopia convolvulus*) and dock (*Rumex* sp.) were recorded along with grasses and grassland herbs including goosegrass (*Galium aparine*), fumitory (*Fumaria officinalis*), buttercups (*Ranunculus* sp.) and vetch/vetchling (*Vicia/Lathyrus* sp.). Wetland plant macrofossils were extremely rare, but nutlets of sedge (*Carex* sp.) and spike-rush (*Eleocharis* sp.) were noted in six samples. Hazel (*Corylus avellana*) nutshell fragments were recorded from twenty-three samples, and other tree/shrub macrofossils included a sloe (*Prunus spinosa*) fruit stone, elderberry (*Sambucus nigra*) 'pips' and a possible fragment of oak (*Quercus* sp.) cupule.

Sample		188	301	251	252	279
Deposit		*1538*	*2695*	*2160*	*2161*	*2555*
Cut (Ditch)		*1541*	*2685*	*1931*	*1931*	*2539*
Feature group		*Enc 1*	*Enc 1*	*Enc 2*	*Enc 2*	*Enc 2*
Cereals						
Avena sp. (grains)	Oat (wild or cultivated)			+cf		
Avena sp. (awn)	Oat (wild or cultivated)	+				
Cereal indet. (grains)		+++	+	+	+	+
Hordeum sp. (grains)	Barley	++	+	+		
Hordeum sp. (rachis nodes)	Barley	+				
H. vulgare L. (asymmetrical lateral grains)	Domesticated barley	+				
Hordeum/Secale cereale type (rachis nodes)	Barley/Rye	+				
Triticum sp. (grains)	Wheat	+	+	+		
Triticum sp. (glume bases)	Wheat	+				
T. dicoccum Schubl. (glume bases)	Emmer wheat			+cf		
T. spelta L. (glume bases)	Spelt wheat	++				
Herbs						
Agrostemma githago L.	Corn cockle	+cf				
Atriplex sp.	Oraches	+	+	+	+	
Bromus sp.	Bromes	+				
Chenopodium album L.	Fat Hen		+			+
Chenopodium ficifolium Sm.	Fig-leaved Goosefoot	+				+
Chenopodiaceae indet.	Goosefoot Family		++			
Fabaceae indet.	Legumes	+				
Fallopia convolvulus (L.)A.Love	Black-bindweed	+		+	+	
Fumaria officinalis L.	Common Fumitory		+			
Galium aparine L.	Cleavers					+
Hyoscyamus niger L.	Henbane			+		
Linum sp.	Flaxes				+	
Medicago/Trifolium/Lotus sp.	Medick/Clover/Bird's Foot Trefoil	+			+cf	
Mentha sp.	Mint	+				
Plantago lanceolata L.	Ribwort Plantain	+				
Small Poaceae indet.	Small-seeded Grass Family	+	+	+	+	+
Polygonum aviculare L.	Knotgrass	+	+			+cf
Polygonaceae indet.	Dock Family		+			+
Ranunculus acris/repens/bulbosus	*cf.* Meadow/Creeping/Bulbous Buttercup				+	
Rumex sp.	Docks	++	+		++	
Sheradia arvensis L.	Field Madder	+				
Stellaria sp.	Campion		+			
Stellaria media (L.)Vill.	Common Chickweed	+	+			
Tree/shrub macrofossils						
Corylus avellana L.	Hazel	+cf				
Other plant macrofossils						
Charcoal <2mm		++	++	++	+	+
Charcoal >2mm		+				
Charred root/rhizome/stem		+	+		+	
Indet. culm nodes		+				
Indet. seeds		+	+		+	
Indet. thorns (*Prunus* type)		+				
Molluscs						
Vertigo sp.					+b	

Sample	188	301	251	252	279
Deposit	1538	2695	2160	2161	2555
Cut (Ditch)	1541	2685	1931	1931	2539
Feature group	Enc 1	Enc 1	Enc 2	Enc 2	Enc 2
Other materials					
Black porous 'cokey' material	++	++	+	++	
Black tarry material			+	+	
Bone	+ +b	+			
Burnt/fired clay	+				
Small coal frags.	+				
Small mammal/amphibian bones	+b				
Vitrified material	++				
Volume of flot (litres)	**<0.1**	**<0.1**	**<0.1**	**<0.1**	**<0.1**
% flot sorted	**100%**	**100%**	**100%**	**100%**	**100%**

Key to Tables 4.16–4.18: + = 1 – 10 specimens; ++ = 10 – 100 specimens; +++ = 100+ specimens; b = burnt; cf = chaff fragment; Enc = Enclosure

Table 4.16 Selected Samples from Middle to Late Iron Age Enclosure 1/2 (Period 3.1)

Other plant macrofossils

Charcoal fragments and pieces of charred root or stem are present throughout the samples at varying densities. Other plant macrofossils are rare, but include indeterminate buds, culm nodes, inflorescence fragments and *Prunus* type thorns. Rare mineral replaced root/stem fragments were noted in some pit fills.

Molluscs

Although specific sieving for molluscan remains was not undertaken, shells were noted in a number of samples. Of these, a proportion are probably modern in origin as they retain delicate surface structures and colouration. However, small assemblages of weathered and abraded shells of predominantly open country species were noted in two samples and a single burnt shell of a probable marshland snail was noted in a sample from a Late Iron Age/Early Roman ditch 1931 forming part of Enclosure 2.

Other materials

The fragments of black porous 'cokey' material and black tarry material, which are present in most samples, are probable residues of the combustion of organic materials at extremely high temperatures. Possible domestic and/or dietary refuse includes bone fragments (some burnt), eggshell and fish bone. Although very rare, some remains possibly related to small scale 'industrial' activities were noted. These included ferrous globules, hammerscale, fragments of burnt or fired clay and vitrified globules.

Results by period

Ponds and palaeochannels

Plant macrofossils and other remains proved to be extremely scarce within all the assemblages taken from a series of natural ponds across the areas. It appears most likely that most, if not all, of the material is derived from small quantities of wind-blown detritus that became accidentally incorporated within the pond fills. As with the ponds, the assemblages from the palaeochannels proved largely negative and therefore not suggestive of cultural activity.

Neolithic and Bronze Age (Period 2)

Sampling of Neolithic and Early Bronze Age contexts produced very sparse charred plant remains. This was especially true of the deposits associated with Early Neolithic pottery and flintwork from one of the hollows/ponds (Pond Q; 16042), which produced only four intermediate charred cereal grains and sparse charcoal. Similarly, sampling of the backfill of the Early Neolithic double inhumation (Burial Group 1) produced only sparse charcoal. Most of the fills of Neolithic and Early Bronze Age pits were similarly impoverished, with the most notable, but still very small, assemblages deriving from pit 15194 (Pit Group 16), which produced a single glume base of one of the prehistoric wheats; emmer (*Triticum dicoccum*) or spelt (*T. spelta*), a single grain and hazel nutshell fragments, and from the upper, Beaker associated, backfill deposit (900) of the 'shaft' in Trench U (Pit Group 7), which produced a small quantity of charred grain, including barley (*Hordeum* sp.) and hazel nutshell. Sampling of one of the fills of putative Middle Bronze Age field system ditches (ditch 2029, Ditch Group 2) yielded very little charred material.

Middle to Late Iron Age (Period 3.1)

Thirty-six contexts of Middle to Late Iron Age date were sampled. The assemblages are characterised by extremely low densities of material (all <0.1 litres), and as a result specific activities are difficult to pinpoint. Small deposits of possible domestic and/or agricultural waste, including grains, weed seeds and dietary refuse were recorded from a few pits and a ditch, the latter forming part of Trackway 1, with small quantities of similar material being scattered throughout a number of other contexts.

Sample 301 from ditch 2685 (fill 2695) associated with Enclosure 1 possibly contains a low density of cereal processing debris, as segetal weed seeds are

129

Sample No		145	147	222	224	226	227	229	228
Context No		1354	1356	1654	1624	1668	1652	1658	1406
Cut (posthole)		1355	1357	1655	1625	1669	1653	1659	1407
Cereals									
Cereal indet. (grains)	Indeterminate cereal grain	++		+	+	+	++	++	++
Hordeum sp. (grains)	Barley	++++	++	+++	++	++	++++	+++++	++++
Herbs									
Anthemis cotula L.	Stinking mayweed					+			
Fallopia convolvulus (L.) A.Love	Black-bindweed						+	+	
Galium aparine L.	Cleavers							+	
Rumex sp.	Docks					+			
Other plant macrofossils									
Charcoal <2mm		++	+	+	+	+	++	++	+
Charcoal >2mm		+	+	+	+	+	+	+	+
Volume of flot (litres)		0.3	<0.1	<0.1	<0.1	<0.1	<0.1	0.1	<0.1
% flot sorted		10%	100%	100%	100%	100%	100%	100%	100%

Table 4.17 Samples from postholes associated with Late Iron Age Corral 1 (Period 3.2)

reasonably common within the assemblage (Table 4.16).

Sample 188 (from ditch 1541, fill 1538) contains a mixture of domestic refuse and possibly cereal processing waste. Grains (principally wheat), chaff and weed seeds are present/common in each along with charcoal and small quantities of dietary refuse. Although chaff is present, spelt chaff, which is frequently predominant in assemblages of Roman date, only occurs in one sample (Sample 188), and then only at a moderate density. This is consistent with the disposal of crop-processing waste which may have been used as animal feed.

Sample 252 from ditch 1931, fill 2161 – associated with Enclosure 2 – may contain a low density of material derived from burnt grass or hay. Although tenuous, the presence of a burnt shell of *Vertigo* sp. perhaps indicates material gathered from damper grassland areas, perhaps close to the River Cam. Possible mixed refuse deposits, including cereal processing waste and domestic debris, came from ditch 1931 (fill 2160) and ditch 2539 (Samples 251 and 279 respectively).

Late Iron Age to Roman (Period 3.2–3.4)

Corral 1
The most productive samples from Late Iron Age features were the eight samples taken from postholes within Corral 1 (Table 4.17) which contained beautifully preserved charred barley grains (and nothing else), some in very large quantities. The flot from Sample 145, fill 1354 of posthole 1355 contained at least 3,000 grains. Barley is a cereal that was commonly used for animal fodder; however, the absence of chaff suggests this was prime barley grain more commonly used for human consumption.

Dog burial in pit 712
Of the few samples taken from contexts of Roman date, only those from pit 712 (Period 3.3) containing

the burial of a dog produced notable assemblages (Table 4.18). Soil samples taken from around the animal's skeleton produced evidence of eggshell, bird and amphibian bones and also include a charred plant assemblage. Pit 712 contained at least three fills: 649, 646 and 486/524; only the lower fill (486/524) was sampled. The pit was cut into a partly-infilled storage pit 461, which also contained three deposits. The burial pit was largely cut through fill 460 and to a lesser extent through 538, both of which seem to have largely been composed of redeposited natural. Two samples were taken: one for the retrieval of the large quantity of amphibian bones present and another that targeted an area rich in charcoal. In contrast to the samples associated with the dog burial, neither sample from the storage pit was found to contain significant charred plant remains and further work was not recommended.

Samples were taken from fill 486/524 from specific areas around the placed dog skeleton: Sample 63 was taken from below the abdomen area of the dog with the aim of retrieving stomach contents. Sample 32 was a general sample of approximately 70% of fill 486 initially taken for the retrieval of eggshell and small bones noted during excavation of the feature. Sample 64 was a small sample of charred material that was noted by the excavator as forming a 'distinct patch of charcoal beneath the dog's paws'.

The plant remains in the samples are preserved by carbonisation (charring) and comprise cereal grains and weed seeds in addition to charcoal. Many of the charred plant remains, particularly the cereal grains, are abraded and have lost their outer testa making identifications tentative. Other preserved items include eggshell and amphibian bones along with snail shells.

A variety of crops is represented including the full range of cereals; rye (*Secale cereale*), barley (*Hordeum vulgare*), wheat (*Triticum* sp.) and occasional oats (*Avena* sp.) along with legumes, possibly peas (*Pisum/Lathyrus* sp.). Preservation is variable; many of the grains are abraded, distorted and/or fragmented.

Sample No.		32	63	64
Context No.		486	486	486
Cut No.		712	712	712
Feature Type		Pit	Pit	Pit
Cereals				
Avena sp. caryopsis	Oats [wild or cultivated]	6	2	
Hordeum vulgare L. caryopsis	Domesticated barley grain	1	34	15
Secale cereale L. caryopsis	Rye	32cf	8cf	2
Triticum cf. *spelta* L. caryopsis	Spelt wheat grain	12		13
Triticum sp. caryopsis	Wheat grain	39		
free-threshing *Triticum* sp. caryopsis	Free-threshing wheat grain	4	8	
cereal indet. caryopsis		117	91	31
Other food plants				
Legume 2–4mm	Pea	2	7	2.5
Tree/shrub macrofossils				
Corylus avellana L. nutshell fragment	Hazel nutshell fragment	2f		
Sambucus nigra L. seed	Elder			2
Other plant macrofossils				
Charcoal <2mm		++	+	++
Charcoal >2mm		+++	+	+++
Charcoal >10mm		++	+	++
Other remains				
Amphibian bones		++++	+++	++
Eggshell		++	++	+
Sample Size (L)		*c.*30	*c.*20	*c.*5
Volume of flot (litres)		100	30	10
% flot sorted		100	100	100

Table 4.18 Samples associated with Latest Iron Age to Early Roman dog burial in pit 712 (Period 3.3)

This may have been the result of being burnt at high temperatures, repeated burning and/or degradation prior to deposition. Diagnostic chaff elements are entirely absent, resulting in identifications being based on grain morphology.

The majority of the wheat grains are compact and have been identified as the free-threshing hexaploid-type bread wheat (*T. aestivum/compactum*) species. Occasional larger grains with a droplet form and a flat ventral surface are probably hulled spelt (*T. spelta*) wheat. The rye grains have a compact morphology and are often only distinguishable from the bread wheat grains by their characteristic sharp keel and elongated embryos. Oat grains have also been identified by their characteristic shape. The diagnostic floret bases are absent, precluding distinction between cultivated and wild varieties. The barley appears to be of the larger-sized hulled variety which would have required parching/pounding/light milling to remove the outer husk if intended for consumption rather than brewing. Small round legumes most resemble peas although may be of the wild sweet-pea (*Lathyrus* sp.) variety rather than cultivated pea (*Pisum sativum*).

The three samples analysed contain differing proportions of cereal varieties despite being taken from the same context. Sample 32 represents the fill around the dog skeleton and has the largest volume of soil processed. Taking this into account, the quantities of cereal grains recovered from Sample 32 and Sample 63 are similar. Sample 32 contains a higher proportion of wheat (both spelt and bread wheat) whereas Sample 63, taken from below the dog, does not contain any recognisable wheat grains but does have a much higher proportion of barley grains. This variation between samples suggests that the fill was not homogeneous and confirms that there were discrete deposits of charred remains. Sample 64, the smallest volume and taken from beneath the dog's paws, contains both spelt wheat and barley. All three samples contain rye grains and legumes.

Elder (*Sambucus nigra*) seeds and hazel (*Corylus avellana*) nutshell fragments are present in low quantities that are too small to suggest that they were being used for food and most probably represent the types of wood being used as fuel. Unusually, no weed seeds were recovered from any of the samples.

The samples taken from around the dog skeleton are sufficiently different to suggest distinct deposits. In general, charred assemblages such as these would also include charred weed seeds and possibly chaff elements that have been burnt along with cereal grains, although no such evidence was found in any of the samples from the deposit surrounding the dog skeleton. Charred assemblages are usually the result of the accidental burning of food during preparation or from floor sweepings in which dropped or discarded grain is swept up and disposed of in a fire. The inclusion of charred remains within a burial context is unexpected, especially where there is visible evidence of a concentration of charred plant remains in a specific area, such as under the dog's paws. The offerings of eggs and fowl (see Section 4.II above) may represent foods that the dog liked to eat, whereas cereals would not normally be considered a dietary constituent for a carnivore. The eggs and fowl bones were not burnt, making it unlikely that the charred grain was included as a food offering; the absence of chaff and weed seeds suggests that the grain was fully processed and stored as clean grain.

It appears that charred cereal grains and legumes were deliberately included in the pit along with eggs and possibly the foot of a chicken, as part of the mortuary process (or ritual) of a dog burial within a formerly utilitarian feature. Dog burials are relatively common on sites of various periods in Britain but rarely have excavations of these deposits included sampling for plant remains. Samples from a similar (Roman) dog burial at Love's Farm, Cambridgeshire (Hinman and Zant 2018) contained sparse charred plant remains including cereals and occasional weed seeds which were interpreted as a background scatter of material that had become incorporated into the deposit during the backfilling of the grave.

IV. Geoarchaeology and palynology
by Steve Boreham

Introduction
This report describes geological and palynological analysis of deposits exposed during excavations at the Genome Campus (Areas A and C) and on the west side of the Cam (Area H) (Fig. 2.1). The results of this work, with a fuller discussion of their implications for understanding the geological and geomorphological history of the upper Cam Valley, have been published elsewhere (Boreham and Rolfe 2009). Assessment of pollen samples from Area J indicated a large amount of post-depositional oxidation, with preservation of organic material being very poor, and consequently these samples were not included in this analysis.

Area A

Palaeochannel 107: Section A
An area of sloping valley side adjacent to a flatter terrace surface above the river floodplain had been cleared of ploughsoil for inspection. The slope was generally underlain by gravelly pellet chalk, interpreted as a periglacial solifluction deposit. However, a number of conspicuous shallow channel-forms filled by red-brown sand forming minor valleys or runnels aligned down-slope were observed.

A trench was cut at 90° to one of the channels in order to inspect the stratigraphy of the slope deposits. Section A was photographed and described from the eastern face of the trench. There was strong evidence for periglacial activity in the floor of the trench where blocks of heaved angular chalk formed polygonal patterning. The contorted gravelly pellet chalk is itself evidence for the mass movement of chalky regolith downslope under permafrost conditions. The brown sand overlying the pellet chalk clearly originated as decalcified slope wash, and must have been contemporaneous with the periglacial activity, since it was heaved by freeze-thaw action into tongues and diapirs within the chalky matrix. The overlying red/brown sand was much less disturbed and filled a small channel-form presumably eroded into the underlying material by running water. A red sand unit formed the core of the channel feature, although the present hillside channel appeared to be superimposed across the line of the older channel-form.

These deposits are interpreted as representing Late Glacial periglacial activity (pellet chalk), climatic amelioration leading to slope wash (brown sand), followed by renewed periglacial activity, perhaps during the Loch Lomond stadial (Younger Dryas) at *c.*12,000 BP, incorporating the brown sand into the chalky matrix. There was then a period of incision and the deposition of red/brown slopewash sand, perhaps at the beginning of the Holocene. The heavily oxidised red sand may represent a time of fully temperate conditions prevailing before vegetation cover had stabilised the soils in the catchment. An erosional channel cutting across the older deposits may relate to (anthropogenic) clearance of trees in the catchment area later in the Holocene.

Debris fan: Section B
At the foot of the sloping valley side on the terrace surface, a patch of brown shelly sand was observed. A trench was cut through this area to investigate the stratigraphy of the deposit. Section B was photographed and described from the north-west face of the trench. The area was floored by brown gravel and sand, overlain by contorted gravelly pellet chalk. Strings, tongues and diapirs of red/brown sand were incorporated into this chalky matrix, indicating that periglacial activity must have re-started after the formation of these slopewash deposits. It seems likely that this sand material originally formed as debris fans at the break in slope between the valley side and the gravel terrace. However, the overlying brown shelly sand was generally less contorted, although it filled several pipes and fissures. The conspicuous shells were identified (by R.C. Preece) as *Arianta arbustorum*, a large terrestrial snail intolerant of very cold conditions.

These deposits are interpreted as representing a gravel terrace overlain by soliflucted Late Glacial pellet chalk incorporating red/brown sand suggesting a short phase of slope wash followed by renewed periglacial activity. The overlying brown sand containing *Arianta* could be Late Glacial or Early Holocene in age, and is clearly a terrestrial rather than aquatic deposit. These deposits are consistent with debris fans formed from slopewash channels at the break in slope between the valley side and the gravel terrace.

Palaeochannel 302: Section C
On the terrace surface some 20m north-west of Section B, a north-east facing section containing charcoal was recorded in a trench. The section at TL 5002 4421 showed context 302 overlying context 304

(both Palaeolithic). The stratigraphy of Section C was as follows:

Below -40cm	Orange clayey sand.
-40 to -5cm	Orange clayey sand, with carbonate mottling, probable Chara tubules. Significant patches of charcoal-stained sand were visible at -25 and -15cm. The datum 0cm represents the base of the archaeological excavation.
-5 to 10 cm	Pale yellow slightly silty sand.
10 to 15cm	Grey sand with charcoal.
15 to 30cm	Black silty sand with abundant charcoal.
30 to 45cm	Dark brown soft silty sand
45 to 130cm	Light orange/brown slightly silty sand with occasional flint pebbles (c.10mm).
130 to 165cm	Ploughsoil (brown silty sand with pebbles).
165cm	Top of section

An attempt to sample charcoal at -25 and -15cm was made, but the material was too superficial. However, a charcoal sample was obtained from the black silty sand at 20–30cm, and has been radiocarbon dated to 3530–3360 cal BC (89% confidence; 4664±42 BP; Wk13861). The full dating results and calibrations appear in Appendix 2. This is an interesting result, since it suggests that burning and clearance was taking place on the valley side and terrace surface at a relatively early date.

This sequence is interpreted as representing initial slopewash and perhaps ponding of water on the terrace surface, indicated by the algae Chara. Charcoal in these sediments may represent episodes of local burning. It is clear that sandy slopewash continued to accumulate, recording the burning event in the Early Neolithic. Further episodes of disturbance and clearance of vegetation on the valley side during later prehistory and/or historic times would appear to have released large quantities of eroding slope material, giving rise to the upper colluvial deposits.

Area C

Pond 3203 (Pond D): Section D

The terrace surface near Section D was underlain variously by gravel and sand, and pellet chalk, and was crossed by shallow channel forms terminating in what appeared to be a series of pool or pond infillings on the terrace surface. One such pond infilling had been partially excavated to reveal a crouched Bronze Age human burial (Burial Group 2; Sk 318).

Section D was described from a south-facing exposure located 1m south of the burial at TL 4982 4446. It was not initially clear whether the burial had been made whilst the pond was still in existence, or whether the burial simply took advantage of the softer ground conditions prevailing on the pond sediment. Evidence from the stratigraphy and the subsequent discovery of a second burial close by, suggests that the latter option is more probable. The stratigraphy of Section D was as follows:

-15 to -9cm	White/orange mottled crumbly pellet chalk.
-9 to 0 cm	Grey/brown silty sand with flint pebbles (c.20mm).
0cm	The datum 0cm represents the base of the archaeological excavation.
0 to 25cm	Grey/black organic silty sand with occasional flint pebbles (c.5mm).
25 to 40cm	Grey/brown slightly silty sand with occasional flint pebbles (10mm).
40 to 63cm	Brown/light brown crumbly silty sand with occasional flints.
63 to 90cm	Light brown clayey sand with angular flints (c.20mm) and flint pebbles (c.10mm).

90-120cm	Ploughsoil (removed).
120cm	Top of section

Pollen samples were taken at 5cm intervals from -5cm to 50cm.

It seems likely that this pond infilling sequence underlain by pellet chalk of the terrace surface represents Late Glacial or Early Holocene slopewash material delivered to the pool or pond by the channels or runnels draining the adjacent valley side. The presence of pebbles, and generally sandy nature of the deposit throughout, hints that sediment delivery was at times by quite high-energy events. Indeed, it is tempting not to view this as a true pond deposit at all, since permanent bodies of standing water tend to accumulate fine-grade organic sediments. The only hint of organic material within this is at 0 to 25cm. It seems more likely that these deposits represent a temporary pool, fed from time to time by run-off from the valley sides carrying colluvial material. The standing water presumably drained through the terrace surface or evaporated. In many respects these deposits may be similar to those of the colluvial debris fan identified in Section B. It is probable that by Bronze Age or Iron Age times, the 'pond' was infilled and simply provided a conveniently dry flat area of soft sediment into which excavations for burials could be made. Thus, the difference in age between the 'pond' sediments and the burial could be as much as 8,000 years.

Area H

On the west side of the River Cam preservation of sediments was better than on the opposing side and these were observed at various stages of the evaluation and excavation in Area H.

Sediments

The gravels exposed at the base of the stratigraphic sequence in this area developed as part of a tunnel valley sequence formed during the Anglian glaciation. The River Cam resides within this valley and its course is restricted both by the chalk ridges which flank the valley and the river's ability to entrain the gravels. These results suggest that the current course of the River Cam in this area is unlikely to have changed much during the course of the Holocene. One of the results of maintaining a stable course is that the River Cam has along its banks preserved a good peat sequence which in the past has been found to include Mesolithic artefacts (Schlee and Robinson 1995). These peat sediments within the development zone vary between 0.6m in depth next to the river, and 0.2m in depth approaching the gravel ridge on the western side of the site. The sequence adjacent to the river provides a good peat stratigraphy sequence in a semi-fibrous state, whilst to the west the sequence is amorphous, dry, slightly friable and – as shown by the pollen assemblage – degraded. Within the peat sequence there are occasional small channels cut into the peat and there is evidence for overbank flooding. The picture is of a zone of wetlands prone to flooding and with banks of reeds lying much as they do today, alongside the river bank.

The peat is overlain by up to 0.5m of alluvial sediment. In the Cam Valley this is commonly associated with deposition resulting from intensive arable farming practices from the Late Iron Age.

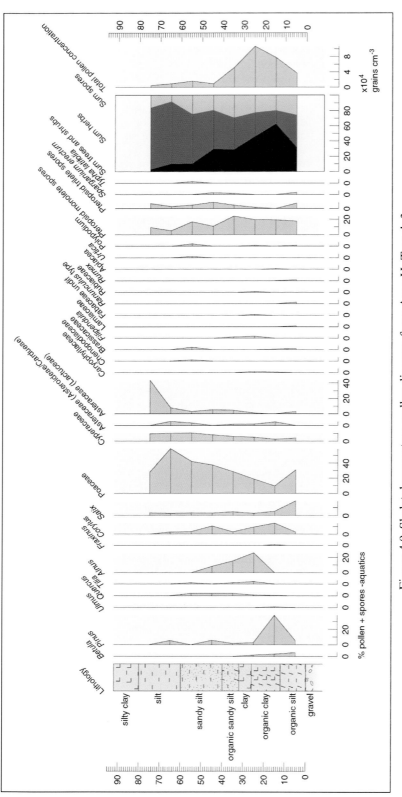

Figure 4.9 Skeletal percentage pollen diagram from Area H, Trench 3

Lab Code	Context	Sample depth (m)	U (PPM)	Th (PPM)	K (%)	Dcosmic (μGy/a-1)*	Moisture (%)	OD (%)**	De (Gy)	Dose rate (μGy/a-1)†	Age (ka)
Shfd14110	15450	0.13	1.26	4.41	0.74	208 ± 10	9	11	7.01 ± 0.18	1425 ± 55	4.92 ± 0.23
Shfd14111	15451	0.3	1.55	5.61	0.98	205 ± 10	10.6	38	6.25 ± 0.27 (23%)	1755 ± 70	3.57 ± 0.21
									15.59 ± 0.86 (25%)		8.88 ± 0.6
									21.28 ± 0.73 (52%)		12.12 ± 0.64
Shfd14112	15452	0.6	1.42	5.45	0.66	201 ± 10	12.5	13	37.7 ± 1.07	1395 ± 58	27.0 ± 1.4

* Cosmic dose is calculated as a linear decay curve at depths below 50 cm. Above this depth, errors in calculation may lead to an underestimation of the cosmic dose contribution.
** OD (overdispersion) is a function which indicates the level of data falling outside the normal distribution that would be expected for well bleached, undisturbed sediment.
† Total dose is attenuated for grain size, density and moisture.

Table 4.19 Details of OSL samples and resulting age estimates

Pollen analysis
Fig. 4.9
At the eastern end of Evaluation Trench 3, close to the modern course of the river, a relatively deep (*c*.1.4m) sequence of alluvial sediments overlying the floodplain gravels was recorded and sampled for pollen analysis (see Fig. 2.1 for location). Samples were taken at 0.1m intervals through a series of deposits which graded upwards from from organic silts and clays to minerogenic sands and silts. Pollen was relatively well-preserved in the lowest 75cm of the sequence, in deposits of organic clays and silts, but was very poorly preserved or absent in samples taken from the upper deposits of inorganic silty clay alluvium.

Pollen preparation, counting and identification were carried out as described by Bennett (1983). Plant taxonomy follows Stace (1997), and incorporates the suggestions of Bennett *et al.* (1994). Where possible a minimum of 300 land-pollen and pores was counted at each level. In the absence of any radiocarbon dates on the sequence, interpretation must be tentative but in general terms the sequence is typical of the Early to Middle Holocene vegetational succession in Southern England.

A grey/brown silt with organic fragments at the base part of the sequence (5cm) was characterised by high frequencies (*c*.20%) of willow (*Salix*), with pine (*Pinus*), birch (*Betula*), hazel (*Corylus*), grass (Poaceae) and fern spores (Pteropsida). This is interpreted as an Early Holocene (Boreal) assemblage, representing local wet woodland (carr) with scattered hazel and birch scrub and stands of trees in an otherwise open grassland environment. The pollen of sedges (Cyperaceae) and bur-reed (Sparganium) suggest that emergent marginal vegetation grew close by.

The black organic clay (15cm) contained abundant pine pollen (*c*.40%) with subordinate birch, hazel, willow and grass. This is interpreted as representing the expansion of boreal woodland during the Early Holocene. In contrast, the pollen signal from the top of the black organic clay and overlying sandy silt (25cm, 35cm, 45cm, 55cm) records the rise of temperate arboreal taxa such as oak (*Quercus*), elm (*Ulmus*) and lime (*Tilia*). Pollen of alder (*Alnus*) and hazel is also important and is accompanied by rising curves for grass, sedges and herbs. This is interpreted as the rise of mixed lime/oak woodland in the catchment and the development of alder carr on the river floodplain.

The overlying mottled brown silt with charcoal (65cm) contained a pollen spectrum dominated by grass, with willow, sedge and herbs. This represents a period of woodland clearance. However, pollen types indicating soil disturbance (*e.g. Plantago lancelota*) and arable activity (cereals) were not found, suggesting that this may not have been associated with extensive cultivation. The pollen sequence from the top of the brown silt unit (75cm) had a very low pollen concentration and was dominated by pollen of Asteraceae (Lactuceae). The super-abundance of these resistant pollen types together with Pteropsid spores is often taken as evidence for post-depositional differential oxidation of pollen.

Notwithstanding the lack of absolute dates to anchor the sequence, it is interpreted as representing much of the Early and Middle Holocene (Boreal and Atlantic periods), apparently terminating with an episode of tree clearance, after which an increase in alluviation and change in hydrology is indicated by the inorganic alluvium. Dating the episode of tree clearance and the onset of alluviation is somewhat speculative, but the clearance attested in the upper pollen sample may equate to the late sub-boreal period (Bronze Age). The overlying alluviation is likely to correlate with increased soil erosion and overbank flooding occasioned by widespread clearance and cultivation but, as outlined in Part II (Clarke *et al.* forthcoming), there is evidence to indicate that these 0.5m of alluvial sediments were developing over a considerable length of time, probably in the region of 1,000 years.

Conclusion
The evidence from Areas A and C is for Late Glacial and Early Holocene periglacial activity and slopewash. A series of channels or runnels drained down the valley side delivering sandy colluvial material to debris fans and pond-like areas on the terrace surface. It is likely that, as vegetation became established on the valley side in the Early Holocene, the amount of colluvial sediment reduced significantly. However, there is direct evidence for Neolithic burning and a suggestion that valley-side channels became active again during later prehistory, delivering a new colluvial regolith onto the terrace surface. On the western bank of the Cam (Area H), the sequence shows the development of Early/ Middle Holocene woodland environments followed by possible clearance activity.

V. Optically simulated luminescence dating
by Mark D. Bateman, with Lawrence Billington
Figs 4.10–4.12

Introduction
Three samples taken from sediments infilling Pond P (Area J) were submitted for luminescence dating. The on-site sampling was undertaken by Dr Samantha Stein and all luminescence work was carried out at the Sheffield Luminescence Laboratory (SLL). Upon arrival, each sample was allocated a Sheffield laboratory number (Table 4.19), which are used throughout this report. This report provides an abbreviated summary of the methods and results of the analyses; fuller reporting and details regarding the individual samples can be found in the project archive.

Paleodose and dose rate calculation
In order to derive an optically stimulated luminescence (OSL) age both the palaeodose (De – the amount of absorbed dose since the sample was buried) and the dose rate (the estimated radiation flux for the sedimentary bodies) have to be determined. Aitken (1998) gives a detailed explanation of both these parameters. To calculate an age, the palaeodose (expressed in Grays) is divided by the annual dose rate (Grays/yr). An inherent assumption in these age calculations is that the sediment was fully reset or 'bleached' by exposure to sunlight during the last transport event or whilst *in situ* prior to burial and that no post-depositional sediment disturbance has occurred.

As the OSL signal measured at the single aliquot level of measurement is an average of 2000 grains, the

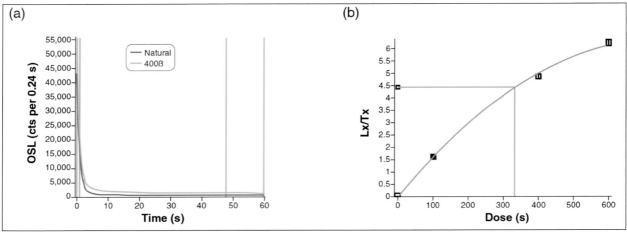

Figure 4.10 Pond P. Examples of single aliquot OSL data for sample SHFD14112

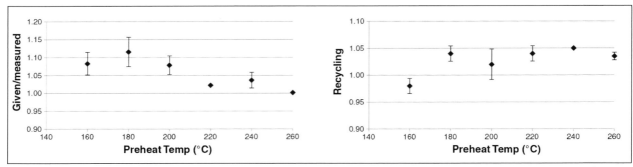

Figure 4.11 Pond P. Results of dose recovery test on sample SHFD14110 used to determine appropriate preheat for SAR protocol

true distribution of De values may be masked. This is of particular significance in heterogeneously dosed samples (*e.g.* poorly reset/bleached) in which grains with a high De signal will dominate the signal at the expense of grains containing a true burial De.

Dose rate analysis

Naturally occurring potassium (K), thorium (Th) and uranium (U) are the main contributors of dose to sedimentary quartz. The concentrations of these elements were determined in the field using an EG&G Micronomad field gamma-spectrometer with a 3" sodium iodide scintillation crystal. Measurement times were 45 minutes per sample. Elemental concentrations were converted to annual dose rates using data from Adamiec and Aitken (1998), Marsh *et al.* (2002), and Aitken (1998). Calculations took into account attenuation factors relating to sediment grain sizes used, density and palaeomoisture. Attenuation of dose by moisture used present-day moisture values with a ±5% error to incorporate fluctuations through time. The contribution to dose rates from cosmic sources was calculated using the expression published in Prescott and Hutton (1994). The dose rates calculated are based on analyses of the sediment sampled at the present day. This assumption is only valid if no movement and/or reprecipitation of the key elements has taken place since sediment burial and the adjacent sediments to those sampled had similar dose rates.

Palaeodose determination

The samples were prepared under subdued red lighting following the procedure to extract and clean quartz outlined in Bateman and Catt (1996). Aliquots were taken from prepared sample material isolated to a size range of 125–180µm for samples Shfd14110 and 14112, and 90–180µm for sample Shfd14111. The samples underwent measurement at the single aliquot level using a Risø DA18 luminescence reader with radiation doses administered using a calibrated ^{90}strontium beta source. For measurement purposes, quartz grains were mounted as a monolayer on 9.6 mm diameter stainless steel discs using silkospray. An array of blue/green LEDs provided the stimulation, and luminescence detection was through a Hoya U-340 filter. Samples were analysed using the single aliquot regenerative (SAR) approach (Murray and Wintle 2000), in which an interpolative growth curve is constructed using data derived from repeated measurements of a single grain which has been given various laboratory irradiations (Fig. 4.10a). Five regeneration points were used to characterise growth curves, with the first three bracketing the natural dose (so that D1 < D2 ≈ De < D3), a zero point (D4), and D5 identical to D1 (Figure 4.10b). The 'recycling ratio' produced by D1/D5 was used to assess the efficacy of the test dose normalisation, with aliquots producing values >10% outside unity being rejected (Murray and Wintle 2000). The most appropriate preheat temperature was selected using a dose recovery preheat plateau test conducted on the sample (Fig. 4.11). This resulted in the selection of a preheat temperature of 220°C for 10 seconds. This was applied prior to OSL measurement to remove any unstable signal generated by laboratory irradiation. The function of the curve fitted to SAR regeneration points is generally most accurately described by the sum of several exponential functions (Bailey *et al.* 1997; Bulur *et al.* 2000). However, a single saturating exponential function is commonly fitted to OSL growth curves for age calculation purposes, of the form given below (where I is the OSL intensity due to dose D, I0 is the saturation intensity and D0 the dose level that is characteristic of the dose response curve).

$I / I0 = (1 - \exp^{-D/Do})$

Adequate description of growth curves with a single saturating exponential function of this form provides confidence they are first-order, *i.e.* they relate only to the fast component signal desired in OSL (Wintle and Murray, 2006). Use of this function also provides a simple means of assessing whether an aliquot is in saturation, *i.e.* unable to retain any more charge. If the De value interpolated is more than twice its D0 component, the aliquot should be considered saturated and the De value treated as a minimum (Wintle and Murray 2006). At doses well below saturation, the OSL growth curve is known to be linear (Murray and Olley 2002). As two of the three samples had low De values an early background subtraction was applied to the measured SAR data.

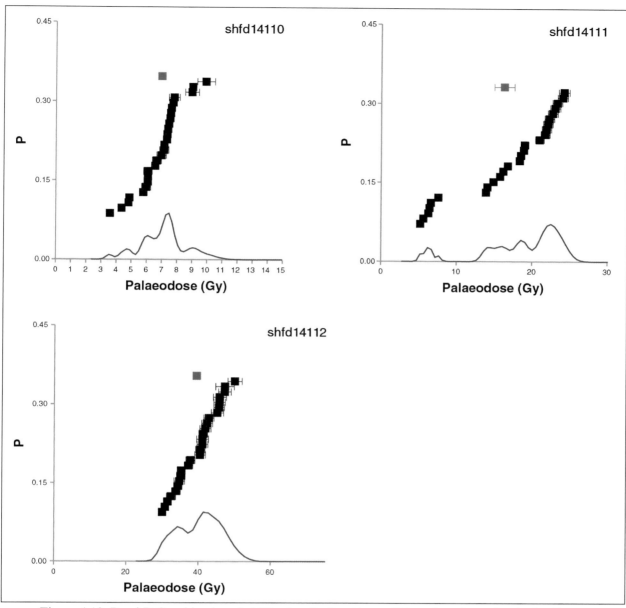

Figure 4.12 Pond P. Combined probability density functions of De values from the single aliquot measurements, showing degree of inter-aliquot variability for all samples

Sample behaviour

Samples exhibited an OSL signal dominated by a fast component (Fig. 4.10a) which grew well with laboratory dose (Fig. 4.10b). Measurements of palaeodose were obtained from 26 aliquots, in order to provide an indication of the reproducibility of the palaeodose measurements and to assess sample bleaching behaviour (see below). Growth curves were fitted with a single saturating exponential curve. Of the 26 aliquots measured for each sample, many were excluded from initial age calculation due to their recycling value (the ratio of first and last dose point) being greater than ±10% outside unity. No aliquots were observed to be in saturation. Calculation of the IR depletion ratio (Duller 2003) revealed that feldspar contamination was not a problem.

Sedimentary bleaching behaviour and sample saturation

The effects of incomplete bleaching of the sediment during the last period of transport or exposure *in situ* can be profound. Typically, poorly bleached sediments retain a significant level of residual signal from previous phases of sedimentary cycling, leading to inherent inaccuracies in the calculation of a palaeodose value. By plotting the replicate De data for the sample as a probability density function some assessment of whether older or younger material has been included in the sample, measurements can be made. In principle a well-bleached sample that has not been subjected to post-depositional disturbance should have replicate De data which is normally distributed and highly reproducible (see Bateman *et al.* 2003, fig. 3; Bateman *et al.* 2007a). Where post-depositional disturbance or incomplete bleaching prior to sample burial has occurred skewing of this distribution may occur and/or replicate reproducibility may be lower (Bateman *et al.* 2007a and b). In the case of poorly bleached material skewing should be evident with a high De tail (*e.g.* Olley *et al.* 2004). High De tails may also be indicative of saturated samples and interpolation of the De

Lab Code	Context	Component/ peak	De (Gy)	Dose rate (μGy/a-1)†	Age (ka before 2014)	Oxcal generated date range 'cal' BP 95% confidence	Oxcal generated date range 'cal' BC 95% confidence
Shfd14110	15450	-	7.01 ± 0.18	1425 ± 55	4.92 ± 0.23	5320–4390 BP	3370–2440 BC
Shfd14111	15451	C	6.25 ± 0.27 (23%)	1755 ± 70	3.57 ± 0.21	3930–3080 BP	1980–1130 BC
		B	15.59 ± 0.86 (25%)		8.88 ± 0.6	10,020–7610 BP	8070–5560 BC
		A	21.28 ± 0.73 (52%)		12.12 ± 0.64	13,340–10,770 BP	11,390–8820 BC
Shfd14112	15452	-	37.7 ± 1.07	1395 ± 58	27.0 ± 1.4	29,740–24,130 BP	

† Total dose is attenuated for grain size, density and moisture.

Table 4.20 OSL age estimates alongside OxCal generated calendrical date ranges

values from the upper, low gradient part of the growth curve (Murray and Funder 2003). It should be pointed out that by making OSL measurement of samples on a 9.6mm diameter aliquot with approximately 2000 grains any heterogeneity in De that individual grains have may be masked.

The De data distribution of samples Shfd14110 (5 outliers) and Shfd14112 (1 outlier) are broadly normally distributed once outliers (defined as those aliquots with De values falling outside two standard deviations of the mean) are excluded. However, dispersion values (OD) on sample Shfd14111 were wide and the De replicates scattered. Therefore, for age calculation purposes Finite Mixture Model (FMM) of Galbraith and Green (1990) was applied. This model attempts to extract the different multiple components contained within the De distributions. Normally for partially bleached samples the lowest component is likely to be the true burial age although where disturbance or bioturbation has taken place the dominant peak may be more reliable (Bateman *et al.* 2007a). FMM from samples Shfd14111 displayed a total of three peaks in the data. These and the resultant ages they produce by are displayed in Table 4.19 along with the proportion of data in each component. Caution should be taken with this sample and other site information used to evaluate the age alternatives.

Age calculation
Ages are quoted in years from the present day (2014) and are presented with one sigma confidence intervals which incorporate systematic uncertainties with the dosimetry data, uncertainties with the palaeomoisture content and errors associated with the De determination. Table 4.19 shows the final OSL age estimates. Aliquot-specific data for each sample can be found in the archive report. The data presented there shows that the palaeodose of the sample is highly reproducible, unsaturated and provides no evidence of partial bleaching or post-depositional disturbance. The best estimates for the samples ages range from 27.03 ± 1.37 to 4.920 ± 0.23 ka, although the age of sample Shfd14111 requires careful interpretation alongside archaeological and stratigraphic data.

Interpretation
by Lawrence Billington
To facilitate the interpretation of the luminescence dates, the final age estimates (expressed as ka before 2014) were processed in OxCal (Version 4.3; Bronk

Ramsey 1995; 2009) to provide calendrical date ranges, at 95% confidence (2 sigma) and rounded outwards to decadal endpoints, equivalent to those generated by radiocarbon dating – allowing ready comparison with radiocarbon-derived date ranges and other calendrical dates. Separate date ranges have been calculated for each of the three distinct peaks/components of sample Shfd14111 (components A, B and C). The original age estimates and the OxCal generated date ranges are set out in Table 4.20. For clarity and ease of comparison with other sites, date ranges falling close to or within the Holocene have been provided in both years BP and BC.

The date range of 29,740–24,130 BP for the emplacement/exposure of the lowest unit within the hollow ('natural' gravel 15452; Shfd14112) indicates a date in the latter part of Marine Isotope Stage (MIS) 3, or the period between GI 4 and GS-3 in terms of the climatic events recorded in the Greenland ice core record (Rasmussen *et al.* 2014). In insular archaeological terms, this equates to the period following the final phase of Early Upper Palaeolithic occupation in Britain (Gravettian), towards the beginning of a long period of absence for human activity between *c.* 33,000 BP and 14,700 BP corresponding to the harsh climatic conditions of the Last Glacial Maximum (see overview in Pettit and White 2012).

The date of a sample taken from the overlying 'silt' layer (15451) is of crucial importance, given that the Terminal Palaeolithic flint assemblage was probably originally deposited on/within this deposit (see Bishop, Chapter 3.I). It is unfortunate, therefore, that the paleodose (De) distribution of this sample (Shf14111) showed three distinct peaks or components of markedly different ages. Component A is the dominant peak (52% of the data), and has the oldest date range: 11,390–8820 BC (13,340–10770 BP), covering the end of the Late Glacial Interstadial (Allerød), the climatic downturn of the Younger Dryas (*c.*10,900–9700 BC) and the beginning of the Holocene – in archaeological terms covering the Final and Terminal Palaeolithic and the Early Mesolithic. Component B (25% of the data) provides a date range in the Early/Middle to Late Mesolithic (8070–5660 BC), whilst Component C (23% of the data) covers a range essentially encompassing the Early and Middle Bronze Age (1980–1130 BC).

The sample (Shf14110) taken from within the uppermost, probably partly colluvial, deposit within the hollow (15450) produced a date range of 3370–

2440 BC – covering the Middle to Late Neolithic period. It is notable that this date range overlaps with a radiocarbon date acquired on a sample of charcoal from a deposit infilling Pond X, interpreted by Boreham as attesting to an episode of clearance and colluviation during the later 4th millennium BC (Boreham, Section IV above).

Interpretation of the sequence and the relationship of the dates to the Terminal Palaeolithic lithic assemblage rests essentially on the multiple date ranges acquired for the silt layer. As set out above by Bateman, where multiple peaks in the data such as this occur, it is normally for the lowest component which is likely to be the true burial age. However, where disturbance or bioturbation has taken place the dominant peak may be more reliable, meaning that careful consideration of the accompanying archaeological and stratigraphic data is required to interpret such samples. Given the close association between the silt layer and the flint scatter – dated on typological/technological grounds to the Terminal Palaeolithic, the preferred interpretation is that the two younger date ranges from the silt deposit (Components B and C) represent evidence for localised post-depositional disturbance (bioturbation) of the deposit, with Component C providing a broad date range for its original formation. Whilst this seems most consistent with the archaeological evidence, the circularity of this argument must be acknowledged. Further discussion of the dates in relation to the archaeological and environmental sequence of the Late Glacial and Early Holocene can be found in Chapter 5.II.

Chapter 5. Discussion

I. Introduction

The prehistoric and Roman remains revealed at the Genome Campus cover a vast sweep of over ten thousand years, from the beginning of the Holocene through to the decades following the incorporation of Southern Britain into the Roman Empire. It is unsurprising, therefore, that the record of activity at the site is uneven and punctuated, and that the character of the evidence for different periods takes very different forms. With this in mind, this chapter is organised chronologically and is structured around three main sections, divided according to the distinctive character of the evidence and specific research themes associated with particular periods.

The first of these sections is concerned exclusively with the assemblage of Terminal Palaeolithic flintwork from Pond P (Area J). Probably representing a single episode of short-lived activity, this scatter is of national significance and must be seen in the specific context of research into the Late Glacial and Early Holocene archaeology of Britain and North-West Europe. The second section is concerned with the much longer sequence of early prehistoric activity at the site from the Mesolithic to the Early Bronze Age. United by the ephemeral character of the evidence for settlement and occupation – invariably represented only by artefact scatters and occasional discrete features – the record of these periods from the Genome Campus attests to episodic activity for over 5,000 years. Against this background of long term activity, there are important individual discoveries – most notably the Early Neolithic scatter/midden (Pond Q) and double burial in Area J, as well as the major Beaker assemblage from the pit/'shaft' investigated in Trench U. The evidence also contributes to an impressive and growing body of evidence relating to prehistoric activity along the Cam Valley which has considerable potential in terms of tracking the changing character and tempo of landscape occupation over the course of these periods. The third and final section is concerned with the Iron Age and Roman remains: this period essentially hinges on the important remains dating to the Late Iron Age and Conquest/Early Roman period, a span of little more than a century covering the late 1st century BC and 1st century AD. Here, the record enters the realm of protohistory, and the sequence and character of the remains must be seen in the context of specific social and political developments, including the Late Iron Age 'tribal' dynamics of Southern and Eastern England and their interactions with Romanised Gaul, together with the subsequent Roman Conquest and occupation, manifested locally by the fort and later town at Great Chesterford.

Alongside this three-fold chronologically based structure there are some wider themes which cut across the various period divisions and which provide at least some common threads to the discussion that follows.

Notable among these, as introduced in Chapter 1, is the theme of routeways, communications and connections – an issue of special importance given the distinctive location of the site, straddling the river and the putative ridgeway route of the Icknield Way, lying within what appears to have been a territorial/cultural border zone during later prehistory and into historic times and now bisected by the Cambridgeshire/Essex county boundary. Aspects relating to this theme will be addressed with reference to specific periods in this chapter, and throughout there is an emphasis on situating the site within its distinctive local and regional context.

II. The Terminal Palaeolithic
by Lawrence Billington, with Barry Bishop and Anthony Haskins

Chronological and cultural context
The technological and typological characteristics and the composition of the large assemblage of flintwork from Pond P leaves little doubt that it belongs to a Terminal Palaeolithic 'Long/Bruised Blade' industry, traditionally dated to the Pleistocene/Holocene transition (see Barton 1989, 1991 and 1998; Barton and Roberts 2004 and 2019; Cooper 2006). In typological terms, such assemblages are characterised by a very low frequency of formal retouched tools (which can, however, include microlithic and tanged points) and by the presence of distinctive 'bruised' blades and flakes (*lames/eclats mâchurées*) displaying extremely heavy edge damage. Technologically, they are based around highly structured Upper Palaeolithic type blade production and are distinguished by the production of regular flat-profiled blades which include exceptionally large pieces referred to as 'long' blades (*Grosseklinge*; >120mm in length) and 'giant' blades (*Riesenklinge*; >150mm in length). In all of these respects the Pond P assemblage is characteristic of Long Blade industries and is distinguishable from other (earlier) Late Upper Palaeolithic assemblages belonging to the Late Glacial interstadial (*i.e.* Final Magdalenian/Creswellian, Hengistbury Type and *Federmesser* industries; see, *e.g.* Barton *et al.* 2003; Jacobi 2004; Barton *et al.* 2009; Conneller and Ellis 2007). Although OSL dating of the sediments containing the scatter produced somewhat ambiguous results (see Chapter 4.V), the current authors' preferred interpretation of the date on the 'silt' layer (context) from which the flint appears to have largely derived is consistent with the typo/technological attribution of the flintwork, with the dominant component of the OSL sample producing a date range covering the end of the Late Glacial and earliest part of the Holocene.

Terminal Palaeolithic activity is known almost exclusively from open air sites in southern and eastern parts of Britain, with major concentrations in the river valleys of the Thames and its tributaries and in East

Anglia (Barton 1998; Barton and Roberts 2004 and 2019). The British sites cannot be seen in isolation and they have long been closely compared with the Belloisian assemblages of Northern France and (Epi-) Ahrensburgian assemblages of the Low Countries and Northern Germany (*e.g.* Barton 1991 and 1998; Cooper 2006). More broadly still, recent work has suggested they should be seen as one part of a single very extensive 'technocomplex' – the 'Flat Blades Technocomplex' (FBT), covering much of Northern Europe and including parts of Southern France as well as extending across the now submerged palaeo-landscapes of the North Sea basin and the English Channel (see Naudinot and Jacquier 2014; Valentin *et al.* 2014; Naudinot *et al.* 2017).

Accurate and precise dating of British Terminal Palaeolithic activity has been hindered both by a scarcity of material suitable for radiocarbon dating and by the wide date ranges produced by calibrated radiocarbon dates falling at the end of the Late Glacial and Early Holocene. This imprecision is important as it has made it difficult to relate Terminal Palaeolithic activity to the climatic and environmental record, and it has often been unclear whether individual episodes of Terminal Palaeolithic activity were taking place within the harsher conditions of the Younger Dryas (the climatic downturn at the end of the Late Glacial period) or during and after the very rapid warming at the beginning of the Early Holocene. This remains a matter of considerable uncertainty, but despite evidence from the continent that the wider FBT appears to have had its origins in the Younger Dryas (*e.g.* Crombé *et al.* 2014), recently acquired high quality dates from small number of British sites (see Conneller and Higham 2015; Conneller *et al.* 2016; Barclay *et al.* 2017), as well as older dates and stratigraphic evidence from earlier discoveries such as Sproughton, Suffolk (Wymer with Rose 1977), hint that much of the record for Terminal Palaeolithic activity in Britain belongs to the first few centuries of the Holocene and may effectively represent communities recolonising Britain following the rapid climatic amelioration from *c.*9700 BC. Equally, an absence of reliable dates falling in the later 10th millennium BC suggest a possible hiatus between the Terminal Palaeolithic and Early Mesolithic, or at the least dramatic changes in lithic technology and lifeways coinciding with climatic fluctuations and environmental changes in the centuries before *c.*9000 BC (Conneller and Higham 2015; *cf.* Conneller *et al.* 2016).

Correlation with the environmental record of the Late Glacial and Early Holocene (and data from the few sites which have produced associated faunal and environmental evidence) suggests that Terminal Palaeolithic communities were operating within an open landscape which, in the Early Holocene, would have been characterised by herb-rich grasslands and the development of juniper and birch scrub/woodland. The few sites associated with faunal assemblages have produced remains of reindeer and, more commonly and abundantly, horse (Lewis with Rackham 2011; Barclay *et al.* 2017; Conneller *et al.* 2016; Jones 2013) and much emphasis has been placed on models of Terminal Palaeolithic communities operating in small highly mobile groups moving in step with herds of migratory animals (*e.g.* Conneller 2007;

Lewis with Rackham 2011; Pettitt and White 2012, 495–501). This model does appear to be supported by recent interpretations of the lithic evidence by continental researchers, with patterns of raw material acquisition and the organisation and techniques of lithic technology appearing to reflect the demands of a highly mobile lifestyle and the specific environmental conditions of the Pleistocene/Holocene transition (Valentin 2008 and 2009; Naudinot *et al.* 2017).

Further insights into patterns of landscape occupation and mobility have come from analysis of the composition of assemblages and their landscape setting. In the insular context, Nick Barton has shown that many Long Blade sites are located in close proximity to sources of high quality flint, often in areas where river valleys cut through the flint-bearing chalk in Eastern and Southern Britain, whilst simultaneously occupying low lying floodplain locations within major river valleys which would have allowed the interception of migratory animals – as well as providing a host of other resources (Barton 1989 and 1991; Barton and Roberts 2019). There is considerable diversity in the composition of Long Blade assemblages and, as discussed below, whilst many appear to represent very short-lived episodes with an emphasis on flintworking, other assemblages do include a wider range of tools, together with evidence for fire settings, which suggest somewhat more extended periods of occupation and the performance of a wider range of tasks – probably including butchery and food preparation, and the manufacture and maintenance of tools, clothing and shelters (see Cooper 2006; Barton and Roberts 2019; Naudinot and Jacquier 2014).

Characterising the occupation
Fig. 5.1

The Terminal Palaeolithic scatter from Pond P and the nature of the activity it represents are best discussed with reference to the small but growing number of well-reported minimally disturbed sites of this date from other parts of Southern and Eastern England. Pre-eminent among these are those from Sproughton, Suffolk (Wymer with Rose 1977); Avington VI, Berkshire (Froom 2005); Launde, Leicestershire (Cooper 2006); Gatehampton Farm, Oxfordshire (Barton 1995); Three Ways Wharf, Uxbridge (Scatters A and C east; Lewis and Rackham 2011); Church Lammas, Staines (Jones 2013); Seamer Carr C, North Yorkshire (Conneller 2007) and Eynsford and Herne Bay, Kent (Anderson-Whymark and Pope 2016; Gardiner *et al.* 2015). These sites do, however, need to be set against a much larger number of more poorly documented assemblages and findspots, which include a relatively large number of sites from the east of England; the latter provide a valuable regional/local context for the Genome Campus assemblage which will be discussed in more detail below.

It should be emphasised from the outset that the 3,817 flints (3,356 excluding microdebitage) from the Genome Campus scatter represents one of the largest Long Blade assemblages in the country to have been recovered under controlled conditions. It is, however, comparable in scale to many of the larger assemblages from the sites referred to above, including Avington VI, Launde, Sproughton and Three Ways Wharf Scatter C East, which (when microdebitage/chips are excluded to allow for differences in recovery methods and taphonomic processes) typically include between 2,500 and 5,000 worked flints. Whilst other scatters are associated with much smaller assemblages of under 1,000 flints (*e.g.* Gatehampton Farm; Lullingstone Country Park), it is notable that individual scatters have not yielded the vast quantities of flint that characterise some Mesolithic scatters (*e.g.* Oakhanger V/VII, Hampshire (Rankine and Dimbleby 1960) or Great Melton, Norfolk (Wymer and Robins 1995)) and this seems likely to reflect the relatively short-lived nature of activity at Terminal Palaeolithic sites, even if there is good evidence for repeated (punctuated) occupations at the same general locale (see below).

The overall distribution and density of the Pond P scatter also compares well with that of the larger Long Blade assemblages known from elsewhere (see Bishop Chapter 3.I; Fig. 5.1). Notwithstanding that the assemblage has experienced some post-depositional disturbance, the core of the scatter (as crudely defined by densities of flintwork of over 10 per 1m grid square) appears to have occupied an area of little more than 10 x 10m (although the original eastern extent of the scatter is unknown due to truncation by later features and uncertainty regarding the extent to which the scatter may have continued outside of the protective environment of the pond/hollow). The scatters at Three Ways Wharf, Avington VI, Sproughton, Launde and Seamer C (Scatters B2, C and F) appear to have been of similar extent. Importantly, at many of these sites there are very well-defined concentrations/areas of higher density within the broader scatter, typically covering areas of 1–2m² (*e.g.* Wymer with Rose 1977, figs 2 and 3; Froom 2005, fig. 2.3). Although the recovery/recording by metre square units allows only relatively coarse plotting of distributions, such concentrations may be discernible within the Pond P scatter, particularly in the case of the outlying high density from grid square K3, on the southern edge of the hollow (see Fig. 5.1). Some of these concentrations may be equivalent to the small and isolated scatters encountered at other sites such as Lullingstone Country Park (Anderson-Whymark and Pope 2016, fig. 2.6), and essentially represent the *in situ* remains of individual episodes of core reduction/flintworking taking place within the larger scatter. Also of note here is the markedly low density of flint from grid square M8, in an area surrounded by much higher densities – it is possible this represents an obstacle of some sort or perhaps even the seating position of an individual knapper, leaving a clear void in the overall distribution. That some of these higher densities do represent areas of intensive *in situ* working is hinted at both by the (limited) refitting evidence – with multiple refits within high density squares M3 and K9 (see Bishop, Chapter 3.I) – and by the relatively high proportion of chips and small working waste (<15mm) in some of the grid squares in or adjacent to the high density grid squares (Fig 5.1: *i.e.* Squares L3 and L10).

A lack of burnt flint, and thus little evidence for fire settings, was once seen as characteristic of Long Blade sites (Barton 1989 and 1998), but it is now recognised that many scatters were organised around one or more hearths (see Barton and Roberts 2019). In the absence of robust hearth settings these have typically been identified through analysis of the distribution of burnt flint, both worked and unworked (*e.g.* Cooper 2006; Lewis with Rackham 2011; *cf.* Sergant *et al.* 2006). Notwithstanding the presence of relatively large quantities of flint in the Pond P assemblage that may have been deliberately heated (Bishop, Chapter 3.I), very little of the worked flint was more heavily burnt/calcined. A somewhat larger amount of unworked burnt flint (120 fragments; 434g) was, however, recovered. This material was thinly distributed (Fig. 5.1, Plot III) with no grid square producing in excess of 26g of burnt flint, although the presence of relatively high densities in three contiguous squares on the north-eastern side of the hollow (N7–9) may suggest that a hearth was located in this area. If so, this may have implications for the overall distribution and extent of the scatter as hearth settings are often found centrally within the distribution of artefacts; this might imply that the scatter originally extended beyond the limit of the pond to the east.

Turning to the composition of the scatter, Bishop's analysis makes it very clear that the assemblage represents intensive flintworking, with all stages of core reduction represented, from the preparation of nodules through to the discard of exhausted cores. Equally, however, there is some evidence that cores may have been transported to the site in a partly prepared/tested state and that other, still-productive cores were taken away from the scatter for further exploitation elsewhere (see Bishop, Chapter 3.I). In very general terms, this emphasis on large-scale flintworking (and a concurrent low proportion of retouched tools) is typical of many Long Blade assemblages, which, traditionally, have been interpreted as representing short-lived 'workshop'-type sites where good quality, locally available raw materials were intensively exploited to produce blades, tool blanks and cores which would be taken away for use and further working. This emphasis on flintworking is consistent with interpretations of the function of the eponymous bruised blades and flakes, with experimental work and use-wear analysis suggesting that many are likely to have been associated with the process of flint knapping itself (used directly as percussors or for honing 'soft stone' hammerstones) rather than being used for other purposes (*e.g.* butchery, woodworking, *etc.*) (Fagnart and Plisson 1997; Froom 2005, 34–8; Jacquier 2014). As noted above, however, recent work has demonstrated considerable variability in the composition of assemblages, with evidence at some sites for more varied activities (see Barton and Roberts 2019) and many of the larger scatters from Southern Britain containing a small but varied range of tool forms including microlithic/backed projectile points, scrapers, burins, truncated pieces and edge-used blades and flakes.

Formal retouched tools are poorly represented in the Pond P assemblage, but include a range of pieces including burins, a scraper, a piercer, truncated blades and notches. Perhaps the most notable feature, however, is the absence of backed points/microliths of the kind which are generally recovered in small numbers from the larger Long Blade scatters. Whilst few in number, these tools do suggest that other activities, perhaps including butchery/food preparation, re-tooling *etc.*, were taking place alongside intensive flintworking, and there is some indication that the quantity of retouched pieces may seriously underestimate the extent of these

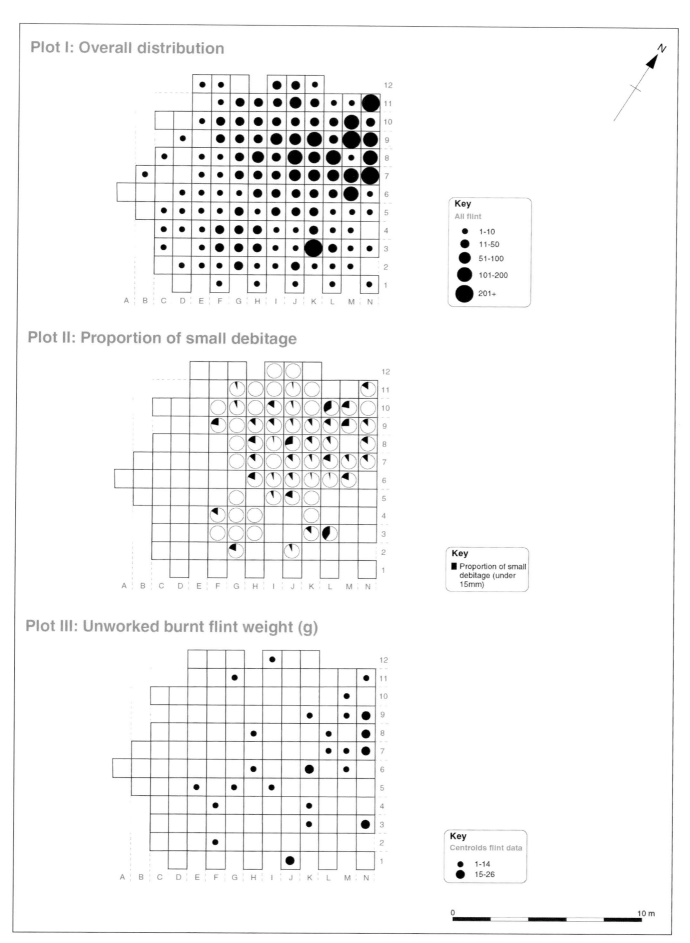

Figure 5.1 Pond P. Distribution plot of Terminal Palaeolithic flint. Scale 1:200

activities given the large number of unretouched blades and flakes which bear macroscopically visible traces of use (Bishop, Chapter 3.I). These include 'true' bruised pieces – which, as noted above, might be associated with flintworking – but the majority display the kind of edge damage more usually seen on pieces used as cutting and scraping tools. A particularly notable find is the large serrated blade (Fig. 3.3, No. 6); serrated pieces/micro-denticulates are generally associated with Mesolithic and Neolithic industries and, although one serrated blade was found at Avington VI, this was found stratified above the main Long Blade scatter and may have been later in date (Froom 2005, 18, fig. 3.3: 8). The size and morphology of the blank on which this Pond P piece is made leaves little doubt that this a genuine Terminal Palaeolithic example, although whether its use can be associated with the working of plant material, as seems to be the case for Mesolithic and Neolithic examples (*e.g.* Levi Sala 1992; Hurcombe 2019), remains unclear.

Regional context and patterns of landscape occupation

The immediate context for the Terminal Palaeolithic scatter at Hinxton is provided by other finds of this date from the Cam Valley and adjacent areas. This is generally a sparse record. A few individual pieces, or very small assemblages, of Upper Palaeolithic type blade-based flints have been recovered at a handful of sites, largely occurring as a small element in larger multi-period lithic assemblages. This includes material from Mill Lane, Sawston (Bishop 2016), Great Wilbraham (Edmonds 2006), Eddington, Cambridge (Billington 2014) and Addenbrookes (Bishop 2015). Not all of this material need date to the Terminal Palaeolithic and some may instead relate to activity during the Late Glacial interstadial, as evidenced by the major Final Palaeolithic (*federmesser*-type) assemblage from Rookery Farm, Great Wilbraham (Conneller 2009). In the lower Cam Valley, on the fen edge, however, there is clearer and more substantial evidence for Terminal Palaeolithic activity in the form of a major ploughzone scatter at Whiteway Drove, Swaffham Prior – discussed in more detail below.

Although far poorer than the record of some parts of Eastern England, the distribution/location of findspots in the Cam Valley is consistent with wider regional trends. Across East Anglia and parts of the East Midlands, material of this date, usually in the form of stray finds of distinctive long/bruised blades and long blade cores, is overwhelmingly found in low-lying river valley locations, together with much smaller number of finds on valley sides/'upland' areas. There are major clusters of findspots in some areas, most notably in the river valleys around Norwich, along the lower Gipping Valley and along some stretches of the river valleys of the Breckland/eastern fen edge (Barton 1998; Robins and Wymer 2006; Billington 2016, 311–20, fig. 7.4). Within these 'clusters' the recovery of multiple assemblages/findspots within relatively restricted areas hint at repeated, episodic, visits to the same locale and, as long recognised (Barton 1989 and 1998), such clusters invariably correspond with the availability of good quality raw materials – usually where river valleys cut through flint-bearing chalk or flint-rich superficial deposits (Billington 2016, fig. 7.5). All of these major clusters of sites have effectively been 'truncated' as a result of Holocene sea level rise, with the limit of the downstream distribution of known findspots corresponding to areas of extensive former wetlands or estuaries, where deep sequences of Holocene sediments seal the Late Glacial and Early Holocene land surface. Beyond, it is likely that the focus or 'heartlands' of activity during this period were in the lower courses of the great river valleys which ran across the now submerged lands of the North Sea.

The location of the Hinxton scatter, at a point where the Cam passes through the chalk escarpment and good quality chalk flint could be collected, resonates with the record of other parts of Eastern England and, although there are no other major assemblages from this part of the Cam Valley, the recovery of occasional/isolated LUP-type blade-based pieces from Hinxton, including a large crested blade from a palaeochannel, suggests that this too may have been a locale which saw repeated visits during the period. As discussed above, the emphasis on riverine environments seen in the regional record and clearly attested to at the Genome Campus seems likely to relate to the major importance of river valley environments in terms of structuring the movements of Terminal Palaeolithic communities. It is possible that seasonal/annual levels of mobility were very high; earlier Final Magdalenian hunter-gatherers, operating within a broadly analogous environment at the beginning of the Late Glacial Interstadial (*c.* 12,700 BC; Jacobi and Higham 2011) have been suggested to have had a seasonal round covering hundreds of kilometres, incorporating upland parts of central England and the Doggerland river valleys (Pettitt 2007, 115; Pettitt and White 2012, 447). In this context, rivers would have provided major corridors of movement – allowing navigation through landscapes with which individuals and communities may have had only a passing familiarity. Certain nodal points along and within these river valley networks, however, appear to have emerged as points which saw repeated episodes of occupation – known places which had acquired a significance, including those where raw materials could be acquired and perhaps where migratory animals could be intercepted or monitored. That this stretch of the Cam Valley, as it passes through the chalk escarpment and onto the lower lying ground beyond, may have been one of these locations is hinted at by the finds from the Genome Campus, but determining whether it approaches the scale of one of the major clusters found elsewhere in the region must await the results of further fieldwork.

If, as seems likely, the Terminal Palaeolithic activity did take place in the context of movement along the Cam Valley, the downstream reaches of the river would have led northwards, passing through what is now the south-east and eastern fens, and skirting the Breckland of Norfolk and Suffolk, before joining the 'Greater Ouse', a major river system fed by the waters of those rivers which now drain into the Wash, and beyond, northwards into Doggerland. The clusters of Terminal Palaeolithic finds on the eastern fen edge and in the Breckland probably attest to activity taking place in the context of movement of these drainage systems, and may have been closely associated with the activity at Hinxton.

Perhaps most relevant here, however, is the evidence, referred to above, from Whiteway Drove,

Swaffham Prior, on the south-eastern fen edge. Here, some 3km south-east of the current course of the Cam and situated adjacent to a network of palaeochannels which fed in to the river from the chalk escarpment to the south, large collections of flintwork of Terminal Palaeolithic date have been collected from the ploughsoil over an area of some 11ha since at least the 1950s. Initially collected on an informal basis by the landowner (the polymath farmer, amateur archaeologist, naturalist and meteorologist, J.W. Clarke – see Bulleid 2014), systematic fieldwalking by Andrew David and Roger Jacobi in the 1980s was able to map the main distribution of the scatter – highlighting the presence of what appeared to represent at least three high density scatters covering areas of c.400m^2 within a larger, lower density, background scatter. The remarkable feature of the Whiteway Drove material is, however, its composition, which is dramatically different to that at the Genome Campus and highly unusual in a national context. Descriptions/summaries of parts of the assemblage (David n.d.; Barton 1986b; cf. Tilley 1979, 10, fig. 6; Cooper 2006, 87, fig. 25), and analysis of all the surviving material from the site (held in collections by the British Museum and the Museum of Archaeology and Anthropology, Cambridge) by one of the present authors (see Billington 2016, 322–8), indicates that the assemblage has an exceptionally large number of retouched tools, together with a high proportion of non-cortical pieces and blades, and relatively little evidence for the early stages of core reduction. The assemblage is substantial, with over 1,800 flints belonging to the Palaeolithic scatters surviving in the museum collections, which include no less than 152 scrapers and 33 burins, together with a range of other tools including a small series of microlithic points (Billington 2016, fig. 6.9).

The contrast between the Whiteway Drove assemblage and that from the Genome Campus hints at considerable complexity in terms of inter-assemblage variability in sites along the Cam Valley: the Genome Campus appears to represent a short-lived episode, dominated by large-scale flintworking – whilst at Whiteway Drove it seems that tools, blades and partly worked cores were brought to and used at a locale where the emphasis was on a different range of activities. This may reflect somewhat longer periods of occupation at the site and, whilst the presence of multiple high density scatters within an extensive area seems likely to reflect repeated visits to a favoured locale, there has been some suggestion that it may have represented a site of seasonal aggregation by multiple groups/communities (see Lewis with Rackham 2011, 205; cf. Cooper 2006, 87). Only further discoveries and reanalysis of poorly documented assemblages will allow the extent and implications of this kind of assemblage variability to be tracked in the region, but it is clear that the area has the potential to provide significant insights into patterns of landscape occupation of relevance and importance to the broader North-West European record (cf. Naudinot and Jacquier 2014).

Conclusions and future prospects

The importance of the Terminal Palaeolithic scatter from the Genome Campus is clear, both in terms of the specific body of research concerning this period in Britain and beyond, as well as in the local context of understanding the extent and character of early occupation in the Cam Valley, with the importance of the river valley as a major conduit of movement prefiguring its role in later prehistory (see below). It is obvious, however, that there remains considerable potential for further work on the assemblage – and in that sense it is hoped that this account is regarded, at least in part, as preliminary. Perhaps most obviously, a major programme of refitting has the potential to provide crucial insights into the taphonomy of the scatters and the character of the occupation, as well as providing a detailed insight into the technology of the lithic industry – whilst the latter could also be explored by more extensive attribute/metric analyses. Beyond this, the potential for use-wear analysis is very high (see Chapter 3.I) and this could provide important data to compare to the few assemblages of this kind to have seen significant programmes of use-wear analysis (cf. Grace 2011; Jacquier 2014). In this context – and with other major assemblages of this date from the region suffering a lack of even basic quantification and reporting (see Billington 2016, 358–60) – it can only be hoped that the assemblage will be recognised as a significant resource for research into the period and that its reporting, as presented here, will represent a springboard for further work.

III. Mesolithic to Bronze Age

Mesolithic

Although there are inevitable uncertainties when dealing with multi-period lithic assemblages of the kind recovered from many of the natural deposits and later features at Hinxton, Mesolithic material appears to have been widespread across the site. There was, however, little evidence for intensive activity, with only a handful of diagnostic retouched tools and a number of small, coherent, individual assemblages – most notably from Pit Group 1 (Area F). As such, the evidence is comparable to that derived from many investigations on the gravel terraces of the Cam and Granta, where small quantities of Mesolithic material are routinely recovered as part of larger assemblages dominated by Neolithic and Early Bronze Age lithics (see Background, Chapter 1.III).

The status of the features making up Pit Group 1 (Fig. 2.3) is uncertain; although deliberately dug pits of Mesolithic date have now been recognised across Britain and Ireland (Blinkhorn et $al.$ 2017), the deposition (or inadvertent incorporation) of Mesolithic material into natural features such as tree throws seems to have been much more common – and most features associated with Mesolithic finds in Eastern England can be demonstrated, or strongly suspected, to be of natural origin (as at Spong Hill, Norfolk, Healy 1988; 2012a, 19; or Peacock's Farm, Cambridgeshire, Smith et $al.$ 1989). In this context, the somewhat irregular, elongated/kidney-shaped plan of the Pit Group 1 features may suggest that they originated as tree throws (cf. Moore and Jennings 1992; Evans et $al.$ 1999) into which material was intentionally deposited.

The lack of diagnostic retouched pieces within the assemblage prevents any more precise dating of the assemblage from Pit Group 1 and the chronology of the Mesolithic activity from the site as a whole is poorly understood. The four microliths from the site included later, 'narrow-blade' Mesolithic forms and there were no clear examples of simple broad-blade forms of the Early Mesolithic, suggesting that the activity here may have largely post-dated *c*.7000 BC (Bishop and Donnelly, Chapter 3.II).

Although the Genome Campus does not appear to have seen the kind of sustained/persistent occupation that characterises some riverside sites elsewhere in the county, such as along the Godwin Ridge at Over/Needingworth (Evans *et al.* 2016), Peacock's Farm, Shippea Hill (Clark *et al.* 1935; Clark 1956; Smith *et al.* 1989), or along the Lower Cam Valley (Reynolds and Kaner 2000; Billington 2016, 102–29), the Mesolithic activity is of some significance in relation to what appears to have been much more extensive activity at the site during the Early Neolithic. The frequency of lithic scatters producing flintwork diagnostic of both the Mesolithic and Early Neolithic in the region, especially in the southern fens has, in the past, led to suggestions that genuinely 'transitional' assemblages may be present at some of these sites, reflecting the gradual uptake of Neolithic lifeways in the region (*e.g.* Hall and Coles 1994, 45–7; Reynolds and Kaner 2000; Evans and Hodder 2006b, 190). More recently – and with improved understanding of the chronology of the two periods – a more sceptical view has been taken of such evidence (*e.g.* Healy 2012a, 3; 2013, 18–19), whilst in some cases detailed analysis of lithic scatters has been able to demonstrate differences in condition or stratigraphic divisions which indicate a chronological separation between episodes of Mesolithic and Neolithic activity (see below). One clear example of this is seen at the Genome Campus, where a small but significant Mesolithic assemblage (including a very finely worked transversely sharpened axe head) was present within the large assemblage of Early Neolithic flintwork from Pond P, but was found almost exclusively in the lowest deposits of the feature and in a spatially restricted area – strongly suggesting that it represents a distinct, earlier phase of activity (Bishop and Donnelley, Chapter 3.II).

If it now seems clear that there is little firm evidence for 'transitional' assemblages or unbroken sequences of occupation across the transition, the frequency with which Neolithic occupation appears to have been superimposed on sites of earlier activity does remain striking. Alongside numerous ploughsoil lithic scatters with mixed assemblages (*e.g.* Edmonds *et al.* 1999), two very similar sequences to that seen at Pond Q have been encountered elsewhere in the county, at Stow-Cum-Quy and on the Fordham Bypass, where natural hollows have produced substantial earlier Neolithic finds assemblages, stratified above and distinguishable from smaller collections of Mesolithic flintwork (Thatcher 2007; Mortimer 2005; Bishop 2012, 140–6). It may be no coincidence that these assemblages are associated with Plain Bowl pottery assemblages, which suggests that they *may* come relatively early in the sequence of Neolithic activity in the region (see below). This pattern resonates to some extent with the much-discussed evidence for Mesolithic scatters found beneath certain Early Neolithic monuments elsewhere in Southern Britain (*e.g.* Saville 1990; Whittle and Benson 2006) and, whilst in some cases this may simply reflect the chance reoccupation of certain favourable locations, it is possible that activities such as clearance and middening associated with earlier occupations may have had long term effects on the ecology and character of particular locales which would have rendered them attractive for later episodes of activity (Bell and Noble 2012). This seems a more convincing interpretation of the evidence for successive occupations such as that from Pond Q (and perhaps also for the superimposition of Mesolithic and Neolithic material within Pond R) than any kind of direct continuity or conscious appropriation of earlier sites of activity, but further examination of this issue in the region will probably require sites where the preservation of organic/environmental remains allows the timing and tempo of occupation and ecological changes to be traced in detail.

Early Neolithic

Overview

In terms of the Mesolithic–Early Bronze Age sequence discussed in this section, the Early Neolithic emerges as the most significant period at the Genome Campus; not only is a very large proportion of the poorly stratified/residual flintwork from across the site thought to relate to this period (see Bishop and Donnelly, Chapter 3.II) (as well as a scatter of pits), two major individual discoveries were made in Area J – the large finds assemblage preserved in Pond P and the double inhumation burial. It is these two major findings these are discussed in detail here, whilst the Early Neolithic activity at the Genome Campus is examined in terms of the broader sequence of Mesolithic–Early Bronze Age occupation of the Cam Valley in the concluding part of this section.

As intimated above, the Early Neolithic occupation may have been prefigured to some extent by a long history of low-intensity use of the river valley by Mesolithic communities. There is little evidence from the site for the environmental conditions of the area during the earlier 4th millennium, or for subsequent periods. Although Boreham's pollen sequence from the floodplain peats in Area H is not anchored by any radiocarbon dating, it seems to be in keeping with the evidence from elsewhere in the region, in that it records a period dominated by deciduous woodland (lime, oak, elm, hazel), with alder growing on the lowest parts of the valley bottom or along the contemporary river channels, which can probably be equated, very broadly with the later Mesolithic and/or earlier Neolithic (see Chapter 4.IV). The scale of Neolithic disturbance/clearance activity within this kind of woodland environment remains uncertain, but is likely to have been relatively limited. Elsewhere on the gravel terraces of the Cam Valley activity appears to have taken place in the context of extensive woodland with localised clearances, some of which hosted monuments and/or areas of settlement activity (Evans *et al.* 2016, 79; Gearey *et al.* 2016, 76), and this is in keeping with the much fuller environmental record from parts of the southern fens (*e.g.* Peglar 2006; Peglar and Waller 1994; Smith *et al.* 1989; Wiltshire 2007). In this context it is significant that a radiocarbon date falling within the late Early Neolithic/early Middle Neolithic (3530–3360 cal BC; Wk13861; Appendix 2) was acquired on a sample from a charcoal-rich probable colluvial deposit in Palaeochannel 302 (Area A). Boreham (Chapter 4.IV) regards this as possible evidence for an episode of clearance at this time and, although some caution is necessary given that the date was acquired on unidentified charcoal, this may be consistent with a picture of localised and episodic clearance activity taking place on the gravel terraces next to the river.

Pond Q

The substantial assemblages of Neolithic finds preserved within the fills of Pond Q, provide valuable evidence for one episode of occupation at the site and offer some insights into the scale and character of Neolithic activity which is otherwise represented only by residual flintwork and occasional cut features. Organic preservation within the hollow deposits was very poor, with no surviving bone and extremely sparse charred plant remains, and there was no material suitable for radiocarbon dating. The fragmentary condition of the pottery dictates that few vessel forms can be reconstructed, but Percival (Chapter 3.VII) suggests that the best comparisons for the assemblage lie with Plain Bowl assemblages such as those from Broome Heath, Norfolk or Eynesbury, Cambs, and there is no clear evidence for the kind of finely finished, open-profiled carinated bowls which appear to characterise the earliest pottery assemblages in the region (*e.g.* Bishop and Proctor 2012; see Healy 2013). The precise date of the assemblage therefore remains unclear, with the use of Plain Bowl pottery (*sensu lato*) appearing to have a long currency, covering much of the earlier and mid 4th millennium BC (see Whittle *et al.* 2011, 756–78) and overlapping with use of Decorated Bowl assemblages – manifested locally by the Mildenhall type pottery best known from causewayed enclosures and some of the major East Anglian pit sites (Healy 2013).

With over 600 sherds of pottery representing at least twenty-one individual vessels and over 2,000 struck flints including a range of tools, the assemblage attests to a significant episode of settlement. It is clear, furthermore, that both the pottery and flint assemblages are partial; most vessels were represented by very small numbers of sherds and, although some refits could be made within the flint assemblage, it appears to have been made up of parts of numerous reduction sequences. Bishop and Donnelly's analysis of the flint suggests (unlike the Terminal Palaeolithic scatter from Pond P) that there is no evidence for *in situ* flintworking here, and that the material is likely to represent material gathered together and dumped/deposited in a midden-like accumulation. This interpretation seems consistent with the partial nature of the assemblages and their varied condition, and suggests that the material may best be seen as an accumulation associated with/within an area of settlement as opposed to representing any kind of 'occupation deposit' or *in situ* activity area. Whilst they remain relatively rare, similar midden-like accumulations have been identified elsewhere in Southern and Eastern England where alluvial/colluvial deposition or earthwork construction has

allowed the preservation of Neolithic land surfaces, as at the Eton Rowing lake, Dorney (Allen *et al.* 2013), Colney, Norfolk (Whitmore 2004), the Stumble, Essex (Wilkinson *et al.* 2012), or, further afield beneath the chambered tombs at Ascott-Under-Wychwood and Hazleton North in the Cotswolds (Saville 1990; Whittle and Benson 2006). In the local/regional setting, the Pond Q scatter can also be compared with the evidence from Early Neolithic scatters from buried soils exposed during excavations in the southern fenland at Sutton Gault (Tabor 2016) and from the infills of analogous periglacial hollows from sites elsewhere in south Cambridgeshire, including New Road, Melbourn (Ladd 2019) and the Babraham Research Campus (Collins 2012). Its closest parallels in terms of scale and the composition/character of its associated finds assemblages lie with the two assemblages from the Fordham Bypass (Mortimer 2005) and Stow-cum-Quy (Thatcher 2007), both of which appear to have represented very similar 'midden-like' deposits preserved within such natural hollows.

Recent discussions of Neolithic settlement in the region have drawn heavily on the evidence from pits (*e.g.* Garrow *et al.* 2005; Garrow 2006; *cf.* Tabor 2016). In large part, this reflects the increase in the record of such features occasioned by developer-funded archaeology and opportunities to investigate other depositional contexts relating to Neolithic activity have been much rarer. As highlighted by Bishop and Donnelly (Chapter 3.II), the midden-like accumulation held in Pond Q is of significance in terms of potentially representing the kind of 'pre-pit context', from which it is invariably suggested that the kinds of finds-rich midden-like fills of many Early Neolithic pits ultimately derive (Garrow 2006). There is indeed a strong sense of equivalence in the character, condition and density of the material from Pond Q and that from contemporary pit deposits, but here it is important to note that the assemblages from Pond Q are equally as 'partial' (*i.e.* a general lack of large parts of individual vessels or full reduction sequences) as those from most pit sites. This is echoed at the other comparable 'midden' sites referred to above and should guard against any expectation that surviving surface deposits will furnish any kind of 'complete' assemblages to complement the partial/'selected' remains recovered from pits. Indeed, when examined in detail (*e.g.* Lambdin Whymark 2008; Allen *et al.* 2013), the depositional and post-depositional histories of surface accumulations seem every bit as complex as those revealed by close grained studies of pit assemblages (*e.g.* Garrow *et al.* 2005; *cf.* Tabor 2016; Beadsmoore *et al.* 2010).

In terms of the nature and duration of the activity represented by the Pond Q assemblage, whilst the pottery assemblage and the wide range of flint tools clearly indicate a range of domestic-type activities, the flint includes evidence for all stages of core reduction, probably reflecting the collection and working of flint cobbles from the gravels in the immediate vicinity of the hollow. Bishop and Donnelly highlight the 'industrial-feel' of the assemblage in terms of the large number of shattered/tested pieces and decortication flakes. Similar material is a feature of some sites in the region which appear to reflect 'specialised' activity with a clear emphasis on the procurement and working of flint – seen perhaps in the large assemblage from a periglacial hollow on the terrace gravels of the Granta at the Babraham Research Campus (the ARES site, Armour 2007), or on the chalk at Wadlow Farm, West Wratting and Heathfields, Duxford (Woodley and Abrams 2013; McFayden 1999a and 1999b; Last 2002). However, in most cases the procurement and primary working of flint appears to have been embedded within what could be described as otherwise typically domestic-type activity (see Bishop 2012, 145–6) – as seen in the material from the hollow at the Fordham Bypass (Mortimer 2005), or Early Neolithic assemblages recovered from elsewhere at the Babraham Research Campus (Collins 2012). The emphasis on flintworking in the Pond Q assemblage does, however, represent one facet of the considerable inter-site variability seen between Early Neolithic flint assemblages in the region (*e.g.* Billington 2016, table 2.17), indicating important differences in the extent of different kinds of activities undertaken at specific locales and carrying an implication that individual assemblages, whether from pits or artefact scatters, may represent relatively short-lived episodes of occupation. This would complement a model of a fairly high frequency of settlement re-location, perhaps best envisaged in terms of models of 'tethered mobility' (Whittle 1997), with communities moving between different locales within a broader zone of settlement and occupation (see Tabor 2016, 184–8).

Double burial
The remains of two individuals held within a single, apparently isolated, grave in Area J (Burial Group 1) have been firmly dated to the Early Neolithic. As discussed in Chapter 2 (and see Appendix 2), combination of the replicate measurements on the two skeletons produced statistically consistent weighted means (at 95% confidence) of 3700–3640 cal BC (Sk 15189) and 3720–3640 cal BC (Sk 15190), indicating a date in the first half of the 37th century BC for their deaths and interment. The human remains where unaccompanied by any artefacts and there were no clear signs that the grave had incorporated any structural elements or furnishings. Despite the poor preservation of the remains, it seems very likely that Sk 15189 had been interred in a fully articulated state, in a tightly flexed position in the eastern half of the grave cut, whilst the remains of Sk 15190 were at least partly disarticulated, with surviving elements appearing to have been 'piled up' in the western part of the cut (Fig. 2.6). Although on a modest scale, the incorporation of semi-/fully articulated and disarticulated remains belonging to multiple individuals resonates with wider patterns in mortuary practice during the earlier 4th millennium BC, best known from monumental contexts such a chambered cairns and non-megalithic long barrows. In the regional context, these include the remains of five individuals interred in the timber mortuary structure sealed by the Foulmire Fen Long Barrow, Haddenham (Evans and Hodder 2006b), and the four individuals probably deposited within a similar timber structure at the centre of one of two plough-levelled monuments at Trumpington Meadows, Cambridge (Evans *et al.* 2018). Perhaps most comparable to Burial Group C, although from somewhat further afield, is the multiple burial deposit

from the Cat's Water sub-site, Fengate, where an isolated trench-like 'flat grave' contained the remains of four individuals in varying states of articulation (Pryor 1976; 1984).

The character and formation of the kind of complex funerary deposits which characterise the earlier part of the period have long been issues of central concern in Neolithic studies, especially in terms of interpreting the combination of individuals and elements in different states of articulation and completeness within such deposits (see Whittle 1991, 94–7). Notwithstanding evidence for considerable variability in mortuary practice (Garwood 2011a, 385–95), modern excavations and analyses of the osteological evidence, coupled with work associated with major dating programmes of some key sites from Southern England (*e.g.* Wysocki and Whittle 2000; Smith and Brickley 2009; Bayliss and Whittle 2007), have shown that at many sites these complex mortuary deposits often resulted from the episodic incorporation of fully articulated bodies into a burial chamber/structure, resulting in disturbance and reorganisation of earlier interments – with a relatively small number of sites showing any clear evidence for the deposition of previously exposed/disarticulated remains (Smith and Brickley 2009; Garwood 2011a, 385). This suggestion certainly seems to hold true in the regional context for the remains found at Trumpington Meadows and Foulmire Fen (Evans *et al.* 2018, 40–41, 82–5; Evans and Hodder 2006b, 192–3), with the preservation of the remains of a timber, box-like, mortuary structure at the latter site providing graphic evidence for the way in which repeated access to such deposits was maintained.

Whether 'non-monumental' mortuary deposits such as the Cat's Water flat grave and the double burial at the Genome Campus should also be seen as the result of repeated acts of deposition is an open question. The Cat's Water burial was originally interpreted as representing a single event, with the previously disarticulated/semi-articulated remains of an adult female and child being deposited alongside the fully articulated body of an adult male (Pryor 1984, 22). A similar interpretation of Burial Group 3 is possible but, given the evidence from more monumental contexts discussed above, it seems equally likely that repeated access to the burial space formed by these ostensibly simple graves could have been maintained over a period of time by the provision of a timber structure, or removable lid/covering: this alternative would situate these 'graves' more closely within wider practices surrounding the treatment of the dead in the period/region, whilst going some way to fulfilling long-held expectations (*e.g.* Kinnes 1975, 20–25) that such somewhat protracted/complex sequences of mortuary activity need not in all cases have been subsequently monumentalised by large-scale earthworks.

Regardless of the issue of successive interments versus single 'burial event', although involving only two individuals, the Hinxton grave provides evidence for the kind of complex mortuary practices that are a hallmark of the period. These practices can be interpreted in many ways and, as emphasised by many researchers, only a (very) small minority of the population were 'processed'/deposited in this way – mortuary rites for most individuals evidently remaining archeologically undetectable. Where available, detailed chronological modelling has indicated that these kinds of complex mortuary deposits invariably accrued over relatively short timespans, spanning decades/generations rather than centuries (Bayliss and Whittle 2007) and, as such, earlier interpretations which emphasised the transformation and integration of individual bodies into the collective, anonymous body of 'ancestral dead' have tended to give way to the idea that in many cases the remains may have represented members of specific lineages/familial groups (see Garwood 2011a, 385). In a local context, this is seen at Trumpington Meadows where, exceptionally, DNA analysis has demonstrated that the individuals from Monument 1 at Trumpington Meadow included a pair of brothers (Scheib *et al.* 2019). Whilst kinship/descent may have been one requisite conditioning the inclusion of certain individuals in these kinds of contexts, the high levels of interpersonal violence exhibited among the remains from some sites (Wysocki and Schulting 2005) raise the possibility that in some cases individuals who had died certain kinds of death may have also been preferentially selected for this kind of treatment.

Our understanding of the precise chronology of Early Neolithic mortuary activity in Eastern England is relatively poor (see Healy *et al.* 2011), but – dating to the first half of the 37th century cal BC – the double burial appears to belong to the beginning of a period of several centuries, *c.*3700–3500, when such practices are best attested (*cf.* Garwood 2011a, 393–4). The burial seems likely to be broadly contemporary (perhaps within one or two generations) of the first interments made into Monument 1 at Trumpington Meadows (Evans *et al.* 2018, 79–80, 84, table 2.26), but probably significantly predates the Foulmire Fen mortuary structure – which is likely to have been constructed and used in the first half of the 36th century BC (Morgan 2006, 183–6). It is also significantly earlier than the unusual isolated and unaccompanied double burial of a woman and infant found locally at Dernford Farm, Sawston, dated to the 35th or 34th centuries cal BC (Newton 2018, 11), which seems more likely to relate to the emergence of more widespread inhumation burial from *c.*3500 cal BC, manifested most clearly by 'Middle Neolithic' individual burials associated with round and oval barrows (see Loveday and Barclay 2010; *cf.* Garwood 2011a, 394–8).

Middle to Late Neolithic
The evidence for Middle and Later Neolithic activity at the Genome Campus is much slighter than for the Early Neolithic but, as discussed further in the concluding part of this section, it is of some significance given a relatively poor record of remains relating to these periods along the terraces of the Cam and Granta Valley (see below).

Although no Peterborough Ware pottery was recovered from the site, activity during the currency of its use in the Middle Neolithic, from (*c.*3400–2900 BC) is indicated by the radiocarbon date of 3120–2920 cal. BC on charred hazelnut shell from one of a pair of pits (Pit Group 16), both associated with small flint assemblages, in Area J. In the same area, the three pits belonging to Pit Group 17 and a further pair of pits forming Pit Group 14 did not produce pottery but their associated flint assemblage (including transverse

arrowheads) can only be attributed a broad Middle or Late Neolithic date. Features within Pit Group 4 and Pit Group 8, however, can be placed more firmly in the Late Neolithic (*c.*2900–2400 cal BC), based on their association with small quantities of Grooved Ware pottery, and a radiocarbon date on animal bone from a feature belonging to Pit Group 4 (pit 691) of 2880–2620 cal BC (Appendix 2).

These small clusters/pair of pits, associated with varying quantities of flintwork and pottery, are typical of the ephemeral traces of Neolithic activity documented across the region (Garrow 2006). Dominant interpretations of such features see them as having been dug and backfilled rapidly as part of practices associated with 'marking' or commemorating episodes of occupation (Thomas 1999; see papers in Anderson-Whymark and Thomas 2012), although other researchers maintain that at least some of these features are likely to have had a primary functional use prior to their deliberate backfilling (see Garwood 2011b). Regardless of debates regarding the function of such features, pits and their associated, often substantial, finds assemblages provide important insights into the tempo and character of individual episodes of occupation/settlement (*e.g.* Garrow *et al.* 2005). The Middle/Late Neolithic pit groups at the Genome Campus are notable, both in terms of the small number of individual features and the very low quantities of pottery recovered; the latter is unexpected given the relatively substantial flint assemblages recovered from some of the pits. Although surely a generalisation, it seems possible that this indicates that these features were associated with somewhat shorter term/less intensive episodes of activity than seen in some contemporary pit sites elsewhere in the region, such as at Over/Needingworth, where Peterborough Ware and Grooved Ware related pit clusters have been found associated with substantial pottery assemblages (see Evans *et al.* 2016; Neil and Evans 2019).

Charred plant remains were poorly preserved and very sparse; although the sample of hazelnut shell from Pit Group 16 returned a Middle Neolithic date, it is a distinct possibility that the very small quantities of charred cereal grain/chaff from these features represent intrusive material (*cf.* Pelling *et al.* 2014) and there is thus no definite evidence for arable agriculture associated with these features. The small animal bone assemblages recovered from the pits are somewhat more informative (see Bates, Chapter 4.II), and in particular the large number of pig bones from features belonging to Pit Group 4 (Grooved Ware associated) is consistent with a wider trend toward a dominance of pig in the Late Neolithic (Serjeantson 2011; Rowley-Conwy and Owen 2011).

Relatively little of the poorly stratified/residual flintwork from the site could be unambiguously attributed to the Middle and/or Late Neolithic but the distribution of features does suggest fairly widespread activity across the site and the presence of surface scatters/middens is implied by the small assemblages of later Neolithic flintwork from Pond H, located close to (and potentially associated with) Late Neolithic Pit Group 4.

Beaker to Bronze Age

Three distinct facets of Beaker associated activity were found at the Genome Campus, the first the midden-like deposit in the upper fill of the pit/'shaft' in Trench U (Pit Group 7), the second a series of finds-poor features in Area J (which may have included the remains of a post-built structure; Structure 1; Pit Groups 13 and 15) and, finally, two semi-complete Beaker vessels recovered from a small pit in Area C (pit 352, Pit Group 12). Whilst the remains from the Trench U feature and those in Area J seem closely related to domestic activity, the vessels from Area J seem more likely to relate to some kind of ceremonial/funerary activity, and may have formed the focus for later burials, including a Bronze Age inhumation.

The character of the remains thought to be associated with domestic-type activity highlights some of the problems associated with the identification and characterisation of Beaker-associated settlement in the region. Domestic structures belonging to this period generally remain as elusive as those of earlier periods, whilst the tradition of pit digging and associated depositional practices appears to have been less widespread than at least during certain parts of the Neolithic (Garrow 2006, 137–8, 152). Thus, whilst the Beaker settlement record in the region is relatively rich when compared to that of other areas of Southern England (*cf.* Allen and Maltby 2012) and does include important assemblages from pits and pit cluster sites (*e.g.* Chapman *et al.* 2005; Hummler 2005; Ashwin 2001; Evans *et al.* 2009; 2016), many of the more important sites are represented by surface artefact scatters and ephemeral features fortuitously preserved/protected by fenland deposits (Bamford 1982; Healy 1996; Tabor 2015) or by later earthworks, as from beneath round barrows at Chippenham, Cambs (Gibson 1980) and Weasenham Lyngs and Reffley Wood, Norfolk (Petersen and Healy 1986). At the Genome Campus, the deposition of material in the hollow formed by the infilling of the Trench U shaft therefore represents the kind of serendipity that has produced most of the more significant domestic Beaker assemblages from the region, whilst the finds-poor features in Area J may have been associated with relatively intensive activity that has – typically – simply left very little trace in terms of the artefacts form earthfast features.

The origin of the pit/shaft (902) excavated in Trench U remains unclear in terms of whether it was deliberately cut or instead represented a natural geological feature (*i.e.* a solution hole). With a dearth of finds from its lower fills (aside from a *possibly* utilised quartzite cobble), the Beaker pottery from its uppermost fill is likely to have been deposited at a considerably later date than that of the original formation/excavation and initial infilling of the feature itself, which at this point was probably visible only as a relatively shallow hollow. The typology and affinities of the substantial assemblage of Beaker pottery from this upper fill are discussed in detail by Last and Percival (Chapter 3.VI) and in those terms require little further comment here. One of the most striking aspects of the assemblage is the large number of vessels represented – with an estimated 30 vessels, more than the total recovered from Neolithic midden in Pond Q but represented by just 144 sherds compared to the

643 sherds present in Pond Q. The composition of the assemblage, with a large number of vessels represented by relatively few sherds, including relatively fresh, larger portions of some pots alongside many vessels represented by single or small numbers of weathered and abraded sherds is – as discussed in detail by Mark Knight (Knight 2016, see also Knight 2009, 160–2) – a recurrent one among the major assemblages of Beaker pottery from the region. Knight regards this distinctive characteristic of Beaker assemblages as providing important evidence for the scale and tempo of Beaker-related settlement, attesting to extended and complex taphonomic histories during which individual pots were exposed to significant levels of attrition and dispersal. One implication of this is that comparisons of the size (in term of sherd count/weight) of such assemblages with those of other periods may often significantly underestimate the scale of the pottery assemblage represented – as seen in the totals from the Trench U pit/shaft and Pond Q. Equally, the complex taphonomic processes evidenced by Beaker assemblages such as that from the pit/shaft deposit may suggest that associated occupation was of longer duration and/or saw repeated episodes of occupation at the same specific locale than was typical for earlier periods.

In stark contrast to the pit/shaft material, the Beaker vessels from the small pit (352) in Area C, although poorly preserved, appear to have originally been deposited as a pair of complete or at least substantially complete vessels (see Chapter 2; Fig. 2.11). They lay against one edge of this small oval-shaped feature, which measured little more than 0.5m long. The deposition of complete Beaker vessels as grave goods accompanying inhumation burials is, of course, well-known and given how rarely they occur in non-funerary contexts, Percival (Chapter 3.VII) suggests it is likely that they were originally associated with a burial. Elsewhere, otherwise 'empty' pits containing Beaker vessels found during the investigation of round barrows and ring ditches clearly represent graves with no surviving skeletal material (*e.g.* Ashwin and Bates 2000; Wymer 1996; *cf.* Last 2007, 168–70), and given the position of the Beakers in pit 352, at one end of the feature, it seems very possible that they originally accompanied a burial. The major issue with this interpretation is the size of the pit, which seems too small to have held a crouched adult inhumation, and it would have to be presumed that the grave was that of a child/infant. In this context it may be significant that the more complete of the two Beakers from the pit was a cordoned vessel bearing some rusticated decoration, and hence unlike the finely and profusely decorated pots more familiar from Beaker funerary contexts. In their review of Beaker/Early Bronze Age burial practices at Raunds, Northamptonshire, Harding and Healy point to a possible pattern, which can be traced across large parts of Eastern and Southern England, for child burials to be accompanied by 'atypical' plain or rusticated pots (Harding and Healy 2007, 250). The burial of a child and the consequently fragile nature of any associated skeletal remains would also make the absence of any traces of a burial in this feature more explicable.

A further argument in favour of pit 352 having been a grave rests on evidence for later funerary activity at this specific location, with two inhumation burials lying within 20m to its north-west. One of these was the burial of an adult female (Sk 218; Burial Group 2) dated to the Early or Middle Bronze Age, 1750–1430 cal BC (95% confidence; Wk-12598; 3303±68 BP), whilst the second was that of an adult male, dated to the Late Iron Age or Early Roman period (Burial Group 4; see below). The Bronze Age individual represented by Sk 218 seems likely to have died and been interred some time, probably several centuries, later than the deposition of the Beakers in pit 352. Recent modelling of Beaker-associated radiocarbon dates from England (largely from funerary contexts) suggests the end of their use sometime between c.1900 and 1700 cal BC (Jay et al. 2019; Healy 2012b), whilst a more critical appraisal of the dates suggests there is in fact very little evidence for Beakers being used and deposited post c.1950 cal BC (see Parker Pearson et al. 2019, 174). If this sequence of burials is not to be seen as purely coincidental, it seems likely that the original position of pit 352 was marked, perhaps by a low, unditched mound, of the kind known to have covered Beaker burials elsewhere (see Garwood 2007), and often suspected to have originally overlain Beaker 'flat graves' discovered in locations which have seen a long history of cultivation (cf. Last 2007, 164–5; in the local context see Evans et al. 2018, 47).

The radiocarbon date for Sk 218 is an imprecise one but, whether regarded as belonging to the Early or Middle Bronze Age, it falls within a period when inhumation burials have traditionally been seen as rare, with cremation appearing to have been the dominant funerary rite. However, in recent years, in the context of a major expansion of fieldwork and an increase in the radiocarbon dating of otherwise undated/unaccompanied burials, examples of inhumation burials belonging to these periods have become more common (e.g. Evans et al. 2016, 252–3; Luke 2016, 171–87; Phillips and Blackbourn 2019; cf. Harding and Healy 2007, 237–8) and a regional scale reappraisal of Bronze Age funerary practices is now required to contextualise these new discoveries.

Regardless of its precise date, this burial provides the only firm evidence for probable post-Beaker activity at the site prior to the remains of occupation in the Middle Iron Age. Although the investigations have identified a series of stratigraphically early east-to-west aligned ditches which could represent the remains of a Middle Bronze Age field system (Ditch Groups 1 and 2), this attribution is extremely tentative, but potentially gains some credence from the recent recognition of probable Middle Bronze Age ditched boundaries on the valley sides to the north of the Wellcome Genome Campus during extensive evaluation of land to the west of Hinxton Grange (Jones 2017; see Chapter 1.III). Nor does the lack of datable finds necessary imply a major hiatus in settlement in the area during the later 2nd millennium BC, and Middle/Late Bronze Age activity is clearly evinced nearby at Hinxton Quarry at the location of an earlier ring ditch by a very substantial lithic assemblage including many retouched and utilised tools, interpreted as essentially 'domestic in character' (Pollard 1998, 67).

Conclusions: Mesolithic to Early Bronze Age land use and settlement in the Cam Valley

Although the episodic character of occupation and activity at the Genome Campus over the course of the later Mesolithic to Early/Middle Bronze Age has been emphasised here, the record revealed by the excavations is a relatively full one, in the sense that remains belonging to most of the traditionally used chronological/period divisions are represented. When seen in the wider context of the Upper and Middle Cam Valley, this provides an opportunity to reflect briefly on the longer term patterns in the intensity and character of prehistoric occupation in the area. Any such exercise is hampered by major variations in the archaeological visibility of different periods – chiefly due to important differences in depositional practices and the use of material culture – and major biases in terms of the extent and methods of archaeological fieldwork, but it is possible to identify some trends and issues which are at least deserving of further research.

As noted above, Early Neolithic activity, belonging to the first half of the 4th millennium BC, is well-represented at the Genome Campus site and the remains of this period are certainly more extensive than those of the Later Mesolithic or Middle and Late Neolithic. At a broader scale, this is true of the gravel terraces right along the Middle and Upper Cam Valley as a whole – where an increasing number of sites have produced evidence for Early Neolithic settlement in the form of pits and finds from surface scatters/preserved soil horizons (see Chapter 1; e.g. Paul et al. 2016; Newton 2018) – alongside the 'riverside' monuments at Trumpington Meadows (Evans et al. 2018) and the newly discovered causewayed enclosure at Great Shelford (Small 2017), the latter located immediately adjacent to the river floodplain. The contrast with the evidence of Middle and Neolithic activity is particularly striking; whilst remains of Late Neolithic settlement are now known from several sites on the gravels of the Granta Valley to the north (e.g. Clarke and Gilmour forthcoming), there are no real equivalents along the Cam – the modest pit groups from the Genome Campus making an important contribution in this respect. The evidence so far amassed from the excavations in the Addenbrookes/Trumpington environs to the south of Cambridge currently provides the best illustration of this pattern, with the quantities of Plain Bowl/Mildenhall type Early Neolithic pottery from the major excavations in this landscape dwarfing those of Peterborough Ware and Grooved Ware (Knight 2018, 61–2, table 2.13). This disparity could be explained by differences in depositional practice – with more extensive digging and backfilling of pits during the Early Neolithic as opposed to later periods (see Garrow 2006) – but significant pit sites of Middle and (especially) Late Neolithic date are known from elsewhere in the region and the dominance of Early Neolithic material appears to hold good when considering less robust remains such as surface scatters and residual finds – as at the Genome Campus itself where Early Neolithic pits were actually few and relatively unproductive in terms of finds.

The probability that Early Neolithic occupation was more intensive on the terraces of the river valleys than during the later 4th and early 3rd millennium BC has wider implications, especially in terms of current models of dramatic changes in population and land use over the period at a national scale. Recent large scale analyses of radiocarbon dates and environmental evidence have suggested that a major expansion in population at the beginning of the Neolithic, strongly associated with the new agricultural economy and with evidence for widespread cereal cultivation, was brought to a halt in the mid 4th millennium, with a decline in population and the adoption of essentially pastoralist economies prior to renewed agrarian and demographic expansion in the Early to Middle Bronze Age (*e.g.* Stevens and Fuller 2012; Bevan *et al.* 2017). Although this model has been subject to critique, especially in the context of the evidence from specific local/regional areas (*e.g.* Bishop, R.R. 2015), it may provide at least a partial explanation for some aspects of the Neolithic record from the Cam Valley. It is important, however, to decouple the growing body of evidence for major changes in economy over the course of the 4th millennium BC from the evidence for population decline, which essentially relies on an acceptance that the gross quantity of radiocarbon dates can act as a useful proxy for population levels. It may instead be the case that changing patterns of landscape occupation/site location associated with changes in economy and land use may underlie the relative dearth of Middle and Late Neolithic activity in the riverine settings of the gravel terraces – and evidence for this may be emerging in south Cambridgeshire in the form of several extensive swathes of Late Neolithic pits at specific spring line/head locations on the lower slopes of the chalk escarpment; notably at the foot of the Gog Magog Hills south-east of Cambridge (Billington in prep; Gilmour 2017) and to the south of Melbourn (Ladd 2019). This may reflect new priorities in terms of site location and more complex and wide ranging mobility patterns associated with the exploitation of a diverse range of domestic livestock and of wild resources, leading to less intensive use of the gravel terraces which appear to have been the core areas of Early Neolithic settlement (Billington in prep.).

Regardless of the scale of Middle and Late Neolithic activity along the valley, it seems possible that in the specific case of the Genome Campus, more sustained episodes of activity at the site occurred during the later 3rd millennium, associated with the use of Beaker pottery and – as during the Early Neolithic – this includes evidence for probable funerary/ceremonial activity as well as settlement. Given the problems of identifying Beaker settlement, it is unsurprising that the local context for the Beaker activity is provided largely by evidence for funerary activity on the gravel terraces of Cam – perhaps broadly comparable to and contemporary with that represented by pit 352. As noted in Chapter 1, two Beaker vessels, presumably related to one or more burials, were recovered during antiquarian investigations at Great Chesterford (Medlycott 2011a, 9), whilst a Beaker-accompanied inhumation is also known from Whittlesford Station (Lethbridge and O'Reilly 1937). Further upstream, in the Addenbrookes/Trumpington environs, similar activity is attested by a double Beaker burial at Trumpington Meadows, but here large-scale excavations have also produced evidence for settlement, with Beaker-associated pits being found at

sites including Trumpington Meadows, the Park and Ride site and Clay Farm.

In the context of Beaker/Early Bronze Age land use it is also important to consider the major concentrations of ring ditches and round barrows in the area – found not only on the gravel terraces of the river but also in large numbers on adjacent parts of the chalk downland (see Chapter 1.III). Unfortunately, with the region's archaeological agenda in recent years driven largely by the exigencies of development, there has been very little opportunity to investigate any of the monuments on the chalk which, beyond their strictly 'archaeological' interest, have considerable potential in terms of proving evidence for local land use and environmental conditions (*cf.* French *et al.* 2007; Allen 1997). Nonetheless, given that at least some of these monuments are likely to have their origins in the Chalcolithic/earlier part of the Early Bronze Age, it seems likely that they indicate increasingly widespread clearance outside of the river valleys in this period, in areas potentially at some remove from areas of contemporary settlement (*cf.* Last 2000). Whether, as has long been suggested, the association between the distribution of 'chalkland' round barrows and the putative routeway of the Icknield Belt can any longer be sustained remains open to debate (*cf.* Evans *et al.* 2018, 424–5; Bell 2020, 195–7), but this may have been a period of major importance in terms of a growing potential for the establishment of both local and longer distance networks of movement and communication across the interfluves and uplands of the chalk (Harding and Healy 2007, 285–6).

IV. Late Iron Age and Romano-British

Introduction

Despite the evidence for Middle Iron Age and later Roman activity, the floruit of the later prehistoric and Roman sequence at the Genome Campus covers the Late Iron Age and immediate aftermath of the Roman invasion, during the later 1st century BC and 1st century AD. A period of major political and social change, this is also the earliest period in which archaeological remains are supplemented by the evidence from written sources and numismatic evidence, providing some glimpses into the political history of the region. Although, as is so often the case, it is a difficult task to map the archaeological evidence onto the framework of historical 'events', the archaeology of this period at the Genome Campus must be seen in the context of these wider social and political changes.

This issue is particularly important given the location of the site which, as set out in Chapter 1, lay on the course of the Cam–Stort corridor – long seen as marking the boundary between the Late Iron Age tribal polities of the Trinovantes and Catuvellauni (Medlycott 2011a, 9–10; see Rippon 2018, 43–75) – and equally significantly, within an area marking a major, if diffuse, boundary between the Late Iron Age societies of South-East England, which shows strong influence from contacts with Romanised Gaul, and those to the west and north where there was more limited or selected uptake of continentally inspired customs. In archaeological terms, the differences between such communities are most apparent in the appearance, in the south-east, of Aylesford-Swarling type cremation burials, together with the increasing dominance of wheel-thrown/finished pottery, including Roman and Gallo-Belgic imports, also being reflected by major differences in the architecture and character of settlement, and in terms of political/social organisation (see Hill 2002; 2007). In the immediate context of Eastern England this contrast falls between the communities of what Hill (2002) has termed 'Southern' and 'Northern' East Anglia, with the former broadly corresponding to modern Hertfordshire and Essex (and the territories of the Catuvellauni and Trinovantes respectively) and the latter equating to much of Cambridgeshire, Norfolk and Suffolk. The location of the Genome Campus at this major fault line or interface in the geography of the Late Iron Age of Southern Britain is, as discussed below, reflected at the site by what appears to have been the selective appropriation of novel forms of architecture and material culture familiar from the heartlands of 'Southern East Anglia', deployed alongside what appear to be more locally specific, and perhaps traditional, cultural practices.

Whilst the relatively close dating of some pottery forms belonging to this period allows a measure of chronological control rarely possible in earlier periods, it remains the case that there are significant uncertainties regarding the precise chronology and sequence of the remains that have been attributed to Period 3. In large part, this reflects the complexity of the remains belonging to this relatively short period, attesting both to intensive activity at the site and to major changes in land use/organisation over the course of these politically turbulent times. This section begins, therefore, with a review of the sequence of Late Iron Age and Roman activity at the site – providing a thumbnail sketch of the site's sequence – before moving on to consider specific elements of the Late Iron Age and Roman archaeology and, finally, briefly considering their significance in the wider local/regional context in terms of the vexed and much rehearsed issue of the 'Romanisation' of Iron Age communities.

Sequence and site development
In interpreting the Late Iron Age and Roman sequence at the Genome Campus, it is crucial to recognise the partial nature of the investigation, particularly in relation to the very limited (trench-based) investigations in the areas lying immediately adjacent to the modern floodplain of the river to the west of Areas A–D. This issue is particularly important in terms of tracing the origins of Iron Age occupation at the site, with hints that remains predating the enclosure/trackway complex in Areas D and I may have been present in this riverside zone. That said, the earliest evidence for Iron Age activity came from the pit groups associated exclusively with handmade Middle Iron Age pottery in Area J, one of which was associated with a radiocarbon date of 330–200 cal BC (pit 15066; Pit Group 28). Although the finds associated with these scattered features (including pottery, fired clay and animal bone) surely relate to domestic-type activity, it is difficult to assess the scale of occupation. They could represent features on the periphery of an area of more extensive

settlement or relate to brief/small-scale episodes of activity. Whilst there is a stark contrast between these features and the more substantial remans of enclosed settlements widely known elsewhere in the region, they are consistent with the record of Middle Iron Age settlement from the immediate area, with relatively small groups of pits also known from Pepperton Hill and Hinxton Road, Duxford (see Chapter 1, Fig. 1.2).

Whether these Middle Iron Age remains should be seen as marking the beginning of continuous activity at the site into the Late Iron Age and Early Roman period is an open question, and it remains possible that the Period 3.1 trackways, which played a major role in structuring activity at the site, had their origins in the Middle Iron Age. This may also be implied by the evidence for the reworking/modification of the ditches associated with Trackway 1 to accommodate the construction of Enclosures 1–3. Given, however, that there is no evidence that the enclosures were built and used prior to the final decades of the 1st century AD (see below), it seems equally possible that the trackways could belong to the earlier part of the Late Iron Age and/or could be broadly contemporary with the 'transitional' assemblage of Middle to Late Iron Age pottery from the boundary ditch encountered during trial-trenching to the west of Area B (see Percival, Chapter 3.VII). This latter assemblage implies some occupation in this riverside zone at a time when Late Iron Age type pottery was first beginning to circulate in the region – which present evidence suggests can be placed no earlier than c.50 BC (Sealey 2007, 27–31).

The major set of trackside enclosures (Enclosures 1/2 and 3) attributed to Period 3.1 (and probably by analogy the trench-investigated sub-square Enclosure 4) does seem, however, to belong to a more advanced phase of the Late Iron Age and it is these features that provide the most abundant evidence for Late Iron Age activity at the Genome Campus site. The dating of the original cut of the square enclosure appended to Trackway 1 (Enclosure 1) rests essentially on a radiocarbon date of 120 cal BC – cal AD 60 at 94% confidence (OxA-29573; 2039±27 BP; Appendix 2) which derives from a burial cut into the base of the ditch (and hence very soon after its original construction) and the relatively substantial pottery assemblage recovered from its fills. Whilst the radiocarbon date associated with the burial provides little more than a *terminus ante quem* of AD 60 for the beginning of the ditch's infilling, the character of the pottery strongly implies a date no earlier than the latest years of the 1st century AD; dominated by 'Belgic' style Late Iron Age forms, it includes locally produced copies of Gallo-Belgic beakers which were not circulated or imitated in the region until c.15 BC at the earliest (Brown, Chapter 3.VII; see Hill 2002, 148). Indeed, it is entirely possible that the enclosure was constructed in the earlier part of the 1st century AD and, although its complex fill sequence and the major episode of recutting represented by Enclosure 2 suggests a somewhat extended period of use, the character of the pottery suggests that its primary use did not extend much beyond the first half of the 1st century AD. In this context it is important to note that, whilst the presence of kiln furniture belonging to a pre-Flavian pottery kiln in the upper fills of the ditch marking the southern side of Enclosure 2 is a significant find, it is probably best interpreted as representing a discrete episode of later activity as opposed to attesting to the longevity of the enclosure's use. The construction and use of pottery kilns in the decades immediately following the Conquest is increasingly well documented in southern Cambridgeshire, and in most cases they appear to have been located within areas of earlier (Late Iron Age) field systems/enclosures and at some remove from areas of contemporary settlement/activity (Anderson and Woolhouse 2016, 64; *cf.* Evans *et al.* 2008, 127–33). The use and subsequent dismantling/deposition of a pottery kiln located somewhere within or around what was by this point an abandoned earthwork, but adjacent to the contemporary routeway represented by Period 3.2 Trackway 3, seems a likely context for this material – especially given the lack of pottery from the site which could be readily identified as the product of such a kiln.

Other elements of the Late Iron Age and Roman remains at the Genome Campus rarely produced substantial assemblages of pottery such as those from Enclosures 1–3, and are consequently less well dated. At this stage of the site's development, in the pre-Conquest period, it seems clear that activity was structured around the major east-to-west aligned routeway (represented by Trackway 1), which equates very broadly with the putative, southern, route of the Icknield Way/Belt. Significantly, during the final stages of the preparation of this volume a continuation of the trackway was exposed during trial-trenching of the area immediately to the east in the proposed Wellcome Genome Campus Expansion Land (Fig. 1.2, No. 21; Robinson-Zeki 2019), and its presence here strongly suggests that a feature originally interpreted as a field lynchet at the Uttlesford crematorium site represents its continuation on the higher ground of the valley side (Fig. 1.2, No. 12; Network Archaeology 2017). Further east its course is unknown, but it may have continued as one route across the chalk downlands south of Great Abington, crossing the interfluve to provide a link with the communities of the Granta Valley.

Given the importance this east-to-west route appears to have had in terms of the layout of Enclosures 1–3, its apparent slighting by the north-to-south aligned ditches of Trackway 3 in Period 3.2 represents a major fault line in the site's sequence which seems to have been associated with the extensive, if fragmentary, remains of field/enclosure systems as well as the probable 'track-side' shrine (Period 3.3). A relative poverty of datable finds renders the precise chronology of these developments over the course of Period 3.2 and 3.3 unclear, although it is tempting to associate them with major changes in land use in the mid to later 1st century AD occurring as a result of the Roman Conquest. The new trackway's north-to-south alignment (paralleling the course of the river itself, as well as the historic road network of the modern village) seems likely to have formalised existing routes along the river valley, perhaps in direct response to the foundation, upstream, of the military fort and subsequent town at Great Chesterford, which may have been provisioned from riverside farms and settlements in its hinterland, including the Early Roman farmstead complex partially investigated at Hinxton Quarry (Fig 1.2, No. 7; Gibson 2003; Mortimer and Evans 1996,

Chapter 1.III) and other probable major farmsteads/settlements known from aerial survey in the valley to the north of the Wellcome Genome Campus (Chapter 1.III; Fig. 1.2, Nos 7, 20, 22). That the slighting of the earlier east-to-west aligned routeway at the subject site may have reflected changes in routeways and land use across the wider landscape is also implied by the manner in which its eastwards continuation, noted at the Wellcome Genome Campus Expansion Land, appears to have had a similar relationship to a later set of sinuous, north-to-south aligned set of trackway ditches (see Fig. 1.2, No. 21; Robinson-Zeki 2019, 36), as well as probably having been cut across by the route of the Roman road leading from Great Chesterford to Worsted Lodge.

Throughout Periods 3.2 and 3.3, and despite the presence of fairly substantial assemblages of animal bone and some pottery, there was little direct evidence for occupation within the investigated areas, and the site instead appears to have been characterised by a well-developed system of fields, corrals and interconnecting trackways, relating to agricultural activity. This agricultural usage appears to have continued into the Middle and Late Roman periods, whilst the north-to-south alignment of Trackway 3 proved to be of enduring significance in terms of later, Anglo-Saxon, settlement and land use at the site (see Part II).

Aspects of ceremony and settlement

In the following discussion of selected aspects of the Iron Age and Roman remains, a broad two-fold distinction is made between aspects of mortuary and ceremonial/ritual activity, and those relating to land use and agricultural practices. Whilst this is a useful heuristic device, it should be emphasised that the problems of maintaining a rigid distinction between 'ritual' and 'mundane' activities is well known, and is clearly manifested in the character of the most significant remains belonging to Period 3 (trackside Enclosures 1–3), where ceremonial/mortuary practices appear to have been accompanied by what should probably be regarded as evidence for more quotidian settlement-type.

Ceremonial and mortuary activity

A Late Iron Age ceremonial/mortuary complex? (Period 3.1)
Over the course of the project, interpretation of the Late Iron Age enclosures (Enclosures 1–4), has oscillated between the extremes of regarding them as domestic/settlement compounds or as overtly ritual/ceremonial spaces. However, as the excavation and analysis progressed, the unusual nature of Enclosure 1/2 became clearer and, given the traces of what might normally be regarded as domestic-type activity, the evidence suggests a special status for these features in terms of playing host to ceremonial/funerary rites.

As noted above, the location of the larger enclosure adjacent to Trackway 1 – a potential incarnation of one route of the Icknield Way – must be of some significance. It suggests that the ability to travel to and from nearby settlements (or perhaps further afield) was fundamental to the purpose of the enclosure. Moreover, the fact that it was necessary to divide the entranceway spatially from the trackway (into the 'annex' of Enclosure 3) from the inner enclosed space (Enclosure 1/2) suggests that different levels of access to the inner space were required or that different activities took place here. A similar secondary enclosure entrance, albeit used for settlement and associated craft activity, was evident in one phase of the major Iron Age enclosure complex at Fison Way, Norfolk (Gregory 1992, 41–88).

Whilst it is acknowledged that the substantial assemblages of pottery and animal bone from Enclosures 1/2 clearly attest to major episodes of food preparation and consumption, very possibly in the context of a resident household, it seems clear that, from its inception, it was used as a place for disposing of and/or dealing with the dead. Sub-square enclosure for the purpose of burial was relatively common both in Southern Britain and in Northern France during this period (Haselgrove 2007, 496–9), although specific rites changed significantly between each settlement, meaning that each example should be analysed on an individual basis (Carr 2007, 451). The mortuary rites associated with human remains are discussed in more detail below and, whilst it would be difficult to argue that the two inhumation burials and five deposits of disarticulated bone found associated with Enclosure 1/2 constitute a formal 'cemetery', the frequency of human remains is very high, especially given that the enclosure ditches saw only partial excavation. Notwithstanding that the recovery of isolated burials and small quantities of disarticulated human bone is by no means uncommon in Middle to Late Iron Age settlement-associated contexts in the region (*e.g.* Evans 2003, 227–32; see Anderson *et al.*, Chapter 4.1), the frequency of human remains strongly suggests a special role for the enclosure, although whether this related specifically to mortuary practice, or to a broader set of ceremonies/rituals within which the processing and deposition of remains of the dead played an important role remains far from certain.

The shrine (Period 3.3)
Fig. 5.2
Located a short distance to the north of the Middle to Late Iron Age enclosures discussed above, on the opposite (northern) side of the Icknield Way, it could be argued that the putative shrine in some way represents a continuation of the ceremonial/funerary activity witnessed there in the Late Iron Age. However, its clear relationship to the major reorganisation of the site represented by Trackway 3 and its more overtly 'Romanised' form makes it more likely that its construction and use was bound up with new concerns which emerged in the context of the post-Conquest period in the mid to late 1st century AD.

Interpretation as a shrine is based on the enclosure or building's distinctive single *cella* design, with an ambulatory surviving on its west and south sides and the suggestion of an enclosed entrance. Figure 5.2 shows the shrine alongside other similar contemporary examples from the wider region, including those from the adjoining settlements at Duxford (Lyons 2011, 36–7 and 116–8, figs 27 and 62) and Great Chesterford (Medlycott 2011a, 133–4, fig 10.4). No finds or burials were found within the Hinxton example which, although this may be in part due to

the severe truncation it had suffered, is also typical of Late Iron Age/Conquest period shrines in the region (Evans and Hodder 2006a, 327; Lyons 2011, 116–8). Unlike many local examples, however, two complete posthole rows (and the suggestion of a third) survived within the enclosed space at Hinxton. These could have been the remains of a small room or inner chamber. No other evidence for how the shrine was constructed has survived but most known examples were built with upright timbers in a shallow bedding trench, with wattle and daub walls and a thatched roof (Wait 1985, 172). The lack of finds, however, makes it difficult to comment on how this particular building was used by the community. The only possible direct clue as to which gods and goddesses were worshipped at Hinxton (although perhaps within the household rather than at a communal shrine), came in the form of the lower part of a small, solid-cast figurine (Howard-Davis, Chapter 3.III, SF 144, Fig. 3.9); this item was recovered unstratified during the Genome Campus (HINGC02, Areas A–D) excavations. The figure probably represents Fortuna, who was associated with good fortune and was a popular household deity amongst soldiers and civilians alike (Henig 1984, 77–8, 172).

Burial practices and ritual deposition
with Louise Loe, Helen Webb and Andrew Bates
The human remains from Enclosure 1/2 (Period 3.1) included both disarticulated remains and formal burials. The disarticulated material comprises the partial remains of three adults found in the lower fills of the enclosure and those of two very young children recovered from pits within its interior. It is suggested that these disarticulated remains were the result of a defleshing mortuary process, probably excarnation. No evidence for excarnation was, however, observed on the bones, such as scavenging or cut marks: the small size of the assemblage and surface abrasion may explain this absence. It is also possible that excarnation had been performed by methods other than exposure, for example, defleshing by boiling, short term burial in the ground (or possibly middens), or deposition in a mortuary structure/building – potentially sited within the enclosure itself.

Supplementing the disarticulated remains was the burial of an older male, interred in a grave in the north-east corner of the enclosure ditch and found alongside disarticulated human bone from another individual (but perhaps deriving from the later ditch fills). This grave also contained a single cow humerus that was located above the head of the interred individual, although whether this was a deliberate inclusion remains uncertain. No butchery marks were visible on the cow humerus, but this may have been the result of the level of erosion to the surface of the bone or the skill of the butcher. The placement of single species food offerings within graves has pre-Roman origins. Offerings of pork are more commonly found, with the bones of cattle and sheep being less frequent (Philpott 1991). In a Romano-British context, such offerings are more frequently found in rural settings, and may indicate a survival of this pre-Roman belief system (*ibid.*). A second inhumation burial of an adolescent of unknown sex (Burial Group 3C) was found close to the north-west corner of the enclosure, inserted

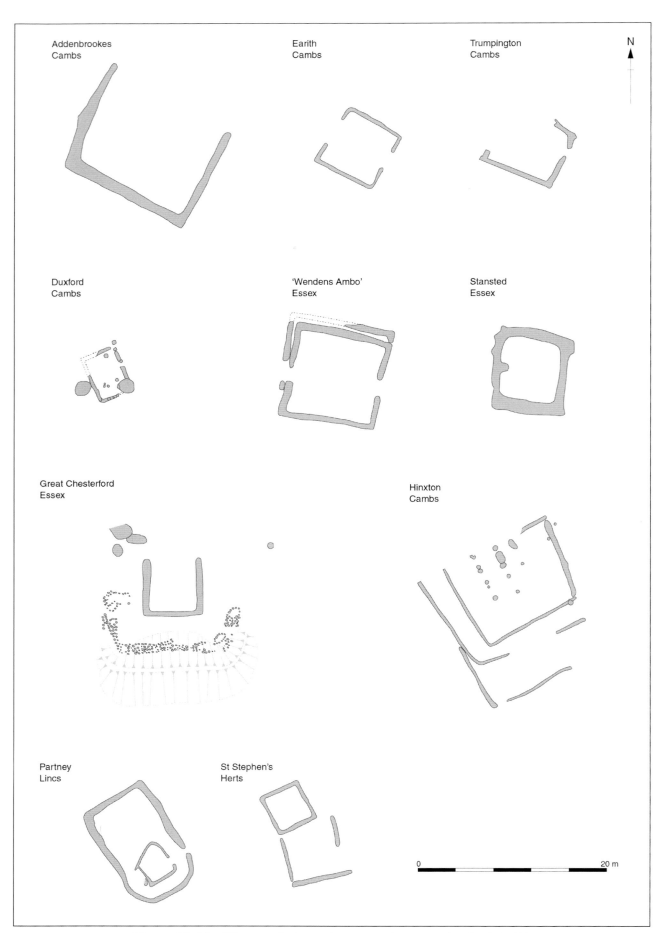

Figure 5.2 The Hinxton shrine and comparative examples. Scale 1:400

into the top of an existing pit. Both of the inhumation burials were supine with their arms by their sides, while the adolescent had their legs fully extended. The adolescent was broadly orientated north-east to south-west and the older male east to west.

A third inhumation burial, in Area C (Sk 1231; Burial Group 4; Period 3.3), constitutes the only human remains belonging to Period 3 located away from the trackside enclosures and, although tentatively attributed to Period 3.3, has been radiocarbon dated to 170 cal BC – cal AD 70 and may be broadly contemporary with the remains from the enclosures. Significantly this individual, a middle/old adult male again laid out in an extended, supine position, was interred in close proximity to what has been suggested to have been the visible remains of a small earthwork associated with much earlier funerary activity (see above).

Despite lying within the northernmost distribution of Aylesford-Swarling type cremation cemeteries (Rippon 2018, fig. 2.9), including the nearby cemetery at Hinxton Quarry (which probably dates somewhat earlier than the main phase of Late Iron Age activity at the Genome Campus; see Hill *et al.* 1999) and those known from environs of Great Chesterford (see Chapter 1; Medlycott 2011a), cremation burials were absent from the Genome Campus and the only formal interments appear to have taken the form of these supine, extended, inhumation burials. The presence of similar inhumation burials in Early Roman cemeteries more normally exclusively associated with cremation burial has been recognised as a distinct characteristic of the area (see Evans *et al.* 2008, 12, 137). The evidence from the Genome Campus provides further evidence that this practice had its origins in the Late Iron Age, as best attested very locally at Duxford where a small Late Iron Age to Early Roman cemetery including analogous inhumation burials was found in association with a shrine (Lyons 2011).

Aside from the deposition of human remains, other possible instances of ritual deposition are rare, and much of the semi-articulated animal bone from Enclosure 1/2 or from other features on the site could more readily be interpreted as butchery waste (see Chapter 4.II, Table 4.6). One major exception to this was the articulated dog skeleton buried in a small pit (712) that had been cut into the infill of a much larger storage pit (Pit Group 26) at some point in the Late Iron Age to Early Roman period (assigned here to Period 3.3). It comprised the complete skeletal remains of an adult male dog, excluding some of the phalanges, placed at the base of the pit with two (possibly whole) eggs placed on top of the body (presumably as food offerings). No butchery marks were present upon the dog bones and the body of the animal appears to have been deposited intact and with respect. Other bones from the same deposit include the left and right tarso-metatarsus of a young domestic fowl, suggesting a possible food offering for the dog. The degree of organisation and care taken with this animal burial suggests that it was a favourite pet. Indeed, dogs are known to have been afforded 'special' treatment by the Romans, perhaps due to their social proximity to humans (Hill 1995, 103).

Dog burials are common finds on Iron Age and Romano-British sites across the region, probably reflecting their importance both as guardians (of the stock animals and homesteads) and also in hunting (Evans and Hodder 2006a, 224). Other indications of the importance of dogs in Roman society come from Lydney in Gloucestershire where nine iconographic images of dogs were connected with the god of hunting and healing (*ibid.*, 394). The very similar burial of dog in a disused storage pit or silo was found nearby to the north at a contemporary site at Duxford (Lyons 2011, 25, 121), while at the Hutchison Site in Cambridge a dog burial was found within a small mixed rite Early Roman inhumation/cremation cemetery (Evans *et al.* 2008, 47–55). Slightly further afield, a dog buried at Love's Farm, St Neots, was buried with a stone marking its eye (Hinman and Zant 2018, 118, 130–31) and other examples from the region include five dogs found in association with Middle Iron Age settlement at Prickwillow Road, Ely (Atkins and Mudd 2003, 52) and a single immature Iron Age dog from Biddenham Loop, Bedfordshire (Luke 2008, 55).

Settlement, agriculture and exchange

Towards a stock-management regime
by Andrew Bates and Alice Lyons
During the latest Iron Age and Early Roman period at the Wellcome Genome Campus site there was evidently extensive exploitation of the slightly higher ground to the east of the River Cam. The local topography allowed a well-developed system of fields, corrals and interconnecting trackways to be established, with the main 'spine' formed by a new track aligned north-to-south during Period 3.2 (Trackway 3). The Hinxton field systems are similar to those identified at later Iron Age and Romano-British sites in the Upper Thames Valley, such as Farmoor, Claydon Pike and Thornhill Farm which appear to have been specialist seasonal pastoral settlements (*e.g.* Jennings *et al.* 2004; Lambrick and Robinson 1979; Miles and Palmer 1990), although this process of land division has been observed over most of Southern Britain (Knight 2007, 192). The development of this complex at Hinxton represents a fundamental reorganisation of the agrarian landscape on a large scale, which arguably saw a major re-alignment of the landscape (from east-to-west to north-to-south) towards the fort and later town at Great Chesterford (but also referencing the natural topography of the Cam Valley). The enclosures or fields were demarcated by short sections of narrow ditches, often re-dug several times, with gaps (presumably fenced) to facilitate the movement of stock between fields. In one place (in the north of Area B; Pit Group 29) a length of enclosure ditch was re-enforced with an alignment of pits, one of which may initially have been a well.

It has been suggested that in the Thames Valley 'enclosures, rectilinear field systems, and networks of pit alignments are interrelated phenomena, indicative of increasing pressures upon finite pasture and arable resources and a growing demand for tighter control of the valley environment' (Knight 2007, 214). The same pressures may have been factors in the Cam Valley, necessitating development in response to a rising population as the town at Great Chesterford became established. Indeed, larger populations of both people and livestock would probably have required more formal methods of animal management (droveways, batch-handling stock yards, corrals *etc.*) to provide for a local economy focusing on more than self-sufficiency (Evans and Hodder 2006a, 315).

Analysis of the faunal assemblage indicates that during the Middle and Late Iron Age, cattle and sheep were the principal domestic stock animals, alongside pig. It is likely that cattle husbandry involved a mixed strategy, with the majority of males probably being culled after gaining meat weight after three years of age. A population of older adult dairy cows and working animals would also have been maintained. A small number of cattle were evidently slaughtered as very old animals at the end of their working life. The sheep were generally culled before four years of age. Significant numbers of older animals indicating a wool flock appear to be absent at Hinxton and it is likely that meat was an important factor in the husbanding of sheep. The pigs were slaughtered young, as is typical in an animal exploited primarily for its meat and secondary products.

Discovery of at least two well-preserved corrals at Hinxton is of note as on current evidence they appear to be unique within the local landscape, although examples are known in the Thames Valley (Knight 2007). More locally at Steeple Morden (*c.*30km to the west) a long Roman track or hollow way was associated with beam slot structures (akin to shepherd's huts; although no stock enclosures were found), which may have had a similar stock control function (Atkins and Hurst 2014, fig. 6). Modern-day ethnographic parallels are also very similar in layout and design which allows the proposal that Corral 1 was perhaps designed primarily for smaller animals such as sheep or goats and Corral 2, with its circular layout, designed for large animals such as cattle and or horses. A demand for increasing efficiency also led to demand for an increase in levels of specialisation within farming generally and animal husbandry specifically. At Hinxton it appears that cattle and sheep were the primary stock animals, mainly raised for their meat, while the presence of dog remains probably also reflects the need to guard and herd these animals.

Crop production and consumption
with Val Fryer
Preservation of macrobotanical remains and pollen was poor in pre-Anglo-Saxon deposits at Hinxton. It does appear, however, that although of course necessary to feed both the people and animals of Hinxton, cereal production was not the primary activity undertaken within the excavated areas. The environmental samples are characterised by extremely low densities of material (all <0.1 litres), as a result of which specific activities are difficult to pinpoint. However, small deposits of possible domestic and/ or agricultural waste, including grains, weed seeds and dietary refuse, were found in a few samples, with small quantities of similar material being scattered throughout a number of other contexts. A sample from one of the ditches forming part of Late Iron Age Enclosure 1/2 yielded a low density of material derived from burnt grass or hay. Although tenuous, the presence of a burnt shell of *Vertigo* sp. may indicate material gathered from damper grassland areas, possibly close to the River Cam. Another ditch produced a low density of possible cereal processing debris, since segetal weed seeds are reasonably common within the assemblage. Associated with Corral 1 in Area C was a significant deposit of burnt barley and, although prime 'cleaned' barley is normally associated with human consumption, its context here may suggest that it was destined to be good quality animal feed.

On the western side of the river (Area H) lay an interesting group of enclosures and what appear to have been small riverside fields (Ditch Group 15). While there is no environmental, artefactual or ecofactual evidence to suggest a use for these atypical fields it is possible that they were used to grow a hydroponic crop. These small divided fields are remarkably similar to modern watercress beds, suggesting that the Romans may have grown it here. Pliny the Elder, who lived from AD 23–79, listed over forty medicinal uses for watercress, and included the belief that the smell of watercress would drive away snakes and neutralize scorpion venom! Another venerable Roman, Varro, stated that it is profitable near a city to have a garden on a large scale so as to grow produce suitable for sale in the local market (Alcock 2001, 63) and watercress may have served this purpose. Cultivation of watercress is practical on a large scale – the species thrives in water that is slightly alkaline and is frequently produced around the headwaters of chalk streams (similar to the conditions at Hinxton). Once harvested, watercress stays fresh for only a short time and its production therefore requires a readily accessible market, such as the town at Great Chesterford.

Processes of 'Romanisation' at Hinxton
Beyond the value of individual aspects of the Late Iron Age and Roman remains at the Genome Campus in terms of providing important evidence for, amongst other matters, mortuary practice, ceremonial/ritual behaviour and agricultural production, the sequence as a whole provides an insight into, or at least an individual case study of, the trajectory and dynamics of social change in the years either side of the Roman invasion at a location on the margins of the developed Late Iron Age 'polities' of South-East England.

The Late Iron Age remains from the Genome Campus, especially the main trackside enclosure complex, show very clearly that the communities living here around the turn of the 1st century AD were strongly influenced by – and in close contact with – the Late Iron Age societies living within the modern counties of Essex/Hertfordshire. Especially notable is the overwhelming dominance of 'classically' Late Iron Age pottery; there is little indication here of the kind of 'resistance' to the adoption of new ceramic technologies exhibited by many Late Iron Age communities in areas further north (see Hill 2007), where pottery in the Middle Iron Age tradition continued in use up until and after the Roman Conquest, and here by the early 1st century AD a broadly wholesale replacement of the domestic repertoire of storage, preparation and serving vessels appears to have taken place. In Chapter 3.VII Brown notes that the affinities of the pottery from Enclosures 1–3 (and perhaps the ultimate source of both pottery and potters) lie firmly with assemblages known from the west – in Hertfordshire – as opposed to those from Essex. Whilst it is difficult to speculate on what the implications of this are in terms of tribal politics in the territories of the Catuvellauni and Trinovantes (*cf.* Creighton 2006), this observation may be of some significance in relation to indicating contacts to the west of the Cam Valley, and hence probably relating to established routes of communication and exchange along the Icknield Belt – the eastern extension of routes which have previously been shown to have been of major significance in terms of the location and distribution of Late Iron Age settlements in northern Hertfordshire (Bryant 1999, 183–95, 423, fig 5.5).

In a local context, the Late Iron Age activity at the Genome Campus can be paralleled with the evidence from a string of broadly contemporary sites along the Cam Valley where the use of wheel-thrown/Late Iron Age type pottery appears to have been taken up on a large scale. Extending upstream as far as Cambridge, and including the 1st-century AD assemblage from Castle Hill, Cambridge (Alexander and Pullinger 2000), these include an increasing number of sites in the southern hinterlands of the modern city, such as Trumpington Park and Ride (Billington in prep.) and the Hutchison site (Evans *et al.* 2008), as well as sites further south such as Dernford Farm (Newton 2018). Parallels between these sites can also be drawn in terms of the architecture/morphology of the enclosures at the Genome Campus – the regular rectangular form of Enclosure 1/2 bearing comparison with the three-sided rectangular compounds or larger conjoined rectangular enclosures found at many of these sites. Such features provide a contrast with the irregular/ organic complexes associated with Late Iron Age settlement in northern parts of the county (although note the evidence for occasional appropriation of the conventions of 'rectangular architecture' among the otherwise 'conservative' communities of northern East Anglia (*e.g.* Gregory 1986 and 1992; Martin 1993)).

Closer inspection of the evidence from the Genome Campus, however, reveals that rather than representing any kind of direct emulation or mimicry of communities to the south, here, as elsewhere in this 'transitional zone' of northern Essex and south Cambridgeshire, local communities drew upon the novel repertoire of 'Romanised' material culture, architectural conventions and cultural practices in a selective manner, contingent on specific local circumstances and social dynamics (see Hill 2002 and 2007). Thus, the Late Iron Age pottery assemblage from Enclosures 1–3, whilst so clearly distinct from the traditions of the Middle Iron Age, contains a relatively restricted range of vessels, especially in terms of imitations of Gallo-Belgic table wares, which are virtually restricted to beakers – contrasting with the diverse range of vessels including platters, cups, flagons and flasks familiar from sites in Essex and Hertfordshire (see Hill 2002, 148). A similar pattern was observed at the Hutchison site, Cambridge (Webley and Anderson 2008), suggesting that communities in south Cambridgeshire drew selectively on this range on new vessel forms, presumably in the context of their own specific (and perhaps traditional) practices in terms of the serving and consumption of food and drink (*cf.* Hill 2002, 148–51; Pitts 2005). Another striking aspect of the Late Iron Age at the Genome Campus is the relative lack of metalwork, especially in the form of brooches and coins (see

Howard-Davis, Chapter 3.III). Marked disparities in the occurrence of coins and brooches at Late Iron Age settlements in Eastern England have been used as a crude index of the relative 'Romanisation' of different communities (see Evans *et al.* 2008, 139, table 2.46), and the low numbers present here compared to sites in Essex and Hertfordshire and to some other sites in south Cambridgeshire (notably Castle Hill; Alexander and Pullinger 2000), whilst potentially informing on the relative status of the community at Hinxton, also suggest that new fashions in dress may have been largely spurned, and that engagement in monetised transactions was avoided or restricted. Coupled with these patterns in terms of material culture, the mortuary practices evidenced at the Genome Campus (see above), in terms of the absence of cremations and the presence of inhumation burials of a kind documented at other sites in south Cambridgeshire, but which are otherwise very unusual in the regional context, provide a further important point of contrast with those known from areas to the south (and, equally, from communities to the north and west). It may also be significant that the only burial not associated with the main enclosure complex was that from Area C, where it is thought very likely to have been located in reference to an earlier monument/marker of some kind and this may relate to a desire for the community to demonstrate their associations, perhaps in terms of specific imagined genealogies or a more general sense of ancestry/origins, with earlier communities in the local area as opposed to emphasising more distant and 'exotic' influences.

If the details discussed above suggest that the Late Iron Age community at the Genome Campus, and elsewhere in southern Cambridgeshire, retained a degree of cultural and political autonomy in the face of the growing power and influence of the communities to the south, the reorganisation of the site initiated in Period 3.2 may represent the point that this independence was swept away in the aftermath of the Roman invasion. It has been argued above that it is likely that developments associated with Periods 3.2 and 3.3 were directly associated with the foundation of the fort and later town at Great Chesterford – although the precise chronology of these events remains obscure. Regardless of the specific timing, however, the end of the use of the trackside enclosures and the development of an intensively utilised agricultural landscape seems likely to have involved at the very least the rapid adaption of local communities to the new realities and power structures of the post-Conquest period – if not seeing a degree of coercion, and perhaps more punitive episodes of clearance and resettlement, by the Roman military and/or newly empowered local leaders.

V. Conclusions

Although the prehistoric and Roman sequence revealed at the Genome Campus is a rich and full one, it has not been possible, nor seen as desirable, to construct a long term narrative of the occupation of this particular area of the riverside terraces of the Upper Cam Valley. Rather, it has been emphasised how the inevitably partial coverage of the excavations, the vagaries of preservation and the specific character of the remains of different periods have dictated that certain episodes of the site's use have fallen into sharper focus, whilst for other periods evidence is entirely lacking or of a character which defies detailed interpretation. Equally important is the manner in which it has only been possible to interpret these remains in terms of explicit reference to the wider local/regional record, beyond the almost entirely arbitrary physical limits of the site.

In acknowledging the crucial importance of networks of movement, exchange and communication in interpreting the site's remains, it is appropriate to end here by revisiting the observations made at the beginning of this volume, in terms of the site's location in an area marked by important geographical and cultural boundaries and routeways. What seems clear is that, although the major landscape features represented by the river and the boundary between the chalk escarpment and the lower lying land to the north and west remained of perennial importance throughout the site's history, the specifics of the ways in which they structured patterns of land use, communication and settlement were contingent on the character of the various periods and episodes of occupation in evidence at the Genome Campus.

Thus, whilst the river valley's role as a major corridor of movement and communication is a constant theme throughout the sequence, there are major, self-evident, differences in the way this played out in different periods, from the manner in which the valley structured the long distance movements of groups of hunters at the end of the last Ice Age, to linking the emerging urban centre at Great Chesterford within its agricultural hinterland in the aftermath of the Roman Conquest. Meanwhile, in terms of the location of the site on the chalk escarpment, although this clearly provided special opportunities for earlier prehistoric communities, such as access to flint sources, it has been difficult to detect any major significance in the boundary/routeways of the Icknield belt prior to the Late Iron Age, when it does seem to have played a major role in defining an important cultural/political boundary zone and in structuring movement and contacts at a local and regional scale. It is in this context of providing evidence for specific episodes of occupation and activity, set in the context of their relationship to the local landscapes of the Upper Cam Valley, that the excavations described here have contributed to an increasingly richly documented regional record.

Appendix 1: List of archaeological works (grey literature) undertaken or commissioned by OA East (CCC AFU, CAM ARC) at the Hinxton Hall and Genome site

Site	Date	Reports
Geophysical Survey at Hinxton Hall Park: Phase 1	1993	Shiel, D., 1993, *Report on Geophysical survey: Hinxton Hall Park*, Geophysical Surveys of Bradford Rep 93/87
Geophysical Survey at Hinxton Hall Park: Phase 2	1993	Shiel, D., 1993, *Report on Geophysical survey: Hinxton Hall Park*, Geophysical Surveys of Bradford Rep 93/100
Hinxton Hall: Desktop study	1993	Leith, S and Reynolds, T., 1993, *Hinxton Hall: An Archaeological Desktop Study*, CCC AFU Rep ?A10
Hinxton Hall: Assessment by Excavation: Phase 1	1993	Leith, S., 1993, *An Archaeological Assessment at Hinxton Hall*, CCC AFU Rep A18
Hinxton Hall: Assessment by Excavation: Phase 2	1993	Leith, S., 1993, *Phase II Archaeological Assessment at Hinxton Hall*, CCC AFU Rep A25
New Lake Site: Excavations: Phase 1	1994	Leith, S., 1995, *Archaeological Recording at Hinxton Hall: The New Lake Site Phase I*, CCC AFU Rep A45
Ickleton: Archaeological Desktop Study	1994	Robinson, B., 1994, A*bbey Farm, Ickleton, Cambridgeshire: An Archaeological Desktop Study*, CCC AFU Rep A34
Ickleton: Metal Detector Survey	1995	Robinson, B., 1995, *Metal Detector Rally at Abbey Farm, Ickleton, Cambridgeshire*, unpublished report
Hinxton Hall excavations 1993–4: summary statement	1995	Spoerry, P., 1995a, *Hinxton Hall excavations 1993-4: summary statement 1995*, CCC AFU Special Report
New Lake Site: Excavations: Phase 2	1995	Leith, S., 1995, *Archaeological Recording at Hinxton Hall: The New Lake Site Phase II*, CCC AFU Rep A69
Evaluation along the Hinxton Hall to Gt. Chesterford Watermain	1995	Roberts, J., 1996, *Archaeology and Alluvium along the Hinxton Hall to Great Chesterford New Main*, CCC AFU Rep A81
Hinxton Hall: Earthwork Survey	1995	Spoerry, P., 1995b, *An Anglo-Saxon Settlement at Hinxton Hall*, draft report
Review of excavation at Hinxton Hall	1996	Spoerry, P. and Leith, S., 1996, *Excavations at Hinxton Hall 1993–5*, CCC AFU Rep
Aerial Photography Assessment	1996	Palmer, R., 1996, *Hinxton: field centred TL500443: Cambridgeshire: Aerial photographic assessment*, Air Photo Services (Cambridge) Rep R084
Evaluation in North Parkland Hinxton Hall	1996	Kenney, S., 1996, *19th-Century Garden Features in the North Parkland Hinxton Hall, Hinxton, Cambridgeshire*, CCC AFU Rep A094
Analysis of the Neolithic Shaft and Beaker assemblage	1997	Last, J., 1997, *A Late Neolithic Shaft and Beaker Assemblage from Hinxton Hall, Cambridgeshire*, unpublished
Evaluation of the Hinxton Hall Northern Ha-Ha	1997	Heawood, R., 1997, *The Northern Ha-ha at Hinxton Hall, Hinxton, Cambridgeshire: An Archaeological Investigation*, CCC AFU Rep B011
Hinxton Riverside: Desktop Study	1997	Leith, S., 1997, *Hinxton Riverside: An Archaeological Desk-top Study*, CCC AFU Rep A69
		Leith, S. and Spoerry, P., 1997, *Hinxton Riverside: An Archaeological Desk-Top Study*, CCC AFU Rep 139
Evaluation at Genome Campus extension, Hinxton	1998	Spoerry, P., 1998, *Specification for Archaeological Evaluation at the Genome Campus, Hinxton, Cambridgeshire*, CCC AFU
		Kemp, S. and Spoerry, P., 2002, *Evaluation of Iron Age, Roman and Saxon Archaeology at the proposed Wellcome Trust Genome Campus Extension, Hinxton, Cambridgeshire. TL500433. Environmental Statement. Technical Annex C*, CCC AFU Rep 149 (x 3 editions)
Evaluation Genome Campus extension, Hinxton	2002	Kemp, S. and Spoerry, P.S., 2002, *Specification for Archaeological Excavation at the Genome Campus, Hinxton, Cambridgeshire*, CCC AFU
		Thomas, A, 2002, *Brief for Archaeological Investigation, Genome Campus Extension, Hinxton (Construction Phases 1–3)*, Archaeology Section, Cambridgeshire County Council
		Kenney, S., 2002, *Multi-period Remains on the site of the Proposed Genome Campus Extension. Hinxton: An Archaeological Evaluation*, CCC AFU Rep A206
Evaluation at Genome Camp extension, west of the River Cam	2002	Kemp, S.N., 2002, *Archaeological evaluations at the Hinxton Campus Extension, West of the River Cam. TL 4980/4420*, CCC AFU Rep A214
The South Field Project Genome Campus, Hinxton	2003	Derek Lovejoy Partnership and Kemp, S.N., 2003, *The South Field Project Genome Campus, Hinxton Phase 1: Management Strategy for Archaeological Protection Areas*

Site	Date	Reports
Genome Campus: Excavation	2007	Kenney, S., 2007, *Hinxton Genome Campus Extension Excavations and Wetlands Area Assessment and Monitoring 2002–2003*, CCC AFU Rep 891
Proposed Extensions at the Genome Campus, Hinxton: Desk Based Assessment	2008	Kenney, S., 2008, *Proposed Extensions at the Genome Campus, Hinxton, Cambridgeshire*, OA East Rep 1042
Proposed Extensions at the Genome Campus, Hinxton: Environmental Statement	2009	Kenney, S. and Spoerry, P., 2009, *The Wellcome Trust Genome Campus Extensions Phases 2 & 3 Environmental Statement Technical Annex 2*, OA East Rep 1089
Genome Campus: Excavations	2011	Spoerry, P., 2011, *Specification for Archaeological Excavation: Hinxton Genome Campus Technical Hub*
		Fletcher, T., 2012, *Hinxton Genome Campus Technical Hub, Post-Excavation Assessment and Updated Project Design*, OA East Rep 1323
Hinxton South Field (Phase 3)	2015	Haskins, A. and Clarke, R., 2015, *Hinxton South Field, Phase 3. Post-excavation Assessment and Updated Project Design*, OA East Rep 1659
	2016	Bishop, B., Clarke, R. and Haskins, A., 2016, *A Late Upper Palaeolithic Lithic Assemblage from Hinxton, Cambridgeshire. Catalogue and Overview Report*, OA East Rep 1995

Appendix 2: Radiocarbon dating

All radiocarbon dates acquired over the course of the project are listed opposite. The calibrated date ranges have been calculated by the maximum intercept method (Stuiver and Reimer 1986), using the program OxCal v4.4 (Bronk Ramsey 1995; 2001; 2009) and the IntCal20 data set (Reimer *et al.* 2020), and are quoted in the form recommended by Mook (1986), with date ranges rounded outwards to decadal endpoints.

Site Code	Area	Period	EAA part	Lab. Code	Context	Cut	Radiocarbon years BP	δ13C	Material	Calibrated date range
HINGEL14	J	Neo (2.1)	I	OxA-30872	15190	15188	4919 ± 34	-20.88	Bone (human)	**3640–3370 cal BC (95.4%)**
HINGEL14	J	Neo (2.1)	I	OxA-33463	15189	15188	4892 ± 34	-20.47	Bone (human)	**3770–3630 cal BC (95.4%)**
HINGEL14	J	Neo (2.1)	I	OxA-33619	15190	15188	4883 ± 35	-20.75	Bone (human)	**3770–3620 cal BC (92.1%)** 3560–3530 cal BC (3.4%)
HINGEL14	J	Neo (2.1)	I	OxA-30871	15189	15188	4877 ± 35	-20.59	Bone (human)	**3770–3620 cal BC (89.2%)** 3570–3530 cal BC (6.2%)
HINGEL14	J	Neo (2.1)	I	OxA-33462	15189	15188	4873 ± 33	-20.59	Bone (human)	3770–3740 cal BC (1.8%) **3720–3620 cal BC (85.8%)** 3580–3530 cal BC (7.9%)
HINGC02	A	-	I	Wk-13861	Palaeochannel 302		4664 ± 42	-25	Unid. charcoal	3610–3580 cal BC (1.9%) **3530–3350 cal BC (93.5%)**
HINGEL14	J	Neo (2.1)	I	SUERC-64624	15195	15194	4427 ± 29	-22.3	Charred hazelnut shell	3330–3230 cal BC (20.2%) 3190–3150 cal BC (3.3%) **3110–2920 cal BC (71.9%)**
HINGC02	C	Neo (2.1)	I	SUERC-64619	687	691	4138 ± 33	-23	Bone ?Bos prim	**2880–2620 cal BC (91.9%)** 2610–2580 cal BC (3.6%)
HINGC02	C	BA (2.2)	I	Wk-12598	318	319	3303 ± 68	-23.6	Bone (human)	**1750–1430 cal BC (95.4%)**
HINGEL14	J	M/LIA (2.3)	I	SUERC-64620	15065	15066	2230 ± 29	-23.1	Barley grain (Hordeum sp.)	390–340 cal BC (22.3%) **330–200 cal BC (73.1%)**
HINGC02	D	M/LIA (2.3)	I	OxA-29573	1964	2147	2039 ± 27	-19.44	Bone (human)	150–130 cal BC (1.5%) **120 cal BC–60 cal AD (94%)**
HINGC02	C	LIA 3.3	I	Wk-12599	1231	1232	2029 ± 49	-21.9	Bone (human)	**170 cal BC–120 cal AD (95.4%)**
HINGEC11	I	MS (4.2)	II	OxA-X-2565-12	5518	5519	1320 ± 45	-19.65	Bone (human)	**640–780 cal AD (92.4%)** 790–830 AD (3%)
HINGC02	C	MS (4.2)	II	OxA-29574	241	242	1288 ± 25	-19.73	Bone (human)	**660–780 cal AD (95.4%)**
HINGEL14	J	MS (4.2)	II	OxA-30873	15777	15778	1235 ± 26	-20.22	Bone (human)	750–680 cal AD (33.2%) **890–770 cal AD (62.2%)**
HINGC02	D	M/LS (5.1)	II	OxA-29572	355	369	1230 ± 25	-19.65	Bone	680–750 cal AD (25.4%) **770–890 cal AD (70.1%)**
			II	SUERC-64625			883 ± 29	-24.9	Barley grain (Hordeum)	1040–1110 cal AD (19.8%) **1120–1230 cal AD (75.6%)**

Bibliography

Abrams, J. and Ingham, D., 2008
Farming on the Edge: Archaeological Evidence form the Clay Uplands to the West of Cambridge, E. Anglian Archaeol. 123

Adamiec, G. and Aitken, M., 1998
'Dose-rate conversion factors: update', *Ancient TL* 16, 37–50

Aitken, M.J., 1998
An Introduction to Optical Dating: the dating of Quaternary sediments by the use of photon-stimulated luminescence (Oxford, Oxford Univ. Press)

Albarella, U., 2002
'Size matters: how and why biometry is still important in zooarchaeology', in Brothwell, D., *Bones and the Man: studies in honour of Don Brothwell*, 51–62 (Oxford, Oxbow)

Albarella, U., 2003
'Animal bone', in Germany, M. (ed.), *Excavations at Great Holts Farm, Boreham, Essex, 1992–1994*, E. Anglian Archaeol. 105, 193–200

Albarella, U., Johnston, C. and Vickers, K., 2008
'The development of animal husbandry from the Late Iron Age to the end of the Roman period: a case study from South-East Britain', *J. Archaeol. Sci.*, 35, 1828–48

Alcock, A., 2001
Food in Roman Britain (Tempus)

Alcock, L., 1971
'Excavations at south Cadbury Castle, 1970: a summary report', *Antiquaries J.* 51, 1–7

Alexander, J. and Pullinger, J., 2000
'Roman Cambridge: Excavations on Castle Hill 1956–1988', *Proc. Cambridge Antiquarian Society* 88

Allason-Jones, L., 1989
Ear-rings in Roman Britain, Brit. Archaeol. Rep. Brit. Ser. 201 (Oxford)

Allen, C., 2008
'Pottery', in Luke, M., *Life in the Loop: Investigation of a Prehistoric and Romano-British Landscape at Biddenham-Loop, Bedfordshire*, E. Anglian Archaeol. 125, 113–15

Allen, M.J., 1997
'Landscape, land-use and farming', in Smith, R.J.C., Healy, F., Allen, M.J., Morris, E.L., Barnes, I. and Woodward, P.J., *Excavations along the Route of the Dorchester By-pass, Dorset, 1986–8*, Wessex Archaeol. Rep. 11, 277–83 (Salisbury)

Allen, M.J. and Maltby, M., 2012
'Chalcolithic land-use, animals and economy – a chronological changing point?', in Allen, M.J., Gardiner, J., and Sheridan, A. (eds), *Is there a British Chalcolithic? People, place and polity in the late 3rd millennium*, Prehist. Soc. Res. Pap. 4, 281–97 (Oxford)

Allen, T., Barclay, A., Cromarty, A.M., Anderson-Whymark, H., Parker, A., Robinson, M. and Jones, G., 2013
Opening the Wood, Making the Land. The archaeology of a Middle Thames Landscape. Mesolithic, Neolithic and Early Bronze Age, Oxford Archaeol. Thames Valley Landscapes Monogr. 38 (Oxford)

Anderson, K. and Woolhouse, T., 2016
'Continental potters? First-century Roman flagon production at Duxford, Cambridgeshire', *Britannia* 47, 43–69

Anderson, S., 2007
'Human Skeletal Remains', in Kenney, S., *Hinxton Genome Campus Extension Excavations and Wetlands Area Assessment and Monitoring 2002-2003, Post-excavation Assessment and Updated Project Design*, CAMARC Rep. 891, 98–112 (unpubl.)

Anderson-Whymark, H. and Pope, M., 2016
Late Quaternary (Upper Palaeolithic, Mesolithic and Later Prehistoric) Human Activity in the Darent Valley at Lullingstone Country Park, Eynsford, Kent, SpoilHeap Publications Occ. Pap. 5 (Portslade)

Anderson-Whymark, H. and Thomas, J. (eds), 2012
Regional Perspectives on Neolithic Pit Deposition: Beyond the Mundane (Oxford, Oxbow)

Armour, N., 2007
The ARES site, Babraham Research Campus, Cambridgeshire, An Archaeological Excavation, CAU Rep. 752 (unpubl.)

Arthur, P.R., 2004
'The pottery from the 1973 excavation', in Blagg, T.F.C., Plouviez, J.H. and Tester, A., *Excavations at a Large Romano-British Settlement at Hacheston, Suffolk, 1973–74*, E. Anglian Archaeol. 106, 160–71

Ashwin, T., 2001
'Exploring Bronze Age Norfolk: Longham and Bittering' in Brück, J. (ed.), *Bronze Age Landscapes Tradition and Transformation*, 23–32 (Oxford, Oxbow)

Ashwin, T. and Bates, S., 2000
Excavations on the Norwich Southern Bypass, 1989–91. Part I: Excavations at Bixley, Trowse, Cringleford and Little Melton, E. Anglian Archaeol. 91

Atkins, R. and Hurst, V., 2014
'"Avenell Way": an ancient track across south Cambridgeshire?', *Proc. Cambridge Antiq. Soc*, 103, 83–106

Atkins, R. and Mudd, A., 2003
'An Iron Age and Romano-British settlement at Prickwillow Road, Ely, Cambridgeshire: Excavations 1999–2000', *Proc. Cambridge Antiq. Soc.* 92, 5–55

Aufderheide, A.C. and Rodriguez-Martin, C., 1998
The Cambridge Encyclopaedia of Human Paleopathology (Cambridge, Cambridge Univ. Press)

Austin, L. and Sydes, R., 1998
'Potential recognition: evaluating lithic scatters – curators' concerns', *Lithics* 19, 19–23

Bacher, A., 1967
'Vergleichend morphologische Untersuchungen an Einzelknochen des postkranialen Skeletts', *Mitteleuropa vorkommender Schwäne und Gänse* (München)

Bailey, R.M., Smith, B.W. and Rhodes, E.J., 1997
'Partial bleaching and the decay form characteristics of quartz OSL', *Radiation Measurements* 27, 123–36

Baker, J. and Brothwell, D., 1980
Animal Diseases in Archaeology (London, Academic Press)

Bamford, H., 1982
Beaker Domestic Sites in the Fen Edge and East Anglia, E. Anglian Archaeol. 16

Barclay, A., Bello, S., Bradley, P., Harding, P., Higbee, L., Manning, A., Powell, J., Macphail, R., Roberts, A., Stewart, M. and Barton, N., 2017
'A new Later Upper Palaeolithic open-air site with articulated horse bone in the Colne Valley, Berkshire', *Antiquity* 91(360), E4 doi:10.15184/aqy.2017.216

Barton, R.N.E., 1986a
'Experiments with long blades from Sproughton, near Ipswich, Suffolk', in Roe, D. (ed.), *Studies in the Upper Palaeolithic of Britain and North-west Europe*, Brit. Archaeol. Rep. Int. Ser. 296, 129–41 (Oxford)

Barton, R.N.E., 1986b   *A Study of Selected British and European Flint Assemblages of Late Devensian and Early Flandrian Age* (unpubl. PhD thesis, Univ. Oxford)

Barton, R.N.E., 1989   'Long blade technology in southern Britain', in Bonsall, C. (ed.), *The Mesolithic in Europe: Papers Presented at the Third International Symposium, Edinburgh 1985*, 264–71 (Edinburgh, John Donald)

Barton, R.N.E., 1990   'The en *éperon* technique in the British Late Upper Palaeolithic', *Lithics* 11, 31–3

Barton, R.N.E., 1991   'Technological innovation and continuity at the end of the Pleistocene in Britain', in Barton, R.N.E., Roberts, A.J. and Roe, D.A., (eds), *The Late Glacial in North-west Europe: Human Adaptation and Environmental Change at the End of the Pleistocene*, Counc. Brit. Archaeol. Res. Rep. 77, 234–45 (York)

Barton, R.N.E., 1992   *Hengistbury Head Dorset. Volume 2: the Late Upper Palaeolithic and Early Mesolithic sites*, Oxford Univ. Cttee Archaeol. Monogr. Ser. 34 (Oxford)

Barton, R.N.E., 1995   'The long blade assemblage', in Allen, T.G., *Lithics and Landscape: archaeological discoveries on the Thames Water pipeline at Gatehampton Farm, Goring, Oxfordshire 1985–92*, 54–64 (Oxford, Oxford Archaeol. Unit/Oxbow)

Barton, R.N.E., 1998   'Long blade technology and the question of British late Pleistocene/early Holocene lithic assemblages', in Ashton, N., Healy, F. and Pettitt, P. (eds), *Stone Age Archaeology. Essays in honour of John Wymer*, Oxbow Monogr. 102, 158–64 (Oxford, Oxbow)

Barton, R.N.E., Ford, S., Collcutt, S., Crowther, J., Macphail, R., Rhodes, E. and Van Gijn, A., 2009   'A Final Upper Palaeolithic site at Nea Farm, Somerley, Hampshire (England) and some reflections on the occupation of Britain in the Late Glacial Interstadial', *Quartär* 56, 7–35

Barton, R.N.E., Jacobi, R.M., Stapert, D. and Street, M. J., 2003   'The Late-glacial reoccupation of the British Isles and the Creswellian', *J. Quaternary Sci.* 18 (7), https://doi.org/10.1002/jqs.772

Barton, R.N.E. and Roberts, A.J., 1996   'Reviewing the British Late Upper Palaeolithic: new evidence for chronological patterning in the late glacial record', *Oxford J. Archaeol.* 15 (3), 245–65

Barton, R.N.E. and Roberts, A., 2004   'The Mesolithic period in England: current perspectives and new research', in Saville, A. (ed.), *Mesolithic Scotland and its Neighbours*, 339–58 (Edinburgh, Soc. Antiq. Scot.)

Barton, R.N.E. and Roberts, A., 2019   'The transition from the Younger Dryas to the Pre-Boreal in southern Britain: some new perspectives on the spatial patterning and chronology of long blade sites', in Montoya, C., Fanart, J.P. and Locht J-L. (eds), *Préhistoire de l'Europe du Nord-Ouest: mobilité, climats et identités culturelles, Actes du 28è congrès préhistorique de France d'Amiens (30 mai–4 juin 2016) Vol. 2 : Paléolithique supérieur ancien, Paléolithique final – Mésolithique*, 381–9 (Paris, Société Préhistorique Française)

Bass, W.M., 1987   *Human Osteology. A laboratory and field manual*, Missouri Archaeol. Soc. Special Publi. No. 2 (Columbia, Mo)

Bateman, M.D. and Catt, J.A., 1996   'An absolute chronology for the raised beach and associated deposits at Sewerby, East Yorkshire, England', *J. Quaternary Sci.* 11, 389–95

Bateman, M.D., Boulter, C.H., Carr, A.S., Frederick, C.D., Peter, D. and Wilder, M., 2007a   'Detecting post-depositional sediment disturbance in sandy deposits using optical luminescence' *Quaternary Geochronology* 2, 57–64

Bateman, M.D., Boulter, C.H., Carr, A.S., Frederick, C.D., Peter, D., and Wilder, M., 2007b   'Preserving the palaeoenvironmental record in Drylands: bioturbation and its significance for luminescence-derived chronologies', *Sedimentary Geology* 195, 5–19

Bateman, M.D., Frederick, C.D., Jaiswal, M.K. and Singhvi, A.K., 2003   'Investigations into the potential effects of pedoturbation on luminescence dating', *Quaternary Sci. Reviews* 22, 1169–76

Bates, A., Mulville, J. and Powell, A., 2012   'The animal bone', in Allen, T., Donnelly, M., Hardy, A., Hayden C. and Powell, K., *A Road Through the Past: Archaeological discoveries on the A2 Pepperhill to Cobham road-scheme in Kent*, 259–73 (Oxford, Oxbow)

Bateson, J.D., 1981   *Enamel Working in Iron Age, Roman and Sub-Roman Britain. The products and techniques*, Brit. Archaeol. Rep. Brit. Ser. 93 (Oxford)

Baxter, I., 2011   'Faunal remains, Temple Precinct', in Medlycott, M., *The Roman Town of Great Chesterford*, E. Anglian Archaeol. 137, 320–44

Bayliss, A. and Whittle, A. (eds), 2007   'Histories of the dead: building chronologies for five southern British long barrows', *Cambridge Archaeol. J.* 17 (Supplement S1)

Bayliss, A., Bronk Ramsey, C. and Crowson, A., 2004   'Interpreting chronology', in Crowson, A., *Hot Rocks in the Norfolk Fens: the excavation of a burnt flint mound at Northwold*, E. Anglian Archaeol. Occ. Pap. 16

Beadsmoore, E., 2005   *The Flintwork from Linton Village College*, CAMARC Rep. (unpubl.)

Beadsmoore, E., 2006   'Earlier Neolithic flint', in Garrow, D., Lucy, S. and Gibson, D., *Excavations at Kilverstone, Norfolk; an episodic landscape history*, E. Anglian Archaeol. 113, 53–70

Beadsmoore, E., Garrow, D. and Knight, M., 2010   'Refitting Etton: space, time, and material culture within a causewayed enclosure in Cambridgeshire', *Proc. Prehist. Soc.* 76, 115–34

Bell, M., 2020   *Making One's Way in the World: the footprints and trackways of prehistoric people* (Oxford, Oxbow)

Bell, M. and Noble, G., 2012   'Prehistoric woodland ecology', in Jones, A.M., Pollard, J., Allen, M.J. and Gardiner, J. (eds), *Image, Memory and Monumentality: archaeological engagements with the modern world*, Prehist. Soc. Res. Pap. 4, 80–92 (Oxford, Oxbow)

Bennett, K.D., 1983   'Devensian Late-Glacial and Flandrian vegetational history at Hockham Mere, Norfolk, England. I. Pollen percentages and concentrations', *New Phytologist* 95, 457–87

Bennett, K.D., Whittington, G. and Edwards, K.J., 1994   'Recent plant nomenclatural changes and pollen morphology in the British Isles', *Quaternary Newsletter*, 73, 1–6

Bergman, C.E., Barton, R.N.E., Collcut, S.N. and Morris, G., 1987   'Intentional breakage in a late Upper Palaeolithic assemblage from southern England', in Sieveking, G. De G. and Newcomer, M.H. (eds), *The Human Uses of Flint and Chert*, 21–36 (Cambridge, Cambridge Univ. Press)

Berry, A.C. and Berry, A.J., 1967   'Epigenetic variation in the human cranium', *J. Anatomy* 101, 361–79

Bevan, A., Colledge, S., Fuller, D., Fyfe, R., Shennan, S. and Stevens, C., 2017 'Holocene fluctuations in human population demonstrate repeated links to food production and climate', *Proc. National Academy Sci.* 114(49), 10524–31

Biddulph, E., 2007 'Strood Hall (Sites 9 and 44)', in Timby, J., Brown, R., Biddulph, E., Hardy, A. and Powell, A., *A Larger Slice of Rural Essex: archaeological discoveries from the A120 between Stansted Airport and Braintree* (Oxford, Wessex Archaeol.)

Billington, L., 2014 'Upper Palaeolithic', in Cessford, C. and Evans, C., *North West Cambridge Archaeology. University of Cambridge 2012–13 Excavations. Introduction and Prehistory*, (NWC Report No. 3, Part 1), CAU Rep. 1225, 23 (unpubl.)

Billington, L., 2016 *Lithic Scatters and Landscape Occupation in the Late Upper Palaeolithic and Mesolithic: a case study from eastern England* (unpubl. PhD thesis, Univ. Manchester)

Billington, L., in prep. *Cambridge Park & Rides: three places in a prehistoric landscape* (working title), E. Anglian Archaeol.

Bishop, B., 2000 *Lithic Assessment: Excavations at Babraham Road Park and Ride*, CAMARC Rep. (unpubl.)

Bishop, B., 2012 *The Grimes Graves Environs Survey: Exploring the Social Landscapes of a Flint Source* (unpubl. PhD thesis, Univ. York)

Bishop, B., 2015 'Lithics', in Phillips, T., *Bronze Age – Roman Remains at Cambridge Biomedical Campus: The Circus and Piazza and Papworth Trust Sites. Post-Excavation Assessment and Updated Project Design*, OA East Rep. 1726, 59–69 (upubl.)

Bishop, B., 2016 'Prehistoric lithics', in Paul, S., Colls, K. and Chapman, H., *Living with the Flood: Mesolithic to post-medieval archaeological remains at Mill Lane, Sawston, Cambridgeshire*, 29–38 (Oxford, Oxbow)

Bishop, B., Clarke, R. and Haskins, A., 2016 *A Late Upper Palaeolithic Lithic Assemblage from Hinxton, Cambridgeshire. Catalogue and Overview Report*, OA East Rep. 1995 (unpubl.)

Bishop, B. and Proctor, J., 2011 *Settlement, Ceremony and Industry on Mousehold Heath*, PreConstruct Archaeol. Monogr. 13 (London)

Bishop, M. and Coulston, J., 1993 *Roman Military Equipment from the Punic Wars to the Fall of Rome* (London, Batsford)

Bishop, R.R., 2015 'Did Late Neolithic farming fail or flourish? A Scottish perspective on the evidence for Late Neolithic arable cultivation in the British Isles', *World Archaeol.* 47(5), 834–55

Bland, R. and Burnett, A., 1988 'Normanby, Lincolnshire', in Bland, R., and Burnett, A., (eds), *The Normanby Hoard and other Roman Coin Hoards*, Coin Hoards from Roman Britain VIII, 114–215 (London, British Museum Publications)

Blinkhorn, E., Lawton-Matthews, E. and Warren, G., 2017 *Creuser au Mésolithique / Digging in the Mesolithic: Actes de la séance de la Société préhistorique française de Châlons-en-Champagne (29–30 mars 2016)*, Achard-Corompt, N., Ghesquière, E. and Riquier, V. (eds), Séances de la Société préhistorique française 12, 211–24 (Paris, Société Préhistorique Française)

Boessneck, J., 1969 'Osteological differences between Sheep (*Ovis aries* Linne) and Goat (*Capra hircus* Linne)', in Brothwell, D. and Higgs, E. (eds), *Science and Archaeol.* 2, 131–58 (London)

Boreham, S. and Rolfe, C.J., 2009 'Holocene, Weichselian Late-glacial and earlier Pleistocene deposits of the upper Cam valley at the Hinxton Genome Campus, Cambridgeshire, UK', *Netherlands J. Geosciences*, 88 (2), 117–25

Bouts, W. and Pot, T.J., 1989 'Computerized recording and analysis of excavated human dental remains', in Roberts, C.A., Lee, F. and Bintliff, J. (eds), *Burial Archaeology: current research, methods and developments*, Brit. Archaeol. Rep. Brit. Ser. 211, 113–28 (Oxford)

Brickley, M. and McKinley, J., 2004 *Guidelines to the Standards for Recording Human Remains*, IFA Pap. 7 (Reading, Brit. Assoc. Biological Anthropol. Osteoarchaeol./ Inst. Field Archaeologists)

Brickstock, R.J., 2004 *The Production, Analysis and Standardisation of Romano-British Coin Reports* (London, English Heritage)

Briscoe, G., 1949 'Combined Beaker and Iron Age sites at Lakenheath, Suffolk', *Proc. Cambridge Antiq. Soc.* 42, 92–111

Briscoe, G., 1960 'Giant Beaker and rusticated ware from Lakenheath, Suffolk, and reproduction of ornament', *Proc. Cambridge Antiq. Soc.* 53, 1–7

Britnell, W.J., 2000 'Small pointed blades', in Barrett, J.C., Freeman, P.W.M., and Woodward, A., *Cadbury Castle, Somerset. The later prehistoric and early historic archaeology*, English Heritage Archaeol. Rep. 20, 183–6 (London)

Bromley, R.G. and Ekdale, A.A., 1986 'Flint and fabric in the European Chalk', in Sieveking, G. De C. and Hart M.B. (eds), *The Scientific Study of Flint and Chert*, 71–82 (Cambridge, Cambridge Univ. Press)

Bronk Ramsey, C., 1995 'Radiocarbon calibration and analysis of stratigraphy: the OxCal program', *Radiocarbon* 37(2), 425–30

Bronk Ramsey, C., 2001 'Development of the radiocarbon calibration program', *Radiocarbon* 43 (2A), 355–63

Bronk Ramsey, C., 2009 'Bayesian analysis of radiocarbon dates', *Radiocarbon* 51(1), 337–60

Brothwell, D.R., 1981 *Digging Up Bones*, 3rd edn (London, British Museum (Natural History))

Brown, N. and Glazebrook, J. (eds), 2000 *Research and Archaeology: A Framework for the Eastern Counties 1. research agenda and strategy*, E. Anglian Archaeol. Occ. Pap. 8

Brück, J., 1999 'What's in a settlement? Domestic practice and residential mobility in Early Bronze Age southern England', in Brück, J. and Goodman, M. (eds), *Making Places in the Prehistoric World: themes in settlement rrchaeology*, 52–75 (London, UCL Press)

Brudenell, M., 2004 *Granta Park, Great Abington, Cambridgeshire: The Rickett Field Site*, CAU Rep. (unpubl.)

Brudenell, M., 2012 *Pots, Practice and Society: an investigation of pattern and variability in the Post-Deverel Rimbury ceramic tradition of East Anglia* (unpubl. PhD thesis, Univ. York)

Bryant, S., 2000 *Settlement and Landscape in the Late Iron Age of Hertfordshire and the Northern Chilterns* (unpubl. PhD thesis, Univ. Sheffield)

Buikstra, J.E. and Ubelaker, D.H. (eds), 1994 *Standards for Data Collection from Human Skeletal Remains*, Arkansas Archaeol. Survey Res. Ser. 44 (Arkansas)

Bulleid, A. and Grey, H. St G., 1917 *The Glastonbury Lake Village ii* (Glastonbury, Glastonbury Antiq. Soc.)

Bulleid, J., 2014   'John Walter Clarke 1926–2013', *Nature in Cambridgeshire* 56, 84–6

Bulur, E., Botter-Jensen, L. and Murray, A.S., 2000   'Optically stimulated luminescence from quartz measured using the linear modulation technique', *Radiation Measurements* 32, 407–11

Byers, S.N., 2005   *Introduction to Forensic Anthropology*, 2nd edn (New York, Pearson)

Carr, G., 2007   'Excarnation to cremation: continuity or change?', in Haselgrove, C. and Moore, T. (eds), *The Later Iron Age in Britain and Beyond*, 444–53 (Oxford, Oxbow)

Carr, G. and Knüsel, C., 1997   'The ritual framework for excarnation by exposure as the mortuary practice of the early and middle Iron Ages of central southern Britain', in Gwilt, A. and Haselgrove C. (eds), *Reconstructing Iron Age Societies*, Oxbow Monogr. 71, 167–73 (Oxford)

Cessford, C. and Mortimer, R., 2004   *Sawston Police Station, Sawston: an archaeological evaluation and watching brief*, CAU Rep. 596 (unpubl.)

Chapman, A., Carlyle, S. and Leigh, D., 2005   'Neolithic and Beaker pits and a Bronze Age landscape at Fenstanton, Cambridgeshire', *Proc. Cambridge Antiq. Soc.* 94, 5–20

Clark, J.G.D., Godwin, H. and M.E. and Clifford, M.H., 1935   'Report on recent excavations at Peacocks Farm, Shippea Hill, Cambridgeshire', *Antiquaries J.* 15, 284–319

Clark, J.G.D., 1956   'A microlithic industry from the Cambridgeshire fenland and other industries of Sauveterrian affinities from Britain', *Proc. Prehist. Soc.* 21, 3–20

Clark, J.G.D., Higgs, E.S. and Longworth, I.H., 1960   'Excavations at the Neolithic Site at Hurst Fen, Mildenhall, Suffolk (1954, 1957 and 1958)', *Proc. Prehist. Soc.* 26, 202–45

Clarke, D.L., 1970   *Beaker Pottery of Great Britain and Ireland* (2 vols.) (Cambridge, Cambridge Univ. Press)

Clarke, D.L., 1976   'Mesolithic Europe: the economic basis', in Sieveking, G., Longworth I.H. and Wilson, K.E., (eds), *Problems in Economic and Social Archaeology*, 449–82 (London, Duckworth)

Clarke, G., 1979   *Pre-Roman and Roman Winchester Part II – The Roman Cemetery at Lankhills*, Winchester Studies 3 (Oxford, Oxford Univ. Press)

Clarke, R. and Gilmour, N., forthcoming   *Linton in Context: investigations of five millennia of human interaction with the landscape of the Granta Valley. Excavations at Linton Village College, Cambridgeshire 2004–10*, E. Anglian Archaeol.

Clarke, R., Leith, S. and Spoerry, P., forthcoming   *Hinxton, Cambridgeshire: Part 2. Excavations at the Genome Campus 1993–2014: Anglo-Saxon and medieval activity in the Cam Valley*, E. Anglian Archaeol.

Cleal, R., 1992   'Significant form: ceramic styles in the earlier Neolithic of southern England' in Sharples, N. and Sheridan, A. (eds), *Vessels for the Ancestors* (Edinburgh, Edinburgh Univ. Press), 286–304

Clutton-Brock, J., 1992   *Horse Power* (London, Natural History Museum)

Cohen, A. and Serjeantson, D., 1996   *A Manual for the Identification of Bird Bones from Archaeological Sites* (London, Archetype)

Collins, M., 2012   *Babraham Research Campus, Cambridgeshire, the R and D land. Archaeological Excavation*, CAU Rep. 1130 (unpubl.)

Conneller, C., 2007   'Inhabiting new landscapes: settlement and mobility in Britain after the Last Glacial Maximum', *Oxford J. Archaeol.* 26(3), 213–37

Conneller, C., 2009   'Investigation of a Final Palaeolithic Site at Rookery Farm, Great Wilbraham, Cambridgeshire', *Proc. Prehistoric Soc.* 75, 167-188

Conneller, C., Bayliss, A., Milner, N. and Taylor, B., 2016   'The resettlement of the British landscape: towards a chronology of Early Mesolithic lithic assemblage types', *Internet Archaeol.* 42. Available: https://doi.org/10.11141/ia.42.11. Accessed: 17.10.22

Conneller, C. and Ellis, C., 2007   'A Final Upper Palaeolithic Site at La Sagesse Convent, Romsey, Hampshire', *Proc. Prehist. Soc.* 73, 191–227

Conneller, C. and Higham, T., 2015   'Dating the Early Mesolithic: new results from Thatcham and Seamer Carr', in Ashton, N. and Harris, C. (eds), *No Stone Unturned: Papers in honour of Roger Jacobi*, Lithic Studies Soc., Occ. Pap. 9, 157–66 (London)

Cooke, N., Brown, F. and Phillpotts, C., 2008   *From Hunter Gatherers to Huntsmen. A history of the Stansted landscape*, Framework Archaeol. Monogr. 2

Cooper, L.P., 2006   'Launde, a Terminal Palaeolithic Camp-site in the English Midlands and its North European Context', *Proc. Prehist. Soc.* 72, 53–93

Creighton, J.D., 2006   *Britannia: The Creation of a Roman Province* (Abingdon, Routledge)

Crombé, P., Sergant, J., Verbrugge, A., De Graeve, A., Cherretté, B., Mikkelsen, J., Cnudde, V., De Kock, T., Huisman, H.D., van Os, B.J. and Van Strydonck, M., 2014   'A sealed flint knapping site from the Younger Dryas in the Scheldt valley (Belgium): bridging the gap in human occupation at the Pleistocene–Holocene transition in W Europe', *J. Archaeol. Sci.* 50, 420–39

Crowfoot, G.M., 1945   'The bone 'gouges' of Maiden Castle and other sites', *Antiquity* 19, 157–8

Crummy, N., 1983   *The Roman Small Finds from Excavations in Colchester 1971–9*, Colchester Archaeol. Rep. 2 (Colchester)

Cunliffe, B., 1992   'Pits, preconceptions and propitiatory in the British Iron Age', *Oxford J. Archaeol.* 11, 69–84

Cunliffe, B. and Poole, C., 1991   *Danebury: An Iron Age Hillfort in Hampshire. Vol. 5 The finds (excavations 1979–88)*, Brit. Archaeol. Rep. Brit. Ser. 73 (Oxford)

Cunliffe, B.W. and Phillipson, D.W., 1968   'Excavations at Eldon's Seat, Encombe, Dorset', *Proc. Prehist. Soc.* 34, 191–237

Cunnington, M.E., 1923   *The Early Iron Age Inhabited Site at All Cannings Cross Farm, Wiltshire* (Devizes, George Simpson)

David, A., n.d.   *Swaffham Prior* (unpubl. typescript)

Davis, S.J.M., 1992   *A Rapid Method for Recording Information about Mammal Bones from Archaeological Sites*, Anc. Monument Lab. Rep. 19/92 (unpubl.)

Davis, S.J.M., 1996   'Measurements of a group of adult female Shetland sheep skeletons from a single flock: a baseline for zooarchaeologists', *J. Archaeol. Sci.* 23, 593–612

Dawson, M., 2005   *An Iron Age Settlement at Salford, Bedfordshire*, Bedfordshire Archaeol. Monogr. 6 (Bedford, Albion Archaeol.)

Dean, B., 2012 — *Human Remains from Hinxton Genome Campus. HIN GC02*, OA East Rep. (unpubl.)

Dickson, A., forthcoming — 'The Later Neolithic flintwork', in Clarke, R. and Gilmour, N., *Linton in Context: investigations of five millennia of human interaction with the landscape of the Granta Valley*, E. Anglian Archaeol.

Dobney, K.M, Jaques, S.D. and Irving, B.G., 1996 — *Of Butchers and Breeders: Report on the vertebrate remains from various sites in the City of Lincoln*, Lincoln Archaeol. Stud. 5 (Lincoln)

Dobney, K.M., Jaques, D. and Johnston, S., 1999 — *A Protocol for Recording Vertebrate Remains from Archaeological Sites*, Environmental Archaeol. Unit Rep. 99/15 (unpubl.)

Dodwell, N., Anderson, K. and Lucy, S., 2008 — 'Burials', in Evans, C., Mackay, D. and Webley, L., *Borderlands. The Archaeology of the Addenbrooke's Environs, South Cambridge*, CAU Landscape Archives: New Archaeologies of the Cambridge Region (1), 47–57

Duhig, C., 2011 — 'Human skeletal remains', in Lyons, A.L., *Life and Afterlife at Duxford, Cambridgeshire: Archaeology and History in a Chalkland Community*, E. Anglian Archaeol. 141, 68–72

Duller, G.A.T., 2003 — 'Distinguishing quartz and feldspar in single grain luminescence measurements', *Radiation Measurements* 37, 161–5

Duncan, H.B. and Mackreth, D.F., 2005 — 'Spinning and weaving', in Dawson, M., *An Iron Age Settlement at Salford, Bedfordshire*, Bedfordshire Archaeol. Monogr. 6, 125–6 (Bedford, Albion Archaeol.)

Duncan, H. and Riddler, I.D., 2011 — 'Worked bone objects', in Lyons, A.L., *Life and Afterlife at Duxford, Cambridgeshire: Archaeology and History in a Chalkland Community*, E. Anglian Archaeol. 141, 66–7

Eckhardt, H., and Crummy, N., 2008 — *Styling the Body in Late Iron Age and Roman Britain: a contextual approach to toilet instruments*, Monographies Instrumentum 36 (Editions Mergoil)

Edmonds, M., 2006 — 'The lithics', in Evans, C., Edmonds, M. and Boreham, S., "Total archaeology' and model landscapes: excavation of the Great Wilbraham causewayed enclosure, Cambridgeshire, 1975–76', *Proc. Prehist. Soc.* 72, 130–4

Edmonds, M., Evans, C. and Gibson, D., 1999 — 'Assembly and collection – lithic complexes in the Cambridgeshire fenlands', *Proc. Prehist. Soc.* 65, 47–82

Elsdon, S., 1992 — 'East Midlands scored ware', *Trans. Leicestershire Archaeol. Hist. Soc.* 66, 83–91

English Heritage, 1997 — *English Heritage Archaeology Division Draft Research Agenda* (unpubl.)

Etté, J. and Lucas, G., 2006 — 'Loomweights', in Evans, C. and Hodder, I., *Marshland Communities and Cultural Landscapes from the Bronze Age to the Present Day*, The Haddenham Project Vol. 2, 197–201 (Cambridge, McDonald Inst. Archaeol. Res.)

Evans, C., 1993 — *Archaeological Investigations at Hinxton Quarry, Cambridgeshire*, CAU Rep. 88 (unpubl.)

Evans, C., 2003 — *Power and Island Communities: Excavations at the Wardy Hill Ringwork, Coveney, Ely*, E. Anglian Archaeol. 103

Evans, C., with Beadsmoore, E., Brudenell, M. and Lucas, G., 2009 — *Fengate Revisited, Further Fen-Edge Excavations, Bronze Age Fieldsystems and Settlement and the Wyman Abbott/Leeds Archives*, CAU Landscape Archives: Historiography and Fieldwork (No. 1) (Cambridge, McDonald Inst. Archaeol. Res.)

Evans, C. and Hodder, I., 2006a — *Marshland Communities and Cultural Landscapes from the Bronze Age to Present Day*, The Haddenham Project, Volume 2 (Cambridge, McDonald Inst. Archaeol. Res.)

Evans, C. and Hodder, I., 2006b — *A Woodland Archaeology: Neolithic sites at Haddenham*, The Haddenham Project, Volume 1 (Cambridge: McDonald Inst. Archaeol. Res.)

Evans, C. and Knight, M., 2001 — 'The 'Community of Builders': the Barleycroft post alignments', in Brück, J. (ed.), *Bronze Age Landscapes: Tradition and Transformation*, 83–98 (Oxford, Oxbow)

Evans, C. and Knight, M., 2002 — "A Great Circle': investigations at Arbury Camp', *Proc. Cambridge Antiq. Soc.* 91, 23–54

Evans, C. and Knight, M., 2008 — 'Further investigations at Arbury Camp, Cambridge: the eastern entrance – a monumental architecture', *Proc. Cambridge Antiq. Soc.* 97, 7–30

Evans, C., Lucy, S. and Patten, R., 2018 — *Riversides: Neolithic Barrows, a Beaker grave, Iron Age and Anglo-Saxon burials and settlement at Trumpington, Cambridge*, CAU Landscape Archives: New Archaeologies of the Cambridge Region (2) (Cambridge, McDonald Inst. Archaeol. Res.)

Evans, C., Mackay, D. and Webley, L., 2008 — *Borderlands – The Archaeology of the Addenbrooke's Environs, South Cambridge*, CAU Landscape Archives: New Archaeologies of the Cambridge Region (1)

Evans C., Pollard J. and Knight M., 1999 — 'Life in Woods: 'Tree-throws, 'Settlement' and Forest Cognition', *Oxford J. Archaeol.* 18, 3, 241–54

Evans, C., with Tabor, J. and Vander Linden, M., 2016 — *Twice-crossed River. Prehistoric and palaeoenvironmental investigations at Barleycroft Farm/Over, Cambridgeshire*, CAU Landscape Archives Ser., The Archaeology of the Lower Ouse Valley, Vol. III (Cambridge, McDonald Inst. Archaeol. Res.)

Evans, K., 1994 — 'Fortnightly review: diagnosis and management of sinusitis', *British Medical J.* 309, 1415–22

Fagnart, J-P. and Plisson, H., 1997 — 'Fonction des pièces mâchurées du Paléolithique final du basin de la Somme: caractères tracéologiques et donées contextuelles', in Fagnart, J.-P. and Thévenin, A. (eds), *Le Tardiglaciaire en Europe du Nord-Ouest. Actes du 119ème Congrès National des Sociétés Historiques et Scientifiques*, 95–106 (Paris, Comité des Travaux Historiques et Scientifiques)

Farrar, R.A.H., Hull, M.R. and Pullinger, J., 1999 — 'The Iron Age pottery', in Alexander, J.A., and Pullinger, J., 'Roman Cambridge: Excavations on Castle Hill 1956–1988', *Proc. Cambridge Antiq. Soc.* 88, 117–30

Ferembach, D., Schwidetzky, I. and Stloukal, M., 1980 — 'Recommendations for age and sex diagnoses of skeletons', *J. Human Evolution* 9, 517–49

Finlay, N., 2000a — 'Deer Prudence', *Archaeol. Review from Cambridge* 17 (1), 67–79

Finlay, N., 2000b — 'Microliths in the making', in Young, R. (ed.), *Mesolithic Lifeways: current research from Britain and Ireland*, Leicester Archaeol. Monogr. 7, 23–31

Finnegan, M., 1978 — 'Non-metric variation of the infracranial skeleton', *J. Anatomy* 125, 23–37

Fletcher, T., 2012 — *Hinxton Genome Campus Technical Hub, Post-Excavation Assessment and Updated Project Design*, OA East Rep. 1323 (unpubl.)

Flitcroft, M., 2001 *Excavation of a Romano-British Settlement on the A149 Snettisham Bypass, 1989*, E. Anglian Archaeol. 93

Fosberry, R. 2012 'Environmental samples', in Fletcher, T., *Hinxton Genome Campus Technical Hub, Post-Excavation Assessment and Updated Project Design*, OA East Rep. 1323, 90–95 (unpubl.)

Fosberry, R. 2015 'Environmental samples', in Haskins, A. and Clarke, R., *Hinxton South Field, Phase 3. Post-excavation Assessment and Updated Project Design*, OA East Rep. 1659, 125–37 (unpubl.)

Fox, C.F., 1923 *Archaeology of the Cambridge Region* (Cambridge, Cambridge Univ. Press)

French, C., Cyganowski, N.D., Evans, C., Gdaniec, K., Hanks, B., Hill, J.D., Lewis, H., Miracle, P., Oswald, A., Pattison, P. and Shell, C., 2004 'Evaluation survey and excavation at Wandlebury ringwork, Cambridgeshire, 1994–7', *Proc. Cambridge Antiq. Soc.* 93, 15–66

French, C., Lewis, H., Allen, M., Green, M., Scaife, R. and Gardiner, J., 2007 *Prehistoric Landscape Development and Human Impact in the Upper Allen Valley, Cranborne Chase, Dorset* (Cambridge, McDonald Inst. Archaeol. Res.)

Froom, R., 2005 *Late Glacial Long Blade Sites in the Kennett Valley: excavations and fieldwork at Avington VI, Wawcott XII and Crown Acres*, British Museum Res. Publications 153 (London))

Fryer, V., 1993 *Macrobotanical and other remains from Hinxton Genome Campus, Cambridgeshire* (unpubl.)

Fryer, V. and Murphy, P., forthcoming 'Plant macrofossils', in Clarke, R., Leith, S. and Spoerry, P., forthcoming, *Hinxton, Cambridgeshire: Part 2. Excavations at the Genome Campus 1993-2014: Anglo-Saxon and Medieval Activity in the Cam Valley*, E. Anglian Archaeol.

Galbraith, R.F. and Green, P.F., 1990 'Estimating the component ages in a finite mixture', *Nuclear Tracks and Radiation Measurements* 17, 197–206

García-Díaz, V. and Verbaas, A., 2014 *Use-wear and Residue of the Palaeolithic Long Blade Assemblage from Hinxton*, Leids Archeospecialistisch Bureau Rep. 44 (unpubl.)

Gardiner, J., Allen, M.J., Lewis, J.C., Wright, J. and Macphail, R.I., 2015 *A Long Blade Site at Underdown Lane, Herne Bay, Kent and a Model for Habitat Use in the British Early Postglacial*, Wessex Archaeol. Rep. (unpubl.) Available: http://www.kentarchaeology.org.uk/10/016.pdf, accessed: 17.10.22

Garrow, D., 2006 *Pits, Settlement and Deposition during the Neolithic and Early Bronze Age in East Anglia*, Brit. Archaeol. Rep. Brit. Ser. 414 (Oxford)

Garrow D., Beadsmoore E. and Knight, M., 2005 'Pit clusters and the temporality of occupation: an earlier Neolithic site at Kilverstone, Thetford, Norfolk', *Proc. Prehist. Soc.* 71, 139–57

Garrow, D., Lucy, S. and Gibson, D., 2006 *Excavations at Kilverstone, Norfolk: an episodic landscape history*, E. Anglian Archaeol. 113

Garwood, P., 2007 'Before the hills in order stood: chronology, time and history in the interpretation of Early Bronze Age round barrows', in Last, J. (ed.), *Beyond the Grave: new perspectives on round barrows*, 30–52 (Oxford, Oxbow)

Garwood, P., 2011a 'Making the dead', in Hey, G., Garwood, P., Robinson, M., Barclay, A. and Bradley, P. (eds), *The Thames Through Time, Vol. 1(2): Earlier Prehistory*, 383–432 (Oxford, Oxbow)

Garwood, P., 2011b 'Early prehistory: hunter-gatherers and early agriculturalists in Kent', in Booth, P., Champion, T., Foreman, S., Garwood, P., Glass, H., Mumby, J. and Reynolds, A. (eds), *On Track: the archaeology of the High Speed 1*, section 1, 37–150 (Oxford, Oxford/Wessex Archaeol.)

Garwood, P. and Barclay, A., 1998 'The chronology of depositional contexts and monuments', in Barclay, A. and Haplin, C., *Excavations at Barrow Hills, Radley, Oxfordshire. Volume 1: The Neolithic and Bronze Age Monument Complex*, Thames Valley Landscapes Volume 11, 175–329 (Oxford, Oxford Archaeol. Unit)

Gearey, B., Hopla, E-J., Krawiec, K., Reilly, E. and McKenna, R., 2016 'Palaeoenvironmental analyses', in Paul, S., Colls, K. and Chapman, H., *Living with the Flood: Mesolithic to post-medieval archaeological remains at Mill Lane, Sawston, Cambridgeshire*, 67–78 (Oxford, Oxbow)

Getty, R., 1975 *Sisson and Grossman's the Anatomy of the Domestic Animals*, 5th edn (Philadelphia)

Gibbard, P.L., 1986 'Flint gravels in the Quaternary of south-east England', in Sieveking, G. De C. and Hart, M.B. (eds), *The Scientific Study of Flint and Chert*, 141–9 (Cambridge, Cambridge Univ. Press)

Gibson, A., 1980 'A re-interpretation of Chippenham Barrow 5, with a discussion of the Beaker-associated pottery', *Proc. Cambridge Antiq. Soc.* 70, 47–60

Gibson, A.M., 1982 *Beaker Domestic Sites, a study of the Domestic Pottery of the Late Third and Early Second Millennium BC in the British Isles*, Brit. Archaeol. Rep. Brit. Ser. 107 (Oxford)

Gibson, A.M., 2005 'Neolithic and Beaker pottery', in Chapman, A., Carlyle, S. and Leigh, D., 'Neolithic and Beaker Pits and a Bronze Age Landscape at Fenstanton, Cambridgeshire', *Proc. Cambridge Antiq. Soc.* 94, 9–12

Gibson, A.M., forthcoming 'The pottery', in Pendleton, C. and Gibson, A., 'An excavated Beaker assemblage, including a bronze flat axe, from Worlingham, Suffolk', *Proc. Prehist. Soc.*

Gibson, A.W. and Woods, A., 1990 *Prehistoric Pottery for the Archaeologist* (Leicester, Leicester Univ. Press)

Gibson, C., 2003 *Lordship Farm, Hinxton, Cambridgeshire. An Archaeological Excavation. Final Report*, Hertfordshire Archaeol. Trust Rep. 1271 (unpubl.)

Gilmour, N., 2017 *Late Neolithic Pits on Land Adjacent to Peterhouse Technology Park, Cherry Hinton, Cambridgeshire: Excavation Report*, OA East. Rep. 2034 (unpubl.)

Grace, R., 2011 'Use-wear analysis of the lithic assemblages, in Lewis, J.S.C. with Rackham, J., *Three Ways Wharf, Uxbridge: A Late Glacial and Early Holocene hunter-gatherer site in the Colne Valley*, Museum of London, Monogr. 51, 171–80 (London)

Grant, A., 1982 'The use of tooth wear as a guide to the age of domestic ungulates', in Wilson, R., Grigson, C. and Payne, S. (eds), *Ageing and Sexing Animal Bones from Archaeological Sites*, Brit. Archaeol. Rep. Brit. Ser. 109, 91–108 (Oxford)

Green, B. and Rogerson, A., 1978 *The Anglo-Saxon Cemetery at Bergh Apton, Norfolk*, E. Anglian Archaeol. 7

Gregory, T., 1986   'Enclosures of 'Thornham' type in Norfolk', in Gregory, T. and Gurney, G., *Excavations at Thornham, Warham, Wighton and Caistor St. Edmund, Norfolk*, E. Anglian Archaeol. 30, 32–7

Gregory, T., 1992   *Excavations in Thetford, 1980–1982, Fison Way, Volume 1*, E. Anglian Archaeol. 53

Gregory. T. and Elsdon, S.M., 1996   'Romano-British pottery', in May, J., *Dragonby. Report on excavations at an Iron Age and Romano-British settlement in north Lincolnshire*, Oxbow Monogr. 61, 513–85 (Oxford)

Gresham, C.A., 1939   'Spettisbury Rings, Dorset', *Archaeol. J.* 96, 114–31

Griffiths, D.R., Bergman, C.A., Clayton, C.L., Ohnuma, K., Robins, G.V. and Seeley, N.J., 1987   'Experimental investigation of the heat treatment of flint', in Sieveking, G. De G. and Newcomer M.H. (eds), *The Human Uses of Flint and Chert*, 43–52 (Cambridge, Cambridge Univ. Press)

Grigson, C., 1982   'Sex and age determinations of some bones and teeth of domestic Cattle: a review of the literature', in Hands, A.R. and Walker, D.R. (eds), *Ageing and Sexing of Animal Bones from Archaeological Sites*, Brit. Archaeol. Rep. Brit. Ser. 109, 7–23 (Oxford)

Gwilt, A. and Haselgrove C., (eds), 1997   *Reconstructing Iron Age Societies*, Oxbow Monogr. 71 (Oxford)

Hall, D. and Coles, J., 1994   *Fenland Survey: An Essay in Landscape and Persistence* (London, English Heritage)

Halstead, P. and Collins, P., 1995   *Sheffield Animal Bone Tutorial: Taxonomic identification of the principal limb bones of common European farmyard animals and deer*, Archaeology Consortium, TL TP, University of Glasgow (unpubl.)

Halstead, P., 1985   'A study of mandibular teeth from Romano-British contexts at Maxey', in Pryor, F., French, C., Crowther, D., Gurney, D., Simpson, G. and Taylor, M., *Fenland Project, No 1: Archaeology and Environment in the Lower Welland Valley, Vol. 1*, E. Anglian Archaeol. 27, 219–24

Harding, J. and Healy, F., 2007   *The Raunds Area Project: A Neolithic and Bronze Age Landscape in Northamptonshire* (Swindon, English Heritage)

Harrison, S., 2003   'The Icknield Way: some queries', *Archaeol. J.* 160 (1), 1–22

Hartley, B.R., 1957   'The Wandlebury Iron Age hillfort: excavations of 1955–6', *Proc. Cambridge Antiq. Soc.* 50, 1–27

Haselgrove, C., 2007   'The Age of Enclosure: Later Iron Age settlement and society in northern France', in Haselgrove, C. and Moore, T. (eds), *The Later Iron Age in Britain and Beyond*, 492–522 (Oxford, Oxbow)

Haselgrove, C., Armit, I., Champion, T., Creighton, J., Gwilt, A., Hill, J.D., Hunter, F. and Woodward, A., 2001   *Understanding the Iron Age: an agenda for action* (Salisbury, Iron Age Research Seminar / Council of the Prehistoric Society)

Haskins, A. and Clarke, R., 2015   *Hinxton South Field, Phase 3. Post-excavation Assessment and Updated Project Design*, OA East Rep. 1659 (unpubl.)

Hattatt, R., 1989   *Ancient Brooches and Other Artefacts* (Oxford, Oxbow)

Healy, F., 1988   *The Anglo-Saxon Cemetery at Spong Hill, North Elmham. Part VI: Occupation in the seventh to second millennia BC*, E. Anglian Archaeol. 39

Healy, F., 1996   *The Fenland Project, Number 11: The Wissey Embayment: Evidence for pre-Iron Age Occupation*. E. Anglian Archaeol. 78

Healy, F., 2012a   'Starting something new: the Neolithic in Essex', *Trans Essex Soc. Archaeol. Hist.* 3 (4th Ser.), 1–25

Healy, F., 2012b   'Chronology, corpses, ceramics, copper and lithics', in Allen, M.J., Gardiner, J. and Sheridan, A., *Is there a British Chalcolithic? People, place and polity in the late 3rd millennium*, Prehist. Soc. Res. Pap. 4, 144–64

Healy, F., 2013   'In the shadow of hindsight: pre-Iron Age Spong Hill viewed from 2010', in Hills, C. and Lucy, S., *Spong Hill IX: chronology and synthesis*, 12–21 (Cambridge, McDonald Inst. Archaeol. Res.)

Healy, F., Bayliss, A., Whittle, A., Pryor, F., French, C., Allen, M.J., Evans, C., Edmonds, M., Meadows, J. and Hey, G., 2011   'Eastern England', in Whittle, A., Healy F. and Bayliss, A., *Gathering Time: Dating the Early Neolithic enclosures of Southern Britain and Ireland*, 263–347 (Oxford, Oxbow)

Heawood, R. and Robinson, B., 1998   *A Romano-British Site East of Hinxton Grange: A11 Stump Cross to Four Wentways Improvement Scheme*, CCC AFU Rep. 114 (unpubl.)

Henig, M., 1984   *Religion in Roman Britain* (London, Routledge)

Hill, J.D., 1995   *Ritual and Rubbish in the Iron Age of Wessex*, Brit. Archaeol. Rep. Brit. Ser. 242 (Oxford)

Hill, J.D., 2002   'Just about the potter's wheel? Using, making and depositing middle and later Iron Age pots in East Anglia', in Woodward, A. and Hill, J.D. (eds), *Prehistoric Britain: The Ceramic Basis*, 143–60 (Oxford, Oxbow)

Hill, J.D., 2007   'The dynamics of social change in Later Iron Age eastern and south-eastern England c. 300 BC–AD43', in Haselgrove, C. and Moore, T. (eds), *The Later Iron Age in Britain and Beyond*, 16–40 (Oxford, Oxbow)

Hill, J.D. and Horne, L., 2003   'Iron Age and early Roman pottery', in Evans, C., *Power and Island Communities: Excavations at the Wardy Hill Ringwork, Coveney, Ely*, E. Anglian Archaeol. 103, 145–84

Hill, J.D., Evans, C. and Alexander, M., 1999   'The Hinxton Rings – a Late Iron Age cemetery at Hinxton, Cambridgeshire, with a reconsideration of northern Aylesford-Swarling distributions', *Proc. Prehist. Soc.* 65, 243–73

Hobbs, R., 1996   *British Iron Age Coins in the British Museum* (London, British Museum Press)

Hobbs, R., 2011   'Coins from Great Chesterford', in Medlycott, M., *The Roman Town of Great Chesterford*, E. Anglian Archaeol. 137, 255–64

Hodder, I. A., 1982   *Wendens Ambo. The Excavations of an Iron Age and Romano-British Settlement*, The Archaeology of the M11, Vol. 2 (London, Passmore Edwards Museum)

Hummler, M., 2005   'Before Sutton Hoo: the prehistoric settlement (c.3000 to c.AD 550)', in Carver, M., *Sutton Hoo: A seventh-century princely burial ground and its context*, Rep. Res. Cttee Soc. Antiq. Lond. 69, 391–458 (London, British Museum Press)

Humphrey, J., 2003 'The utilization and technology of flint in the British Iron Age', in Humphrey, J. (ed.), *Researching the Iron Age: selected papers from the proceedings of the Iron Age research student seminars, 1999 and 2000*, Leicester Archaeol. Monogr. 11, 17–23

Hurcombe, L., 2019 'Microwear analysis of selected flint tools', in Clark, P., Shand, G. and Weekes, J., *Chalk Hill: Neolithic and Bronze Age discoveries at Ramsgate, Kent*, 96–103 (Leiden, Sidestone Press)

Hutton, J., 2008 *The Red Lion, Whittlesford. Archaeological Evaluation*, CAU Rep. 836 (unpubl.)

Hutton, J., 2010 *The Red Lion, Whittlesford. An Archaeological Excavation*, CAU Rep. 969 (unpubl.)

Hylton, T. and Williams, R.J., 1996 'Tile', in Williams, R.J., Hart, P.J. and Williams, T.L., *Wavedon Gate: A Late Iron Age and Roman Settlement in Milton Keynes*, Bucks. Archaeol. Soc. Monogr. Ser. 10, 153–4

Ingle, C. and Saunders, H., 2011 *Aerial Archaeology in Essex: the role of the National Mapping Programme in interpreting the landscape*, E. Anglian Archaeol. 136

Inizan, M-L., Reduron-Ballinger, M., Roche, H. and Tixier, J., 1999 *Technology and Typology of Knapped Stone* (Translated by J. Feblot-Augustines), Cercle de Recherches et d'Etudes Préhistoriques Tome 5 (Nanterre)

Jacobi, R.M., 1976 'Britain inside and outside Mesolithic Europe', *Proc. Prehistoric Soc.* 42, 67–84

Jacobi, R.M., 1978 'The Mesolithic of Sussex', in Drewett, P.L. (ed.), *Archaeology in Sussex to AD1500*, Counc. Brit. Archaeol. Res. Rep. 29 (London)

Jacobi, R.M., 1980 'The Mesolithic of Essex', in Buckley, D.G. (ed.), *Archaeology in Essex to AD 1500*, Counc. Brit. Archaeol. Res. Rep. 34, 14–25 (London)

Jacobi, R.M., 2004 'The Late Upper Palaeolithic lithic collection from Gough's Cave, Cheddar, Somerset and human use of the cave', *Proc. Prehist. Soc.* 70, 1–92

Jacobi, R.M. and Higham, T., 2011 'The Later Upper Palaeolithic recolonisation of Britain: new results from AMS radiocarbon dating', *Developments in Quaternary Sci.* 14, 223–47

Jacobi, R.M., Martingell, H.E. and Huggins, P.J., 1978 'A Mesolithic Industry from Hill Wood, High Beach, Epping Forest', *Essex Archaeol. and History* 10, 206–19

Jacquier, J., 2014 'Analyse fonctionnelle des outillages lithiques et interpretations socio-économique du statut des sites tardiglaciaires du Buhot à Calleville (Eure) et de la Fosse à Villiers-Charlemagne (Mayenne)', in Langlais, M., Naudinot, N. and Peresani, M. (eds), *Les groupes culturels de la transition Pléistocène-Holocène entre Atlantique et Adriatique. Actes de la séance de la Société préhistorique française de Bordeaux, 24–25 mai 2012*, Séances de la Société préhistorique française, 3 (Paris)

Jay, M., Richards, M.P. and Marshall, P., 2019 'Radiocarbon dates and their Bayesian modelling', in Parker Pearson, M., Sheridan, A., Jay, M., Chamberlain, A., Richards, M.P. and Evans, J., *The Beaker People: Isotopes, mobility and diet in prehistoric Britain*, Prehist. Soc. Res. Pap. 7, 43–80

Jennings, D., Muir, J., Palmer, S. and Smith, A., 2004 *Thornhill Farm, Fairford, Gloucestershire: an Iron Age and Roman Pastoral Site in the Upper Thames Valley*, Oxford Archaeol. Thames Valley Landscapes Monogr. 23 (Oxford)

Jones, G.J., 2002 'Tooth eruption and wear observed in live sheep from Butser Hill, the Cotswold Farm Park and Five Farms in the Pentland Hills, UK', in Ruscillo, D. (ed.), *Recent Advances in Ageing and Sexing Animal Bones, Proceedings of the 9th Conference on the International Council of Archaeozoologists, 2002*, 155–78 (Oxford)

Jones, M., 2017 *Land South of Hinxton Grange, Hinxton, Cambridgeshire: An Archaeological Evaluation*, Pre-Construct Archaeol. Rep. 12845 (unpubl.)

Jones, P., 2013 *Upper Palaeolithic Sites in the Lower Courses of the Rivers Colne and Wey: Excavations at Church Lammas and Wey Manor Farm*, SpoilHeap Publications Monogr. 5 (Woking)

Jurmain, R.D., 1999 *Stories from the Skeleton – Behavioural Reconstruction in Human Osteology* (Netherlands, Gordon and Breach)

Kaufmann-Heinimann, A., 1998 *Götter und Laurarien aus Augusta Raurica, Herstellung, Fundzusammenhänge uns sakrale Function figürlicher Bronzen in einer römischen Stadt*, Forschungen in Augst, 26 (August)

Kemp, S., 2002 *Archaeological Evaluations at the Hinxton Campus Extension, West of the River Cam. TL 4980/4420*, CCC AFU Rep. A214 (unpubl.)

Kemp, S., 2007 'Other lithics', in Kenney, S., *Hinxton Genome Campus Extension Excavations and Wetlands Area Assessment and Monitoring 2002–2003: Post-Excavation Assessment and Updated Project Design*, CAM ARC Rep. 891, 68–70 (unpubl.)

Kemp, S. and Spoerry, P., 2002 *Evaluation of Iron Age, Roman and Saxon Archaeology at the proposed Wellcome Trust Genome Campus Extension, Hinxton, Cambridgeshire. TL500433. Environmental Statement. Technical Annex C*, CCC AFU Rep. 149 (unpubl.)

Kenney, S., 2002 *Multi-period Remains on the site of the Proposed Genome Campus Extension. Hinxton: An Archaeological Evaluation*, CCC AFU Rep. A206 (unpubl.)

Kenney, S., 2007 *Hinxton Genome Campus Extension Excavations and Wetlands Area Assessment and Monitoring 2002-2003*, CCC AFU Rep. 891 (unpubl.)

Kenney, S. and Lyons, A., 2011 'An Iron Age banjo enclosure and contemporary settlement at Caldecote', *Proc. Cambridge Antiq. Soc.* 100, 67–84

Kenney, S. and Spoerry, P., 2002 *Evaluation of Iron Age, Roman and Saxon Archaeology at the proposed Wellcome Trust Campus extension, Hinxton, Cambridgeshire. TL500433, Environmental Statement. Technical Annex C*, CCC AFU Rep. 149 (unpubl.)

Kinnes, I., 1975 'Monumental function in British Neolithic burial practices', *World Archaeol.* 7(1), 16–29

Knight, D., 2007 'From open to enclosed', in Haselgrove, C. and Moore, T. (eds) *The Later Iron Age in Britain and Beyond*, 190–218 (Oxford, Oxbow)

Knight, M., 2009 'Prehistoric pottery overview (Edgerley Drain Road – Fengate North)', in Evans, C. with Beadsmoore, E., Brudenell, M. and Lucas, G., *Fengate Revisited, Further Fen-Edge Excavations, Bronze Age Fieldsystems and Settlement and the Wyman Abbott/ Leeds Archives*, CAU Landscape Archives: Historiography and Fieldwork (No. 1), 155–64 (Cambridge, McDonald Inst. Archaeol. Res.)

Knight, M., 2016   'Pottery dynamics: case-study', in Evans, C., with Tabor, J. and Vander Linden, M., *Twice-crossed River. Prehistoric and palaeoenvironmental investigations at Barleycroft Farm/Over, Cambridgeshire*, CAU Landscape Archives Ser., The Archaeology of the Lower Ouse Valley, Vol. III, 164–6 (Cambridge, McDonald Inst. Archaeol. Res.)

Knight, M., 2018   'Pottery', in Evans, C., Lucy, S. and Patten, R., *Riversides: Neolithic Barrows, a Beaker grave, Iron Age and Anglo-Saxon Burials and Settlement at Trumpington, Cambridge*,. CAU Landscape Archives Ser., New Archaeologies of the Cambridge Region (2), 52–62 (Cambridge, McDonald Inst. Archaeol. Res.)

Knüsel, C.J., 2000   'Bone adaptation and its relationship to physical activity in the past', in Cox, M. and Mays, S., *Human Osteology in Archaeology and Forensic Science*, 381–40 (London, Cambridge Univ. Press)

Kratochvil, Z., 1969   'Species criteria on the distal section of the tibia in *Ovis ammon* F. *aries* L. and *Capra aegagrus* F. *hircus* L.', *Acta Veterinaria (Brno)* 38, 483–90

Kufel-Diakowska, B., 2011   'The Hamburgian Zinken perforators and burins – flint tools as evidence of antler working', in Baron, J. and Kufel-Diakowska, B. (eds), *Written in Bones: studies on technological and social contexts of past faunal skeletal remains*, 233–40 (Wrocław, Uniwersytet Wrocławski Instytut Archeologii)

Ladd, S., 2019   *Land East of New Road, Melbourn, Cambridgeshire: Excavation Report*, OA East. Rep. 2199 (unpubl.)

Ladd, S. and Mortimer, R., 2017   'The Bran Ditch: Early Iron Age origins and implications for prehistoric territories in South Cambridgeshire and the East Chilterns', *Proc. Cambridge Antiq. Soc.* 106, 7–22

Lambdin-Whymark, H., 2008   *The Residues of Ritualised Action: Neolithic depositional practices in the Middle Thames Valley*, Brit. Archaeol. Rep. Brit. Ser. 466 (Oxford)

Lambrick, G., 2009   *The Archaeology of the Gravel Terraces of the Upper and Middle Thames, Late Prehistory: 1500 BC – AD 50*, Thames Valley Landscapes Monogr. 29 (Oxford, Oxford Archaeol.)

Lambrick, G.H. and Robinson, M.A., 1979   *Iron Age and Roman Riverside Settlements at Farmoor, Oxfordshire*, Counc. Brit. Archaeol. Res. Rep. 32 (Oxford)

Last, J., 1997   *A Late Neolithic Shaft and Beaker Assemblage from Hinxton Hall, Cambridgeshire*, CCC AFU Rep. (unpubl.)

Last, J., 2000   '9: The Bronze Age', in Kirby, T. and Oosthuizen, S. (eds), *An Atlas of Cambridgeshire and Huntingdonshire History* (Cambridge, Centre for Regional Studies, Anglia Polytechnic Univ.)

Last, J., 2002   *Heathfield, Thriplow, Cambs, an Archaeological Excavation. Final Report*, Archaeological Solutions Rep. 1745 (unpubl.)

Last, J., 2007   'Covering old ground: barrows as closures', in Last, J. (ed.), *Beyond the Grave: new perspectives on round barrows*, 156–80 (Oxford, Oxbow)

Laws, K., 1981   'The worked bone and antler', in Sharples, N.M., *Maiden Castle. Excavations and Field Survey 1985–6*, English Heritage Archaeol. Rep. 19, 234–8 (London)

Leaf, C.S., 1940   'Further excavations in Bronze Age barrows at Chippenham, Cambridgeshire', *Proc. Cambridge Antiq. Soc.* 39, 29–68

Leith, S., 1993a   *An Archaeological Assessment at Hinxton Hall*, CCC AFU Rep. A18 (unpubl.)

Leith, S., 1993b   *Phase II Archaeological Assessment at Hinxton Hall*, CCC AFU Rep. A25 (unpubl.)

Leith, S., 1995a   *Archaeological Recording at Hinxton Hall: The New Lake Site Phase I*, CCC AFU Rep. A45 (unpubl.)

Leith, S., 1995b   *Archaeological Recording at Hinxton Hall: The New Lake Site Phase II*, CCC AFU Rep. A69 (unpubl.)

Lethbridge, T.C. and O'Reilly, M.A., 1937   'Archaeological Notes', *Proc. Cambridge Antiq. Soc.* 37, 74–5

Levine, M.A., 1982   'The use of crown height measurement and eruption-wear sequences to age horse teeth', in Wilson, R., Grigson, C. and Payne, S. (eds), *Ageing and Sexing Animal Bones from Archaeological Sites*, Brit. Archaeol. Rep. Brit. Ser. 109, 223–50 (Oxford)

Levine, M.A., Whitwell, K.E. and Jeffcott, L.B., 2005   'Abnormal thoracic vertebrae and the evolution of horse husbandry', *Archaeofauna* 14, 93–109

Levi Sala, I., 1992   'Functional analysis and post-depositional alterations of microdenticulates', in Barton, R.N.E., *Hengistbury Head, Dorset, Volume 2: The Late Upper Palaeolithic and Early Mesolithic Sites*, 238–46 (Oxford, Oxford Univ. Cttee for Archaeol.)

Lewis, J.S.C. with Rackham, J., 2011   *Three Ways Wharf, Uxbridge: A Late Glacial and Early Holocene hunter-gatherer site in the Colne Valley*, Museum of London Monogr. 51 (London)

Lister, A.M., 1996   'The morphological distinction between bones and teeth of Fallow Deer (*Dama dama*) and Red Deer (*Cervus elaphus*)', *Int J. Osteoarchaeol.* 6, 119–43

Longworth, I., 1971   'The Neolithic pottery', in Wainwright, G.J. and Longworth, I.H., *Durrington Walls Excavations 1966 to 1968.* 48–155 (London, Soc. Antiq.)

Loveday, R. and Barclay, A., 2010   'One of the most interesting barrows ever examined. Liffs Low revisited', in Leary, J., Darvill, T. and Field, D. (eds), *Round Mounds and Monumentality in the British Neolithic and beyond*, 108–29 (Oxford, Oxbow)

Luff, R., 1985   'The fauna', in Nesbitt, R., *Sheepen: an early Roman industrial site at Camulodunum*, Counc. Brit. Archaeol. Res. Rep. 57, 143–9 (London)

Luke, M., 2008   *Life in the Loop: Investigations of a prehistoric and Romano-British landscape at Biddenham Loop, Bedfordshire*, E. Anglian Archaeol. 125

Luke, M., 2016   *Close to the Loop: Landscape and settlement evolution beside the Biddenham Loop, west of Bedford*, E. Anglian Archaeol. 156

Lyons, A., 2008   'Kiln bars', in Willis, S., Lyons, A., Popescu, E. and Roberts, J., 'Late Iron Age/Early Roman pottery kilns at Blackhorse Lane, Swavesey, 1998–99', *Proc. Cambridge Antiq. Soc.* 97, 57–9

Lyons, A., 2009   *Becoming Roman and Losing your Temper, a petrological study of Early Roman pottery from Cambridgeshire* (unpubl. Masters dissertation, Univ. Southampton)

Lyons, A., 2011   *Life and Afterlife at Duxford, Cambridgeshire: archaeology and history in a chalkland community*, E. Anglian Archaeol. 141

172

Mackreth, D.F., 1996 'Brooches', in Potter, T.W., *Excavations at Stonea, Cambridgeshire, 1980–85*, 296–326 (London, British Museum Press)

Mackreth, D.F., 2011 *Brooches in Late Iron Age and Roman Britain* (2 vols) (Oxford, Oxbow)

Malim, T., 1998 'Prehistoric and Roman Remains at Edix Hill, Barrington', *Proc. Cambridge Antiq. Soc.* 86, 13–56

Malim, T., 2000 '27: The Anglo-Saxon Dykes', in Kirby, T. and Oosthuizen, S. (eds), *An Atlas of Cambridgeshire and Huntingdonshire History* (Cambridge, Centre for Regional Studies, Anglia Polytechnic Univ.)

Maltby, J.M., 1981 'Iron Age, Romano-British and Anglo-Saxon animal husbandry – a review of the faunal evidence', in Dimbleby, G. and Jones, M., *The Environment of Man: the Iron Age to the Anglo-Saxon Period*, Brit. Archaeol. Rep. Brit. Ser. 87, 155–203

Maltby, J.M., 1996 'The exploitation of animals in the Iron Age: the archaeozoological evidence', in Champion, T.C. and Collis, J.R. (eds), *The Iron Age in Britain and Ireland: recent trends*, Sheffield Excav. Rep. 4 (Sheffield)

Manning, W.H., 1985 *Catalogue of the Romano-British Iron Tools, Fittings and Weapons in the British Museum* (London, British Museum Press)

Margary, I.D., 1973 *Roman Roads in Britain*, 3rd edn (London, John Baker)

Marsh, R.E., Prestwich, W.V., Rink, W.J. and Brennan, B.J., 2002 'Monte Carlo determinations of the beta dose rate to tooth enamel', *Radiation Measurements* 35, 609–16

Martin, E., 1993 'The Iron Age enclosure at Barnham', in Martin, E. (ed.), *Settlements on Hill-tops: Seven Prehistoric Sites in Suffolk*, E. Anglian Archaeol. 65, 1–22

Martin, E.A. and Denston, C.B., 1976 'The excavation of two tumuli on Waterhall Farm, Chippenham, Cambridgeshire, 1973', *Proc. Cambridge Antiq. Soc.* 66, 1–22

Martingell, H., 1990 'The East Anglian Peculiar? The 'squat' flake', *Lithics* 11, 40–43

Mays, S. and Steele, J., 1996 'A mutilated skull from Roman St Albans, Hertfordshire, England', *Antiquity* 70, 155–61

McFadyen, L., 1999a *An Archaeological Evaluation at Heathfields, Duxford*, CAU Rep. 326 (unpubl.)

McFadyen, L., 1999b *Archaeological Fieldwalking at Heathfields, Duxford*, CAU Rep. 339 (unpubl.)

McKinley, J.I., 2004 'Compiling a skeletal inventory: cremated human bone', in Brickley, M. and McKinley, J.I. (eds), *Guidelines to the Standards for Recording Human Remains*, IFA Pap. 7, 9–13 (Reading, Brit. Assoc. Biological Anthropol. Osteoarchaeol./Inst. Field Archaeologists)

Medlycott, M., 2011a *The Roman Town of Great Chesterford*, E. Anglian Archaeol. 137

Medlycott, M. (ed.), 2011b *Research and Archaeology Revisited: a revised framework for the East of England*, E. Anglian Archaeol. Occ. Pap. 24

Mepham, L.N., 2004 'The pottery', in Ellis, C.E. (ed.), *A Prehistoric Ritual Complex at Eynesbury, Cambridgeshire: Excavation of a Multi-period Site in the Great Ouse Valley, 2000–2001*, E. Anglian Archaeol. Occ. Pap. 17, 47–8

Miles, A.E.W., 1962 'Assessment of the ages of a population of Anglo-Saxons from their dentitions', *Proc. Royal Soc. Medicine* 55, 881–6

Miles, A.E.W., 2001 'The Miles method of assessing age from tooth wear revisited', *J. Archaeol Sci.* 28, 973–82

Miles, D. and Palmer, S. 1990 'Claydon Pike and Thornhill Farm', *Current Archaeology* 121, 19–23

Mook, W.G., 1986 'Business meeting: Recommendations/ resolutions adopted by the Twelfth International Radiocarbon Conference', *Radiocarbon* 28, 799

Moore, J. and Jennings, D., 1992 *Reading Business Park: a Bronze Age landscape* (Oxford, Oxford Archaeol. Unit)

Moore-Colyer, R.J., 1994 'The Horse in British prehistory: some speculations', *Archaeology J.* 151, 1–15

Morgan, R., 2006 'Tree ring results', in Evans, C. and Hodder, I., *A Woodland Archaeology: Neolithic sites at Haddenham*, The Haddenham Project, Volume 1, 177–87 (Cambridge, McDonald Inst. Archaeol. Res.)

Mortimer, R., 2005 *Neolithic, Bronze Age, Iron Age and Romano-British Occupation along the route of the Fordham Bypass, Fordham, Cambridgeshire. Post-Excavation Assessment*, CCC AFU Rep. 816 (unpubl.)

Mortimer, R., 2006 *Bronze Age Enclosures at Sawston Police Station*, CCC AFU Rep. 831 (unpubl.)

Mortimer, R. and Evans, C., 1996 *Archaeological Excavations at Hinxton Quarry, Cambridgeshire – The North Field*, CAU Rep. 168 (unpubl.)

Mullins, C., 2007 'Socketed longbone points: a study of the Irish material with reference to British and continental examples', *J. Irish Archaeol.* 16, 35–60

Murray, A.S. and Funder, S., 2003 'Optically stimulated luminescence dating of a Danish Eemian coastal marine deposit: a test of accuracy', *Quaternary Science Reviews* 22, 1177–83

Murray, A.S. and Olley, J.M., 2002 'Precision and accuracy in the optically stimulated luminescence dating of sedimentary quartz: a status review', *Geochronometria* 21, 1–16

Murray, A.S. and Wintle, A.G., 2000 'Luminescence dating of quartz using an improved single-aliquot regenerative-dose protocol', *Radiation Measurements* 32, 57–73

Naudinot, N. and Jacquier, J., 2014 'Socio-economic organisation of Final Palaeolithic societies: new perspectives from an aggregation site in Western France', *J. Anthropological Archaeol.* 35, 177–89

Naudinot, N., Tomasso, A., Messager, E., Finsinger, W., Ruffaldi, P. and Langlais, M., 2017 'Between Atlantic and Mediterranean: changes in technology during the Late Glacial in Western Europe and the climate hypothesis', *Quaternary International* 428, Part B, 33–49

Needham, S., 2005 'Transforming Beaker Culture in North-West Europe: processes of fusion and fission', *Proc. Prehistoric Soc.* 71, 171–217

Needham, S., 2012 'Case and place for the British Chalcolithic', in Allen, M.J., Gardiner, J. and Sheridan, A., *Is there a British Chalcolithic? People, place and polity in the late 3rd millennium*, Prehist. Soc. Res. Pap. 4, 1–27

Neil, B. and Evans, C., 2019 *Willingham Mere-Side Investigations, 2018 Excavations within Hanson's Over/ Needingworth Quarry Sites XI &XV*, CAU Rep. 1421 (unpubl.)

Network Archaeology, 2017 *Uttlesford Crematorium, Great Chesterford, Essex. Interim Report for Archaeological Controlled Strip and Excavation* (unpubl.)

Newton, A.S., 2018   *Small Communities: Life in the Cam Valley in Neolithic, late Iron Age and Early Anglo-Saxon times. Excavations at Dernford Farm*, E. Anglian Archaeol. 168

Niblett, R., 1999   *The Excavation of a Ceremonial Site at Folly Lane, Verulamium*, Britannia Monogr. Series 14 (London)

OA East (forthcoming)   *Prehistoric and Romano-British Occupation along Fordham Bypass, Cambridgeshire, 2004*, E. Anglian Archaeol.

O'Brien, L., 2016   *Bronze Age Barrow, Early to Middle Iron Age Settlement and Burials, and Early Anglo-Saxon Settlement at Harston Mill, Cambridgeshire*, E. Anglian Archaeol. 157

O'Connor, T.P., 2003   *The Analysis of Urban Animal Bone Assemblages. A handbook for archaeologists* (York, York Archaeol. Trust)

Olivier, A., 1996   'Brooches of silver, copper alloy and iron', in May, J., *Dragonby. Report on Excavations at an Iron Age and Romano-British Settlement in North Lincolnshire* (2 vols), 231–63 (Oxford, Oxbow)

Olley, J.M., De Deckker, P., Roberts, R.G., Fifield, L.K., Yoshida, H. and Hancock, G., 2004   'Optical dating of deep-sea sediments using single grains of quartz: a comparison with radiocarbon', *Sedimentary Geology* 169, 175–89

Olsen, S.L., 2003   'The bone and antler artefacts: their manufacture and use', in Field, N. and Parker Pearson, M., *Fiskerton. An Iron Age Timber Causeway with Iron Age and Roman Votive Offerings: the 1981 Excavations*, 92–110 (Oxford, Oxbow)

Ortner, D.J., 2003   *Identification of Pathological Conditions in Human Skeletal Remains* (San Diego, Academic Press)

Parker, A.J. 1988   'The birds of Roman Britain', *Oxford J. Archaeol.* 7(2), 197–226

Parker Pearson, M., Needham, S. and Sheridan, A., with Gibson, A., 2019   'The Beaker People project individuals, their funerary practices and their grave goods', in Parker Pearson, M., Sheridan, A., Jay, M., Chamberlain, A., Richards, M.P and Evans, J., *The Beaker People: Isotopes, mobility and diet in prehistoric Britain*, Prehist. Society Res. Pap. 7, 115–210

Partridge, C., 1980   'Excavations at Puckeridge and Braughing 1975–1979', *Hertfordshire Archaeol.* 7, 28–132

Partridge, C.L., 1981   *Skeleton Green. A late Iron Age and Romano-British site*, Britannia Monogr. Ser. 2 (London)

Partridge, C. 1989   *Foxholes Farm: a multi-period gravel site* (Hertford, Hertfordshire Archaeol. Trust)

Paul, S., Colls, K. and Chapman, H., 2016   *Living with the Flood. Mesolithic to post-medieval remains at Mill Lane, Sawston, Cambridgeshire* (Oxford, Oxbow)

Payne, S., 1973   'Kill-off patterns in sheep and goat mandibles: the mandibles of Asvan Kale', *Anatolia Studies*, 23, 281–303

Payne, S., 1985   'Morphological distinctions between the mandibular teeth of young sheep, *Ovis*, and goats, *Capra*', *J. Archaeol. Sci.* 12, 139–47

Payne, S. and Bull, G., 1988   'Components of variations of measurements of pig bones and teeth, and the use of measurements to distinguish wild from domestic pig remains', *Archaeozoologia* 2, 27–66

Peglar, S., 2006   'The Ouse Channel Flandrian sequence', in Evans, C. and Hodder, I.A., *A Woodland Archaeology; Neolithic Sites at Haddenham*, The Haddenham Project Volume I, 26–9 (Cambridge, McDonald Inst. Archaeol. Res.)

Peglar, S. and Waller, M., 1994   'The Ouse channel, Haddenham', in Waller, M. (ed.), *The Fenland Project, Number 9; Flandrian Environmental Change in Fenland*, E. Anglian Archaeol. 70

Pelling, R., Campbell, G., Carruthers, W., Hunter, K. and Marshall, P., 2014   'Exploring contamination (intrusion and residuality) in the archaeobotanical record: case studies from central and southern England', *Vegetation History and Archaeobotany* 24, 85–99

Percival, J.W., 2002   'Neolithic and Bronze Age occupation in the Yare Valley: excavations at Three Score Road, Bowthorpe 1999–2000', *Norfolk Archaeol.* 44, 59–89

Percival, S., 2005   *The Prehistoric Pottery: Linton Village College LINVIC04*, report for OA East (unpubl.)

Petersen, F. and Healy, F., 1986   'The excavation of two round barrows and a ditched enclosure on Weasenham Lyngs, 1972', in Lawson, A.J., Bown, J., Healy, F., Le Hegarat, R. and Petersen, F., *Barrow Excavations in Norfolk, 1950–82*, E. Anglian Archaeol. 29, 70–103

Pettitt, P.B., 2007   'Cultural context and form of some of the Creswell images: an interpretative model', in Pettitt, P., Bahn, P. and Ripoll, S. (eds), *Palaeolithic Cave Art at Creswell Crags in European Context*, 112–39 (Oxford, Oxford Univ. Press)

Pettitt, P. and White, M., 2012   *The British Palaeolithic: human societies at the edge of the Pleistocene world* (London, Routledge)

Phillips, T., 2015   'Bronze Age and Iron Age settlement and land-use at the Milton landfill and Park & Ride sites', *Proc. Cambridge Antiq. Soc.* 104, 7–30

Phillips, T. and Blackbourn, K., 2019   'Field End, Witchford: Middle–Late Bronze Age funerary activity, settlement and bronze-working on the Isle of Ely', *Proc. Cambridge Antiq. Soc.* 108, 7–32

Phillips, T. and Mortimer, R., forthcoming   *The Archaeology of Clay Farm, Trumpington: A Landscape Study*, E. Anglian Archaeol.

Philpott, R., 1991   *Burial Practices in Roman Britain*, Brit. Archaeol. Rep. Brit. Ser. 219 (Oxford)

Pickstone, A. and Mortimer, R., 2012   'War Ditches, Cherry Hinton: Revisiting an Iron Age hillfort', *Proc. Cambridge Antiq. Soc.* 101, 44–5

Pitts, M.W., 1978   *Towards an Understanding of Flint Industries in Post-Glacial England*, Bull. Inst. Archaeol. 15, 179–97

Pitts, M., 2005   'Pots and pits: drinking and deposition in late Iron Age south east Britain', *Oxford J. Archaeol.* 24 (2), 143–61

Pitts, M.W. and Jacobi, R.M., 1979   'Some aspects of change in flaked stone industries of the Mesolithic and Neolithic in southern Britain', *J. Archaeol. Sci.* 6, 163–77

Pollard, J., 1996   'Worked flint', in Mortimer, R. and Evans, C., *Archaeological Excavations at Hinxton Quarry, Cambridgeshire 1995 – North Field*, CAU Rep. 168 (unpubl.)

Pollard, J., 1998   'Prehistoric settlement and non-settlement in two southern Cambridgeshire river valleys: the lithic dimension and interpretative dilemmas', *Lithics* 19, 61–7

Pollard, J., 1999   "'These places have their moments': thoughts on settlement practices in the British Neolithic', in Brück, J. and Goodman, M. (eds.) *Making Places in the Prehistoric World: themes in settlement archaeology*, 76–93 (London, Univ. Coll. London Press)

Pollard, J., 2002   'The ring-ditch and the hollow: excavation of a Bronze Age 'shrine' and associated features at Pampisford, Cambridgeshire', *Proc. Cambridge Antiq. Soc.* 91, 5–21

Pollard, J., 2006   'A community of beings: animals and people in the Neolithic of southern Britain', in Serjeantson, D. and Field, D. (eds), *Animals in the Neolithic of Britain and Europe*, Neolithic Studies Group Seminar Pap. 7, 135–48 (Oxford, Oxbow)

Poole, C., 1991   'Objects of bone and antler', in Cunliffe, B. and Poole, C., *Danebury. An Iron Age Hillfort in Hampshire. Volume 5. The Excavations, 1979–1988: the Finds*, Counc. Brit. Archaeol. Res. Rep. 73, 354–68 (London)

PCRG, 1995   *The Study of Later Prehistoric Pottery: general policies and guidelines for analysis and publication* (London, Prehist. Ceramics Res. Group)

Prescott, J.R. and Hutton, J.T., 1994   'Cosmic-ray contributions to dose-rates for luminescence and ESR dating - large depths and long-term time variations', *Radiation Measurements* 23, 497–500

Price, J., Brooks, I.P. and Maynard, D.J., 1997   *The Archaeology of the St Neots to Duxford Gas Pipeline 1994*, Brit. Archaeol. Rep. Brit. Ser. 255 (Oxford)

Prosser, L. and Murray, J., 2001   *Land at Priory Farm, Back Lane, Ickleton, Cambridgeshire. An archaeological evaluation*, Hertfordshire Archaeol. Trust (unpubl.)

Prummel, W. and Frisch, H-J., 1986   'A guide for the distinction of species, sex and body side in bones of sheep and goat', *J. Archaeol. Sci.* 13, 567–77

Pryor, F., 1976   'A Neolithic multiple burial from Fengate, Peterborough', *Antiquity* 50 (199), 232

Pryor, F., 1980   *Excavation at Fengate, Peterborough, England: the Third report*, Northamptonshire Archaeol. Soc. Monogr. 1, Royal Ontario Museum Archaeol. Monogr. 6 (Leicester/Toronto)

Pryor, F., 1984   *Excavation at Fengate, Peterborough, England: the Fourth Report*, Northamptonshire Archaeol. Soc. Monogr. 2, Royal Ontario Museum Archaeol. Monogr. 7 (Leicester/Toronto)

Rankine, W.F., 1952   'A Mesolithic chipping floor at the Warren, Oakhanger, Selborne, Hants.', *Proc. Prehist. Soc.* 18, 21–35

Rankine, W.F. and Dimbleby, G.W., 1960   'Further excavations at a Mesolithic site at Oakhanger, Selborne, Hants.', *Proc. Prehist. Soc.* 26, 246–62

Rasmussen, S.O., Bigler, M., Blockley, S.P., Blunier, T., Buchardt, S.L., Clausen, H.B., Cvijanovic, I., Dahl-Jensen, D., Johnsen, S.J., Fischer, H. and Gkinis, V., 2014   'A stratigraphic framework for abrupt climatic changes during the Last Glacial period based on three synchronized Greenland ice-core records: refining and extending the INTIMATE event stratigraphy', *Quaternary Science Reviews* 106, 14–28

Reece, R., 1991   *Roman Coins from 140 Sites in Britain*, Cotswold Studies 4 (Cirencester)

Reimer, P., Austin, W.E., Bard, E., Bayliss, A., Blackwell, P.G., Bronk Ramsey, C., Butzin, M., Cheng, H., Edwards, R.L., Friedrich, M., Grootes, P.M., Guilderson, T.P., Hajdas, I., Heaton, T.J., Hogg, A.G., Hughen, K.A., Kromer, B., Manning, S.W., Muscheler, R., Palmer, J.G., Pearson, C., Van Der Plicht, J., Reimer, R.W., Richards, D.A., Scott, E.M., Southon, J.R., Turney, C.S.M., Wacker, L., Adolphi, F., Büntgen, U., Capano, M., Fahrni, S.M., Fogtmann-Schulz, A., Friedrich, R., Köhler, P., Kudsk, S., Miyake, F., Olsen, J., Reinig, F., Sakamoto, M., Sookdeo, A. and Talamo, S., 2020   'The IntCal20 Northern Hemisphere radiocarbon age calibration curve (0–55 kcal BP)', *Radiocarbon* 62 (4), 725–57

Resnick, D., (ed.), 1995   *Diagnosis of Bone and Joint Disorders*, 3rd edn (London, Harcourt)

Reynolds, T. and Kaner, S., 2000   'The Mesolithic of southern fenland: a review of the data and some suggestions for the future', in Young, R. (ed.), *Mesolithic Lifeways: Current Research from Britain and Ireland*, Leicester Archaeol. Monogr. 7, 191–7 (Leicester)

Riddler, I., 2007   'Objects of antler and bone', in Mays, S., Harding, C. and Heighway, C., *The Churchyard, Wharram. A Study of Settlement on the Yorkshire Wolds, XI*, York Univ. Archaeol. Publi. 13, 313–17 (York)

Rigby, V., 1988   'The late prehistoric, Roman and later wares', in Longworth, I.H., Ellison, A.B. and Rigby, V.A., *Excavations at Grimes Graves, Norfolk, 1972–1976. Fascicule 2. The Neolithic, Bronze Age and Later Pottery*, 100–10 (London, British Museum)

Rigby, V., 1989   'Pottery from the Iron Age cemetery', in Stead, I.M. and Rigby, V., *Verulamium. The King Harry Lane site*, English Heritage Archaeol. Rep. 12, 112–210 (London)

Rippon, S., 2018   *Kingdom, Civitas, and County: the evolution of territorial identity in the English landscape* (Oxford, Oxford Univ. Press)

Roach Smith, C., 1849   'Recent discoveries made at Ickleton and Chesterford, on the borders of Essex and Cambridgeshire, by the Hon. R.C. Neville, FSA, etc.', *J. Brit. Archaeol. Assoc.* 4, 356–78

Roberts, C. and Cox, M., 2003   *Health and Disease in Britain from Prehistory to the Present Day* (Stroud, Sutton)

Roberts, C. and Manchester, K., 1995   *The Archaeology of Disease* (Stroud, Sutton)

Roberts, J., 1996 — *Archaeology and Alluvium along the Hinxton Hall to Great Chesterford New Main*, CCC AFU Rep. A 81 (unpubl.)

Robertson, A., Barker, B. and Roy, M., 2003 — *Sewage Treatment Works, Great Chesterford, excavation & watching brief*, Essex County Council Field Archaeol. Unit Rep. (unpubl.)

Robins, P. and Wymer, J.J., 2006 — 'Late Upper Palaeolithic (long blade) industries in Norfolk', *Norfolk Archaeol.* 45 (1), 86–95

Robinson, B., 1994 — *Abbey Farm, Ickleton, Cambridgeshire: An Archaeological Desktop Study*, CCC AFU Rep. A34 (unpubl.)

Robinson-Zeki, L., 2019 — *Wellcome Genome Campus Development Project, Hinxton, Cambridgeshire*, OA East Rep. 2269 (unpubl.)

Rogers, J. and Waldron, T., 1995 — *A Field Guide to Joint Disease in Archaeology* (Chichester, Wiley)

Rowley–Conwy, P. and Owen, A.C., 2011 — 'Grooved Ware feasting in Yorkshire: Late Neolithic animal consumption at Rudston Wold', *Oxford J. Archaeol.* 30(4), 325–67

Saville, A., 1980 — 'On the measurement of struck flakes and flake tools', *Lithics* 1, 16–20

Saville, A., 1981 — *Grimes Graves, Norfolk. Excavations 1971–2, Volume II: The Flint Assemblage*, Dept of Environment Archaeol. Rep. 11 (London)

Saville, A., 1990 — *Hazleton North: The excavations of a Neolithic long cairn of the Cotswold-Severn group* (Swindon, English Heritage)

Scheib, C.L., Hui, R., D'Atanasio, E., Wohns, A.W., Inskip, S.A., Rose, A., Cessford, C., O'Connell, T.C., Robb, J.E., Evans, C. and Patten, R., 2019 — 'East Anglian early Neolithic monument burial linked to contemporary Megaliths', *Annals of Human Biology*, 46(2), 145–9

Schiffels, S., Haak, W., Paajanen, P., Llamas, B., Popescu, E., Loe, L., Clarke, R., Lyons, A., Mortimer, M., Sayer, D., Tyler-Smith, C., Cooper, A. and Durbin, R., 2016 — 'Iron Age and Anglo-Saxon genomes from East England reveal British migration history', *Nature Communications*, doi: 10.1038/ncomms10408

Schlee, D. and Robinson, B., 1995 — *An Archaeological Evaluation of Land Adjacent to Duxford Mill, Duxford. Late Mesolithic / Early Neolithic Activity on the Floodplain of the River Cam*, CCC AFU Rep. 113 (unpubl.)

Schmid, E., 1972 — *Atlas of Animal Bones for Prehistorians, Archaeologists and Quaternary Geologists*, (Amsterdam, Elsevier)

Scheuer, L. and Black, S., 2000 — *Developmental Juvenile Osteology* (Oxford, Elsevier Academic Press)

Seager Smith, R., 2000 — 'Worked bone and antler', in Lawson, A.J., *Potterne 1982–5: Animal Husbandry in Later Prehistoric Wiltshire*, Wessex Archaeol. Rep. 17, 222–34 (Salisbury)

Sealey, P.R., 1996 — 'The Iron Age of Essex', in Bedwin, O.R. (ed.), *The Archaeology of Essex: Proceedings of the Writtle Conference*, 46–68 (Chelmsford)

Sealey, P.R., 2011 — 'The Middle and Late Iron Age pottery', in Kenney, S. and Lyons, A., 'An Iron Age Banjo Enclosure and Contemporary Settlement at Caldecote', *Proc. Cambridge Antiq. Soc.* 100, 24–33

Sealey, R.R., 2007 — *A Late Iron Age Warrior Burial from Kelvedon, Essex*, E. Anglian Archaeol. 118

Sellwood, L., 1984 — 'Objects of bone and antler', in Cunliffe, B.W., *Danebury. An Iron Age Hillfort in Hampshire*, Counc. Brit. Archaeol. Res. Rep. 52, 317–95 (London)

Sergant, J., Crombé, P. and Perdaen, Y., 2006 — 'The 'invisible' hearths: a contribution to the discernment of Mesolithic non-structured surface hearths', *J. Archaeol. Sci.* 33 (7), 999–1007

Sergeantson, D., 1996 — 'The animal bones', in Needham, S. and Spence, A. (eds.), *Refuse and Disposal at Area 15 East Runnymede. Runnymede Bridge Research Excavations*, Vol. 2, 194–222 (London, British Museum Press)

Serjeantson, D., 2011 — *Review of Animal Remains from the Neolithic and Early Bronze Age of Southern Britain (4000–1500 BC)*, English Heritage Res. Dept Rep. Ser. 29-2011 (Portsmouth)

Shiel, D., 1993a — *Report on Geophysical survey: Hinxton Hall Park*, Geophysical Surveys of Bradford Rep. 93/87 (unpubl.)

Shiel, D., 1993b — *Report on Geophysical survey: Hinxton Hall Park*, Geophysical Surveys of Bradford Rep. 93/100 (unpubl.)

Silver, I.A., 1969 — 'The ageing of domestic animals', in Brothwell, D. and Higgs, E. (eds), *Science in Archaeology*, 283–302 (London, Thames and Hudson)

Small, F., 2017 — *Great Shelford, Cambridgeshire. Great Shelford Neolithic Causewayed Enclosure*, Historic England Res. Rep. Ser. 3-2017 (Portsmouth)

Smith, A.G., Whittle, A., Cloutman, E.W. and Morgan, L.A., 1989 — 'Mesolithic and Neolithic activity and environmental impact on the south-east fen edge in Cambridgeshire', *Proc. Prehist. Soc.* 55, 207–49

Smith, M. and Brickley, M., 2009 — *People of the Long Barrows: life, death and burial in the Earlier Neolithic* (Stroud, History Press)

Spoerry, P. and Leith, S., 1996 — *Excavations at Hinxton Hall 1993-5*, CCC AFU Rep. (unpubl.)

Spoerry, P., 1995a — *Hinxton Hall Excavations 1993–4: summary statement 1995*, Cambridgeshire Archaeol. Special Rep. (unpubl.)

Spoerry, P., 1995b — *An Anglo-Saxon Settlement at Hinxton Hall*, draft report

Stace, C., 1997 — *A New Flora of the British Isles*, 2nd edn (Cambridge, Cambridge Univ. Press)

Stead, I.M. and Rigby, V., 1989 — *Verulamium: the King Harry Lane site*, English Heritage Archaeol. Rep. 12 (London)

Stevens, C.J. and Fuller, D.Q., 2012 — 'Did Neolithic farming fail? The case for a Bronze Age agricultural revolution in the British Isles', *Antiquity* 86 (333), 707–22

Stirland, A., 2000 — *Raising the dead: the skeleton crew of Henry VIII's great ship, the Mary Rose* (Chichester, John Wiley and Sons)

Stuart-Macadam, P., 1991 — 'Anaemia in Roman Britain: Poundbury Camp', in Bush, H. and Zvelebil, M. (eds) *Health in Past Societies: Biocultural Interpretations of Human Skeletal Remains in Archaeological Contexts*, 101–13 (Oxford)

Stuiver, M. and Reimer, P.J. 1986 'A computer program for radiocarbon age calibration', *Radiocarbon* 28(2B), 1022–30

Swan, V., 1984 *The Pottery Kilns of Great Britain*, Roy. Comm. Hist. Mon., Suppl. Ser. 5 (London, HMSO)

Swift, E., 2011 'Personal adornment', in Allason-Jones, L. (ed), *Artefacts in Roman Britain. Their purpose and use*, 194–218 (Cambridge, Cambridge Univ. Press)

Tabor, J., 2015 'Late Neolithic and Early Bronze Age activity at North Fen, Sutton Gault, Cambridgeshire', *Proc. Cambridge Antiq. Soc.* 104, 31–54

Tabor, J., 2016 'Early Neolithic pits and artefact scatters at North Fen, Sutton Gault, Cambridgeshire', *Proc. Prehist. Soc.* 82, 161–91

Taylor, A., 1981 'The barrows of Cambridgeshire', in Lawson, A.J., Martin, E.A. and Priddy, D. (eds), *The Barrows of East Anglia*, E. Anglian Archaeol. 12, 108–20

Taylor, C.C., 1998 *Archaeology of Cambridgeshire. Volume 2: South East Cambridgeshire and the Fen Edge* (Cambridge, Cambridgeshire County Council)

Taylor, C. and Arbon, A., 2007 'The Chronicle Hills, Whittlesford, Cambridgeshire', *Proc. Cambridge Antiq. Soc.* 96, 26–40

Thatcher, C., 2007 *Neolithic Flint and Pottery at Main Street, Stow-Cum-Quy, Cambridgeshire*, CCC AFU Rep. 899 (unpubl.)

Thomas, A., 2002 *Brief for Archaeological Investigation*, CCC Archaeology Section (unpubl.)

Thomas, J.S., 1999 *Understanding the Neolithic* (London, Routledge)

Thomas, S.C., 1996 'Differentiation of selected frog (*Rana*) and toad (*Bufo*) bones using morphological and osteometric traits', *Canadian Zooarchaeol.* 10, 2–24

Thompson, I., 1982 *Grog-tempered 'Belgic' Pottery of South-eastern England*, Brit. Archaeol. Rep. Brit. Ser. 108 (Oxford)

Thompson, I., 1984 (on-line version of Thompson 1982, above). Available: https://www.kentarchaeology.org.uk/16/000.htm. Accessed: 24.03.21

Tilley, C.Y., 1979 *Post Glacial Communities in the Cambridge Region*, Brit. Archaeol. Rep. Brit. Ser. 66

Tomber, R. and Dore, J., 1998 *The National Roman Fabric Reference Collection. A Handbook*, MoLAS Monogr. 2 (London)

Tringham, R., Cooper, G., Odell, G., Voytek, B. and Whitman, A., 1974 'Experimentation in the formation of edge damage: a new approach to lithic analysis', *J. Field Archaeol.* 1, 171–96

Trotter, M., 1970 'Estimation of stature from intact long bones' in Stewart, T.D. (ed.), *Personal Identification in Mass Disasters*, 71–83 (Washington, Smithsonian Inst. Press)

Trump, D.H., 1956 'The Bronze Age barrow and Iron Age settlement at Thriplow', *Proc. Cambridge Antiq. Soc.* 49, 1–12

Tyers, P., 1999 *Roman Pottery in Britain*, 2nd edn (London, Routledge)

University of Southampton, 2003 *Animal Bone Metrical Archive Project (ABMAP)* [data-set]. York: Archaeology Data Service [distributor] doi.org/10.5284/1000350

Uí Choileáin, Z., 2014 *Assessment of human skeletal remains. HINGEL14*, OA East Rep. (unpubl.)

Valentin, B., 2008 *Jalons pour une paléohistoire des derniers chasseurs, XIVe-VIe millénaire avant J.-C*, Vol. 1 (Paris, Publications de la Sorbonne)

Valentin, B., 2009 'Éléments de paléohistoire autour du basculement Pléistocene-Holocène' in Crombé, P., Van Strydonck, M., Sergant, J., Boudin, M. and Bats, M. (eds), *Chronology and Evolution within the Mesolithic of North-West Europe: Proceedings of an International meeting, Brussels, May 30th–June 1st 2007*, 23–38 (Newcastle on Tyne, Cambridge Scholars Publishing)

Valentin, B., Weber, M.J. and Bodu, P., 2014 'Initialisation and progression of the core reduction process at Donnemarie-Dontilly (Seine-et-Marne, France), site of the Belloisian tradition: new interpretative key for comparisons with contemporaneous industries and 'Federmesser-Gruppen' assemblages', *Bulletin de la Société préhistorique française*, 659–78

Van Arsdell, R.D., 1989 *Celtic Coinage of Britain* (London, Spink)

von den Driesch, A., 1976 *A Guide to the Measurement of Animal Bones from Archaeological Sites*, Peabody Museum Bull. 1 (Cambridge, Mass., Harvard Univ.)

Wainwright, G.J., 1972 'The excavation of a Neolithic settlement on Broome Heath, Ditchingham, Norfolk', *Proc. Prehist. Soc.* 38, 1–97

Wait, G.A., 1985 *Ritual and Religion in Iron Age Britain*, Brit. Archaeol. Rep. British Ser. 149 (Oxford)

Ward, G.K. and Wilson, S.R., 1978 'Procedures for comparing and combining radiocarbon age determinations: a critique', *Archaeometry* 20(1), 19–31

Webb, H., 2012 *Hinxton – HINGEC11. The Human Remains*, OA East Rep. (unpubl.)

Webley, L. and Anderson, K., 2008 'Late Iron Age and Roman pottery', in Evans, C., Mackay, D. and Webley, L., *Borderlands. The Archaeology of the Addenbrooke's Environs, South Cambridge*, CAU Landscape Archives. New Archaeologies of the Cambridge Region (1), 63–75 (Cambridge, McDonald Inst. Archaeol. Res.)

Webley, L., 2007 'Prehistoric, Roman and Saxon activity on the Fen hinterland at Parnwell, Peterborough', *Proc. Cambridge Antiq. Soc.* 96, 79–114

West, S.E., 1990 *West Stow: The Prehistoric and Romano-British Occupations*, E. Anglian Archaeol. 48

Weston, P., Newton, A.A. and Nicholson, K., 2007 'A Late Bronze Age enclosure at Lynton Way, Sawston, Cambridgeshire', *Proc. Cambridge Antiq. Soc.* 96, 7–20

Wheeler, R.E.M., 1943 *Maiden Castle, Dorset*, Rep. Res. Cttee Soc. Antiq. London 12

Whimster, R., 1981 *Burial Practices in Iron Age Britain*, Brit. Archaeol. Rep. Brit. Ser. 90 (Oxford)

White, R. H., 1988 *Roman and Celtic Objects from Anglo-Saxon Graves*, Brit. Archaeol. Rep. Brit. Ser. 191 (Oxford)

Whitmore, D., 2004 'Excavations at a Neolithic site at The John Innes Centre, Colney, 2000', *Norfolk Archaeol.* 44 (3), 406–31

Whittle, A., 1991 'Wayland's Smithy, Oxfordshire: excavations at the Neolithic tomb in 1962–63 by R.J.C. Atkinson and S. Piggott', *Proc. Prehist. Soc.* 57 (2), 61–101

Whittle, A., 1997 'Moving on and moving around: Neolithic settlement mobility', in Topping, P. (ed.), *Neolithic Landscapes*, Neolithic Studies Group Seminar Papers 2/Oxbow Monogr. 86, 15–22 (Oxford, Oxbow)

Whittle, A. and Benson, D., 2006 *Building Memories. The Neolithic Cotswold Severn Long Barrow at Ascott under Wychwood* (Oxford, Oxbow)

Whittle, A., Healy, F. and Bayliss, A. (eds), 2011 *Gathering Time: dating the Early Neolithic enclosures of southern Britain and Ireland* (Oxford, Oxbow)

Wilkinson, T.J., Murphy, P.L., Brown N. and Heppell. E.M., 2012 *The Archaeology of the Essex Coast, Volume 2: excavations at the prehistoric site of the Stumble*, E. Anglian Archaeol. 144

Willis, S., Lyons, A., Shepherd Popescu, E. and Roberts, J., 2008 'Late Iron Age/Early Roman pottery kilns at Blackhorse Lane, Swavesey, 1998-99', *Proc. Cambridge Antiq. Soc.* 97, 53–76

Wilson, B., 1996 *Spatial Patterning among Animal Bones in Settlement Archaeology*, Brit. Archaeol. Rep. Brit. Ser. 251 (Oxford)

Wiltshire, P., 2007 'Palynological analysis of palaeochannel sediments', in Gdaniec, K., Edmonds, M. and Wiltshire, P., *A Line Across Land: Fieldwork on the Isleham-Ely pipeline, 1993–4*, E. Anglian Archaeol. 121, 62–77

Wintle, A.G. and Murray, A.S., 2006 'A review of quartz optically stimulated luminescence characteristics and their relevance in single-aliquot regeneration dating protocols', *Radiation Measurements* 41, 369–91

Woelfle, E., 1967 *Vergleichend morphologische Untersuchungen an Einzelknocken des postcranialen Skelettes in Mitteleuropa vorkommender Enten, Halbgänse und Säger* (Unpubl. dissertation München)

Woodley, N.C. and Abrams, J., 2013 'A multi-period landscape at Wadlow Farm, West Wratting', *Proc. Cambridge Antiq. Soc.* 102, 7–28

Woodward, A., 2002 'Beads and Beakers: heirlooms and relics in the British Early Bronze Age'. *Antiquity* 76, 1040–47

Worley, F., 2011 'Northfleet Roman villa', in Barnett, C., McKinley, J.I., Stafford, E., Grimm, J.M. and Stevens, C.J., *Settling the Ebbsfleet Valley. High Speed 1 excavations at Springhead and Northfleet, Kent – the late Iron Age, Roman, Saxon and medieval landscape. Vol. 3: Late Iron Age to Roman human remains and environmental reports*, 42–50 (Oxford and Salisbury, Oxford Wessex Archaeol.)

Woudhuysen, M., 1998 'Pottery', in Malim, T., 'Prehistoric and Roman remains at Edix Hill, Barrington, Cambridgeshire', *Proc. Cambridge Antiq. Soc.* 86, 33–8

Wright, J., Leivers, M., Seagar Smith, R. and Stevens, C.J., 2009 *Cambourne New Settlement: Iron Age and Romano-British Settlement on the Clay Uplands of West Cambridgeshire* (Salisbury, Wessex Archaeol.)

Wyman Abbott, G. and Smith, R., 1910 'The discovery of prehistoric pits at Peterborough and the development of Neolithic Pottery', *Archaeologia*, 62 (1), 333–52

Wymer, J.J., 1996 'The excavation of a ring-ditch at South Acre', in Wymer, J.J. (ed.), *Barrow Excavations in Norfolk, 1984–88*, E. Anglian Archaeol. 77, 59–89

Wymer, J.J. and Robins, P., 1995 A Mesolithic Site at Great Melton. *Norfolk Archaeol.* 42 (2), 125–47

Wymer J.J. with Rose J., 1977 'A long blade industry from Sproughton, Suffolk and the date of the buried channel deposits at Sproughton', in West S.E. (ed.), *Suffolk*, E. Anglian Archaeol. 3, 1–15

Wysocki, M. and Whittle, A., 2000 'Diversity, lifestyles and rites: new biological and archaeological evidence from British Earlier Neolithic mortuary assemblages', *Antiquity* 74(285), 591–601

Wysocki, M.P. and Schulting, R.J., 2005 '"In this chambered tumulus were found cleft skulls...": an assessment of the evidence for cranial trauma in the British Neolithic', *Proc. Prehist. Soc.* 71, 107–38

Yalden, D., 1999 *The History of British Mammals* (London, Poyser)

Yates, D.T., 2007 *Land, Power and Prestige: Bronze Age Field Systems in Southern England* (Oxford, Oxbow)

Young, R. and Humphrey, J., 1999 'Flint use in England after the Bronze Age: time for a re-evaluation?', *Proc. Prehist. Soc.* 65, 231–42

Ytrehus, B., Carlson, C.S. and Ekman, S., 2007 'Etiology and pathogenesis of osteochrondrosis', *Veterinary Pathology* 44, 429–48

Hinman, M. and Zant, J., 2018 *Conquering the Claylands: Excavations at Love's Farm, St Neots, Cambridgeshire*, E. Anglian Archaeol. 165

Zeepvat, R.J., 1987 'Tiles', in Mynard, D.C. (ed.), *Roman Milton Keynes: excavations and fieldwork 1971–82*, Bucks. Archaeol. Soc. Monogr. Ser. 1, 118–25

178

Index

Page numbers in *italics* denote illustrations. Places are in Cambridgeshire unless indicated otherwise.

A2 Pepperhill–Cobham road scheme (Kent), animal bones 125
Abington, flint 80
Addenbrookes site
  burials 113, 114, 152
  dog burial 157
  flint 144
  pottery 151, 159
  prehistoric settlement 1, 4
  shrine *156*
agriculture 157–8; *see also* animal bones; field systems; plant remains
anaemia 108
animal bones
  assemblage 114
  butchery 119, 123, 124, 125
  description
    Neolithic–Bronze Age 115–16, 149
    Middle/Late Iron Age–Conquest period 116–18, *117, 118*
    Conquest period–Roman 118–19, *118*
  discussion 125–6, *126*, 155, 157, 158
  discussion by context
    Corral 1 37
    Ditch Group 15 45
    Enclosure 1/2 32
    Pit Group 4 22
    Pit Group 31 42–3
    shaft/pit 25
    Trackway 1 29–30
  discussion by species
    amphibians 125
    birds 125
    cattle 119–20, 120–1, 122–3, *121*
    deer 124
    dog 124
    equids 123–4
    pig 120, 121–2, *122*
    sheep/goat 120, 121, *121, 122*, 123
    small mammals 125
  methodology 114–15
  quantification and distribution 115, 116
  taphonomy 115
  see also antler fragments; butchery waste; fish bones
antler fragments 22, 25, 124
anvil 25, 60
Arbury Camp hillfort 4
arrowheads
  barbed-and-tanged 25, 63, 66, *72*, 78
  leaf-shaped *18*, 24, 63, 65, 66
  transverse
    discussion 63, 66, 75, *76*
    excavation evidence 20, 21, 24, 30
Ascott-under-Wychwood (Oxon), Neolithic land surface 147
Avington VI (Berks), flint 141, 144
awl, bone 106, *106*
axe fragments, Neolithic
  discussion *19*, 66, *68*, 69, 70–1, *71*
  excavation evidence 23, 24
axe/adze, Mesolithic
  discussion *16*, 63, 65, 67, *68*, 69, 146
  excavation evidence 16
Babraham
  Copley Hill, long barrow 3
  flint 147, 148
bangles, copper alloy 81, *82*, 83, 85
Barham (Kent), pottery 95
barrow mound 26
Biddenham Loop (Beds)

dog burial 157
  pottery 92, 95
blade, bone 106–7, *106*
Bottisham, pottery 92
Boudican revolts 5
boundaries, territorial 3, 152
boundary, Roman *46*, 47, *47*
Bourn Bridge, flint 80
Bowthorpe (Norfolk), pottery 92
Bramble Shot Field, burials 5
Breckland 144
brooches, Iron Age–Roman 81, *82*, 83, 84–5, 159
Broome Heath (Norfolk)
  flint 63–4, 79
  pottery 93, 147
buckle plate, copper alloy *82*, 83
Burial Group 1
  discussion 148–9
  excavation evidence *17*, 19, *20*
  human bones 108, 110
  plant remains 129
Burial Group 2
  discussion 151
  excavation evidence *23, 26, 27*
  human bones 108–9, 110
Burial Group 3A
  excavation evidence 28, *28, 31*, 32
  human bones 109, 110
Burial Group 3B
  animal bones 117–18, 125, 155
  discussion 155
  excavation evidence 28, *28*, 30, *31*, 33–4, *33*
  human bones 109, 110, *112*
Burial Group 3C
  discussion 155–7
  excavation evidence 28, *28, 31, 33*, 34
  human bones 109–12
Burial Group 4
  discussion 151, 157
  excavation evidence *27, 40*, 41–2, *42*
  human bones 111, 112–13, *112*
butchery 119, 123, 124, 125
butchery waste 32, 42, 119, 121, 157

Cadbury Castle (Som), burials 114
Caldecote, pottery 96, 98
Cam, River 1, 3, 133, 152
Cam Valley, landscape occupation
  Terminal Palaeolithic 144–5
  Mesolithic 146
  Neolithic 146, 151–2
  Late Iron Age–Roman 157, 159
Cambridge
  flint 64, 144
  pottery 97, 159
  see also Addenbrookes site; Trumpington
Catuvellauni 152, 153, 159
ceramic building material 104
cereal processing 129–30, 158
charcoal 129, 133
Chippenham, round barrow 92, 150
Claydon Pike (Glos), field system 157
cobbled surfaces 45
cobbles
  quartzite 25, 150
  sandstone *19*, 60
coins
  Iron Age 85
  Roman 48, 85–6, 159
Colchester (Essex), animal bones 126

East Anglian Archaeology

is a serial publication sponsored by ALGAO EE and English Heritage. It is the main vehicle for publishing final reports on archaeological excavations and surveys in the region. For information about titles in the series, visit **https://eaareports.org.uk**. Reports can be obtained from:

Oxbow Books, **https://www.oxbowbooks.com/oxbow/eaa**

or directly from the organisation publishing a particular volume.

Reports available so far:

No.1, 1975 Suffolk: various papers
No.2, 1976 Norfolk: various papers
No.3, 1977 Suffolk: various papers
No.4, 1976 Norfolk: Late Saxon town of Thetford
No.5, 1977 Norfolk: various papers on Roman sites
No.6, 1977 Norfolk: Spong Hill Anglo-Saxon cemetery, Part I
No.7, 1978 Norfolk: Bergh Apton Anglo-Saxon cemetery
No.8, 1978 Norfolk: various papers
No.9, 1980 Norfolk: North Elmham Park
No.10, 1980 Norfolk: village sites in Launditch Hundred
No.11, 1981 Norfolk: Spong Hill, Part II: Catalogue of Cremations
No.12, 1981 The barrows of East Anglia
No.13, 1981 Norwich: Eighteen centuries of pottery from Norwich
No.14, 1982 Norfolk: various papers
No.15, 1982 Norwich: Excavations in Norwich 1971–1978; Part I
No.16, 1982 Norfolk: Beaker domestic sites in the Fen-edge and East Anglia
No.17, 1983 Norfolk: Waterfront excavations and Thetford-type Ware production, Norwich
No.18, 1983 Norfolk: The archaeology of Witton
No.19, 1983 Norfolk: Two post-medieval earthenware pottery groups from Fulmodeston
No.20, 1983 Norfolk: Burgh Castle: excavation by Charles Green, 1958–61
No.21, 1984 Norfolk: Spong Hill, Part III: Catalogue of Inhumations
No.22, 1984 Norfolk: Excavations in Thetford, 1948–59 and 1973–80
No.23, 1985 Norfolk: Excavations at Brancaster 1974 and 1977
No.24, 1985 Suffolk: West Stow, the Anglo-Saxon village
No.25, 1985 Essex: Excavations by Mr H.P.Cooper on the Roman site at Hill Farm, Gestingthorpe, Essex
No.26, 1985 Norwich: Excavations in Norwich 1971–78; Part II
No.27, 1985 Cambridgeshire: The Fenland Project No.1: Archaeology and Environment in the Lower Welland Valley
No.28, 1985 Norfolk: Excavations within the north-east bailey of Norwich Castle, 1978
No.29, 1986 Norfolk: Barrow excavations in Norfolk, 1950–82
No.30, 1986 Norfolk: Excavations at Thornham, Warham, Wighton and Caistor St Edmund, Norfolk
No.31, 1986 Norfolk: Settlement, religion and industry on the Fen-edge; three Romano-British sites in Norfolk
No.32, 1987 Norfolk: Three Norman Churches in Norfolk
No.33, 1987 Essex: Excavation of a Cropmark Enclosure Complex at Woodham Walter, Essex, 1976 and An Assessment of Excavated Enclosures in Essex
No.34, 1987 Norfolk: Spong Hill, Part IV: Catalogue of Cremations
No.35, 1987 Cambridgeshire: The Fenland Project No.2: Fenland Landscapes and Settlement, Peterborough–March
No.36, 1987 Norfolk: The Anglo-Saxon Cemetery at Morning Thorpe
No.37, 1987 Norfolk: Excavations at St Martin-at-Palace Plain, Norwich, 1981
No.38, 1988 Suffolk: The Anglo-Saxon Cemetery at Westgarth Gardens, Bury St Edmunds
No.39, 1988 Norfolk: Spong Hill, Part VI: Occupation during the 7th–2nd millennia BC
No.40, 1988 Suffolk: Burgh: The Iron Age and Roman Enclosure
No.41, 1988 Essex: Excavations at Great Dunmow, Essex: a Romano-British small town in the Trinovantian Civitas
No.42, 1988 Essex: Archaeology and Environment in South Essex, Rescue Archaeology along the Gray's By-pass 1979–80
No.43, 1988 Essex: Excavation at the North Ring, Mucking, Essex: A Late Bronze Age Enclosure
No.44, 1988 Norfolk: Six Deserted Villages in Norfolk
No.45, 1988 Norfolk: The Fenland Project No. 3: Marshland and the Nar Valley, Norfolk
No.46, 1989 Norfolk: The Deserted Medieval Village of Thuxton
No.47, 1989 Suffolk: West Stow: Early Anglo-Saxon Animal Husbandry
No.48, 1989 Suffolk: West Stow, Suffolk: The Prehistoric and Romano-British Occupations
No.49, 1990 Norfolk: The Evolution of Settlement in Three Parishes in South-East Norfolk
No.50, 1993 Proceedings of the Flatlands and Wetlands Conference
No.51, 1991 Norfolk: The Ruined and Disused Churches of Norfolk

No.52, 1991 Norfolk: The Fenland Project No. 4, The Wissey Embayment and Fen Causeway
No.53, 1992 Norfolk: Excavations in Thetford, 1980–82, Fison Way
No.54, 1992 Norfolk: The Iron Age Forts of Norfolk
No.55, 1992 Lincolnshire: The Fenland Project No.5: Lincolnshire Survey, The South-West Fens
No.56, 1992 Cambridgeshire: The Fenland Project No.6: The South-Western Cambridgeshire Fens
No.57, 1993 Norfolk and Lincolnshire: Excavations at Redgate Hill Hunstanton; and Tattershall Thorpe
No.58, 1993 Norwich: Households: The Medieval and Post-Medieval Finds from Norwich Survey Excavations 1971–1978
No.59, 1993 Fenland: The South-West Fen Dyke Survey Project 1982–86
No.60, 1993 Norfolk: Caister-on-Sea: Excavations by Charles Green, 1951–55
No.61, 1993 Fenland: The Fenland Project No.7: Excavations in Peterborough and the Lower Welland Valley 1960–1969
No.62, 1993 Norfolk: Excavations in Thetford by B.K. Davison, between 1964 and 1970
No.63, 1993 Norfolk: Illington: A Study of a Breckland Parish and its Anglo-Saxon Cemetery
No.64, 1994 Norfolk: The Late Saxon and Medieval Pottery Industry of Grimston: Excavations 1962–92
No.65, 1993 Suffolk: Settlements on Hill-tops: Seven Prehistoric Sites in Suffolk
No.66, 1993 Lincolnshire: The Fenland Project No.8: Lincolnshire Survey, the Northern Fen-Edge
No.67, 1994 Norfolk: Spong Hill, Part V: Catalogue of Cremations
No.68, 1994 Norfolk: Excavations at Fishergate, Norwich 1985
No.69, 1994 Norfolk: Spong Hill, Part VIII: The Cremations
No.70, 1994 Fenland: The Fenland Project No.9: Flandrian Environmental Change in Fenland
No.71, 1995 Essex: The Archaeology of the Essex Coast Vol.I: The Hullbridge Survey Project
No.72, 1995 Norfolk: Excavations at Redcastle Furze, Thetford, 1988–9
No.73, 1995 Norfolk: Spong Hill, Part VII: Iron Age, Roman and Early Saxon Settlement
No.74, 1995 Norfolk: A Late Neolithic, Saxon and Medieval Site at Middle Harling
No.75, 1995 Essex: North Shoebury: Settlement and Economy in South-east Essex 1500BC–AD1500
No.76, 1996 Nene Valley: Orton Hall Farm: A Roman and Early Anglo-Saxon Farmstead
No.77, 1996 Norfolk: Barrow Excavations in Norfolk, 1984–88
No.78, 1996 Norfolk:The Fenland Project No.11: The Wissey Embayment: Evidence for pre-Iron Age Occupation
No.79, 1996 Cambridgeshire: The Fenland Project No.10: Cambridgeshire Survey, the Isle of Ely and Wisbech
No.80, 1997 Norfolk: Barton Bendish and Caldecote: fieldwork in south-west Norfolk
No.81, 1997 Norfolk: Castle Rising Castle
No.82, 1998 Essex: Archaeology and the Landscape in the Lower Blackwater Valley
No.83, 1998 Essex: Excavations south of Chignall Roman Villa 1977–81
No.84, 1998 Suffolk: A Corpus of Anglo-Saxon Material
No.85, 1998 Suffolk: Towards a Landscape History of Walsham le Willows
No.86, 1998 Essex: Excavations at the Orsett 'Cock' Enclosure
No.87, 1999 Norfolk: Excavations in Thetford, North of the River, 1989–90
No.88, 1999 Essex: Excavations at Ivy Chimneys, Witham 1978–83
No.89, 1999 Lincolnshire: Salterns: Excavations at Helpringham, Holbeach St Johns and Bicker Haven
No.90, 1999 Essex: The Archaeology of Ardleigh, Excavations 1955–80
No.91, 2000 Norfolk: Excavations on the Norwich Southern Bypass, 1989–91 Part I Bixley, Caistor St Edmund, Trowse
No.92, 2000 Norfolk: Excavations on the Norwich Southern Bypass, 1989–91 Part II Harford Farm Anglo-Saxon Cemetery
No.93, 2001 Norfolk: Excavations on the Snettisham Bypass, 1989
No.94, 2001 Lincolnshire: Excavations at Billingborough, 1975–8
No.95, 2001 Suffolk: Snape Anglo-Saxon Cemetery: Excavations and Surveys
No.96, 2001 Norfolk: Two Medieval Churches in Norfolk
No.97, 2001 Nene Valley: Monument 97, Orton Longueville
No.98, 2002 Essex: Excavations at Little Oakley, 1951–78
No.99, 2002 Norfolk: Excavations at Melford Meadows, Brettenham, 1994
No.100, 2002 Norfolk: Excavations in Norwich 1971–78, Part III
No.101, 2002 Norfolk: Medieval Armorial Horse Furniture in Norfolk
No.102, 2002 Norfolk: Baconsthorpe Castle, Excavations and Finds, 1951–1972
No.103, 2003 Cambridgeshire: Excavations at the Wardy Hill Ringwork, Coveney, Ely
No.104, 2003 Norfolk: Earthworks of Norfolk

No.105, 2003 Essex: Excavations at Great Holts Farm, 1992–4
No.106, 2004 Suffolk: Romano-British Settlement at Hacheston
No.107, 2004 Essex: Excavations at Stansted Airport, 1986–91
No.108, 2004 Norfolk: Excavations at Mill Lane, Thetford, 1995
No.109, 2005 Fenland: Archaeology and Environment of the Etton Landscape
No.110, 2005 Cambridgeshire: Saxon and Medieval Settlement at West Fen Road, Ely
No.111, 2005 Essex: Early Anglo-Saxon Cemetery and Later Saxon Settlement at Springfield Lyons
No.112, 2005 Norfolk: Dragon Hall, King Street, Norwich
No.113, 2006 Norfolk: Excavations at Kilverstone
No.114, 2006 Cambridgeshire:Waterfront Archaeology in Ely
No.115, 2006 Essex:Medieval Moated Manor by the Thames Estuary: Excavations at Southchurch Hall, Southend
No.116, 2006 Norfolk: Norwich Cathedral Refectory
No.117, 2007 Essex: Excavations at Lodge Farm, St Osyth
No.118, 2007 Essex: Late Iron Age Warrior Burial from Kelvedon
No.119, 2007 Norfolk: Aspects of Anglo-Saxon Inhumation Burial
No.120, 2007 Norfolk: Norwich Greyfriars: Pre-Conquest Town and Medieval Friary
No.121, 2007 Cambridgeshire: A Line Across Land: Fieldwork on the Isleham–Ely Pipeline 1993–4
No.122, 2008 Cambridgeshire: Ely Wares
No.123, 2008 Cambridgeshire: Farming on the Edge: Archaeological Evidence from the Clay Uplands west of Cambridge
No.124, 2008 *Wheare most Inclosures be*, East Anglian Fields: History, Morphology and Management
No.125, 2008 Bedfordshire: Life in the Loop: a Prehistoric and Romano-British Landscape at Biddenham
No.126, 2008 Essex: Early Neolithic Ring-ditch and Bronze Age Cemetery at Brightlingsea
No.127, 2008 Essex: Early Saxon Cemetery at Rayleigh
No.128, 2009 Hertfordshire: Four Millennia of Human Activity along the A505 Baldock Bypass
No.130, 2009 Norfolk: A Medieval Cemetery at Mill Lane, Ormesby St Margaret
No.131, 2009 Suffolk: Anglo-Saxon Settlement and Cemetery at Bloodmoor Hill, Carlton Colville
No.132, 2009 Norfolk: Norwich Castle: Excavations and Historical Survey 1987–98 (Parts I–IV)
No.133, 2010 Norfolk: Life and Death on a Norwich Backstreet, AD900–1600: Excavations in St Faith's Lane
No.134, 2010 Norfolk: Farmers and Ironsmiths: Prehistoric, Roman and Anglo-Saxon Settlement beside Brandon Road, Thetford
No.135, 2011 Norfolk: Romano-British and Saxon Occupation at Billingford
No.136, 2011 Essex: Aerial Archaeology in Essex
No.137, 2011 Essex: The Roman Town of Great Chesterford
No.138, 2011 Bedfordshire: Farm and Forge: late Iron Age/Romano-British farmsteads at Marsh Leys, Kempston
No.139, 2011 Suffolk: The Anglo-Saxon Cemetery at Shrubland Hall Quarry, Coddenham
No.140, 2011 Norfolk: Archaeology of the Newland: Excavations in King's Lynn, 2003–5
No.141, 2011 Cambridgeshire: Life and Afterlife at Duxford: archaeology and history in a chalkland community
No.142, 2012 Cambridgeshire: Extraordinary Inundations of the Sea: Excavations at Market Mews, Wisbech
No.143, 2012 Middle Saxon Animal Husbandry in East Anglia
No.144, 2012 Essex: The Archaeology of the Essex Coast Vol.II: Excavations at the Prehistoric Site of the Stumble
No.145, 2012 Norfolk: Bacton to King's Lynn Gas Pipeline Vol.1: Prehistoric, Roman and Medieval Archaeology
No.146, 2012 Suffolk: Experimental Archaeology and Fire: a Burnt Reconstruction at West Stow Anglo-Saxon Village
No.147, 2012 Suffolk: Circles and Cemeteries: Excavations at Flixton Vol.I

No.148, 2012 Essex: Hedingham Ware: a medieval pottery industry in North Essex; its production and distribution
No.149, 2013 Essex: The Neolithic and Bronze Age Enclosures at Springfield Lyons
No.150, 2013 Norfolk: Tyttel's *Halh*: the Anglo-Saxon Cemetery at Tittleshall. The Archaeology of the Bacton to King's Lynn Gas Pipeline Vol.2
No.151, 2014 Suffolk: Staunch Meadow, Brandon: a High Status Middle Saxon Settlement on the Fen Edge
No.152, 2014 A Romano-British Settlement in the Waveney Valley: Excavations at Scole 1993–4
No.153, 2015 Peterborough: A Late Saxon Village and Medieval Manor: Excavations at Botolph Bridge, Orton Longueville
No.154, 2015 Essex: Heybridge, a Late Iron Age and Roman Settlement: Excavations at Elms Farm 1993–5 Vol.1
No.155, 2015 Suffolk: Before Sutton Hoo: the prehistoric remains and Early Anglo-Saxon cemetery at Tranmer House, Bromeswell
No.156, 2016 Bedfordshire: Close to the Loop: landscape and settlement evolution beside the Biddenham Loop, west of Bedford
No.157, 2016 Cambridgeshire: Bronze Age Barrow, Early to Middle Iron Age Settlement and Burials, Early Anglo-Saxon Settlement at Harston Mill
No.158, 2016 Bedfordshire: Newnham: a Roman bath house and estate centre east of Bedford
No.159, 2016 Cambridgeshire: The Production and Distribution of Medieval Pottery in Cambridgeshire
No.160, 2016 Suffolk: A Late Iron-Age and Romano-British Farmstead at Cedars Park, Stowmarket
No.161, 2016 Suffolk: Medieval Dispersed Settlement on the Mid Suffolk Clay at Cedars Park, Stowmarket
No.162, 2017 Cambridgeshire: The Horningsea Roman Pottery Industry in Context
No.163, 2018 Nene Valley: Iron Age and Roman Settlement: Rescue Excavations at Lynch Farm 2, Orton Longueville, Peterborough
No.164, 2018 Suffolk: Excavations at Wixoe Roman Small Town
No.165, 2018 Cambridgeshire: Conquering the Claylands: Excavations at Love's Farm, St Neots
No.166, 2018 Norfolk: Late Bronze Age Hoards: new light on old finds
No.167, 2018 Norfolk: A Romano-British Industrial Site at East Winch
No.168, 2018 Cambridgeshire: Small Communities: Life in the Cam Valley in the Neolithic, Late Iron Age and Early Anglo-Saxon Periods. Excavations at Dernford Farm, Sawston
No.169, 2019 Suffolk: Iron Age Fortification Beside the River Lark: Excavations at Mildenhall
No.170, 2019 Cambridgeshire: Rectory Farm, Godmanchester: Excavations 1988–95, Neolithic monument to Roman villa farm
No.171, 2020 Norfolk: Three Bronze Age Weapon Assemblages
No.172, 2020 Suffolk: Excavations at Stoke Quay, Ipswich: Southern Gipeswic and the parish of St Augustine
No.173, 2020 Nene Valley: Prehistoric Burial Mounds in Orton Meadows, Peterborough
No.174, 2021 Suffolk: Provisioning Ipswich: Animal Remains from the Saxon and Medieval Town
No.175, 2021 Norfolk: Crownthorpe: a Boudican Hoard of Bronze Vessels from Early Roman Norfolk
No.176, 2022 Norfolk: Fransham: people and land in a central Norfolk parish
No.177, 2022 Suffolk: Living with Monuments: Excavations at Flixton Vol.II
No.178, 2023 Cambridgeshire: Hinxton Part I, Excavations at the Wellcome Genome Campus: Late Glacial Lithics to the Icknield Way